Political Investments in Food Production

POLITICAL INVESTMENTS IN FOOD PRODUCTION

Edited by Barbara Huddleston and Jon McLin

Published in Association with the American Universities Field Staff

INDIANA UNIVERSITY PRESS
Bloomington & London

Library of Congress Cataloging in Publication Data
Main entry under title:
Political investments in food production.

   Mostly papers presented at a seminar held at the
American Universities Field Staff Center for Mediter-
ranean Studies in Rome in April 1978.
   1. Food supply—Congresses. 2. Underdeveloped
areas—Food supply—Congresses. 3. Agriculture—
Economic aspects—Congresses. I. Huddleston,
Barbara, 1939— II. McLin, Jon B. III. American
Universities Field Staff.
HD9000.1.P644   338.1'9   79-5025
ISBN 0-253-16219-X
ISBN 0-253-28197-0 pbk.

CONTENTS

Preface

The project which led to publication of this book had as its purpose to produce and disseminate a body of descriptive material about the politics of food problems in a representative group of nations and the relation of those national political decisions to others taken at, or effective at, the international level. Called simply "The Politics of Food," it was undertaken by the American Universities Field Staff, supported by grants from the Rockefeller Brothers Fund, The Rockefeller Foundation, and the Tinker Foundation.

The American Uniersities Field Staff is two organizations in one: a career corps of foreign correspondents dedicated to in-depth reporting on social, political, and economic events in Europe, Africa, Asia, and Latin America; and a consortium of U.S. educational institutions. In early 1977 it established a study group consisting of those staff members who cover a representative set of countries and who over a period of time have developed an interest and competence in issues of agricultural policy.

The work of the study group in the first year of the project was organized in the context of a working seminar in which a number of outside specialists and nationals of developing countries also participated. It was held at the AUFS Center for Mediterranean Studies, in Rome, in April 1978. Most of the papers contained in this volume were presented at or, as in the case of Barbara Huddleston's overview, were informed by that seminar; that of Bruce Stone was prepared following the seminar in order to add a statistical perspective to the discussion of Chinese agriculture.

As the project's title suggests, the study group set out to shed light on the political determinants of food policies rather than on the technical soundness of those policies. Why do political elites appear not to perceive as clearly or take as seriously as some outsiders their countries' "food problems"—in any of the meanings that phrase may have? Why are policies that appear favorable to the accelerated production or more equitable distribution of food not more widely followed? These were questions the authors were asked to bear in mind as they examined *inter alia* the politics surrounding such questions as investment priorities, pricing policies, and land tenure practices. As the project evolved, the sharpness of the distinction between determinants and content of policy turned out to be blurred by the rich variety of the case material. Description of policies and their effects thus became a quite important vehicle for revealing the underlying politics.

By focusing on the political forces which influence food policy choices differently in different countries, and discussing the impact of these choices on efforts to expand domestic food production and to distribute it more equitably, the AUFS project hopes to bring a new perspective to international discussion of the issues involved. Most Field Staff Associates have served for some years as full-time correspondents in the countries about which they write, and the other contributors have extensive experience in the non-Western world. However, all of us are affected in our perceptions by the values and attitudes of our own cultures. The contributors to this volume have chosen to concentrate on the internal process of supplying food to malnourished population groups in developing countries. It should be recognized that political leaders in developing countries are faced with a whole range of considerations with respect to food, and their emphasis might be somewhat different. While acknowledging this possible bias, the contributors believe that the content of this collection is sufficiently rich to enable each reader to arrive at his or her own value judgments regarding policy choices for the future.

The country study papers have previously appeared as *American Universities Field Staff Reports*, and a project-oriented issue of the AUFS quarterly *Common Ground* reflected the discussion at the 1978 seminar. In addition, the information gathered and conclusions reached have been utilized by a separate AUFS project, namely a series of PBS programs on "The Fight for Food" produced in collaboration with public television station WQED of Pittsburgh and broadcast in November 1978.

A word is in order about the respective roles of the two co-editors in the realization of this volume. As coordinator of the project, Jon McLin worked during 1977-78 with members of the study group to shape the first year's collective research effort and organize the Rome seminar. The task of fashioning the raw material of seminar papers into the current book has been performed almost entirely by Barbara Huddleston, in collaboration with the respective authors.

Despite the probably invidious character of selective expressions of gratitude, we cannot fail to acknowledge the roles of a number of individuals and institutions whose efforts have made this volume possible: the authors, especially the non-AUFS contingent, which lacked the Field Staff's proprietary interest, the Rome seminar participants; the sponsoring foundations; E.A. Bayne and Patricia Weaver of the Center for Mediterranean Studies; and the International Food Policy Research Institute, which made available the services of Barbara Huddleston and her research assistant, Eileen Harris. The American Universities Field Staff also provided indispensable help. Manon Spitzer in particular provided valuable editorial assistance and critical comment to both authors and editors throughout the life of the project, and John M. Thompson, as home office coordinator, gave essential backup support to the entire effort.

Barbara Huddleston
Jon McLin

Foreword

Keith Griffin

Never before have so many poor countries grown as fast as they have in the last quarter century. Never before has food and agricultural output in the tropics increased so rapidly. Yet despite the fact that in most countries, most of the time, per capita income and the per capita availability of food have increased, large sections of the poor have experienced little improvement in their standards of food consumption and some have experienced a decline.

We can say straight away that the "food problem" is not primarily an agronomic problem: farmers have demonstrated that they know how to grow more food. This does not imply that further agronomic research in the Third World is unnecessary. Clearly it is. Research on the obstacles to higher production in tropical areas has been long neglected and this deficiency has begun to be corrected on a significant scale only within the past 15 years or so. Much more needs to be done, but it would be a mistake to believe that the solution to the problem of world hunger awaits a technological breakthrough or miracle.

Equally, the "food problem" is not a demographic problem. The specter of Malthus can safely be laid to rest. There is little evidence, outside parts of Africa, that the long-term rate of growth of food production is less than that of population increase. Moreover, it now appears that fertility rates have in many countries begun to fall, and thus demographic pressure on available food supplies should in future diminish.

The "food problem" is essentially a problem of political economy: a classic problem of "who gets what, for how much?" In this sense it is an aspect of the wider problem of poverty.

In many of the countries examined in this volume, the politics of production is a substantial part of the politics of food, and in the few cases where food production has stagnated, notably in Egypt and Mexico, the politics of production is of great significance. In most of the country studies reported in this volume, however, food output has at least kept pace with population growth. This is the case, for example, in India, the Philippines, Venezuela, and China, and in countries such as these the politics of food is essentially the politics of distribution.

Posing the issue in this way naturally encourages one to think in conflictive terms and to anticipate that politics may be resolved, at least in the short run, by policies which reflect the outcome of bargaining processes. The different authors included in this volume have approached the issue of conflict in different ways. No doubt this reflects in part the predilections of the observer and in part the nature of the societies observed.

Thus some authors indicate the regional dimension of conflict: the wheat regions of India have been treated differently by government from the rice regions: the neo-*latifundia* regions of northern Mexico have been favored in comparison with the central and southern regions where *ejidos* predominate. Others view the conflict as one between rural food producers and urban consumers. In this formulation the politics of food becomes essentially a struggle over the internal terms of trade. The food politics of Egypt and the Philippines can be understood in part in this way.

Overriding regional and sectoral conflicts, however, is the clash of interests between the rich and the poor, between those, on the one hand, whose wealth and income and access to the machinery of government give them both purchasing and political power and those, on the other, who do not possess these attributes.

Time and again in the chapters which follow we are informed of policies which served the interest of the rich, even when they were introduced in the name of the poor. Often, delicately, these are described, for example, as production policies biased in favor of "middle class foods" (as in Venezuela), agrarian reform policies captured by the "middle class" (as in Egypt) or credit policies (as in the Philippines) which in the name of production discriminate against the small and in favor of the middle-sized farmer.

In preparing their contributions to this volume each author was asked to examine in some detail three specific aspects of the politics of food, namely, pricing policies, investment patterns, and institutional arrangements. Widely applicable generalizations about these are difficult to formulate and perhaps are uninstructive. It should become clear to the reader, however, that in the domain of food governments have not been at all reluctant to intervene in the market. Taxes, subsidies, quotas, and rationing through administrative arrangements proliferate everywhere. Most prices that matter in the food sector are political prices, not prices determined exclusively by economic forces. No one who peruses this volume is likely to go away believing that agriculture in the Third World is a textbook example of the perfectly competitive industry.

A great deal of information on the volume of investment in the agricultural sector is contained in the country studies. It is arguable, however, that the investment issue has not always been posed in the most helpful way. The question to

my mind is not one of agriculture versus industry or of what proportion of investment occurs in one sector compared to another. The major issues are, first, whether the actual process of industrialization strengthens the agricultural sector or occurs at its expense and, second, within agriculture, whether the patterns of investment and technical change that occur are biased in favor of the large landowner or in favor of the small peasant and worker.

In all the countries analyzed in this volume, a redistribution of land has been proclaimed as government policy. Only in China and Japan, however, can land reform be considered a success. Elsewhere, in India, Egypt, the Philippines, Mexico, and Venezuela the reforms were limited in scope, or only partially enforced or even undermined by the government itself. Moreover, in most cases the peasantry largely were left to fend for themselves, unorganized. The rapidly rising number of landless rural workers is a manifestation of the failure of institutional arrangements to provide an adequate livelihood to a large proportion of the rural population.

Nonetheless, it is evident that there are several paths to prosperity and equity in rural areas. The experience of China, Taiwan, and Japan can be cited as examples of what can be done. It is equally evident, however, that most of the countries of the Third World are traveling on a different path and will almost certainly reach a different destination. Indeed, there are signs that in many countries the present systems of production and distribution are coming under increasing strain verging on breakdown.

Discussions of the politics of food, in this book and elsewhere, tend to concentrate on the policies of governments. One should not forget, however, the high degree of violence in many rural areas; the murder, imprisonment and torture of many peasant leaders; the suppression of many *campesino* organizations; and the cancerous spread of repressive regimes throughout Asia, Latin America, and Africa. These, too, form part of the politics of food.

Turning to international aspects of the politics of food, the following points are likely to command considerable agreement. First, flows of foreign aid from rich countries to poor are low and in real terms per head of the population are falling. Second, assistance to agriculture has increased in the past decade, but it appears to have reached a peak around 1976 and may now be on a slight decline. Third, the lending activities of the World Bank on balance probably exacerbate international inequality in the distribution of income among Third World countries. That is, the distribution of World Bank loans to the Third World probably is even less equal than the distribution of income among the countries so classified. Fourth, the likelihood of a negotiated international agreement on world food security is negligible.

The conclusion, then, seems inescapable: whether or not financial "self-reliance" is desirable, for most countries it is unavoidable. This in itself neither increases nor diminishes the dimensions of the food problem. A self-reliant community can be as hungry as a dependent one. A resolution of the problem of hunger awaits an improvement in the distribution of purchasing power, international and particularly national. Until then it will continue to be true that many of those who are hungry, perhaps even a majority of the malnourished, obtain their livelihood as landless laborers, tenant farmers, and *minifundistas*—growing food.

List of Contributors

Michael W. Donnelly, Assistant Profesor of Political Science, University of Toronto. Author of "Setting the Price of Rice: A Case Study in Political Decision-Making," in T.G. Penpel (ed.) *Policy-Making in Contemporary Japan* and other articles on Japanese agricultural policy and Canadian-Japanese agricultural trade.

Marcus Franda, American Universities Field Staff Associate for India and Bangladesh, is a former Professor of Political Science at Colgate University. Author of *Radical Politics in West Bengal* and *India's Rural Development*, etc.

Brewster Grace is an American Universities Field Staff Consulting Associate for Southeast Asia. He is completing a book, begun as AUFS Scholar-in-Residence at The Asia Society, on the politics of income distribution among ASEAN nations.

Keith Griffin, Acting Warden, Queen Elizabeth House, University of Oxford; formerly World Employment Program, International Labor Organization. Author of *Political Economy of Agrarian Change, Underdevelopment in Spanish America*, etc.

Howard Handelman, an American Universities Field Staff Faculty Associate for Latin America, is an Associate Professor of Political Science at the University of Wisconsin-Milwaukee. Author of *Struggle in the Andes; Peasant Political Mobilization in Peru*, etc.

Barbara Huddleston, Research Fellow at the International Food Policy Research Institute (IFPRI), was formerly Director of the Trade Negotiations Division of the U.S. Department of Agriculture. Ms. Huddleston has published two occasional papers—*Commodity Trade Issues in International Negotiations* and *Potential of Agricultural Exports to Finance Increased Food Imports in Selected Developing Countries* (with Alberto Valdés) and one research report—*Food Security: An Insurance Approach* (with Panos Konandreas and Virabongsa Ramangkura).

Jon McLin, American Universities Field Staff Associate for European Community and International Organizations from 1968-1978, served as Director of the AUFS study group on the "Politics of Food." Author of *Canada's Changing Defense Policy, 1957-1963,* he is completing a book on international organizations and alternative means for managing interdependence.

Albert Ravenholt, American Universities Field Staff Associate for East and Southeast Asia, is a specialist on tropical agriculture. Author of *The Philippines; a Young Republic on the Move*, etc.

Thomas G. Sanders, American Universities Field Staff for Latin America, is a former Professor of Religious Studies at Brown University. Author of *Secular Consciousness and National Conscience* and *Mexico's Development Decade*, etc.

Bruce Stone, Visiting Researcher, International Food Policy Research Institute (IFPRI), is conducting research on agricultural policy in the People's Republic of China.

Richard Stryker, Associate Professor of Political Science, Indiana University. Author of *Neo-Colonialism as a Development Strategy: The Political Economy of the Ivory Coast*, etc.

John Waterbury is an American Universities Field Staff Consulting Associate for the Arab World. Author of *Egypt: Burdens of the Past, Options for the Future* and *The Hydropolitics of the Nile Valley*, etc.

A Summary View of Food Production Systems in Five Developing Countries and Some Perspectives on Foreign Assistance Strategy

Barbara Huddleston

A quick glance at a map reveals significant differences in the topography and climate of the five developing countries under review: Mexico, Venezuela, Egypt, the Philippines, and India. Historically, the geographic characteristics of each country have played an important role in determining the major food crops grown and have influenced the evolution of institutional arrangements governing the use of the land. While there are variations in physical characteristics and environment, the patterns of institutional arrangements in rural areas, particularly in regard to land tenure, are more similar.

It seems likely that the application of technology will narrow the differences in agricultural systems among countries even further. As the use of high-yielding varieties of wheat, maize, and rice becomes more widespread—especially when it is accompanied by improved irrigation systems—the physical environment appears to be less and less a constraint. Thus, despite their significant geographic and cultural differences, it should be possible to look for similarities among these countries in their efforts to increase food production and improve the nutritional status of low-income classes.

Before we consider these similarities at greater length, it may be useful to look briefly at the characteristics of the agricultural environment in each country.

Mexico

In Mexico two volcanic ranges border the semiarid flatlands of the north, moving southward until they converge in the central plateau which was traditionally and is still today the heartland of the country. Beyond Mexico City to the south the mountains gradually taper off until a low-lying tropical region takes their place (Figure 1, page 22). On this land Mexico produces a wide variety of crops, along with cattle, under a number of different institutional arrangements. It is hard to generalize about types of farming in different parts of the country, since a variety of geographical zones and farming systems occur within each broad region (Figure 2, page 23). Livestock, wheat, subsistence crops (beans, maize, and rice) and cash crops (cotton, coffee, bananas, and tomatoes) are all grown in scattered regions throughout the country. But broadly speaking, as the Mexican case study points out, livestock, wheat, and fruits and vegetables dominate the north, subsistence agriculture with some commercial agriculture the central highlands, and tropical cash crops the low-lying coastal regions of the south.

Interestingly enough, the pattern of land settlement appears not to have been dictated by agroclimatic considerations. Before the arrival of the Spaniards, the population was concentrated almost entirely on the central plateau and was already beginning to experience food problems, owing to the lack of water and the relatively poor quality of the soil. During the colonial period plantation agriculture and ranching developed in the north, and major irrigation projects have in recent times been concentrated in that region. The most fertile, water-abundant areas in the south are the least populated, and land resettlement schemes have met with little success. Under these circumstances, the challenge which Mexico's land and water constraints presents to the development of its food production system is doubly difficult.

Like the other countries under review, Mexico has attempted to restructure its agricultural production system by implementing a land reform program. Mexico's program is the oldest of the five, dating back to the Revolution of 1910-1921 and enacted into law in 1922. Agrarian reform in Mexico had the objective of restoring previously expropriated lands to peasant communities; in the initial phase the majority of estates affected were in the central highland areas of high population density, but later the reform spread to commercial crop and range lands in other parts of the country. Most of the redistributed lands were granted to communal groups called *ejidos*, but within the *ejidos* the cropland was then parceled out among member families who farmed it individually. Only a few relatively large *ejidos* organized collectively to produce crops.

By 1960, land had been distributed to nearly half the Mexican peasantry. While this reform represented a significant accomplishment, it by no means solved the land problem. Although the number of farm families increased from 2.2 to 3.6 million between 1940 and 1960, the number of landless workers and private smallholders more than doubled. The pressure of these poor peasants to obtain land for themselves led to additional redistribution during the 1960s, but the land available for this purpose was largely semiarid eroded land with low productive potential.

By 1970 the proportion of the rural population belonging to *ejidos* had risen to 66 percent, but most of the land controlled by them was classified either as barren, forested or inaccessible, or as pasture. Thus large numbers of Mexican peasants still had access only to small plots of relatively poor farmland from which to feed themselves and their growing families.

One of the most important policy responses to the plight of these families has been the family planning drive initiated in the early 1970s. In a major policy turnaround President Echeverria announced his intention to create a government-organized national family planning program. This policy was adopted into law in late 1973 and was made a constitutional right in 1974. Since then use of contraceptives and other family planning services sponsored by the government has spread rapidly. By 1977, 9 percent of all women age 15 to 49 were using contraceptives regularly, and the number was expected to increase to 20 percent by 1982. Although it will not provide immediate relief, a significant decline in the birthrate could eventually do much to relieve the pressure of population growth on Mexico's scarce arable land resources.

As in the case of Venezuela, Philippines, and, to a lesser extent, India, agricultural policies have been oriented toward the needs of farmers holding relatively better land, and farming units of five hectares or more in size (one hectare = 2.47 acres). These larger farms have been the primary beneficiaries of major irrigation projects and have on the whole had better access to both commercial and public credit than the small farmers. Since 1971 guaranteed prices for all major crops have been increased substantially, but a marked rise in production occurred only in irrigated areas where relatively better-off farmers also had access to credit and agricultural extension services.

Resources generated by Mexico's recently discovered petroleum reserves could be used in part to provide additional financial resources to aid small farmers, through investment in infrastructure projects in poorer regions and subsidized credit programs for relatively high-risk borrowers. Yet, such investments are likely to be costly, and Mexico's experience to date suggests that in regions where the quality of the land has deteriorated badly and the peasant culture is still highly traditional, the payoff in terms of increased agricultural productivity will be low.

The Mexican government can also consider using petroleum earnings to create nonagricultural employment opportunities in densely populated rural areas. Whereas small-farm agriculture can provide a viable economic base for the development of local industry in countries such as Egypt, Philippines, and India, this is not likely to be the case in Mexico. More probably, farm family members who cannot obtain adequate subsistence from poor unproductive plots will gradually drift to urban areas and to regions offering petroleum-related employment. The movement of illegal migrants across the border into the United States will also continue to provide some relief.

That the flight from agriculture has already begun is indicated by a World Bank staff paper which suggests that the number of landless agricultural workers has probably declined significantly since 1960, due to the combined effect of additional land distribution and out-migration. To the extent that general industrialization also provides alternative employment opportunities to smallholders farming one to four hectares of land, Mexico's agricultural policy problem will become the more manageable one of organizing viable small landholders, both on and off *ejidos*, so that they can obtain a larger share of existing credit and extension services. While sizable problems will remain for some time to come, such a strategy could eventually enable the most impoverished elements of Mexico's rural population to improve their incomes and their ability to purchase food through off-farm employment, and give agricultural producers the necessary incentives to produce marketable surpluses to meet the growing demand.

Venezuela

Venezuela is by far the richest of the five countries under review, with a per capita income of $2,280 in 1975 compared to $1,050 in Mexico, $260 in Egypt, $380 in the Philippines, and $140 in India. Like its corn and cattle, Venezuela's oil and mineral wealth is also a product of the land, and helps to account for the relatively low priority accorded to agriculture in recent history. Much of the land, moreover, is not well-suited to agriculture. The southern third of the country is a mountainous forested region. It merges into the upper reaches of the Amazon basin, producing a tropical rainforest in the far southwest. This region is sparsely populated and nonproductive, though it is reputedly rich in mineral resources and moist, fertile land. The central plains, which

account for another third of the land area and a fifth of the population, are hot and dry, subject from time to time to torrential rains during the spring and summer months, and suitable mostly for cattle. The Andean Highlands occupy much of the northern third of the country, leaving only scattered areas on the slopes of the mountains and in the Lake Maracaibo valley for the cultivation of food and cash crops (Figure 3, page 44).

Although agriculture declined in importance after the discovery of petroleum in the 1920s, production of cash crops for export is still an important feature of Venezuelan agriculture. These crops include coffee, cocoa, sugar, bananas, tobacco, sisal, hides and skins. Production of food crops for domestic consumption is also important, but much of this production takes the form of subsistence agriculture, with maize, beans, rice, and root crops predominating (Figure 4, page 45). As the agricultural population has declined, production of these crops for sale to low-income workers in the cities has become increasingly important, although the country has also been importing wheat in increasing amounts. Despite the country's high per capita income level, the nutritional condition of the urban workers is poor. An agricultural policy aimed at increasing food production could help meet their needs, and improve the economic condition of the remaining peasant farmers. But this is not the course pursued by the Venezuelan government in the past, and it is not yet clear whether the announced intention to devote increased petroleum revenues to agriculture will produce the desired result.

Land reform in Venezuela differs markedly from the programs undertaken in the other four countries under review. Whereas programs in the other countries all involve expropriation of land belonging to large proprietors, with appropriate compensation, and redistribution to tenants and peasant smallholders, usually in plots of five hectares or less, Venezuela has proceeded to distribute land to subsistence farmers primarily by resettling them in small plots on previously uncultivated public lands. Thus the pattern of land distribution, which is heavily skewed in favor of large estates, has not been significantly altered.

This policy has proved feasible in part because the agricultural population is steadily declining, comprising today only about 20 percent of the total, and in part because Venezuela's geography afforded the country large areas of unused public pastureland suitable for distribution. It has not been a production-oriented policy, however. To increase yields of small peasant farmers, Venezuela would have to provide support services in addition to distributing land. Such services include irrigation, road systems, credit for the purchase of fertilizer and high-yielding varieties of seed, and readily accessible extension services. Despite public pronouncements to the contrary, the Venezuelan case study makes abundantly clear that this kind of support for the small farm sector has not been forthcoming. Irrigation districts were situated primarily in areas where high-value commercial crops are grown; as of 1972, the United Nations Food and Agriculture Organization (FAO) estimated that the amount of credit available was adequate to finance no more than half the country's capital needs for agriculture; and the number of extension personnel available to service resettlement areas is seriously deficient. Because land resettlement took place wherever peasants grouped together and requested allotments, the sites are scattered in relatively inaccessible regions not well-served by existing infrastructure. Under these circumstances it is not surprising that agricultural productivity on small farms has shown little improvement.

The expansion of crop area resulting from the land reform did result in an increase in production of major staple crops during the 1960s, but this was followed by declining growth rates throughout the 1970s. To make up for the domestic production deficit, Venezuela has therefore had to begin importing maize and sorghum as well as wheat.

Not all of this increased supply has necessarily gone for direct human consumption. A by-product of the sudden increase in the value of Venezuela's oil has been a sharp increase in urban demand for livestock products. Although the domestic cattle industry has been a consistent beneficiary of Venezuela's agricultural support policies, it has only recently begun to be a heavy user of feedgrains and soybean meal. Thus the pressure on domestic corn producers to meet market demand stems not only from the increasing number of workers desiring to purchase maize for food use, but also from the expanding requirements of the cattle feeders.

In 1974 the newly elected Perez administration pledged to make increased food production a major government goal. Minimum price supports have been extended to virtually all major food crops produced in Venezuela, with the government bearing the cost of subsidizing consumer prices when necessary. The more important aspect of this new policy emphasis on food production has been the significant increase in the amount of money being plowed into agricultural credit and input subsidies. But loose administrative control over the agrarian credit program and structural difficulties impeding extension of farm program benefits to resettlement areas may mean that increases in grain and livestock production will take place primarily on large estates, while the productive potential of the peasantry remains largely unexploited.

In a sense, Venezuela is already experiencing the effects of a policy choice similar to the one Mexico is now facing. Blessed with substantial oil reserves, Venezuela has chosen, through the decisions of numerous individual landowners and investors, to allow its rural population to migrate to the cities and form a growing industrial working class. Peasant agriculture is viewed less as a productive resource and more as a form of welfare employment for a low-income group not yet ready to participate fully in a modernizing economy. Whether the social and economic implications of pursuing such a policy will permit the country to continue along this course indefinitely remains to be seen.

Egypt

In Egypt the Nile River is the dominant geographical fact. The Nile Valley and its Delta, together comprising less than one-quarter of the country's total land area, offer the only cultivable surface except for a few oases and artificially irrigated areas in the vast desert to the West (Figure 5, page 64). For centuries Egyptian *fellaheen* farmed in accordance with the river's annual flood cycle. Water supplies far exceeded the amount needed in the fields during the high water season (July-November) but were insufficient to produce a second crop during the spring and early summer.

In order to encourage cultivation of cotton and sugar cane in the Lower Valley, in the early nineteenth century Egyptian rulers developed a system of deep canals. This system was later extended throughout much of the Delta, and in the regions served by these canals, two and three crops per year became possible. Still, in the Upper Valley, only one crop per year could be produced. Even though this irrigation system helped to regularize the flow of water during the course of the year, the total amount available remained subject to the level of the annual flood. Thus the crop mix and the average yields could vary considerably, depending on the adequacy of the year's water supply.

Egyptian agriculture produces a variety of crops, among which cotton, clover (*berseem*), wheat, rice, and coarse grains dominate in terms of acreage, and sugar cane, pulses, vegetables, and orchard fruits also figure importantly in terms of value (Figure 6, page 65). With an adequate water supply, profitable summer crops (cotton, rice, and summer corn) could be produced in abundance. In years of low flood, however, farmers would shift the acreage to fallow or produce low-yielding crops during the summer months.

Construction of the Aswan High Dam, which began operations in 1965, was intended to help alleviate this problem. By creating a natural reservoir behind the dam (Lake Nasser), the annual as well as the seasonal flow of water could be controlled. Thus water supply would no longer be dictated by the flood cycle. The Aswan Dam has improved the prospects for Egyptian agriculture, but it has also been a source of difficulty.

In addition to regularizing the annual flow of water to regions already served by irrigation canals, the High Dam has increased the potential cultivable acreage in the Nile Valley and has made multiple cropping possible in regions where previously only one crop per year could be grown. This could increase the productive potential of Egyptian agriculture significantly, enabling the country to reverse the decline in the amount of cultivable land available per farmer. However, much of the new land on the fringes of the Valley has yet to be reclaimed, and by most accounts the process will be quite costly in relation to anticipated output, since the quality of the soil is poor. In regions served by the canal system, overirrigation and lack of adequate drainage has also created serious problems, owing to waterlogging and increasing salinity. In some areas yields have fallen from 30 to 100 percent on this account. Finally, flood control has also necessitated an increase in fertilizer usage, since the silt deposits that restored fertility to the soil each year as the flood waters receded are now collecting in the reservoirs rather than on the land.

Whether or not institutional developments since Nasser's Socialist Revolution in 1952 will be able to cope with these problems is open to question. As the Egyptian case study points out, the government has intervened heavily in agriculture; for a time it apparently followed a deliberate policy of taxing agriculture to pay for industrial development. As in Mexico, population pressure and increasing dependence on imported wheat to feed its urban inhabitants have forced a rethinking of the country's agricultural policy, but the interplay of physical and institutional factors suggests a different outcome.

The early focus of Nasser's agricultural policy was on land reform, and on the creation of cooperatives that would provide credit and inputs to farmers and market their crops for them at harvest time. In this regard Egypt is considerably ahead of the Philippines and India, where such efforts are still in an experimental phase. Before 1952, most Egyptian peasants farmed plots of less than half a hectare, either as owners or, more frequently, as tenants. The land reform undertook to redistribute land held in parcels of more than 84 hectares to tenants and smallholders farming less than two hectares. Later legislation reduced the ceiling for a single landowner to 24 hectares. In eliminating very large landholdings and redistributing the land to smaller farmers, the land reform was largely successful. However, the middle-sized landowners farming parcels averaging around ten hectares increased their control over the land and the institutional arrangements governing its use more than did the peasant holders of very tiny plots.

The land reform also offered protection to peasants who did not convert from tenancy to ownership. This group, which still constitutes an important part of Egypt's agricultural population, benefited from the maximum rent and security-of-tenure provisions of the new legislation. However, the increased political influence of the larger landholders receiving the rents has recently led to a substantial increase in the valuation of the land for tax purposes, to which rents are tied. Thus some tenants may now be forced to abandon agriculture entirely or convert to share-cropping.

The movement toward greater influence of middle-sized landowners on agricultural policy, and a reduction of government intervention, is also evident in the current debate about freeing up the credit and pricing system. For a variety of reasons, farmers have increasingly failed to use the cooperative system as intended. Although many of them still rely on the coop to supply inputs—in particular, subsidized fertilizer and seeds—a large number no longer follow the prescribed crop rotations, selling nonprescribed crops at more profitable prices outside the cooperative system. Again, the middle-sized farmers are in the best position to operate in this way and thereby reap higher profits than the smallholders still locked into the state system.

Recognizing that the cooperatives are an increasingly cumbersome and ineffective instrument for carrying out the government's agricultural policies, a decision has already been taken to reintroduce commercial credit into the countryside, and abolition of delivery quotas and administered prices is being considered. Egyptian agriculture is feeling the pressure of a shift in the relative prices of the numerous crops it is capable of producing. High-value foodstuffs, fruits and vegetables, and poultry are more profitable than the old standbys, cotton, wheat, and rice. This means either that the government must reverse its long-standing policy and begin to throw more

resources into agriculture than it gets back, or it must give up hope of improving the country's capacity to feed itself and resort to industrial exports to pay for increased food imports.

Certainly the Sadat regime seems committed to attempting to pursue the former course of action. Even though it loosens up its control of credit and prices, the government could still provide valuable assistance to smallholders by investing in the extension of tile drainage to all irrigated areas; by continuing to subsidize the use of improved cultivating machinery, high-yielding seed varieties, and fertilizer, particularly for farmers holding less than two hectares; by increasing and improving the quality of extension services; and by encouraging increased production of new fodder crops such as soybeans and sugar beets so that poultry production can be significantly increased to meet rapidly growing urban demand. Such a policy could have an important by-product in terms of the ability of small farmers to improve their own nutrition, since the beneficiaries should be able to increase their yields of important subsistence crops such as maize, millet, and barley as well as of targeted crops. Some increase in wheat production could be expected from this approach, but continued imports would almost certainly be required to provide the quantities needed to supply the government-subsidized bread ration in urban areas. This is, however, a high-cost policy, and it is not readily apparent that Egypt commands the resources to realize fully the productive potential which its agricultural sector offers.

Philippines

The Philippines is the only island country among the five selected for the study. Like the others it possesses a varied geography, and its agriculture is conditioned by its physical environment. Much of the country is mountainous, hilly, or elevated plateau. This high country is heavily forested, but where agriculture is practiced, dryland rice and corn are produced. In the coastal areas and lowland river basins, tropical agriculture predominates, with wetland rice being the primary staple (Figures 7 and 8, pages 86 and 87). Among the country's important export crops, coffee, sugar cane, and tobacco occupy a relatively small portion of the agricultural land area, while coconuts are cultivated more extensively.

Traditionally, much of the country's agricultural land has been held by a small number of wealthy families who dominate the agricultural system. In some areas cash-crop plantations employ relatively large numbers of agricultural workers, and these workers or members of their families may farm small plots as tenants or smallholders on the fringes of the estate land. In other cases, the cash crop itself may be produced by tenants, who then use a portion of the rented plot to produce staples for their own subsistence. As of 1971 roughly half the farm operators in the country were tenants.

Efforts to implement a land reform program prior to imposition of martial law in 1972 were pursued on a limited scale; the declaration of land reform areas was confined to areas of serious agrarian unrest. Wealthy landowners provided much of the political leadership for the country, and concessions to peasant pressure for change involved primarily the creation of a leasehold system assuring security of tenure and a legally fixed rent for their tenants. Various attempts to provide credit to small farmers were initiated, but for the most part the funds ended up being used for export crops rather than for food production.

One of President Marcos' first policy initiatives was the imposition of a national land reform program. The reform, which applies only to rice and cornlands, provides that ownership of landholdings exceeding seven hectares will be transferred to tenants. Implementation has been slow, however, and even if completed the program will affect only half the tenant population.

The Philippines has increasingly come to recognize the importance of improving the productivity of the small farmers who comprise the majority of the population, if the country's food needs are to be met. But there is some question whether completion of the land reform is a prerequisite for agricultural progress. Although a few families constitute a landed elite in the Philippines, on the whole land ownership is not highly concentrated, and most small farmers

producing staple food crops do have effective control of their land, whether or not they own it.

More important than land reform itself may be the government's commitment to provide adequate irrigation, transport systems, credit, and agricultural support services to the mass of small farmers who have, until recently, received relatively little benefit from public investments in agriculture. Historically, the Philippines had been able to increase production by expanding cultivated area, principally by clearing forests. Today, however, cultivable forest land is becoming more and more scarce; poor soil management practices have led to erosion and loss of fertility in many recently cleared tracts; and inadequate irrigation and drainage facilities in the wet lowland areas are causing the quality of the soil to deteriorate. The government thus feels impelled to make a conscious effort to manage its farming system more efficiently than it has done in the past.

Improved varieties of rice have been bred for the Philippines and their use is spreading. These new varieties, coupled with proper fertilization, have brought about striking increases in yields, but only in those limited areas with adequate irrigation and drainage facilities. The Philippines' water problem is not inadequate supply—rainfall is plentiful. But the rains are often very irregular and water supply management is vitally important. Consequently, providing adequate irrigation to Filipino farmers is as much a training function as it is a public works program. Not only does a network of irrigation canals and supply ditches need to be constructed, but local officials need to learn how to maintain them and how to regulate the flow of water to individual users so that maximum benefits will be obtained. The government has created several pilot projects to organize farmers into water management associations and to demonstrate proper irrigation techniques, but still this program reaches a relatively small number. Similarly, the government has adopted a credit program (Masagana-99), as a complement to high-yielding varieties, fertilizer, and irrigation for accelerating the country's rice output, small, high-risk rice farmers who are among the principal beneficiaries of the land reform stand to gain from Masagana-99, but this program too is reaching only a portion of those who need its benefits.

The difficulties the government faces in trying to make modern technologies available to small farmers in ways which will increase their productivity and improve their welfare stem from the long legacy of semifeudal organization of the countryside. As long as a few families controlled the institutions that serviced the small farmers, the peasants did not need to concern themselves with the operation of these institutions nor to weigh the advantages and disadvantages of different methods of farming their land. Government efforts to improve the productive capacity of peasant farmers have therefore focused on the organization of cooperatives to replace the previous network of private merchants and moneylenders. However, a program of this type involves major social changes and its progress is slow. Initiative to date has been provided largely by the central government. As local leadership begins to grow stronger, the cooperative movement may eventually gain real control over the supply of credit and services to peasant farmers and the marketing of their crops. Until this occurs, other policies the government might pursue on behalf of the small producer are likely to have relatively little effect.

India

India is a large country composed of several distinct geographical regions, including, like Mexico, a large plateau, a desert, and a high mountain range. India nevertheless offers a more promising environment for agriculture because its land is more fertile and its water supply is abundant. The northern plain formed by the Ganges River basin has traditionally been India's major wheat-producing region, while the inhabitants of the central and southern highlands have eaten coarse grains (maize, millet, and sorghum) and the coastal peoples rice. A large part of the land area in these three regions is devoted to crops. Nomads pasture cattle even in the Great Indian Desert which forms the northwestern border of the country, and livestock and wheat grow in the Indus Valley of the Himalaya region to the far north (Figures 9 and 10, pages 108 and 109).

Although India has an abundance of fertile land, the uncertainty of rainfall and its uneven distribution throughout the country have in the past caused periodic crop failures and famines. As in Egypt, though for different reasons, irrigation is a necessary feature of successful agriculture in most parts of the country. Indian peasants have built wells, tanks, canals, and dams from ancient times, but the introduction of Green Revolution technology into India in the mid-1960s and the accompanying shift in government policy in favor of incentive prices for farmers have given added importance to irrigation development.

The effects of Green Revolution technology for small farmers in India can be discussed with some degree of confidence. One of the important questions frequently raised about this new technology is its net effects on agricultural employment in low-income areas. The record by now clearly indicates that irrigation development creates jobs whereas mechanization ordinarily displaces workers. It is an important distinction, particularly since access to a reliable water supply contributes far more to improved yields than the substitution of mechanical for human labor. Whereas in Mexico, Venezuela, and the Philippines, the poorest regions have not been primary targets for irrigation projects, this has not necessarily been the case in India. Particularly in regions where canals provide equitable access to water to all farmers within a reasonable distance, availability of improved varieties has produced changes in cropping patterns and significant increases in yields per hectare.

Some of India's major irrigation investments have been criticized on the grounds that they have been underutilized and wasteful compared to the gains that might have been obtained from investing larger sums in small-scale projects such as tubewells, which can be owned and operated by individual farmers. But as the Indian case study notes, major irrigation schemes involve construction of hand-dug canals for distribution of water to the fields. Such projects provide large numbers of poor workers with employment. Further, once completed, these schemes make it relatively easy for poor farmers with no capital and little credit to draw small amounts of water from the canal when needed; tubewell systems are usually situated on the property of relatively well-off middle-sized farmers and are not easily accessible to poor farmers, either physically or financially. The Janata government has made a commitment to double expenditure on irrigation schemes, with the increase in irrigated acreage divided roughly equally between canal and tube-well type schemes. This commitment, if carried out, should have positive benefits for agricultural productivity and farmer welfare in the affected areas.

Although India has been pursuing a land reform program since 1948, implementation of policy recommendations rests with the states, and progress has been rather slow. Because of the complexity of landlord-tenant relationships, imposition of landholding ceilings and redistribution of estate lands to poor peasants has been difficult to accomplish unless accompanied by other institutional changes which provide the communal services previously supplied by the landlord. Despite this difficulty, the reform programs have succeeded in virtually abolishing feudal and semifeudal landholdings, and have given most cultivators at least nominal title to the land they till. Numerous exemptions from the landholding ceilings have produced a substantial class of middle-to-large-sized landowners, however, and the plots allotted to peasants in poorer regions are frequently too tiny to provide adequate subsistence for the owner and his family. Average farm size varies considerably from one state to another—from a low of 0.85 hectares in Kerala to a high of 6.07 hectares in Rajasthan. For the nation as a whole the average was 2.67 hectares in 1960-61, with over two-thirds of the holdings amounting to less than 2 hectares each. In the more successful agricultural areas farm size averages around 4 to 5 hectares and many holdings run to 12 or more hectares. Farmers operating holdings of this size are best situated to take advantage of state irrigation projects and have frequently mechanized. It is also on their lands that most of the impressive increases in agricultural output have taken place.

How to enable small farmers to obtain similar improvements in their productivity and improve the incomes of the rural poor is one of the critical policy issues facing the Indian government today. A plot of at least two hectares is considered the minimum necessary for a viable, self-sustaining farm unit. Yet many poor peasants with as little as half a hectare could make a living if they can raise a cow or two, some poultry, or higher value vegetables, and find supplementary off-farm employment.

The government recognizes that further improvements in the provision of credit and extension services to small farmers will be required. Although India offers some outstanding examples of successful agricultural cooperatives, the tradition of letting the larger landowners dominate local cooperative and credit societies has carried over from the feudal period to the present in many areas. Finding ways to provide leadership which will overcome this problem remains a difficult and much-debated issue for the central government.

India has had some success with its price policies since the decision was taken in the late sixties to fix procurement prices at a reasonably high level so as to provide market incentives to farmers to invest in increasing production. This has meant some drain on the budget, since India also pursues a policy of subsidizing food prices for certain vulnerable sections of the population through the operation of fair price shops. These food price subsidies do not necessarily benefit the most impoverished classes, since these classes rely heavily for their subsistence on coarse grains not sold through the public distribution system. For a variety of reasons, price policy has favored wheat over rice, and it is in the northern and eastern wheat-growing regions of the country where production has shown the most striking gains. Where there is opposition to higher procurement prices, it tends to come from middle-income consuming classes who do not qualify for access to the fair price shops and who do not want to see higher market prices for food.

The argument is frequently made that pricing policies which favor farmers, both high procurement prices and subsidized input prices, tend to channel disproportionate gains to a relatively small group of well-to-do landowners. Since the policies seem to be producing the desired response, this does not seem a sufficient reason to abandon them. Removal of other constraints preventing small farmers from taking advantage of high procurement prices for their grain would seem a more advisable course to pursue. In some respects the situation India faces is much like that of Mexico; with fairly ample foreign exchange resources, at least for the moment, and a small farmer class which has been left out of the progress experienced in the rural sector to date, the question is how to use available resources to benefit this large and potentially important class without disrupting the political balance of the society as a whole.

Conclusions

An important issue raised by all the papers under review has been the policy attitudes of governments toward improving the agricultural productivity and standard of living of small farmers. Nowhere is the small farmer sharply defined, however. The meaning implied throughout this book refers to the class of farmers, whether owners or tenants, cultivating plots of land so small that subsistence is barely provided to the farmer and his family. By this definition, the middle-sized farmer is any proprietor or tenant who is farming enough land to feel that his survival is secure, and may include some farmers who are quite well off. The number of hectares that divides a small farmer from a middle-sized farmer varies from country to country and from region to region within countries, as does average farm size (Table 1, page 15). The quality of the land, the type of crop grown, and the productivity of the land will all affect its value to the farmer. In general, however, the farmer cultivating somewhere between two and five hectares of land can be reasonably successful, particularly in areas where he has access to irrigation and credit. Yet his is still a small farm and large numbers of these viable small farmers are still inadequately served by infrastructure and support services financed through official agricultural development programs. This generalization holds true regardless of the extent to which land reform has successfully converted tenants and landless workers to land ownership.

Intensity of land use differs markedly among these countries (Table 2, page 16). The two Latin American cases, with a high proportion of arable land devoted to pasture, do not farm very intensively. On the other hand, the combination of climate and controlled water supply permits Egypt to sustain a highly intensive agricultural system. In South and Southeast Asia expansion of irrigated area and introduction of new seed varieties could greatly increase the extent of multiple cropping. Multiple cropping widens the production choices open to farmers. FAO points out, for example, that while in some areas double or even triple cropping of high-yielding rice may be the most efficient use of the land, in other areas, a four-crop rotation including rice, a pulse, sweet potatoes, and a vegetable or a second cereal may prove more productive. The increases in per hectare yields which result from multiple cropping will, of course, reduce the amount of land an individual farmer needs to till in order to provide his own subsistence plus a marketable surplus.

The Green Revolution technology that makes possible this kind of improvement has been criticized as bringing disproportionate benefits to large farmers and widening income disparities in rural areas. It has unquestionably been the case that in the first years after introduction of the new technology, large farmers with a solid capital base and the ability to withstand the risks associated with a change in farming method have been the quickest to plant high-yielding varieties. Recent research on the spread of these varieties in Mexico, India, Philippines, and elsewhere indicates, however, that as farmers become familiar with the results, more and more of the smaller cultivators adopt the new seeds and apply additional fertilizer. Where these smaller cultivators have access to irrigation and credit, the improvement in their productivity is as great or greater than that of larger, more highly mechanized farms. Particularly in India and the Philippines, the prospects for significant improvement in the productivity and well-being of small farmers are quite good if the irrigation and credit constraints can be removed. As the case study papers demonstrate, however, removal of this constraint is not just a technical problem. To give strength to the claim of the rural poor to a larger share of public resources, some social changes will be required—through formation of cooperatives, small farmers' associations, local planning organizations, or through the central government's imposition of policies having redistributional consequences, or some combination of both.

The small farmers to which these generalizations apply are not the marginal subsistence farmers cultivating one hectare or less. They are the group referred to earlier as farming plots of two to five hectares in size. There is no clear evidence that new technologies can provide significant benefits to marginal farmers through improved staple crop production, and it is this group which has probably experienced the worst deterioration of income relative to other social classes, and for which, along with the urban unemployed, the food problem is most serious.

Whether the solution is to keep these marginal farmers on the land is not clear. For some, effective implementation of land reform policies and government investment in infrastructure, credit, and extension services could transform them into successful and productive small farmers. As part of an overall effort to help this group, the importance of continued investment in infrastructure projects, particularly irrigation and transport, needs to be emphasized. Large-scale, capital-intensive infrastructure projects have been criticized as benefiting primarily the rich. Yet, without them, provision of credit, seeds, fertilizer, extension, and marketing services to poor farmers is not likely to produce the desired results, either in terms of increased productivity or higher incomes and improved welfare.

Even if more public funds are channeled their way, not all these marginal farmers will be able to improve their lot by staying on the land, particularly as rural populations continue to grow. Rapid growth in agricultural production on somewhat larger farms can provide additional employment for landless laborers, particularly if efforts are made to discourage labor-displacing investment in tractors and farm machinery. Employment in industries and services that supply farmers' nonfood needs will also increase as farm incomes rise. Thus off-farm migration and an increase in wage employment are not necessarily a sign of deterioration of living standards in the countryside. Rather, an increase in off-farm jobs accompanying agricultural production growth should be a sign of health for backward rural areas.

The effects of price policy on agricultural production and food consumption cannot be clearly discerned from the country studies under review. Only in the case of Egypt does it seem fairly obvious that consumer price subsidies and artificially low producer prices have encouraged increased consumption of imported wheat and discouraged domestic production. Recent increases in producer prices in Mexico and India seem to have produced some response, and the Indian and Venezuelan cases show that governments can separate procurement price policy from food subsidy programs for vulnerable groups, if they choose to do so.

In all five countries, the results of modernization in terms of the overall growth rate for staple crop production have been favorable (Table 3, page 17). Three in fact exceeded 3.5 percent per year for the period 1960-1975—a respectable figure by most standards. To achieve food self-sufficiency, however, past growth rates must be maintained or increased, and this growth must take place in a way that enhances the nutritional status of the low-income population groups.

Self-sufficiency is not an equally desirable goal for all these countries, however, and the possibility of relying on trade to meet part of the food requirements is a real one for some. As a percent of arable land, cash crops are not land-consuming (Table 4, page 18), although they may use the best land and have better access to credit and modern technologies.

In general, cash-crop exports have a higher value than food-crop imports. Because of absolute land scarcity in Mexico and Egypt, high-value exports are probably worth encouraging along with staple crops, since relatively cheap imported wheat can be used to feed increasing urban populations if necessary. In the Philippines, Venezuela, and to a lesser extent, India, however, the cash-crop sector is already well-developed; while it should not be allowed to deteriorate, increasing food production clearly requires the priority attention of governments.

Keener insights into the complexities of the development process and the role of food production in that process should help in the formulation of foreign assistance strategies at both bilateral and multilateral levels. Unfortunately, the legitimate concern with basic human needs which has surfaced recently, particularly in the United States, could lead to oversimplifications which will hinder rather than help move more food to needy people.

When Western observers view the food problems of the Third World, there are several difficulties that often escape notice, but which are of overriding importance in affecting perceptions and conclusions. First, the political underpinnings of Western analysis, if fully worked out, frequently seem to imply that the food needs of poor countries can only be met if there is a radical restructuring of the country's political system. Yet the solutions such analysts favor are usually evolutionary rather than revolutionary; further, most are careful to acknowledge that the existing governments of developing countries have legitimate political concerns other than food and that the resolution of domestic policy conflicts within developing countries themselves has an important bearing on the type of programs for which external assistance is sought.

Development assistance programs which promote the penetration of capitalist-style agriculture in the Third World countries have been criticized as failing to benefit poor farmers; yet the very meaning of the poverty which rural development programs are trying to correct has to do with the lack of participation of large numbers of peasants in the money economy. If, by definition, a farmer is no longer poor and needy as soon as he has reaped the benefits of government programs and modern technology, and if, because of his success we classify him variously as a middle-sized, larger, commercial, or rich farmer and condemn the program because he benefited, then the words we are using are not serving us well.

The problem is particularly acute in considering the situation of farmers owning two to five

hectares, that fuzzy area in which the demarcation between a small, poor, subsistence farmer, and a middle-sized commercial farmer is not very clear. When contrasted with the incomes earned by most middle-class professionals in developed countries, for example, the income levels enjoyed by these small but modernizing farmers are still very low. And when measured against criteria of broader income distribution and economic growth within the developing country, the fact that they are benefiting from agricultural development programs is probably a plus. Thus, suggestions that bilateral and multilateral assistance programs should help the "poorest of the poor" exclusively may run contrary to the very goals of improved welfare and nutrition for the lower income classes in the Third World.

This is not to say that new technologies can be introduced willy-nilly into the countryside without regard for the structure of social organization and the likely level of participation of small farmers in the benefits. It is to say, however, that commercialization of small farmers can be a healthy and is probably a necessary process. Even if this comes about through organization of these small farmers into credit and marketing cooperatives, and their economic power is exercised by them as a group rather than individually, the process is still one in which they receive increased cash income for their food crops and pay more for the production inputs that make increased productivity possible.

A final consideration which is hinted at but not fully developed in the two papers on development assistance contained in this volume is the key role played by the United States, both as regards the conduct of its bilateral programs and as regards its posture in multilateral financial institutions.

Lack of agreement by World Bank Group donors to replenish IDA, for example, can be laid primarily at the feet of the United States, which has consistently refused to pledge the sizable contributions necessary to make possible significant increases in IDA lending. But does this mean that expansion of largely nonconcessionary IBRD loans to those who can afford to pay should be curtailed? Despite the relatively higher level of development of several of the major beneficiaries of World Bank activities, there still remain large numbers of rural and urban poor in these countries who could benefit from multilaterally financed development assistance programs. Rather than arguing for a cutback in World Bank activities in middle-income countries, what needs to be stressed is the serious inadequacy of the U.S. effort, both bilaterally and multilaterally, in relation to its economic and political strength. U.S. foreign assistance is only twice that of Saudi Arabia, the next largest donor, even though Saudi Arabia has but 4 percent of the GNP of the United States. Further, a high proportion of U.S. assistance is concentrated on Israel and Egypt for security reasons. If the United States were really doing its share, its contribution would be 25 times greater than that of the Saudis, and dispersion of substantial amounts to the neediest countries would be possible.

Without question, there is ample room for improvement in the operation of bilateral and multilateral assistance programs, and in the policies and programs of the countries that receive this assistance. However, especially in regard to the World Bank and other multilateral institutions which provide the bulk of the donor community's development assistance, unless caution is exercised critics with legitimate concerns to voice may find themselves unwittingly allied with conservative and isolationist opponents of foreign assistance, who would like to see an end to it altogether. To build support for World Bank

assistance to governments which are gradually trying to evolve to broader participation in political and developmental processes, a balanced approach to what is referred to as "capitalist farming" is in order.

Some of the changes in policy emphasis and in field methods needed to bring the benefits of development to the Third World poor are suggested in the case studies which comprise this volume. Yet the case studies also bring out clearly the magnitude and complexity of the task. Particularly for Americans concerned with world food and equity problems, several points deserve emphasis. First, U.S. policies in trade, aid, military alliances, and other matters have an important effect on the environment within which Third World countries and international financial institutions make their decisions about agricultural development; second, development is a complex political and economic process that requires much of the commercialization and social integration characteristic of modern Western society; third, both developed and developing countries must commit sizable financial and human resources to the process; and finally, Third World political leaders face constraints no less conflicting than Western leadership in accomplishing growth and equity goals. Formulations of programs attuned to these realities will provide the context in which an eventual end to poverty may become possible.

REFERENCES

FAO, *Provisional Indicative World Plan for Agricultural Development*, Rome, 1970.

FAO, *Production Yearbook* and *Trade Yearbook*, Vol. 30, 1976.

World Atlas of Agriculture, Committee for the World Atlas of Agriculture, Instituto Geografico de Agostino, Novara, Italy, 1969, under the aegis of the International Association of Agricultural Economists, four volumes.

K.K. Framji and I.K. Mahajan, *Irrigation and Drainage in the World: A Global Review*. Second Edition, New Delhi: International Commission on Irrigation and Drainage, 1969.

International Rice Research Institute, *Economic Consequences of the New Rice Technology*, Los Banos, Philippines, 1978.

Ralph W. Cummings, Jr., *Land Tenure and Agricultural Development*, LTC No. 17, University of Wisconsin, The Land Tenure Center, July 1978.

Peter Oram, *Criteria and Approaches to the Analysis of Priorities for International Agricultural Research*. Washington, D.C.: International Food Policy Research Institute, Working Paper #1, February 1978.

Land Reform in Latin America: Bolivia, Chile, Mexico, Peru, and Venezuela, World Bank Staff Working Paper No. 275, April 1978.

"Mexico's Population Policy Turnaround," Population Reference Bureau, Inc., Population Bulletin, Vol. 33, No. 5, December 1978.

Fertilizer Situation in Venezuela—1972, FAO Fertilizer Programme Series #2, Rome, 1973.

FAO, *Perspective Study of Agricultural Development for the Arab Republic of Egypt*, ESP/PS/EGY/73/1, Rome, April 1973.

Bent Hansen and Karim Nashashibi, *Foreign Trade Regimes and Economic Development: Egypt*, Chapter 6, "Basic Characteristics of Egyptian Agriculture," New York: National Bureau of Economic Research, 1975, pp. 137-157.

José Encarnacion, Jr., and others, *Philippines Economic Problems in Perspective*, Institute of Economic Development and Research, School of Economics, University of the Philippines, 1976.

David Wurfel, *Philippine Agrarian Policy Today: Implementation and Political Impact*, Institute of Southeast Asian Studies, Occasional Paper No. 46, April 1977.

Asian Development Bank, *Rural Asia: Challenge and Opportunity*, New York: Praeger, 1977.

Government of India, Ministry of Agriculture and Irrigation, *Report of the National Commission of Agriculture: Agrarian Reforms*, Part XV, New Delhi, 1976.

Michael G.G. Schluter, "The Interaction of Credit and Uncertainty in Determining Resource Allocation and Incomes on Small Farms, Surat District, India," Cornell University Ph.D. thesis, August 1973.

John W. Mellor, "Three Issues of Development Strategy—Food, Population, Trade," Washington, D.C. International Food Policy Research Institute, 1978.

Table 1

Land Tenure Patterns

	Total	Population Percent in agriculture	Number of agricultural workers	Index of land concentration	Arable land per farmworker[a]	Average farm size
	(000,000)		(000,000)	(Gini coefficient)	(ha)	(ha)
Mexico				(1960-61)		(1960-61)
1961-65	42.9	50.3	6.3	0.69	3.7	123.90
1975	59.2	40.5	6.9		3.8	(1970) 45.00
Venezuela						1960-61)
1961-65	9.1	30.3	.81	0.936	5.7	81.24
1975	12.2	21.5	.77		6.2	
Egypt						
1961-65	29.4	56.4	4.7	na	.5	1.59
1975	37.5	52.4	5.5		.5	
Philippines				(1960)		
1961-65	32.0	56.9	7.0	0.52	.7	3.59
1975	44.4	49.4	7.8	(1971) 0.51	.7	
India				(1960)		
1961-65	482.4	71.7	142.9	0.59	1.1	2.67
1975	613.2	66.6	159.9	(1971) 0.63	1.0	

a. Arable land per farm worker calculated as total arable cropland divided by economically active population in agriculture. 1965 data are used for earlier period. Average farm size also includes permanent pasture.

Sources: FAO *Production Yearbook*, Vol. 30, 1976 for population and arable land per farm worker.

For average farm size and index of land concentration see *Land Reform*, World Bank Sector Policy Paper, May 1975, Table 1 and Table 1:9; *Land Reform in Latin America: Bolivia, Chile, Mexico, Peru, and Venezuela.* World Bank Staff Working Paper No. 275, April 1978, p. 2, and *Rural Asia: Challenge and Opportunity*, Asian Development Bank, New York: Praeger, 1977, p. 98.

Table 2

Land Utilization

	Total Land Area (000 ha)	Arable Cropland Area[a] (000 ha)		Cropping[b] Intensity Index (percent)	Permanent Cropland Area (000 ha)	Permanent Pasture Area (000 ha)	Forest Area (000 ha)
		Total	Harvested				
Mexico							
1961-65	197,255	23,486	11,954	58[c]	1,422	73,820	80,620
1975		26,220	12,502		1,780	67,000	71,600
Venezuela							
1961-65	88,205	4,580	834	58[c]	637	14,229	
1975		4,760	1,126		557	16,768	47,970
Egypt				(1961-62)			
1961-65	99,545	2,548	4,469[d]	173	78		2
1975		2,862	4,573[d]		132		2
Philippines							
1961-65	29,826	4,840	5,628	(1960)-136	1,967	812	14,700
1975	29,817	5,125	7,728	(1970)-141	2,774	656	12,300
India							
1961-65	296,608	157,185	137,285	(1960)-115	4,813	14,293	58,207
1975		162,500	146,591	(1970)-118	4,700	12,550	67,400

a. Crops harvested on arable land include all those shown in Table 1 except sugar cane, coffee, cocoa, and fibers, which are considered permanent crops. Other permanent crops of importance include bananas, coconuts, palm nuts, and fruit trees. Harvested acreages for 1975 are 1974-1976 averages.

b. Where more than one crop is harvested per year from a given plot of land, the cropping intensity index exceeds 100. Where arable land is left fallow or sown to pasture in some years, the index is less than 100. These indexes may not correspond precisely with proportion of harvested to total area shown in this table, due to difference in data sources.

c. For South America as a region.

d. Includes published figures for harvested area plus unpublished FAO estimate of 1,400,000 ha for area sown to clover.

Sources: *FAO Production Yearbook*, Vol. 30, 1975 for all data except cropping intensity index. For these see FAO, *Provisional Indicative World Plan for Agricultural Development*, Rome, 1970, Vol. I, p. 55 for Latin America; Dana G. Dalrymple, *Survey of Multiple Cropping in Less Developed Nations*, USDA, FEDR-12, October 1971, p. 66 for Egypt, and Asian Development Bank, *Rural Asia: Challenge and Opportunity*, New York, Praeger, 1977, p. 411.

Table 3

Production and Imports of Major Staples, 1961-1965 and 1974-1976
(000 metric tons, cereal equivalent)

	Mexico		Venezuela		Egypt		Philippines		India	
	Production	Net[a] Imports	Production	Net[a] Imports	Production	Net[a] Imports	Production	Net[a] Imports	Production	Net[a] Imports
Wheat										
61-65	1,672	(245)	1	424	1,459	1,507	none	394	11,191	4,514
74-76	2,980	334	1	616	1,959	2,977	none	594	24,539	5,769
Rice, Milled										
61-65	204	(9)	88	(3)	1,199	(327)	2,338	262	34,276	533
74-76	309	22	203		1,559	(151)	3,968	119	44,212	135
Maize										
61-65	7,369	(210)	477	53	1,913	220	1,305	(1)	4,593	111
74-76	8,396	1,601	580	340	2,711	422	2,607	109	6,365	3
Millet & Sorghum[b]										
61-65	452		1		723		none		16,576	
74-76	3,125		114		800		none		18,469	
Roots & Tubers[c]										
61-65	127		145	3	127	(12)	367		1,556	(1)
74-76	209		150	1	225	(15)	435		3,559	(4)
Pulses										
61-65	924	(18)	44	31	411	(31)	35	3	11,700	(9)
74-76	886	(14)	39	35	355	99	29	2	11,134	(3)
Growth Rate (%)										
60-75	4.6		3.5		2.4		3.9		2.5	

a. Parenthesis indicates net exports.
b. Trade figures for millet and sorghum not available.
c. The net import figures relate to potatoes only.

Source: FAO *Trade Yearbook*, Vol. 30, 1976, for production and trade data and IFPRI, *Food Needs of Developed Countries*, Research Report #3, December 1977, for production growth rates.

Table 4

Harvested Acreage, 1961-1965 and 1974-1976

	Mexico	Venezuela	Egypt (000 hectares)	Philippines	India
Wheat					
1961-65	802	2	557		13,402
1974-76	783	2	582		18,901
Rice, paddy					
1961-65	137	79	348	3,147	35,626
1974-76	175	108	456	3,560	38,725
Maize					
1961-65	6,960	441	678	1,978	4,630
1974-76	6,611	483	749	3,588	6,020
Millet & Sorghum					
1961-65	205	1	201		36,793
1974-76	1,150	72	207		35,263
Roots & Tubers					
1961-65	66	65	29	271	797
1974-76	69	78	50	304	1,195
Beans, peas, lentils					
1961-65	2,017	87	209	62	18,225
1974-76	1,952	87	142	49	18,089
Groundnuts					
1961-65	72	2	20	22	7,226
1974-76	51	26	14	49	7,146
Sugar cane					
1961-65	409	45	53	273	2,392
1974-76	487	77	91	495	2,812
Coffee, green					
1961-65	329	330		43	102
1974-76	378	272		65	161
Cocoa beans					
1961-65	69	70		9	
1974-76	82	70		7	
Tea					
1961-65					335
1974-76					363
Tobacco					
1961-65	50	7		92	414
1974-76	40	10		94	404
Fibers					
1961-65		11			1,455
1974-76		11			1,130
Cotton					
1961-65	800	48	738	na	7,987
1974-76	351	68	574	na	7,532
Other					
1961-65	845	102	289	56	11,850
1974-76	1,320	192	399	84	12,593

a. Hemp, jute, sisal.
b. Does not include any permanent crops.

Source: FAO *Production Yearbook*, Vol. 30, 1976.

The Plight of Mexican Agriculture

Thomas G. Sanders

The expectation that Mexico's current population of about 65 million people will probably double within the next 25 or 30 years underlies Mexico's increasingly serious food production problem. Population growth rates of more than 3 percent annually have prevailed since the late 1940s as a result of drops in mortality, especially infant mortality. Despite the ever more ominous necessity of feeding its increasing contingents of people, Mexican society has been unable to respond to the challenge. To the contrary, during the past 10 years food production has increased less than the rate of population growth, and has fallen even farther behind growing demand for food among population groups with rising incomes. The shortage of food, in turn, has contributed to major economic distortions such as high deficits in the balance of payments and an indebtedness that is now straining the nation's capacity to service it.

Although Mexico is a country of medium-range development, inequitable distribution of available food resources among different classes and regions results in an adequate diet for perhaps half the population but serious deficiencies for the other half. The deficiencies are to be found in nearly all parts of the country among the rural and urban lower classes. The traditional basis of the Mexican diet has been corn, beans, and chiles, with corn constituting over 80 percent of total consumption in the poorest segments of the population. Among peasants, who still represent about 40 percent of the nation's inhabitants, the basic staples are supplemented by seasonal fruits, alcoholic beverages like *pulque* (made from the agave plant or *maguey* as it is called),

and a wide range of plants, leaves, roots, insects, birds, and rodents that are considered unacceptable by more affluent people. The common diet is supplemented at fiestas by special foods, usually prepared with a corn base, but which include meat. Among the lower income classes of the cities, commercially produced "junk foods" which are high in sugar and low in nutrient value tend to provide the supplements to corn and beans.

Although the combination of corn and beans has a favorable relationship of amino acids and a high protein content, while chiles are rich in vitamins, millions of Mexicans are still poorly nourished. Milk consumption is almost nonexistent among lower-class children after weaning, because of its high cost and because of cultural inhibitions against its use. A study several years ago indicated that the average Mexican ate only 14 kilos of meat annually, which suggests very low levels among the lower classes. Mexico, with thousands of miles of coastline, is rich in seafood, but production is low because of inadequate marketing facilities, the excessive charges of intermediaries, and its unfamiliarity as a diet item among most of the population.

Serious malnutrition is apparently not very common in the most technologically advanced parts of Mexico (i.e., the Northwest and the area along the border of the United States), but nutritional studies in poor, southern, predominantly peasant states like Chiapas, Oaxaca, Guerrero, and Yucatan have shown that consumption levels average about 1,900 calories per day, including about 50 grams of protein. This falls about 400 calories short of minimum nutritional standards established by FAO and lacks about 12 grams of protein[1]

In times of bad weather or unemployment, consumption of even the basic staples declines. In May 1978, conversations with peasants in the central valley of the state of Oaxaca, which has had inadequate rainfall in the past two years, revealed that families with temporary work were eating beans with their corn only once or twice a week. Those who were unemployed had no money to buy even corn and were subsisting from wild plants gathered in the mountains that are not ordinarily part of the diet, but are resorted to in extreme emergencies to avoid starvation. Doctors in the same area indicate that severe malnutrition among children is common. Other parts of Oaxaca, like the Mixteca and the Mixe regions, are far poorer than the central valley, so that in Oaxaca and other backward parts of Mexico, malnutrition and hunger have apparently reached grave proportions.

By 1971 total agricultural production had increased by 32 percent from the 1961-1965 base period. Food production grew somewhat faster, increasing by 41 percent over the same period. Since 1971 production has stagnated however, resulting in a steady decline in per capita production. The net result in terms of per capita food availability from domestic sources since 1961 has been a virtual standstill (see Table 1).

More important, production of major cereal grains declined sharply in the early 1970s and has not recovered sufficiently to keep up with increasing population. Production and import figures for major cereals shown in Tables 2 and 3 illustrate dramatically what has been happening to Mexico's food supply. Corn production dropped off nearly 10 percent in 1973 and had still not recovered fully by 1976. From 1965 through 1976 corn production declined at an average rate of -0.4 percent per year. Bean production also suffered in 1974 and production declined at a rate of -0.6 percent per year over the 12-year period.

Wheat, rice, barley, and sorghum have not performed so poorly, but they represent a rela-

tively small share of total staple crop consumption. After a spurt in 1969 and 1970, wheat production dropped off in 1971-1973, but picked up again thereafter. Growth rates for the 4 crops from 1965-1976 were 5.3 percent, 4.1 percent, 7.4 percent, and 10.4 percent respectively.

Largely because of the fall-off in domestic corn supply and to a lesser extent because of problems with wheat in the early 1970s, Mexico was forced to increase the volume of its cereal imports substantially. From an average of 198.9 thousand metric tons of cereal imports for the 6 years from 1965 through 1970, the figure jumped to 1,816.9 thousand metric tons for the 1971 through 1976 period.

The poor performance of the agricultural sector has stimulated a wide debate in Mexico. The central issue is how much longer a population that is increasing at a rate now estimated at 3.2 percent, and whose demand for food is rising at about 4.5 percent, can continue to tolerate an agricultural system that is deteriorating rather than expanding.

In recent years, the government has resorted to two types of policies. One, the short-term approach evident from the figures noted above, has been to import food. The second has been to try to stimulate increased food production. Since much of this paper will be dedicated to the second approach, it is useful first to examine the effects on the country's economy from increasing food imports.

In the years preceding 1965, Mexico was practically self-sufficient in basic foodstuffs, and agricultural exports were its most important source of foreign exchange for the ambitious industrialization program under way since 1940. Agricultural production was especially stimulated by two factors: one was an agreement between the Mexican government and the Rockefeller Foundation that set off the "Green Revolution" in wheat and helped improve technology in other crops. The second stimulus was U.S. demand for food products and raw materials like vegetables, shrimp, coffee, sugar, and cotton. As a result, Mexico had a favorable agricultural trade balance until the early 1970s. Though it imported a modest $140 million of food products in 1970, its agricultural exports far exceeded this figure.

During the 1970s, however, production of staple food crops fell off while at the same time world market prices for basic foodstuffs were shooting up sharply. Thus Mexico's food imports rose at an alarming rate, both in amount and in value. The major imports were grains, vegetable oils and oilseeds, and milk products. Between 1972 and 1974 the bill for these items rose from $113 million to $749 million; in 1975 Mexico imported nearly $398 million of corn alone.

Although agriculture was not the only source of Mexico's balance of payments problems, it was a major one. Manageable payments deficits of only a little over $700 million in 1972 and 1973 skyrocketed in 1974, reaching $2.6 billion. The following year the deficit rose to $3.8 billion and still exceeded $3.0 billion in 1976.[2] As a result of this crisis in the Mexican economy, President Luis Echeverria (1970-1976) left office amid a national loss of confidence of which the peso devaluation of the latter part of 1976 was the most vivid symbol. In 1977, under new President José López Portillo, Mexico made an agreement with the International Monetary Fund to carry out an austerity program, so that, despite Mexico's substantial future petroleum potential, the IMF limited the country to an indebtedness during the year of no more than $3 billion.

Mexico underwent a modest economic recovery in 1978, and anticipates that by 1980 petroleum production will be sufficient to relieve its balance of payments problems. Providing an adequate food supply will continue to be one of the nation's principal economic problems however. Thoughtful Mexicans recognize that petroleum earnings, if wisely invested, can be the key to future national industrialization and development; but the same earnings may have to be used to import food if the agricultural sector does not produce sufficiently and provide employment for a respectable portion of the population through more labor-intensive methods and increased production.

The Political Culture of Mexico

It is noteworthy that both Mexican presidents of the 1970s, Echeverria and López Portillo, have identified agricultural growth and increased food production as the number one domestic aim of their administrations. This represents, in theory, a break with the rhetoric and politics of the past three decades. On the rhetorical side, the previous focus on industrialization and its correlate assumption that increased food production would follow in its wake, is now replaced by a recognition that food crops, livestock, and fisheries must receive special attention and allocations. On the political side, the shift seems to suggest that the alliance which had underlain industrialization—built on businessmen, urban labor, technocrats, and politicians—is to be expanded to include the interests of the long-neglected rural sector.

Public rhetoric proclaiming the aims of Mexican presidents and repeated by their conformist followers must always be treated with skepticism in the Mexican context. All presidential administrations bombard the public with an unending, mind-boggling litany of their incomparable achievements and dynamic programs in process. This serves as an instrument by which a rigid authoritarian system has maintained itself in power over 50 years, overwhelming potential opposition criticism and covering up for the failure, corruption, and almost total disinterest in the public welfare that are the chief characteristics of the political bureaucrats who run Mexico.

Thus, in Mexico, to affirm that increasing agricultural production is a central public aim may mean that some government leaders genuinely have an interest in the nourishment of the citizens or in resolving the country's economic problems. It can also mean many other things, such as the following: (1) The country must produce more food to maintain social stability, because violence from starving citizens and rural unemployment can threaten the system itself. (2) Members of the President's political faction can increase their opportunities for personal enrichment through percentages on contracts tendered under new programs and patronage for political supporters who are awarded jobs in the new insti-

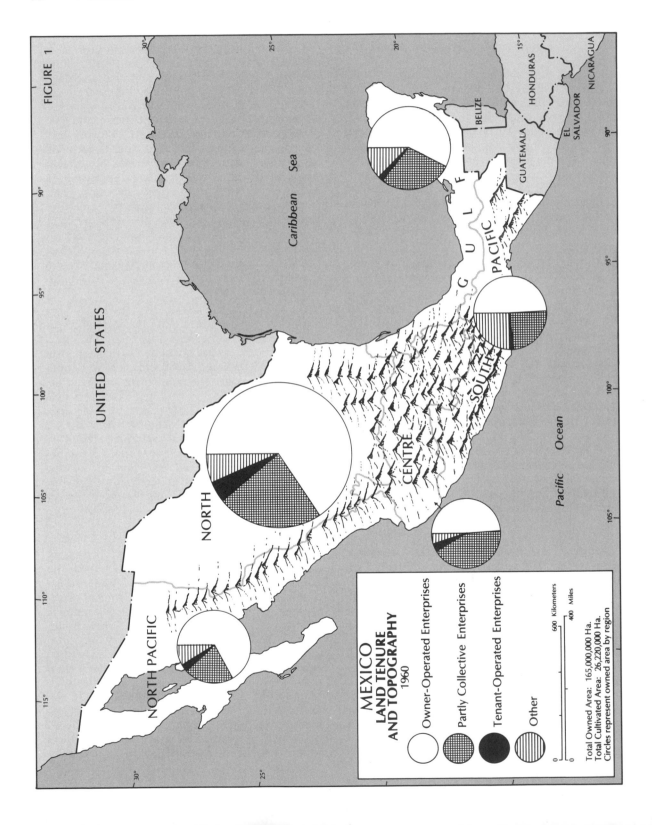

FIGURE 1

MEXICO
**LAND TENURE
AND TOPOGRAPHY**
1960

○ Owner-Operated Enterprises
▦ Partly Collective Enterprises
● Tenant-Operated Enterprises
▥ Other

0   600 Kilometers
0   400 Miles

Total Owned Area: 165,000,000 Ha.
Total Cultivated Area: 26,220,000 Ha.
Circles represent owned area by region

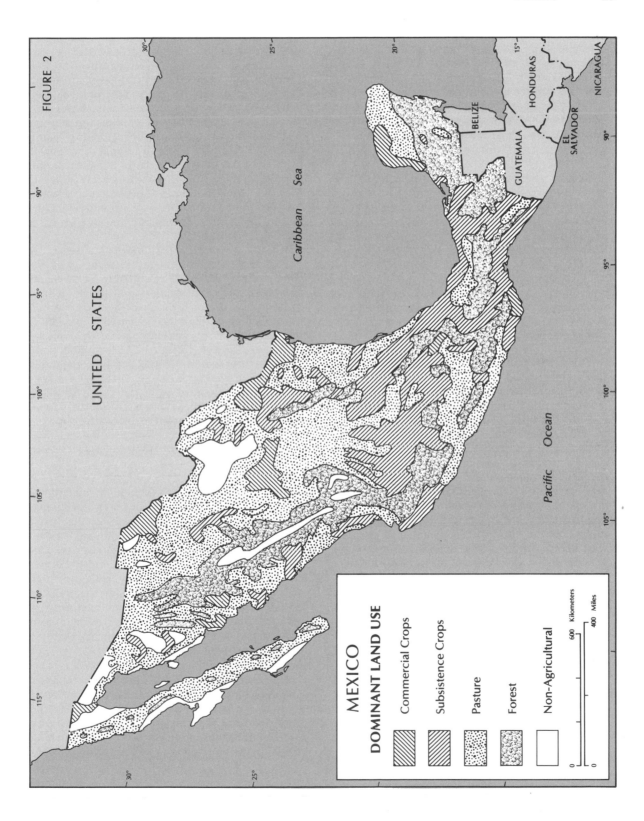

FIGURE 2

tutions created to run these programs. (3) In the struggle among Mexico's many political factions, the support of interest groups and institutional leaders whose power really counts in determining who holds office and can get money requires that lip service be given to increasing agricultural production. (4) A change in rhetoric will work to Mexico's advantage in obtaining support for its programs from the international community.

Despite the presence of a single dominant party in Mexico—the Revolutionary Institutional Party (PRI)—the political system is based on a delicate consensus among major interest groups. Most of them are incorporated into the party itself (except business), and the loyalty of their leaders to the system, rather than to their constituents, is guaranteed by awarding them offices and money. A key skill in Mexican politics is maintaining the support of major groups despite the swings of policy emphasis that mark individual presidential administrations.

This reality helps explain the different "styles" that Echeverría and López Portillo have adopted in dealing with agriculture and the rural population, despite their centrality in the administrative plans of both men. Echeverría came to office in 1970, after at least two decades of growing public criticism that the poor, and especially those in the rural areas, had been neglected in the process of economic development. Production statistics of the previous 5 years, and the decline of government expenditure on agriculture and livestock from an estimated 20 percent of the budget in the early 1950s to about 9 percent, seemed to confirm this analysis. Since every presidential administration tries to distinguish itself rhetorically from the previous one, Echeverría decided to adopt the "populist" route after the parsimonious and repressive terms of his predecessor, Gustavo Díaz Ordaz. Apparently unaware of the complexities of the agricultural scene, Echeverría gave strong verbal support to social change for the poorer peasants and drastically expanded government programs in the countryside. Some of these may have been useful, but others served chiefly as emergency jobs for the unemployed and opened up many lucrative positions in government and chances for corruption by Echeverría's faction.

Whatever Echeverría's personal view of the peasants' situation (he is a native of Mexico City who at no time held an administrative job that would have given him rural exposure), his approach promised to reap rich political dividends by opening up vast new opportunities for jobs and corruption and by gaining the support of the establishment-controlled peasants' syndicate, the Confederacion Nacional Campesina (CNC). His use of populist rhetoric in his drive for domestic political power was intimately linked to the other major emphasis of his administration—his pretentious, quixotic, and ultimately embarrassing quest for international fame as a leader of the Third World bloc.

It is extremely doubtful that the peasants benefited very much, if at all, from Echeverría's approach. Latin American populists are inclined to promote their own political interests through unfulfilled promises to the neglected segments of the population. In this case, since the average Mexican peasant hates the government and wants as little to do with it as possible, expanded government programs to help poorer peasants were virtually doomed from the start. Although millions of words of rhetoric were spilled in favor of the peasants, thousands of politicians and bureaucrats manipulated colonization schemes and rural development programs to benefit themselves.

Furthermore, the long-time political balance that has held Mexico together was upset, and what many observers described as the worst political crisis in decades accompanied Echeverría as he left office. His populist rhetoric confused and alienated the middle and upper classes, both urban and rural, so that they held on to their money or sent it outside the country. In the rural areas, the large and medium-size private landowners regarded the government as a supporter of land invasions, which led them to reduce investment and production.

The new president, López Portillo, is taking a completely different approach. He has continued many of the work-welfare programs among the rural poor and is trying to get them to produce more food, but his emphasis is on re-establishing the old political equilibrium by restoring the confidence of medium- and large-scale producers. He has done this by assuring them against land invasions and promising government sympathy for their role in investment and production. Though the small farmer in the private and *ejidal* (agrarian reform) sectors is not totally neglected, there is no question that the government expects the real results to come from the larger farmers.

Whether López Portillo will be successful or not is too early to determine. Petroleum resources could provide the way out by guaranteeing the means to finance substantial increases in investment in food production. But on the basis of past Mexican experience, the country is more likely to seek the easy way out—importing food instead of producing it, and diverting a large part of the petroleum bonanza into the pockets of government officials and union leaders. The principal government institutions concerned with food such as the Secretariat of Agriculture and Livestock, the Secretariat of Agrarian Reform, the Compañía Nacional de Subsistencias Populares (CONASUPO), and the Banco Nacional de Crédito Rural are all centers of corruption and inefficiency that lose millions of dollars annually. They publish only the most minimum financial data, refuse to grant interviews, and evade any form of public accountability.

The alternative, of course, is an extremely rapid industrialization and development financed by petroleum in the next 20 years, which would greatly reduce the rural population and enable those who stay to be more productive. Given the characteristics of Mexican political culture and the government which is a reflection of it, this is at best a hope and more likely a utopia.

The political culture which is both the creation and curse of Mexico is only one of the problems the country faces in increasing food production. Mexican agriculture is complex and cannot be reduced to a few generalities. The rest of this paper will discuss the physical limitations of the land available for agriculture, then proceed to the land tenure system that has evolved since the Mexican Revolution and is a major obstacle to increasing agricultural production, and finally consider the evolution of official policies toward agriculture during the 1970s and the reasons for their relative ineffectiveness.

Physical Limitations of the Land

For centuries Mexicans thought of their country as one with extraordinary agricultural and livestock potential. The existence of vast tracts of land that were minimally exploited—from cattle ranches in the North to unexplored lowlands in the Southeast—encouraged this belief. In 1900, when the population was 13.5 million, the belief might have had some validity: the regime of President Porfirio Díaz did what it could to transfer as much land as possible to entrepreneurs on the assumption that Mexican prosperity depended essentially on opening up and utilizing the national territory. But now that Mexico's population is nearly five times as large and expected to be nine times as much in the year 2000, we must take a hard look at the genuine limitations of Mexico's cultivable resources.

Topography. A consideration of Mexico's topography provides a quick antidote to optimism. Few countries of the world are as mountainous as Mexico. Of the 196.7 million hectares (one hectare = 2.47 acres) in the country, only 71 million or 36 percent are level or with inclines of less than 25 degrees. Though slopes of more than 25 degrees should not normally be cultivated, in many parts of Mexico the peasants plant them with corn or *maguey* because of the shortage of more suitable land.

Erosion. The common tendency to cultivate hillsides without terracing is one of several factors contributing to erosion, which is another of the physical limitations of the land. Only 34 million hectares of Mexico's total surface are *not* classified as eroded. Of those that are, 25.5 million hectares are totally eroded, 44 million are in an advanced state of erosion, and the rest is moderately eroded.[3]

Unlike many other countries of Latin America that are believed to have considerable untapped agricultural potential, the regions of Mexico with the greatest density of rural population have been cultivated almost constantly for centuries, thus contributing to the exhaustion and erosion of the soil. At the time of the Spanish Conquest many parts of the country were already overpopulated, when measured by land available and techniques of cultivation that were prevalent. Only a combination of constant warfare, human sacrifice, and the migration of ethnic groups helped maintain a reasonable balance between land and population. Population dropped drastically as a result of factors—especially disease—introduced by the Spaniards, but the number of Mexicans today is well over twice as many as the most generous estimate in 1520.

Water. Mexico also has limited supplies of water for agriculture. The country has few major rivers. Available water is poorly distributed in relation to the current patterns of population settlement. The zones of great population concentration, like the Central Highlands and the border with the United States, face water deficits. Though total water potential in these areas has not yet been completely tapped, the combined pressure of agricultural, industrial, hydroelectrical, and domestic demands already exceeds available supply. In contrast, most of the water in Mexico is found at low altitudes, especially in the Southeast, where population is relatively sparse.

About 43 percent of the national territory is classified as arid and 34 percent semiarid. The arid zones cannot be cultivated without irrigation. The semiarid ones can be cultivated during the six-month rainy season, though with considerable insecurity and sometimes a total loss of the crop. About 16 percent of Mexico's land is semi-humid: there one can cultivate crops every year without supplements to the normal rainfall, though irrigation improves production. Finally, 7 percent is humid and can be cultivated without irrigation, although control of excess water is often necessary.[4]

Since the 1920s Mexican policymakers have recognized the need to harness water resources for agriculture and other purposes. As a result Mexico has developed one of the most extensive irrigation systems in the world. A period of massive dam construction from 1945 to 1960 and the use of improved seeds set off the Green Revolution in wheat and contributed satisfactory production increases in other crops during that period. Since 1965, however, though irrigation projects continue to expand, food output has not responded accordingly. Other inhibiting factors have had more effect on the results.

As to the future, further exploitation of water, while possible, will become more difficult and expensive. The easiest rivers have already been harnessed. The decades to come will require more intensive exploitation of surface and sub-surface water deposits, the transfer of water from surplus to deficit regions, and a national policy of conservation of water.

Given the effects of topography, erosion, and water, the total land resources available for agriculture are quite restricted. According to an estimate made in 1974:

The total irrigated area of Mexico can be estimated at 11 million hectares, including 3 million which can be irrigated with subsoil water. Another 19 million can be cultivated by rainfall, in more or less uncertain conditions depending on location, that include 2 million located in the humid zones, which require dams for control and channeling the rivers as well as for blocking, channeling, and draining the land. In sum, the agricultural future of Mexico is based on the exploitation of 30 million hectares.[5]

Though government hydraulic experts have made a more generous estimate that as many as 16 million hectares may possibly be irrigated, this still means that total cultivable land resources may reach only 35 or 40 million hectares. If this is true, a maximum of 20 percent of the country's land area is cultivable, that is, about a half hectare for each of its present 65 million inhabitants. In the early part of the next century, when population is expected to double, only one-fourth hectare per person will be available to grow crops.

Weather. Persistent bad weather in recent years should be understood within the framework of these physical limitations. The most common government explanation of low agricultural production is the weather. For example, the Banco de Mexico's annual report says that "the low level of production in 1976 occurred because of the decline in availability of water in the reservoirs, the intense drought that continued until the month of June, the marked irregularity in the rains, and the presence of frost in the North of the country."[6]

The variety of weather problems stems from the range of agricultural environments and is exacerbated by overpopulation, the poor quality of the soil, and the chronically low rainfall in many parts of the country. Crops are grown in high altitudes approaching 3,000 meters and in tropical rainforests, in regions ranging from aridity to extreme humidity. Harvests on the national level can be affected by too little or too much rain (often in the form of hurricanes) or by heat and cold, depending on the specific environment. In irrigated areas, insufficient precipitation may keep the rivers low and fail to fill the reservoirs, while in nonirrigated zones, inadequate rains may reduce or destroy the harvest. Both of these effects of low rainfall have plagued Mexico in 1977 and 1978. Especially in Mexico's many areas of poor, eroded soil, which often are overcultivated because there is no more land available, the shortage of rain or other adverse weather factors may be the proximate but not the primary cause of a poor or nonexistent harvest. Thus, the official view that poor production in nearly all recent years is due to bad weather should be considered within the total context of fragility in which the peasant operates.

In a small town in the state of Yucatan, for example, many peasants who engage in slash-and-burn agriculture are abandoning that way of life because the effort they must make is no longer worth it. Though they often cite specific weather problems as the cause of their poor harvests, a more basic explanation seems to be the overuse of land and consequent loss of soil fertility stemming from overpopulation. Their Maya ancestors farmed the area, which is extremely rocky, for centuries, but when population was less they could let land lie fallow for 20 years. According to their accounts they had abundant harvests until about two generations ago; now, with an increase in population, land can be left idle for only eight years. Corn crops produce much lower yields and are also seriously affected by any inclement weather; many farmers complain they can no longer grow beans and other traditional crops at all.

The usual reaction of someone who hears about these physical limitations is to think in terms of a technical solution that would organize the Mexican peasants in Israeli or Chinese fashion, making them more efficient farmers and providing them with modern inputs like credit, fertilizer, improved seeds, and small-scale irrigation developments. In the Mexican case, some mobilization and modernization will certainly be necessary in any eventual solution. However, as agricultural scientists often point out, the technology to feed people is already available, but the delivery system, which depends on government commitment and efficiency, is frequently lacking. Mexico has an exceptionally unfavorable situation for improving its agricultural output by technical means because of its political context and land tenure situation.

Land Tenure

A serious obstacle to increased production is the system of land tenure. For over 60 years, Mexico's system of landholding has been and continues to be the product of political impulses and pressures, carried out within an environment of official disinterest, inefficiency, and corruption and peasant distrust and cynicism toward the government. The Mexican land structure, consequently, cannot yet be regarded as an established framework within which to improve production, but rather as an unconcluded process, still characterized by instability, uncertainty, exploitation of the peasants, and political manipulation.

The present land tenure structure has multiple origins, although the Mexican Revolution and the accompanying impulse to agrarian reform have had the most impact in the twentieth century. The Revolution of 1910-1917 took place against a nineteenth-century background of expansion of *latifundios*. During that period land which had previously belonged to the Catholic Church and to the indigenous communities was incorporated into large, private landholdings. The Liberal reformers of the nineteenth century had not intended to create a system of extreme concentration of property. They hoped instead to form a large class of medium-sized farmers. But individuals with power and money, both Mexicans and foreigners, were able to take advantage of the land policies to accumulate vast and minimally utilized properties. By 1910 Mexico had 56,825 *haciendas* and other agricultural properties, 11,117 free villages that were not part of *haciendas*, and about 3 million peasants who usually worked on the *haciendas*.[7]

The Mexican Revolution itself had limited agrarian objectives. The principal victorious leaders came from the Northern part of the country, which was sparsely populated, and some of them were large landholders (*latifundistas*) themselves. The indigenous peasants of the Center and South, in contrast, whose principal chieftain was Emiliano Zapata, took up arms to restore lands that had been taken from them by expanding *haciendas*. Recovery of indigenous community property was the principal emphasis in Zapata's Plan of Ayala in 1911 and in the first revolutionary agrarian legislation of 1915.

Article 27 of the Constitution of 1917, which is still the charter of agricultural policy, reflected the duality between the communal tradition of the indigenous population and the belief in private property that entered Mexico with the Spanish Conquest. On the one hand, Article 27 emphasized the restoration of land to villages or other communities that had been despoiled of it, thus satisfying the interest of many peasants who fought in the Revolution. On the other hand, Article 27 responded to an increasing demand for land redistribution by giving the "Nation" the right to regulate land for the public interest, including such means as dividing large holdings, creating new centers of population, and promoting small-scale private farming.

Until the 1930s, the principal emphasis of agrarian policy was in providing land to communities that fulfilled the established regulations. The presidents in this epoch, however, sympathized with private property and had no intention of breaking up the large estates.

During this stage some of the permanent problems of the agrarian reform had already appeared. Most grants of land took place in the Central Highlands, which were densely populated. There the quality of the soil was often poor and the size of the parcels too small to produce a decent existence. Though the legislative framers proclaimed that they were re-establishing the communal tradition of the indigenous groups by

instituting a cooperative-like system in the form of *ejidos*, the peasants in most cases had long since lost their communal impulses and were interested in farming their own plots. Consequently the *ejidos* did not function in a cooperative manner, but each member received a parcel and cultivated it on his own. Agricultural methods remained traditional—the use of oxen for plowing and the dependence on crops like corn, beans, and chiles—and the government did not allocate money or personnel to experiment with means for augmenting production.

Finally, even though the *ejidos* were formed, the participants usually did not complete the bureaucratic process that would guarantee them definitive title to their land because of the expenses required for surveying and bribes to officials, the voluminous documentation, and the delays imposed by inefficiency and lack of personnel in the system itself. The most dependent and exploited portion of the agricultural population, the *acasillados*, or workers on the *haciendas*, were not even considered by the legislation as eligible for receiving land.

Presidents Alvaro Obregón (1920-1924) and Plutarco Elías Calles (1924-1928) continued the policy of forming *ejidos*, but envisioned that the future agricultural progress of the country would come from the private sector. Many *haciendas* and *latifundios* were left relatively undisturbed by the government, though the total number of property owners greatly increased through private purchase of land. By 1930, the *ejidos* were unquestionably an appreciable part of the agrarian structure, but there were only 8,345 of them, possessing a mere 6.3 percent of the nation's land resources.[8]

With Lázaro Cárdenas (1934-1940) Mexico had its first post-Revolution President who strongly sympathized with *ejidos* and with cooperative and collective forms of exploitation. Whereas *ejidos* had previously been concentrated in some of the poorest and most densely populated parts of the country, Cárdenas expropriated *haciendas* on a massive scale and established *ejidos* in some of the most prosperous commercial districts. Furthermore, he included *hacienda* workers among the beneficiaries of the agrarian reform. Especially where production was already large scale, relatively modernized, and commercially oriented, the *ejidos* were organized collectively. Most, however, continued in the pattern of restricting community ownership to forest or grazing lands while each individual farmed his own plot.

During the Cárdenas administration alone, about twice as much land, over 20 million hectares, was redistributed as in the period from 1915 to 1934. By 1940, 50.2 percent of rural landholders were *ejidatarios*; their portion of the total hectarage had increased to 22.5 percent, including 47.4 percent of the land considered cultivable and 57.4 percent of that with irrigation.[9]

The massive way in which land was distributed under Cárdenas accentuated even more the bureaucratic difficulties of the *ejidatarios*. These difficulties arose from two causes: widespread conflicts over land claims in general in Mexico, and the complicated procedure required for *ejidos* to achieve final possession of assigned land.

Ejidos are supposed to be formed from lands that are available for expropriation and lie within seven kilometers of the petitioning group. However, owing to the haste and carelessness of the surveys over many years, especially when skilled persons were in short supply, there are overlapping claims on much of the *ejidal* land. Settling these disputes is a complex, often almost impossible process.

Many *ejidos* have not followed through on the administrative procedure because of its complexity, expense, and the obstacles placed by corrupt and indifferent officials. Delineation of an *ejido* requires two stages.[10] In the first, the Mixed Agrarian Commission of a state investigates the petition and makes a recommendation based on the petitioners' qualifications and the availability of land. Usually adhering to the position of this report, the governor makes his decision, and if he approves, the boundaries of the *ejido* are provisionally defined, and the peasants can occupy and use the land. Full possession, however, must await a presidential decision, which involves new bureaucratic processes and leads to a definitive determination of *ejidal* boundaries and the presentation of titles that guarantee the right of each individual to his *ejidal* land. The expense of the survey, which the peasants must pay, plus the lengthy delays in making decisions, have had the effect of discouraging the *ejidatarios* from completing the process. In a study of 81 *ejidos*, it was found that the first stage lasted an average of 8 years, and the second, up to the definitive demarcation of the *ejidal* boundaries, 9 years and 6 months. To complete the second stage, with the reception of "rights" to a particular parcel, required a minimum of 20 and a maximum of 40 years. It is not surprising that in the late 1960s, it was estimated that only 7.5 percent of the *ejidos* in the country had concluded the procedure.[11]

The ongoing submission of petitions to the government is a result of the policy, based on social criteria, that every Mexican who works in the countryside but does not possess enough land for an adequate existence has a right to it. Consequently the Secretariat of Agrarian Reform has thousands of claims pending which it does not have time to handle and for which there is little land still remaining, hardly ever within seven kilometers of where the petitioners live.

The capacity of the Mexican government to provide land for all claimants has been undermined by the increase of population in the decades since the agrarian reform began. In 1910, Mexico had an estimated three million landless peasants. Since the national population dropped between 1910 and 1920, it is possible that Mexico could have provided land successfully to its rural population if it had wanted to push ahead rapidly and complete the process between 1920 and 1930. Since then, however, even though the rural percentage of the population has dropped from about 90 to 40, and over 2 million *ejidatarios* have received property, there are now about 4 million landless peasants, few of whom have any chance of eventually owning their parcels. The government itself has aggravated the situation by not admitting frankly that there is no more land available and that it cannot responsibly continue to receive more petitions.

In addition to its incomplete character, the *ejidal* system is composed of small plots that make most *ejidatarios* into *minifundistas*. According to the agricultural census of 1970, out of 1,847,533 *ejidal* parcels, only 166,555 had more than 10 hectares of cultivable land. About 60 percent, or 1,056,858, held 4 or fewer hectares; a total of 327,183 had less than one hectare.[12] The regulations for forming new *ejidos*, since the late 1940s, provide for the minimum grant to be 10 hectares of irrigated or 20 hectares of rainfed land, but since this quantity is rarely available, the petitioners at best receive a smaller amount with rights to expand the *ejido* if additional expropriable property appears. The fact is that further property does not exist, the new *ejidatarios* only increase the number of *minifundistas*, and the Secretariat of Agrarian Reform has its archives filled with requests for expansion of *ejidos*.

The slowness of the agrarian reform process has inhibited possibilities of organizing *ejidos* collectively to encourage production. Since most *ejidatarios* cultivate their own plots, over the years they have tended to differentiate along a spectrum ranging from those who work hard, invest, and achieve a reasonable production to others who give their plots minimal attention because they have other sources of income, or in many cases rent or neglect them.[13] Any program to organize the *ejidos* so as to equalize status would be resisted by those peasants who have struggled to achieve a better relative standard of living. A number of political leaders, including former President Echeverría, advocated the "collectivization" (which is the Mexican term for fulfilling the cooperative potential) of the *ejidos* as a solution to their low levels of production, but their proposals foundered dismally on the practical difficulty of overcoming the established practices of decades.

Furthermore, the record of collective *ejidos* is not encouraging. Though a few do well, others have fallen into a pattern of dependence on the government for organization and credit, politization for purposes of corruption, lack of motivation by the *ejidatarios*, and inefficiency of production.[14]

The pattern of the agrarian reform in turn has affected productivity in the private sector. In addition to the *ejidos* and indigenous communal properties (which are structurally similar to *ejidos*), Mexican legislation allows for *pequeños propietarios* (smallholders). The term itself symbolizes the rejection in principle of large holdings, but obscures the diverse forms that private agricultural property assumes in Mexico.

In 1970, out of 997,324 private holdings, 608,932, or about 61 percent, were less than 5 hectares, while 255,020, or about a fourth, were less than one hectare. These comprise the private (in contrast with *ejidal*) *minifundios*. Another 101,918 had from 5 to 10 hectares.[15]

A second type of *pequeño propietario* is the farmer possessing from 10 to 100 hectares. The census of 1970 records 210,768 of these medium-sized holdings.

Finally, there is a small class of landholders with more than 100 hectares. Most of them have this status legally since the legislation allows a maximum reserve of 100 hectares of irrigated and 200 hectares of rainfed land. A farmer can also retain up to 300 hectares if they are planted in commercial crops like bananas, henequen, sugar cane, coffee, coconuts, cacao, or fruit trees. Anyone who qualifies according to these criteria is automatically a large-scale and probably prosperous farmer. One can also legally own the amount of property necessary to maintain 500 head of cattle. Many large landholdings are formed by combining the land held by several relations into a single enterprise that exceeds the legal limits. Others are clearly illegal because the individual may have enough power in his locality to possess the quantity of land he wants without any action being taken against him.

Although the medium and large landholders play the most important role in Mexico's commercial and export agriculture, they do not fulfill their productive potential in part because of fear of occupation by landless peasants and expropriation for *ejidos*. Though this is especially true among those whose status is illegal, even legal properties are subject to invasions and possible decisions by government that part of the land is expropriable. Livestock producers are especially vulnerable because the criteria for establishing the legal limit are vague and often determined by pressures or the political attitudes of government officials. During the Echeverría administration private landowners became convinced that the government was hostile to them as a class, and consequently they did not make investments to increase their production.

The Mexican policy of dragging out agrarian reform for over 60 years has not solved the problem of land tenure, but exacerbated it. Landholding possibilities are diverse, but insecure, thus inhibiting the long-range investments that farmers make because they are certain of future control over their land. The failure to terminate land expropriations and assure stability is a result of a chain of factors: the ongoing willingness to receive petitions from individuals with a theoretical right to land even though land is not available, the incapacity of government agencies to terminate the thousands of cases still in process, and the failure to decide whether many large holdings are legal or not.[16]

The vast bulk of Mexican landowners, whether they are *pequeños propietarios* or *ejidatarios*, are *minifundistas*. Although smallholdings in many countries provide the basis of a productive agriculture, this has not been so in Mexico. In part this is due to the poor quality of the soil and the dependence of most smallholders on rainfall, but also because the techniques traditionally used by the peasants are inadequate. Rather than try to intensify production, the customary reaction of the Mexican smallholder has been to combine a traditional and marginal farming with other sources of income. Thus, he may try to grow most of the corn and beans he needs for his family's consumption while seeking jobs in his home region or elsewhere. In many instances, he may rent his land to another person, which at least can be considered a positive measure because it means that the renter is trying to work more efficiently with larger units of land. In other instances the owner may simply abandon his land if it is of low fertility and eroded.

Although an exact estimate of their number is not available, landless workers compose 54 percent of the economically active population in agriculture. The landless laborers do not predominantly reside in the highly developed agricultural areas. Most, in fact, reside in the poorer areas, although in states where agriculture is highly developed, landless laborers form a substantial portion of the total rural population.

If they are fortunate, the landless may cultivate the land of their parents who retain ownership to assure security in their old age, or they may rent or sharecrop someone else's property. In many instances, they work for individuals in the community who can pay for occasional assistance. They may migrate to other areas to do seasonal work such as harvesting sugar, cotton, vegetables, and coffee. Many of the Mexicans who work in the rural areas of the United States, either legally or illegally, come from this background.

In regions with irrigated and commercial agriculture, where the rural wage-earning class constitutes a high percentage of the total agricultural work force, landless laborers can earn a relatively decent living. In border states such as Baja California, Sonora, and Coahuila, agricultural laborers can also spend strategic periods as illegal workers in the United States. In the states of the Center like Michoacán, Hidalgo, and Tlaxcala, where rural overcrowding and *minifundios* are common, landless peasants also represent elevated percentages of the total rural population. In these regions the options are fewer, however, and the prospects for making a good living are quite slim.

There is little prospect that those without land can gain access to it. Even on the assumption that parts of some illegal large landholdings are expropriable and that certain areas of the country—the Southeast, for example—still have some land for development, these possibilities can provide for only a small minority of those who would like to acquire agricultural property. According to development theory the landless should have become salaried workers within a productive agricultural system or migrated to the cities. In Mexico the first alternative has been possible for only a portion of the landless because modern agriculture is geographically limited to major irrigation districts. Nor have the cities provided a solution because the rapid tempo of population growth compared with the rate of industrial development prevents their absorption.

The seriousness of the situation of landless laborers is revealed in one estimate that the average number of days they work declined from 194 annually in 1950 to 100 in 1960 and 75 in 1970.[17] This group exercises pressure on the existing landholding system through invasions, rural guerrilla activities, and the countless petitions they submit to the Secretariat of Agrarian Reform for a parcel of land.

Government Policies for Agriculture

The problems of Mexico's political situation, environment, and land tenure underlie the lack of responsiveness by Mexican farmers to recent government policies that under normal circumstances might be expected to stimulate agricultural production. In addition to government expenditure on infrastructure development, policies intended to stimulate production include higher guarantee purchase prices, increased availability of credit, and improved agricultural extension services.

Politicians who represent the populist viewpoint would have the benefits of these policies made widely available to the *ejidatarios* and *pequeños propietarios*. According to this view, the problem of malnutrition in the countryside can only be solved by providing poor peasants with the means to increase their own production of the crops needed to feed themselves. Politician-bureaucrats and experts allied with the interests of commercial agriculture argue, however, that the production increases required to feed Mexico's growing population can only come about by investing in more capital-intensive agriculture on larger landholdings where immediate significant improvements in yields could be achieved. Neither view has won out, although policies intended to stimulate production have thus far been designed and implemented more for the benefit of already viable farm units than to help small, poor peasant farmers. Even so, policy changes have still not proved that effective in bringing about dramatic increases in production.

Prices. One of the most frustrating policy areas has been that of guarantee or minimal purchase prices. In many countries, guarantee prices are considered the most important factor in agricultural production, on the assumption that farmers are rational people who will not risk investing in improved technology unless they are guaranteed at least a minimum income in the event of crop failure, or low market prices.

The Mexican system of guarantee prices is administered by CONASUPO (Compañia Nacional de Subsistencias Populares), which is one of the largest enterprises in Latin America. It aims not only at providing the farmer an adequate price for his product, but through its numerous stores scattered across the country it sells to the consumer at a lower cost than conventional retail outlets and in many instances at less than cost. The company has evolved into its present pattern to counteract the intermediary, the "coyote," who buys cheap, sells expensive, and is regarded as the enemy of both producer and consumer because he pockets a substantial portion of the value of a given commodity. Nevertheless, many producers continue to sell to intermediaries because they provide personal credit, because the product does not fit the quality expectations of CONASUPO, or because the producer cannot transport it easily to CONASUPO reception centers.

During the latter part of the 1960s, although Mexico's agricultural production per capita had begun to decline (Table 1), the prices paid by CONASUPO for basic food commodities remained constant. By the early 70s the advisers of the new President, Luis Echeverría, had focused on two factors they believed were inhibiting output. One was the reduction of government expenditure for agriculture, which had decreased from about 20 percent of the budget in the 1950s to about 9 percent, and the other was the failure to adjust the guarantee prices upward, which reflected a bias against the farmer in favor of the urban consumer.

Beginning in 1973, consequently, guarantee prices were increased, in most cases for the first time in years. This was only the beginning. As Table 4 indicates, in the years immediately following, even more substantial increases took place, which were well ahead of the rate of inflation.[18] But published data on the number of hectares harvested annually, and the average production per hectare show that production did not respond accordingly (Table 5). Though for most crops (corn being a notable exception) the number of hectares cultivated and average production per hectare increased during the period covered, neither criterion changed in a degree proportional to increases in guarantee prices. Data on increases in agricultural production in irrigation districts versus the rest of the country for the period 1970-1974 indicate what has been happening (Table 6). Although cultivated area and agricultural production performance increased significantly in the irrigated districts, they declined in most of the rest of the country. Since corn and beans, the two major staples, are grown primarily on rainfed land, they did not benefit from the increased investment in agricultural production which took place on irrigated land. The foodcrops to benefit most from such investment were wheat, and to a lesser extent corn. However, production of these crops on irrigated land represents a relatively small proportion of staple crop production in Mexico. The disinclination of Mexican farmers to increase the area of corn and bean land under cultivation or to try to increase production by application of improved techniques in response to higher guarantee prices stems in part from the political factors already mentioned, and in part from the failure of complementary credit and extension policies to reach the majority of small farmers on whose lands such crops are primarily grown.

Credit. Available data on provision of agricultural credit indicate that government policy for years has been to increase the amount of credit available to farmers. As the figures in Table 7 indicate, public institutions have predominated with nearly 70 percent of the total granted. During the early 1970s, the amount of money applied and the number of beneficiaries increased significantly. In the period from 1969-70 to 1974, furthermore, public financial institutions increased coverage from 1.8 to 3.3 million hectares, and the beneficiaries went up from 382,000 to 853,000.[19]

Though government policy of the past few years, in theory and rhetoric, has stressed the social desirability of helping smallholders, there are limits to what can actually be accomplished. It was already noted that over a fourth of private holdings and nearly a fifth of *ejidal* parcels are less than one hectare, and that over a half of both are four hectares or less and dependent on rainfall. For all practical purposes, most of these parcels are so small and worn out that they are not worth the effort of the banks, and the owners themselves do not bother to apply for credit because of their small size and penury.

Several other factors discourage applications for credit. One is uncertain titles. Though the private banks do not require a definitive title, they do expect some kind of provisional or probable title. Many private smallholders, who do not have access to public credit and must rely on these banks, cannot produce a satisfactory one. *Ejiditarios* are not eligible for credit from private banks and must rely on the Banco Nacional de Crédito Rural for financing. Numerous *ejidos*, especially those formed in the heady Cárdenas epoch, also lack proper titles, but in recent years, the Banco Nacional has tended to overlook this fact.

A second deterrent, especially applicable to *ejidos*, is lack of organization. The Banco Nacional de Crédito Rural requires *ejidos* or subgroups within them to apply for and disburse credit as a "society." Many *ejidos* are unable or unwilling to organize themselves sufficiently to do this, because of personal conflicts and distrust among the members. In fact, the bank may be contributing to the situation. According to one author, "The Ejidal Bank has from its inception attempted to organize *ejidos* in accordance with its own interests, and always to the detriment of any aggressive and independent peasant leadership."[20]

Third, many peasants who previously had credit are disillusioned because the insurance, which is required, did not pay for crop damages. The insurance company, which is autonomous and separate from the bank, has a monopoly on crop insurance. It has a bad reputation for nonpayment, usually basing the rejection on technicalities, and borrowers do not believe they have adequate coverage in case of damage or loss. When the insurance company does not come through, they must still repay their loans even though they may not have any income that year.

Finally, many farmers are ineligible for loans because they have not paid back previous ones. In a normal year, in the Banco Nacional de Crédito Rural, about 20 percent do not repay. If they do not have a clear justification, they are not eligible in the following year. Over a period of years, this has resulted in disqualification of a sizable number of farmers.

These deterrents to increased lending to small farmers have meant that only farms which are serious productive units could qualify for additional financial resources being made available through both public and private banking systems. Whereas most credit that smallholders get is short-term, from planting time until harvest, bank financing can be obtained by larger farmers to permit major capital improvements. This inequity in the distribution of credit continues to handicap the majority of Mexican landholders in their efforts to increase agricultural production.

Extension. A final policy that might affect agricultural production is the extension service, which is designed to advise farmers on the use of improved seeds, cropping practices, and other means of increasing output. As the figures in Table 8 demonstrate, agricultural extension, research, and educational allotments for training personnel underwent significant budgetary increases in the early 1970s as part of an overall public commitment to agricultural improvement.

The weakest aspect of public agricultural activity has traditionally been the extension service. Before 1970 many states of Mexico had only a handful of extension agents who enjoyed talking with their friends in their offices and occasionally set up demonstrations for a limited clientele. The production increases in the Green Revolution occurred not through public extension activities, but rather because the more progressive farmers adopted new seeds and practices on their own initiative.

The increased investments in agricultural education, both on the secondary and university levels, are in part designed to produce more extension personnel. In 1970, Mexico had less than 800 extension agents, but by the end of 1974 they had increased to 3,500.

Mexico has also been the site of a pilot project called Plan Puebla, which was designed to expand production in the most difficult setting, predominantly corn-producing rainfed small-holdings in the Central Highlands. Begun in 1966, the project was located in a 116,000 hectare region in the state of Puebla, with 47,000 peasants cultivating average plots of 2.5 hectares. At the beginning of the experiment, the average corn yield was 1,300 kilos per hectare. The government concentrated selected extension specialists who recruited a demonstration group, made extensive soil samples, and submitted recommentations for intensifying planting and applying fertilizers.

Though production increased to 2,500-3,000 kilos among the participants, by 1974 only 8,000 peasants with 25,000 hectares were collaborating. Nevertheless, their success had a certain demonstration effect on the nonparticipants, who increased their own output to 1,900-2,500 kilos per hectare.

The results of Plan Puebla encouraged some expansion of this tactic to other areas in central Mexico, but the problems are even more evident than the achievements. In the first place, most of the participants did not follow the recommendations on planting and fertilizer use, so that production did not come up to expectations. Even more striking was the failure of most of the farmers in the region to participate. There are a number of explanations: lack of desire to collaborate in anything involving the government; the greater risk because of increased investment; suspicion of the insurance company; and finally, the fact that many individuals in the region work full or part time in nearby urban centers like Mexico City and Puebla, cultivating their fields only as a sideline.[21]

Experiments like Plan Puebla are very expensive for general application because of the heavy use of personnel. Further, though individual participants doubled their production per unit, the relatively small number of participants means they cannot make a demonstrable difference for overall agricultural production performance.

The previous discussion has shown that a number of policy incentives were applied to an agricultural system that suffered from natural handicaps and from a fragmented, insecure structure of land tenure. There is no doubt that bad weather seriously affected agricultural output during the early 70s, but the system was too rigid to compensate for this adversity by adopting alternative production methods.

At the same time the government was applying incentives, moreover, the agricultural sector was suffering the effects of a major political and psychological disincentive that is also a major explanation of the poor performance of this period, namely, the symbolic effect of the Echeverría administration on investors' confidence. The importance of this factor is suggested by the statistics for 1977 which reveal that agricultural production rose 4 percent, even though rainfall during that year was 22 percent less than normal. Though this result is far from satisfactory, it is still the best in seven years and proves that production can go up despite bad weather and other inhibiting structural factors that have been discussed.

Though Luis Echeverría, more than any recent Mexican president, drew attention to the backwardness of the rural sector and promoted a variety of stimuli to increase production, his efforts were neutralized by the profligacy and corruption of his administration and especially by the insecurity he aroused among the larger farmers who, because of their capacity to innovate, were indispensable in any program to increase production.

The irony of recent Mexican agricultural policy lies in the fact that the incentives which normally should have resulted in increased output were applied in the context of even more powerful disincentives. Increased guarantee prices, for example, aimed at stimulating pro-

ducers to invest precisely at a time when they were afraid to invest. The 1976 Banco de Mexico economic analysis recognizes, in addition to weather, that "another factor that influenced the drop in agricultural production...is related to the stagnation of private investment in this sector,"[22] but it could not, for political reasons, go on to explain why people did not invest. The relevance of this interpretation is illustrated by the disastrous performance of 1976, -8.7 percent, which was the last year of Echeverría's term of office. That year culminated in the expropriation of 100,000 hectares in the rich agricultural state of Sonora for the benefit of landless invaders, an action that was subsequently annulled as illegal by the Supreme Court.

It is still too early to tell whether the improvement in 1977 represents a genuine recovery of confidence—and of Mexican agriculture—or whether it is no more than the inevitable swing back after reaching the bottom in 1976. Many experts argue that Mexico cannot continue concentrating its agricultural policies and financial resources on the larger agricultural enterprises and farms because the more easily developed water resources have already been tapped and extension of cultivated areas is becoming increasingly difficult. Thus policy incentives and investor confidence in the commercial agricultural sector may not be enough. According to this view, further growth of output must increasingly depend on less sophisticated, resource-poor farmers whose productive potential has thus far not been fully exploited. Whatever the case may be, the context of Mexican agriculture is not an easy one, and policies for increasing production may have difficulty overcoming the ongoing political, physical, and historical obstacles that have been described in this paper.

NOTES

1. Salvador Zubirán et al., *La Desnutrición del Mexicano* (México: Fondo do Cultura Económica, 1974), p. 21; United Nations World Food Conference, Assessment of the World Food Situation: Present and Future, E/Conf. 65/3, Rome, November 5-16, 1974, p. 53.

2. Banco de Mexico, *Informes Annales* (Mexico).

3. "Erosión Total o Acelerada, en 69.5 Millones de Hectáreas, y no se Detiene," *Excelsior* (May 24, 1974).

4. Sergio Reyes Osorio, et al., *Estructúra Agraria y Desarrollo Agrícola en Mexico*, Mexico: Fundo de Cultura Economica, 1974, p. 852.

5. Oscar Benassini, "Los Recursos Hidráulicos de México y su Aprovachamiento Racional," *El Escenario Geográfico: Introduccion Ecológica*, ed. Zoltan de Cserna et al. (México: Instituto Nacional de Angropología e Historia, 1974), p. 236.

6. Banco de México, *Informe Anual*, 1976 (México, 1977), p. 39.

7. Reyes Osorio, et al., *op. cit.*, pp. 3, 5.

8. *Ibid.*, p. 55.

9. *Ibid.*

10. For an analysis of the administrative process through which *ejidos* must pass, cf. *ibid.*, pp. 639-644.

11. *Ibid.*, p. 643.

12. *V Censo Agrícola-Ganadero y Ejidal, 1979. Resumen General* (Mexico: Direccion General de Estadística, 1971).

13. I am indebted for this observation to Professor Ramón Fernández y Fernández. On agrarian reform problems, in general, cf. his *Renovacion Agrícola* (Chapingo: Centro de Economia Agrícola, 1977).

14. For a detailed analysis of a collective *ejidal* system and its problems, cf. Thomas G. Sanders, "Henequen: The Structure of Agrarian Frustration," [TGS-3-'77], *AUFS Reports*, North America Series, Vol. V, No. 3, 1977.

15. *V. Censo Agrícola-Canadero y Ejidal, 1970. Resumen General.*

16. A government pilot project to resolve land titles through massive concentration of personnel and resources was begun by López Portillo in the small state of Querétaro. Though originally scheduled for completion in three months, a year has already passed, and it is still not finished. The government intended to extend this strategy to other Mexican states, but at this rate the process would last for decades.
   Early in 1978 the government suddenly changed to a new strategy—the whole question would be handled by the governors rather than by the Secretariat of Agrarian Reform. It is doubtful that this new approach will help to solve the problem, but it illustrates the Mexican tendency constantly to propose new organizational approaches as means of solving problems whose roots are very complex.

17. "El Sector Privado, Principal Beneficiado con el Riego," *Excelsior* (April 23, 1974).

18. Rates of inflation, according to the national consumer price index, during this period were as follows: 1970, 4.8%; 1971, 5.5%; 1972, 5.0%; 1973, 21.5%; 1974, 24.0%; 1975, 16.5%; 1976, 26.2%

19. Secretaria de la Presidencia, *El Sector Agrícola. Comportamiento y Estrategia de Desarrollo*, pp. 42-43.

20. Roger D. Hansen, *The Politics of Mexican Development*, Baltimore: Johns Hopkins University Press, 1971, p. 118.

21. For a more detailed discussion of Plan Puebla, cf. Thomas G. Sanders, "CIMMYT: Agricultural Innovation in Mexico," [TGS-7-'74], *AUFS Reports*, North America Series, Vol. II, No. 6, 1974.

22. Banco de México, *Informe Anual, 1976* (México: 1977), p. 39.

Table 1

Indices of Mexican Agricultural[a] and Food Production: 1964-1975[b]

	1964	1965	1966	1967	1968	1969	1970	1971	1972	1973	1974	1975
Total Agriculture	107	112	114	116	119	117	122	132	130	130	133	131
Per Capita Agriculture	104	105	104	102	102	97	97	102	98	94	94	89
Total Food	105	112	118	122	124	125	132	141	138	140	143	n.a.
Per Capita Food	102	105	107	107	104	102	104	107	101	100	98	n.a.

Source: *Statistical Abstract of Latin America,* Volume 18 (1977), James W. Wilkie, Ed. Los Angeles, UCLA Latin American Center Publications, 1977, pp. 39-41.

a. Includes production of food crops and livestock for human consumption (after deducting for agricultural commodities and imports used in agricultural production) as well as tobacco, industrial oilseeds, rubber, tea, coffee, and vegetable and animal fibers.

b. 1961-1965 equals 100.

Table 2

Production of Major Staple Crops

	1965	1966	1967	1968	1969	1970	1971	1972	1973	1974	1975	1976	Growth Rate '65-76[b] (%)
						(thousand MT)							
Corn	8,936	9,271	8,404	9,062	8,411	8,879	9,786	9,223	8,609	7,784	8,459	8,945	-.43
Wheat	1,659	1,612	2,061	1,780	1,915	2,676	1,831	1,809	2,091	2,789	2,798	3,354	5.3
Beans	761[a]	1,013	980	857	835	925	921	870	1,009	971	1,027	740	-.63[c]
Barley	193	220	203	253	212	238	270	310	392	270	440	460	7.4
Rice (unhusked)	314	362	418	347	395	405	369	375	450	469	717	463	4.1[c]
Sorghum	747	1,411	1,667	2,133	2,456	2,747	2,549	2,590	3,319	3,182	2,843	3,350	10.4
Soybeans	50[a]	95	131	275	287	215	255	377	585	491	699	302	14.7[c]

Source: FAO Printout, July 1978, Production-cereals, IFPRI Statistical Library.
FAO Food Balance Sheets, 1978, IFPRI Statistical Library.

Represents 1961-1965 average.
Logarithmic time trends.
1966-1976.

Table 3

Cereal Imports of Mexico, Volume and Values, 1965-1976

Cereals	1965	1966	1967	1968	1969	1970	1971	1972	1973	1974	1975	1976
						(thousand MT)						
Wheat	11.8	1.0	1.1	1.4	0.6	0.6	177.5	640.5	718.6	975.9	86.4	1.5
Rice	16.8	12.4		0.1	4.9	16.3	0.8	0.7	37.9	71.3	0.0	0.0
Barley	93.6	31.4		1.2	1.1	1.4	1.6	2.3	55.9	122.8	150.2	0.0
Maize	11.2	4.5	5.0	5.5	5.4	760.9	17.2	197.5	1,143.5	1,278.2	2,626.7	902.2
Oats	6.4	8.3	0.1	0.4	2.8	20.8	11.6	16.6	4.0	5.0	8.4	0.8
Pulses	0.6	0.8	1.0	0.7	1.0	9.4	1.0	3.9	18.8	40.2	105.0	1.0
Other Cereals*	34.6	23.0	4.5	60.6	11.7	25.9	17.1	246.5	13.6	427.7	846.3	93.6
Total Cereals	174.4	80.5	13.8	69.2	29.6	825.9	225.9	1,104.3	1,973.8	2,881.1	3,717.9	998.2
						(million dollars)						
Wheat	0.1	0.1	0.1	0.1	0.1	0.0	11.8	46.4	78.1	188.7	17.4	0.2
Rice	2.0	1.7	0.0	0.0	0.8	1.9	0.2	0.1	11.2	26.8	0.0	0.0
Barley	8.1	2.8		0.1	0.1	0.1	0.2	0.3	8.3	27.7	38.6	0.0
Maize	1.7	0.7	0.8	0.9	1.3	58.1	1.9	16.4	124.3	198.9	399.6	104.0
Oats	0.5	0.6	0.0	0.0	0.2	1.5	1.0	1.2	0.4	0.8	1.5	0.1
Pulses	0.2	0.3	0.3	0.2	0.4	2.4	0.4	1.1	4.7	31.4	64.4	0.6
Other Cereals*	2.1	2.1	0.8	4.6	1.8	2.5	2.7	17.5	4.0	64.2	140.5	19.4
Total Cereals	15.6	8.0	2.0	5.8	4.3	64.2	17.8	82.1	226.4	507.3	597.7	123.8

*Includes sorghum, millet, and buckwheat.   Source: FAO Selected Trade Yearbooks.

Table 4

Guarantee Prices for Major Staple Crops, 1971-1977

	1971	1972	1973	1974	1975	1976	1977
Corn							
Nominal price (per ton)	940	940	1,200	1,500	1,900	2,340	2,900
Real price at 1971 values	940	849	892	899	974	954	
Beans							
Nominal price (per ton)	1,750	1,750	2,300	6,000	5,000	5,000	5,000
Real price at 1971 values	1,750	1,581	1,709	3,595	2,572	2,038	
Wheat							
Nominal price (per ton)	913	835	1,200	1,500	1,750	1,750	2,050
Real price at 1971 values	913	754	892	899	900	713	
Rice							
Nominal price (per ton)	1,100	1,100	1,100	3,000	2,500	3,000	3,100
Real price at 1971 values	1,100	994	817	1,797	1,286	1,223	
Sorghum							
Nominal price (per ton)	625	725	775	1,100	1,600	1,760	2,030
Real price at 1971 values	625	655	576	659	823	718	
Safflower							
Nominal price (per ton)	1,500	1,500	1,600	3,000	3,200	3,200	3,900
Real price at 1971 values	1,500	1,355	1,189	1,797	1,646	1.304	
Soybeans							
Nominal price (per ton)	1,600	1,800	3,000	3,500	3,500	3,500	5,500
Real price (per ton)	1,600	1,626	2,229	2,097	1,800	1,427	

Sources: The guarantee prices come from "Los Precios de Garantia," a mimeographed publication of CONASUPO. For price deflators see footnote 18.

Table 5

Changes in Yield and Land Area for Major Staple Crops, 1971-1976

Commodity	1971	1972	1973	1974	1975	1976
(Average annual production per hectare—kilos)						
Corn	1,272	1,264	1,132	1,168	1,264	1,181
Beans	477	515	539	626	586	562
Wheat	2,981	2,634	3,264	3,602	3,596	3,761
Rice	2,402	2,588	2,993	2,843	2,792	2,907
Sorghum	2,695	2,364	2,760	3,096	3,867	3,218
Safflower	1,576	1,364	1,505	1,422	1,466	1,299
Soybeans	1,988	1,700	1,877	1,636	2,029	1,754
(Average land area harvested annually—thousands of hectares)						
Corn	7,652	7,292	6,418	6,720	6,684	6,783
Beans	1,932	1,687	1,870	1,552	1,753	1,315
Wheat	614	687	640	774	778	894
Rice	154	145	150	173	257	159
Sorghum	936	1,083	1,185	1,129	1,445	1,251
Safflower	261	199	198	192	363	185
Soybeans	129	222	312	300	344	172

Sources: Data on production from 1971 to 1974 are derived from Secretaría de la Presidencia, Dirección General Coordinadora de la Programación Económica y Social, *El Sector Agrícola: Comportamiento y Estrategia de Desarrollo* (Mexico 1976). The rest of the data are in the *Boletín Mensual Informativo de Información Económica*, No. 7 (December 1977), published by the Direccion General de Estadística.

Table 6

Increases in Total Agricultural Production, Cultivated Area, and Yields Per Hectare, 1970-1974

	Annual Increase (%)	Area Cultivated (%)	Yields Per Unit [%]
National Agricultural Production	1.8	-2.2	1.1
Irrigation Districts	6.7	3.9	1.1
Rest of Country	-0.8	-3.6	1.2

Source: Secretaría de la Presidencia, *El Sector Agrícola: Comportamiento y Estrategia de Desarrollo*, p. 37.

Table 7

Agricultural Loans by Private and Public Credit Institutions

	Private Credit Institutions	Public Credit Institutions	Total
		(millions of pesos)	
1965	3,174.9	7,460.4	10,635.3
1966	4,089.2	8,599.6	12.688.8
1967	3,870.0	10,155.6	14,025.6
1968	4,583.6	10,772.3	15,355.9
1969	4,827.9	11,360.1	16,188.0
1970	5,581.5	12,113.1	17,694.6
1971	5,951.3	14,489.4	20,440.7
1972			23,540.4
1973			26,165.7
1974			33,902.9
1975	16,728.9	33,832.4	50,561.3
1976	17,877.7	26,922.4	44,800.1

Source: Banco de Mexico.

Table 8

Budget Allocations, Subsecretariat of Agriculture, Secretariat of Agriculture and Livestock

	1970	1971	1972	1973	1974
	(millions of pesos)				
Agricultural Extension		34.5	65.0	78.3	141.2
Agricultural Research	20.8	28.1	46.5	60.0	109.1
National Agricultural School	0.9	5.0	43.9	83.7	65.4

Source: Secretariat of Agriculture and Livestock.

Scarcity Amidst Plenty in Oil-Rich Venezuela

Howard Handelman

For more than two decades, Venezuela has enjoyed one of the highest per capita income levels in Latin America or the Third World. In the wake of the 1973 petroleum price boom, the nation's per capita GNP of over $2,500 places it far ahead of any other country in Latin America. Yet, as in so much of the continent, distribution of wealth is extremely inequitable and per capita averages are a poor indicator of actual living standards. In the late 1960s, the poorest 50 percent of Venezuela's population earned but 14.3 percent of the national income. During the past decade Venezuela's general living standard has clearly improved and there has been some redistribution of wealth from the most affluent 10 percent of the population down to the next 30 percent. But, the relative share of the bottom half has remained virtually unchanged.[1] Thus, amid Caracas' vast wealth, its luxury high-rise apartment buildings, and its imported $40,000 Mercedes Benzs, there still remain perhaps 40 percent of the population who are ill fed and undernourished.

Undoubtedly Venezuela's general nutritional level exceeds the average for most Latin American and Third World nations. Yet, several nations with significantly lower per capita incomes (Uruguay, Philippines, Trinidad, and Tobago) had lower mortality rates for two-year-old children.[2] Venezuela has succeeded in bringing infant mortality rates down to a very low level, but data compiled by the Pan American Health Organization point to a surprisingly high rate of child mortality from nutritional deficiency diseases. Since good nutrition is more likely to be a problem for young children than for infants who have not yet been weaned, the inability of Venezuela to reduce the mortality rate for children ages one to four indicates the seriousness of the malnutrition problem for large segments of the population (see Table 1).

In 1975, Michael Chossudovsky, a British-Canadian sociologist, was commissioned by the Venezuelan government's Council on Development Planning (CORDIPLAN) to conduct a study of socioeconomic conditions within the nation's lower classes. When Chossudovsky's work was completed, however, the government refused to publish his research, labeling its findings excessively critical and "not sufficiently balanced." Ultimately, his study was published commercially in a book entitled, *Misery in Venezuela*.[3] In fact, the book's data on malnutrition and hunger were drawn largely from Venezuelan government statistics and its conclusions, for the most part, are fairly similar to the findings of several other studies of Venezuelan living standards.[4]

Using income distribution figures and average food costs for the nation's urban population (80% of the total), Chossudovsky estimated that 70 percent of all Venezuelans lacked sufficient incomes to afford an adequate diet in terms of requisite calories and protein. Initially, the assertion seems to challenge government statistics showing per capita daily consumption of 2,562 calories (only slightly below the desired level of 2,800) and 68.2 grams of protein (well over the desired minimum). Indeed, by 1971, Venezuela had exceeded FAO's recommended minimum of 2,480 calories.[5] Yet, Chossudovsky insists that average figures are deceptive in that they reflect overconsumption by the affluent, while masking deficiencies among the poor. A Caracas family making over 2,000 Bolivares (Bs.) ($460) per month in 1971, he calculates, consumed 30 to 60 percent above the desired calorie level and 63 to 108 percent above their required protein level. The 45 percent of the urban population with monthly incomes of under Bs. 500 ($115) were consuming only 72 percent of their calorie requirements and received only 60 percent of their protein needs.

While government experts charge Chossudovsky with overstating the problem, they do concede that some 40 to 55 percent of the nation's citizens suffer from insufficient diets, particularly in terms of calorie intake. The nutritional level is obviously most inadequate among the urban and rural poor, with lower-class preschoolers most likely to suffer serious physical consequences.

The most precise available nutritional information on Venezuela is found in a series of surveys conducted by the National Institute of Nutrition (INN). Focusing on a selected sample of families, INN measured their food consumption and calculated the daily consumption of calories, protein, vitamins. A 1966 study of over 7,000 persons in the Caracas metropolitan area—by far the most affluent region in the country—showed daily consumption averaged 2,175 calories. But a subsequent survey of Valencia (then Venezuela's fifth largest city) presented a more somber picture, with consumption averaging 1,523 calories. The most recent INN studies (1974) covering two small rural communities indicate calorie consumption ranging from 1,500 to 1,800 per day—that is, only 65 to 85 percent of the institute's minimal standard of 2,000 calories. In addition, individuals surveyed in these towns were consuming only 65 to 85 percent of their Vitamin C needs and 36 percent of the desired units of Vitamin A.

More extensive, though indirect, nutritional indicators can be drawn from INN's survey of thousands of schoolchildren throughout Venezuela. In 1971-1976, 45-54 percent of the students surveyed were below desired norms of height and weight and, therefore, assumed to be nutritionally deficient. Approximately 15 percent were suffering from severe deficiencies.[6]

In sum, as one expert recently stated, "An adequate diet (now) appears to be within the means of a majority of Venezuelan families; but there is also strong evidence that low income families are often (still) unable to provide proper nourishment especially for their infants.... Infants and young children pay heavily in human suffering."[7]

Evolution of a Food Policy

Venezuela today is overwhelmingly urban, highly dependent on petroleum exports to generate foreign exchange and government revenue, and reliant on agricultural imports to offset internal food deficits. At the turn of the century, the nation had a rural, agriculturally based economy. In 1913, meat, hides, coffee, cocoa, sugar, and other agricultural products constituted 96 percent of Venezuela's limited exports. The nation ranked among the continent's least socially and economically developed countries.

In 1922, after several years of exploration, foreign technicians discovered their first "gusher" in the Los Barros oil field. With that development, the course of Venezuelan destiny was altered dramatically. By 1927, petroleum had become the country's primary export commodity. Within two more years Venezuela had become the world's leading oil exporter![8] Petroleum rose from 2 percent of Venezuela's exports in 1920 to over 90 percent in 1934, where it has remained ever since. At the same time, agriculture's share of exports fell from 96 to 8 percent and continued to fall till it reached its present level of less than 2 percent of export value.[9]

The prospects for agricultural development in Venezuela were never good. Most Venezuelan soil is highly allic (aluminum-based), and this condition, combined with intermittent droughts and floods, made agriculture a costly, high-risk kind of enterprise. On the other hand, the country's "black gold" provided easy access to wealth, and under the circumstances it is not surprising that agriculture was shunted aside and neglected. Although foreign companies dominated the oil fields, compared to coffee and cocoa, there were large profits to be made in oil-related industries.[10] Increasingly large landowners invested their profits in urban commerce or local industry rather than plowing their capital back into the land.

As peasants flocked to the oil fields and the city in search of far higher wages than they could hope to earn in the countryside, the nation's demographic structure also changed dramatically. As recently as 1936, approximately two-thirds of the country's population was rural.[11] By 1950, Venezuela's population was half urban. During the next 2 decades the march to the cities accelerated further so that by 1977 only 20 percent of the nation's population remained in the countryside. Therefore there has been great pressure on the rural sector to increase agricultural productivity so as to feed the ever-growing urban population. While agriculture remained the largest single source of employment into the sixties, by 1961 less than one-third of the labor force was employed in farming, a very low percentage by Third World standards.

Thus, by mid-century, agriculture's contribution to Venezuela's GNP was less than half the proportional share of agriculture in Argentina or Mexico and about one-fourth that of Brazil or Colombia. Venezuela had become the least agriculturally oriented nation in Latin America and remains so today.

When Venezuela embarked on an era of democratic rule in 1958 its new political leaders had to face the cumulative effect of this neglect of the agricultural sector. On January 23 of that year, massive popular demonstrations and a general strike, followed by a military uprising, brought down the regime of Colonel Marcos Pérez Jímenez and ended Venezuela's nearly unbroken history of dictatorial government. Only once before (1945-1948) had the country experienced a government with any substantial base of popular support and aspirations for socioeconomic reform. Elections following the 1958 uprising eventually returned to power Acción Democrática (AD), a reformist, social-democratic party. Since that time, AD has continuously been the largest party in Congress and has won all but

one presidential election. Principal opposition has come from the Christian Social Party (COPEI).

The democratization of Venezuelan politics and the dominant role of Acción Democrática had immediate effects on the agricultural sector. AD President Romulo Betancourt faced two interrelated problems: the spurt in Venezuela's urban population and the country's spiraling dependence on food imports. During Pérez Jímenez's last years, food imports had steadily mounted, reaching a then unprecedented level of 45 percent of total consumption in 1958. Betancourt's first major thrust in the agricultural sector was in the area of agrarian reform, a basic tenet of official AD doctrine since its brief rise to power in the 1940s.[12]

Land Reform and Social Welfare

The case for reform in the countryside seemed overwhelming. Approximately 5,000 large landholders (*latifundistas*) controlled nearly 80 percent of the readily cultivable land. Beyond any social injustice which such a concentration might represent, latifundism seemed to have encouraged a large-scale flight of peasants to the cities. The quadrupling of Caracas' population (from 415,000 in 1941 to 1,500,000 in 1961) had put tremendous strains on housing and urban services, while sharply increasing the urban demand for food. Agrarian reform, it was hoped, would keep more *campesinos* (peasants) back on the farm where they could at least be producing food for themselves rather than merely consuming it. Because of the importance of maintaining food supplies, a basic principle of the reform was that productive agricultural units would generally not be affected. But by distributing unused or inefficiently used lands to the peasantry, it was hoped that agricultural output would in fact increase. In addition, this policy had the objective of increasing rural purchasing power and reducing urban unemployment.

Beyond both economic considerations and AD's ideological commitment to agrarian reform, the party was undoubtedly moved by political considerations. From its inception in the 1940s, Acción Democrática had actively sought peasant votes. Following its return to power in

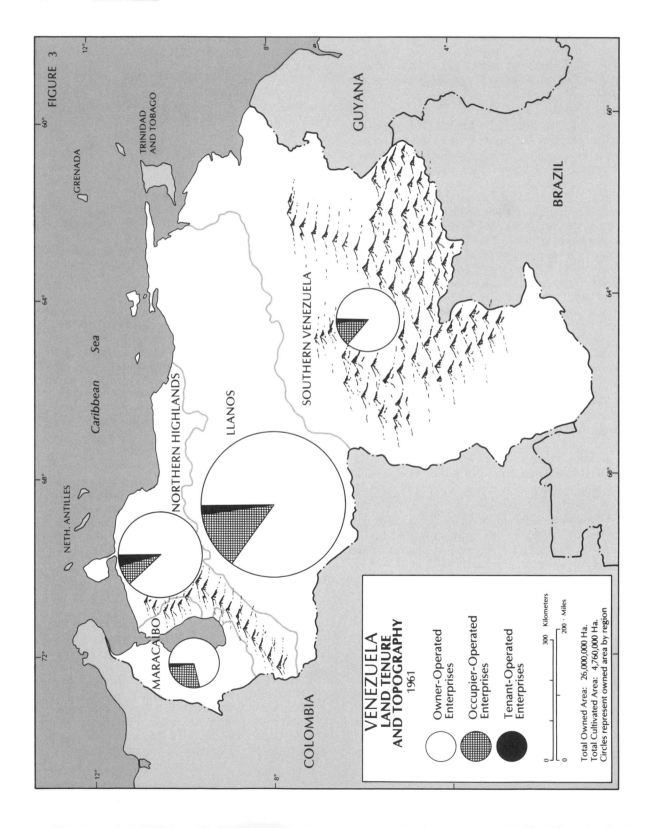

FIGURE 3

VENEZUELA
LAND TENURE
AND TOPOGRAPHY
1961

Owner-Operated
Enterprises

Occupier-Operated
Enterprises

Tenant-Operated
Enterprises

Total Owned Area: 26,000,000 Ha.
Total Cultivated Area: 4,760,000 Ha.
Circles represent owned area by region

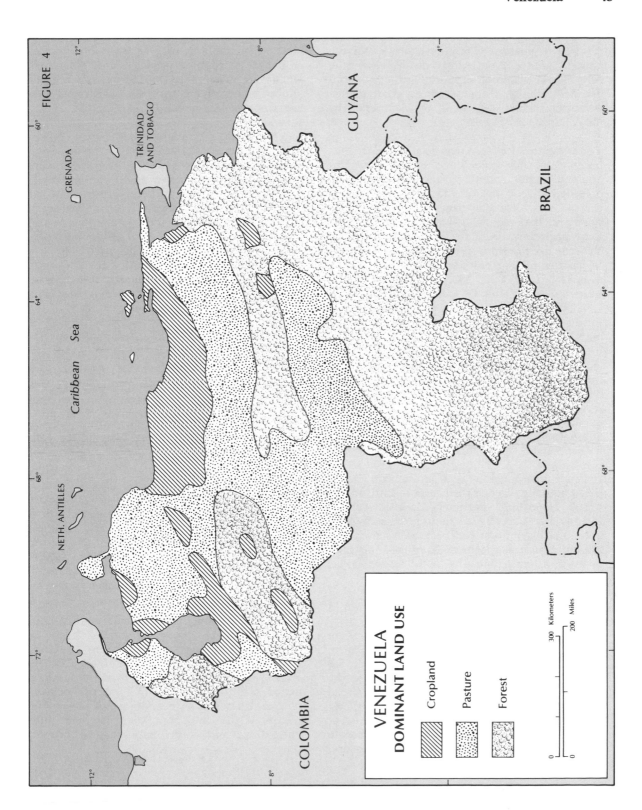

FIGURE 4

GRENADA

TRINIDAD AND TOBAGO

GUYANA

BRAZIL

Caribbean Sea

NETH. ANTILLES

COLOMBIA

VENEZUELA
DOMINANT LAND USE

Cropland

Pasture

Forest

300 Kilometers

200 Miles

1958, the party was closely associated with the creation of peasant federations throughout the nation.[13] Indeed, the rural vote has been the core of AD electoral support for the past two decades. Finally, the case for agrarian reform was given further impetus in the early 1960s by the Alliance for Progress.

During the 1960s, Venezuelan rural reform became a showpiece for the Alliance. Undoubtedly, the extent of land redistribution exceeded that of most Latin American nations except Cuba. Given the dismal record of agrarian reform in that region, however, this constitutes faint praise. In fact, the accomplishments of Venezuela's program were quite disappointing. When the reform bill was passed in 1960, an estimated 280,000 to 380,000 peasant families were in need of land. Ten years later, fewer than 120,000 families had received plots, and over one-third of these had subsequently abandoned their land because of their inability to secure credits from private or public agencies, poor soil, lack of technical assistance, and lack of infrastructure (roads, irrigation, etc.). Moreover, the vast majority of the reform's "beneficiaries" had not received title to their plots and were, consequently, in a very precarious legal position.[14] Subsequent redistributive efforts have been limited except for a spurt of activity in the past two years of the COPEI government (1969-1974). Expenditures for the agrarian reform agency (IAN) actually reached their peak in 1961 and in "real" (constant currency) terms declined steadily thereafter. By 1973, any serious attempts at land redistribution had been terminated. The present administration has distributed less land to the peasantry than any of the four previous democratic regimes.

One of the cornerstones of agrarian reform in Venezuela was an official "social function" clause which separated very clearly the welfare from the productivity objectives of land reform. More specifically, the governing principle for expropriation of private land according to the 1960 law was the nonfulfillment of the social functions of privately owned estates. Criteria such as efficiency in land utilization, allocation of the producer's own labor and other resources to agricultural production, conservation of natural resources, and acceptance and application of labor legislation were used to determine whether or not to expropriate private lands. All public lands were affected by the reform, but the law applied rather high limits below which land area could not be expropriated. For example, ownership of irrigated or humid crop land was to be retained up to 150 hectares, and of dry crop land up to 300 hectares. In addition, land on which the principal export and domestic crops were grown was exempted from expropriation. While in the first three years of the program, emphasis was given to the purchase of private property, from 1963 on priority shifted to utilization of unexploited public lands. As of 1973, only 6 percent of private farm land had been affected.[15] In effect, small farms were created for the poor, mostly from public lands without much expectation of productivity potential, while productivity growth on the bigger farms was facilitated by the social function exemptions for efficiency and by the availability of capital for technical improvements on large farms.[16]

Another aspect of the Venezuelan agrarian reform which underscores the government's lack of concern for modernizing the subsistence sector is the marked trend toward creation of individual small farm operator units rather than the more efficient, larger communal type arrangements. Cooperative efforts were not encouraged, and a 1967 survey indicated that of 96,273 families which received land, 94 percent tilled individual holdings, 4 percent belonged to production coops, and 2 percent were in *asentamientos* not yet subdivided.[17] Despite the fact that landless peasants were given land through the reform program, it seems that the Venezuelan reform process has led principally to a new kind of "minifundismo," and an increase in dualism in agriculture.

An official report to the President in August 1975 summarizes the government's failure to alter the country's rural land tenure structure. The 140,000 families who had been "beneficiaries" through that period had been abandoned, said the report, with no financial or technical assistance. They remain one of the poorest sectors of the rural population and contribute only 10 percent of the nation's food production.[18]

The agrarian reform had never seriously affected the domination of the countryside by large holdings. In 1961, at the start of the reform program, 2.2 percent of the rural landowners controlled 78.8 percent of the cultivable land. A decade later 3.1 percent of the owners controlled 76.5 percent. Moreover, from 1950 through 1971, large estates (of over 100 hectares) increased their share of the value of agricultural production from 36 to 46 percent, while smallholders (less than 20 hectares) saw their share of the market fall from 42 to 28 percent.[19]

Agricultural Production and the "Crisis" of 1972-73

Despite the limits of the agrarian reform program during the 1960s, production of food and other agricultural goods grew steadily from the early 1950s onward. Indeed, if rural output for both 1960 and 1970 are compared to the early 1950s, Venezuela's record seems to compare favorably with other parts of the world (see Table 3). Production consistently exceeded population growth, and the total 135 percent increase in production between the 1952-1956 base period and 1970 significantly surpassed the records of other Latin American nations and of other Third World regions.

Yet, such figures can be deceptive. Since Venezuela was starting off from a low production base (owing to neglect of the agricultural sector from the 1930s through the 1950s), its initial percentage gains are actually somewhat less impressive than they appear on first sight. Indeed, as the base production figures began to increase, percentage growth declined steadily. Agricultural output grew at an annual rate of 7.0 percent during the 1950s, 4.8 percent in the 1960s, and then 4 percent per year from 1969 to 1973.[20]

Moreover, the nation's extremely rapid population growth was consuming most of the additional food output. From 1951-1961, population grew at the astounding rate of 3.75 percent annually, then fell to 3.55 percent in the following decade. Such growth, among the highest in Latin America, far exceeded the rates of the United States (1.6%), Argentina (1.7%), Chile (2.6%), and even Mexico (3.1%) during the 1950s.[21]

A declining infant mortality rate, linked to improvements in public health, produced a very high level of natural population increase. This, in turn, was augmented by significant immigration, both legal (principally from Spain, Portugal, Italy, and more recently, from the southern cone of South America: Uruguay, Chile, Argentina) and illegal (from Colombia). Estimates of the number of illegal Colombian *indocumentados*, for example, range from 500,000 to 1,000,000.[22] If we examine per capita food output, therefore, we find an increase of 22 percent between the base period of 1961-1965 and 1974 (see Table 4). If illegal aliens (mostly Colombian) were included in the population figures (which the census does not do), then per capita gain in that period would be much less.

More serious than the production record (which has shown general long-term growth), is the issue of food distribution. As the nutritional data cited earlier indicate, food production gains have generally benefited those with greater purchasing power. Those persons in the lower 40 percent of the income pyramid continue to lack sufficient purchasing power to improve their diets significantly. During periods of short-term downturns in production, this group may be particularly hard hit. In 1972 and 1973, for example, severe drought, combined with floods in some areas, led to poor harvests. Per capita food production in those years was lower than in any year since 1967.[23]

The drop was particularly serious for corn (used almost exclusively for human consumption in Venezuela) and black beans, the two crops which, along with rice, potatoes, yucca, and plantains constitute the heart of the lower-class diet.[24] Black beans, for example, are the primary source of protein for both rural and urban poor. While rice and potato production fell off badly in 1972, both made a strong recovery in 1973 which has been maintained since. Yucca, on the other hand, began to perform badly in 1973 and production has recovered only gradually (see Table 5). Whereas corn production averaged 679,000 metric tons from 1967 through 1971, it dropped to 540,000 for the period 1972 through 1976. For black beans the 1967-1971 annual average amounted to 49,000 metric tons, whereas for 1972-1976 it came to only 31,000.

Obviously, the 1972-73 food shortages were most likely to hit hardest among the poor, who were least able to sustain added food costs. More important, however, a pattern of stagnation in the peasant sector had been developing for some time. Except for rice, the production growth rate for major food crops in Venezuela for the period 1963-1976 was barely one percent per annum. By contrast, throughout the period production of foods consumed by higher income classes, such as red meat, sugar, and eggs, increased significantly. Thus the increase in average per capita food availability shown in Table 4 does not fully reflect the increasing disparity in its distribution.

The differing performances for what might be called "lower class foods" and "middle class foods" are not due to any technological breakthroughs in the area of egg or meat production, nor to significant changes in yield per acre. Increasing demand for meat and poultry—Venezuela's major "growth" foods in this period—made it profitable to invest in their production. Thus, from 1961 to 1973, the amount of cultivated pasture land in Venezuela nearly doubled while crop lands increased by only 15 percent.[25]

The poor performance of the agricultural sector in the early 1970s, coupled with continuous, high population increases, re-established Venezuela's heavy dependence on imported food. From 1960 through 1970, the country had actually reduced its agricultural imports in terms of "constant" (noninflated) currency. Agricultural imports, which accounted for 25 percent of the value of total consumption in 1960, dropped to only 16 percent. But by 1974 the real value of agricultural imports had doubled and once again over one-fourth of the country's food was produced abroad.[26] The drought of 1972-73 and the resulting increased dependency on food imports came at a particularly unfortunate time since they coincided with a tremendous surge in world food prices. From 1970 through 1973 world prices of wheat, corn, and sorghum—the nation's three largest food (and feed) imports at that time—rose 66, 45, and 109 percent, respectively.[27]

Agricultural Policy (1974-1978)

In March 1974, Carlos Andrés Pérez assumed the Presidency, thereby returning control of Miraflores (the Venezuelan White House) to Acción Democrática after five years of COPEI government. Facing a "minicrisis" in the agricultural sector, CAP, as he is commonly known, made food policy a central component of his administration's development goals. The task facing the new administration was twofold: first, to revive food production from the effects of the 1972-73 drought, and to raise the supply sufficiently to meet both the rapid rate of population growth and an explosion in per capita demand; and, second, to keep the price of food to the consumer from rising too rapidly.

Although Pérez has emphasized agricultural and food policy, he has apparently accepted the proposition that food output can best be increased through the stimulation of large, mechanized agricultural units. The Pérez administration's rural policies have implicitly accepted the widely-held assertion that the social and political case for equity in the countryside (i.e., agrarian reform and land redistribution) conflicts with urban pressures for more food.

By the early 1970s, Venezuela's rate of population growth had slowed (from 3.75% to perhaps 3%) thus easing population pressures on food supply. But per capita demand accelerated tremendously. The oil boom of the early 1970s had produced both an extremely affluent minority and a majority with gradually rising real income. Unlike many Latin American nations, Venezuela had not been greatly troubled by inflation before 1973. But the influx of large amounts of petrodollars, coupled with worldwide inflation, drove prices up rapidly. Despite increasing demand, farmers complained of facing an economic squeeze in which the cost of production inputs (farm machinery, fertilizer, insecticides) was outstripping the selling price of their crops. The new administration therefore set out to find ways to make farming more profitable, while at the same time containing the cost of food for the urban consumer.

If the problems facing the Pérez administration in the wake of the 1972-73 drought were formidable, so too were its resources. The new President took office one year after OPEC embarked on its aggressive policy of petroleum price increases, inheriting a fiscal picture that would make any politician in the world envious. The tax revenues available to the Venezuelan central government in 1974 were triple the amount of the previous year. Simply by increasing its budget correspondingly, Pérez was able to triple the funds available to the Agriculture Ministry in his first year in office.

Beyond its great economic resources, the government was armed with yet another weapon, a tradition of state intervention in the economy. Following nationalization of the petroleum, petrochemical, iron, and steel industries, the state controlled all major sectors of production, and exercised greater control over the economy than in any other Latin American nation outside Cuba. In addition, Acción Democrática's social democratic ideology encouraged a strong governmental role in solving the nation's food problems (as well as other social ills). Development Minister Gumersindo Rodriguez, in presenting the government's "Fifth National Economic Plan" (for 1976-1980), argued that "only government action can alter the devastating and unjust effect on the nation's human resources of unequal distribution of wealth and income...."[28]

Production Incentives

In a special message to Congress on agriculture, delivered just one month after taking office, President Pérez stressed that the price received by farmers must be brought more in line with the costs confronting them.[29] In pursuit of this goal, the government has extended a series of benefits to the grower beyond the wildest dreams of farm lobbies in the industrial nations of the world.

Under the Agricultural Debt Relief Law of 1974, farmers were, in effect, exonerated of all past debts owed to government agencies. In addition, debts to banks and other private lenders could be consolidated through a state loan at 3 percent interest (incredibly low by Venezuelan standards) and up to 30 years to pay. By late 1975, over Bs. 1.5 billion ($350 million) in rural debts had been completely forgiven and approximately Bs. 285 million ($66.5 million) had been renegotiated on favorable terms.[30]

A tax reform decree, issued later in 1974, exempted both farmers and food processors from all income taxes. Equally important, banks were freed from paying taxes on profits made from low interest loans to the agricultural and food processing sectors. Virtually all profits emanating from investments in agriculture are now tax free.

In seeking to reduce food production costs, the government-owned petrochemical industry has sold farmers fertilizers at subsidized (below-cost) prices. Tractors, farm machinery, and a variety of agricultural inputs which Venezuela does not adequately produce have been freed of tariff or other import restrictions. In addition, price controls have been placed on all major "raw materials" needed for farming. As a further means of trying to reduce rural production costs, the government has spent substantial amounts on irrigation, rural roads, and other infrastructural projects. Emphasis has been placed on expanding crop land under cultivation, particularly for sorghum, corn, and other cereals.

The most significant area of government activity, however, has been in the extension of agricultural credits. In June 1974, President Pérez formally created the "Agriculture Livestock Credit Fund" (FCA) to channel nearly Bs. 2 billion ($465 million) of oil revenues into food production. Most of these funds are not loaned directly by the FCA, but rather through private banks or two government agencies: the Agriculture-Livestock Credit Institute (ICAP), whose main function is to provide credits to small and medium-sized farmers; and the Agricultural Development Bank (BANDAGRO) which serves large landowners. Funds are lent at preferential interest rates: 3-5 percent for ICAP, 4.5 percent for BANDAGRO, and 7-7.5 percent for private banks.

Beyond these direct government programs, President Pérez announced in October 1975 measures requiring all private banks to earmark a portion of their loans to the agricultural and food processing sectors. By the close of that year, 5 percent of the banks' loan portfolio had to go to agriculture; that figure would rise to 10 percent by mid-1976 and 20 percent by early 1977. Since private banks had previously been allocating only about 7 percent of their loans to agricultural producers, the President's decree has brought about a substantial increase in rural credits. Initially, the burden on the banks was not really very great, since most of the additional money that they lent to farmers and processors in the first year of the decree was actually channeled to them from the FCA. Moreover, banks were exempted from paying taxes on interest earned from these loans. By 1977, when the proportion legally reserved for rural credits reached 20 percent, most funds were no longer coming from the FCA and bankers were complaining that they couldn't find enough "good credit risks" to meet their agricultural quota.

The result of administration policy has been a dramatic rise in rural credits.

As Table 6 indicates, total credits rose from Bs. 1.8 billion ($420 million) in 1973 to over Bs. 4.8 ($1.12 billion) in 1975, almost doubling between 1974 and 1975 alone. By 1977, loans to agriculture exceeded Bs. 10 billion ($2.34 billion). Two billion of those credits were administered directly through government agencies; Bs. 1.5 billion were channeled from the FCA through private banks; and Bs. 6.5 billion (65% of the total) came directly from private banks out of their government-imposed agrarian loan quota. In all, Pérez administration policies had raised credits to agriculture and food processing by some 560 percent in 4 years. The President's goal of diverting large amounts of petroleum income into food production has been accomplished.

More broadly, the administration's package of subsidized fertilizers, loan forgiveness, low-interest credits, price controls on farm machinery and agricultural "raw materials," and tax exoneration have all combined to reduce production costs (relatively) for the farmer. One more facet of the "increased profitability" equation remained: if production were to increase, the farmer had to be guaranteed a sufficiently attractive selling price for his crop. Basically, this has been accomplished through the government's Agricultural Marketing Corporation (Corparmercadeo or CMA), an agency charged with providing the grower with minimum price levels for cereals and other basic food staples.

In 1973, only five commodities were supported with a minimum price at the farm level, and only three of those crops (rice, corn, and sorghum) were food or animal feed items.[31] By April 1976, the number of price supported crops had risen to 28, of which 24 were foods. Most Venezuelan food staples are affected: meat, fish, poultry, eggs, milk, corn, rice, sorghum, bananas and plantains, potatoes, and black beans. The CMA purchases all or part of the production of these items directly from the grower and resells it to private food processors, middlemen, or food stores.[32] The CMA also imports a significant amount of raw materials for animal feed (sorghum, sesame seed meal, fishmeal) and sells it to processors at a loss.

Because the government's minimum farm price policy has to be balanced with the goal of containing food prices for the urban consumer, virtually all basic foods in Venezuela are price-controlled at the marketplace. Only luxury foods such as choice cuts of meat (tenderloin or porterhouse steak, for example) are uncontrolled. Most of the CMA-purchased products (constituting the bulk of the nation's foodbasket) are resold to wholesalers or retailers at minimal markups or below cost. Thus, the CMA serves as a mechanism for subsidizing foods by guaranteeing the producer an adequate profit while limiting prices at the store.[33]

As in the other areas of food policy, oil revenues have permitted a rapid growth of this subsidization. In 1974, CMA subsidies amounted to Bs. 828 million ($193.5 million); subsidies for the first half of 1977 alone (the latest available data), reached Bs. 1.11 billion ($259.3 million) and will undoubtedly exceed Bs. 2 billion ($467 million) for the year. Moreover, the Corporation's total budget for 1977 of Bs. 2.88 billion ($652 million) will nearly double in 1978.[34]

An essential part of CMA subsidization policy is the recently initiated program of "popular markets" designed to offer the lower classes basic foods at reduced prices. Handling between 60 and 80 basic foods, these markets sell their products at prices averaging 14 percent below those prevailing at private stores (where prices are already government controlled).[35] By the close of 1977, a network of approximately 500 popular markets had been established in low-income urban neighborhoods throughout the country, serving an estimated one million people. While anyone is free to buy at their markets, it is assumed that their location in low-income neighborhoods will guarantee access for the desired clientele.

Evaluating Government Policy

Vast resources are obviously currently being allocated to stimulate food production, and in his 1978 New Year's address to the nation, President Pérez cited increased food production as one of his administration's proudest achievements. While the government points to the record 1977 harvest, spokesmen for COPEI and Movimiento al Socialismo (MAS)—the major leftist opposition party—both depict Pérez' agrarian program as a highly expensive and wasteful failure. In 1977, a group of agricultural experts and leaders issued their analysis of current administration agrarian policy. The title of their book—*CAP: Zero in Agriculture.*

Evaluation of government food policy is particularly difficult. Per capita food production may rise for a period and then fall sharply. Variations in rainfall or other climatic conditions may be more important determinants of short-term agricultural performance than decisions made by either the public or private sector. Since the 1975 harvest was the first to be affected by the Pérez administration's policies, it is somewhat early to pass judgment. Moreover, production trends are not clear.

The 1975 harvest was a fairly good one, but 1976—marred by devastating floods—was a disaster. Rice production fell 25 percent, corn and black beans by 20 percent, and potatoes by 10 percent. Only sorghum—planted after the floods—bucked the trend by registering a spectacular 450 percent gain. Not surprisingly, administration critics spoke of CAP's agrarian *fracaso* (total failure). Yet, one year later near perfect growing weather helped produce a record harvest. Harvests of rice (up 67%), corn (up 60%), sorghum (65%), potatoes (40%), and black beans (185%) all registered spectacular gains.[37]

While the 1977 cereal harvest was indeed very impressive and provides good election year propaganda for AD, it is only fair to point out that the dramatic gains in rice, corn, bean, and sorghum production mentioned above are based on comparisons with the extremely poor harvest of 1976. Nevertheless cereal gains over the past four years have been significant, whereas somewhat surprisingly, livestock has been relatively static. More important, per capita food consumption is 20 percent higher than in the 1961-1964 base period, and because of the relative shift in favor of field crops, more of it is probably going to poor consumers.

Critics of recent food policy insist that these production increases are quite meager in relation to the extensive resources poured into the agrarian sector. This evaluation was stated most vividly to me by Luis Esteban Ray, a journalist and Acción Democrática Deputy who is one of the most articulate critics of his own party. Ray compared recent agrarian programs to a man trying to put out a fire by dousing it with money.

There is general agreement that food policy has been hampered by the usual administrative problems afflicting developing nations—red tape, lack of coordination, bureaucratic incompetence, and corruption. Often agencies such as the Ministry of Agriculture, the National Agrarian Institute (administrator of the land reform), ICAP, and the FCA unknowingly duplicate programs. Technical assistance and training for farmers (particularly smaller ones) is widely discussed but rarely implemented. While neighboring countries such as Colombia have been broadcasting technical information for farmers over commercial radio for years, Venezuela only started in 1974. Often farmers are unaware of infrastructure available to them. One expert estimated several years ago that only 30 percent of Venezuela's installed irrigation capacity was actually being used. Agricultural experts complain that Ministry of Agriculture technicians are often ignored while policy is being introduced by nonexperts.[38]

Critics also question the government's policy of channeling most of its agricultural credits (from the FCA) through private banks. Administration spokesmen justify this policy on the grounds that it is harder for the government to recover its loans and to take action against defaulters than it is for banks. Under the present policy of decentralized loans channeled through private banks, however, there is no coherent planning regarding the use of credits to stimulate particular crops which may be in short supply, or geographical regions which may be in particular need of credits. Huge amounts of funds have been lent with little knowledge of how wisely or effectively they are being spent. Credits are more likely to go to persons having personal contacts or established lines of credit with their local bank than to farmers who might be able to use the funds most productively.

Given the loose administrative control over the agrarian credit program, it is not surprising to find charges that money being lent out under very favorable terms for food production has been used for other purposes. In fact, it is virtually impossible for lending agencies—public or private—to trace what actually happens to the credits they extend. Joseph Mann, a leading foreign correspondent, quotes a large cattleman who told him, "one fellow I know got a one million bolívares ($233,000) loan from the government and sent it straight to Miami" for investment in real estate.[39]

On the whole, there is reason to believe that the net effect of recent agrarian policies has been to reinforce the position of large landowners vis-à-vis the small peasant and to extend the pre-existing trend toward greater domination of the commercial food market by large estates. Debt forgiveness programs, for example, have tended to benefit the medium and large owners who are more likely to know how to deal with the bureaucracy and to handle the extensive paperwork needed to secure debt exoneration. Loan policies have also benefited large farms disproportionately. All too often, peasants lack clear title to the land, or at least the documentation to establish ownership, which is a prerequisite for securing private or public loans. Eighty percent of the peasantry on agrarian reform land have no titles to their plots. As noted, private banks are obviously more prone to lend money to farmers with personal contacts and who are considered "better credit risks." The record of public credit agencies is not much different. Of the first 5,000

farmers to secure loans (through February 1976) from the FCA, 48 percent received loans exceeding Bs. 500,000 ($117,000). The average amount for all 5,000 loans was Bs. 387,000 ($90,000).[40] These loans were not going to small peasants! On balance, credit policy has tended to favor large ranchers and grain producers (who primarily grow animal feed), as well as poultry growers. Thus, loans to the poultry and poultry-feed sectors (with the two often linked in horizontal combinations) have helped three producers—Ralston, Granmovel (General Mills), and Protinal to secure 70 percent of the rapidly expanding egg and poultry market.[41]

Implications for the Future

To be sure, Venezuela's long-term food production increases (1950-1977) have more than kept pace with the nation's rapid population growth and compare favorably with the records of other Third World nations. In the short run, it is obviously too early to determine the efficacy of the current administration's huge investment in agriculture. While recent programs are likely to contribute to increased outputs in the future, many experts feel such gains will not be proportionate to the enormous government expenditure.

At the close of President Pérez's first year in office, the National Agrarian Reform Institute invited René Dumont, the noted French agronomist, to evaluate Venezuela's agricultural programs. In his report, Professor Dumont lamented the tremendous misuse of the country's natural and economic resources. Deforestation, he warned, was advancing at an alarming rate, resulting in serious soil erosion. Burning of pasture land in order to convert it to crop use threatened the countryside's ecological balance. Pastures were being grossly misused or underutilized. Small farmers were not getting the credits or technical education and aid needed to help them produce efficiently.

Examining long-term trends in government agricultural expenditures, Dr. Dumont cited a study conducted by Agriculture Minister Pinto Cohen which indicated that since the 1930s a steadily increasing share of such funds has been siphoned off to urban industrial and commercial interests. Looking more specifically at the new

Pérez administration programs, Dumont described a pattern of wasteful, unnecessary and, even, detrimental policies. Huge amounts of money were being poured into new irrigation projects when most of the existing facilities were lying idle. Loans were being extended to farmers without regard for their effective utilization. Finally, Dr. Dumont objected strongly to the government's debt forgiveness program. The consequence of such a program, he insisted, was to penalize the farmers who had used their loans effectively and reward those who had used theirs incompetently or dishonestly.[42]

Unfortunately, few if any of Dumont's warnings seem to have been heeded. A recent report to the Congress by the Comptroller General's office cites flagrant inefficiency, incompetence, and corruption within the government's seven agrarian institutes, including the agrarian reform agency (IAN), the agricultural marketing office (Corparmercadeo) and, especially, the Agricultural-Livestock Credit Institute (ICAP). "Audits of ICAP's branches in the interior turned up repeated instances in which loans were given to public officials,...relatives of bank employees, and businessmen with no interest whatsoever in the agrarian sector."[43] If the resources of the Venezuelan government were unlimited, then such waste might be less disturbing. But this is not the case. A large budget deficit in 1978 has already forced significant cutbacks in government expenditures (for 1978-79) in the agricultural sector.

Moreover, despite the country's long-term growth in food production, there are some disturbing signs for the future. As noted earlier, the rate of growth per annum has been declining continuously since the 1950s. Those gains that have taken place have come largely through the use of additional acreage. That is, there has been little or no increase in productivity per acre. As René Dumont warns, there are only two million hectares of good land in Venezuela, much less than in Cuba, for example. All the best land is already in use. Consequently, such food production growth based almost entirely on expanding land use cannot continue indefinitely.

Nor can the country sustain imports at the very high levels characteristic of the recent period.

Perhaps the greatest irony of Venezuela's post-1973 petroleum boom—at least as it relates to food—is that at the same time that billions of dollars of oil revenues have been used to stimulate agricultural production, that very same oil wealth has contributed to food shortages and increased dependence on imports. In Caracas and other urban areas, as the middle class and skilled working class have become more affluent, demand for "luxury" foods such as beef and pork has grown tremendously. From 1974-1977, livestock output grew by only 5 percent, while demand for red meat nearly doubled (from 288,000 to 434,000 metric tons). Consequently, imports of beef, once an export product, increased tenfold. Large numbers of live breeding cows and other cattle were imported from Colombia and Central America, but it will take some time before increased cattle numbers affect domestic beef supply. Greater purchasing power has also sifted down to some of the lower class, reflected, for example, in the increased demand for powdered milk. Between 1975 and 1977 demand for all dairy products increased by 65 percent and imports tripled (from 33,000 to 111,000 tons).

The pressure of increased consumer demand for food became particularly acute following the disastrous 1976 harvest. By the middle of the year, serious shortages had developed in the supply of meat, milk, eggs, poultry, beans, rice, coffee, and other staples. Because CMA, the government agency charged with importing all foods, was unable to handle the crisis, restrictions were lifted on food importation by the private sector. CMA Director, General Giselo Payares, was removed from his post by President Pérez, allegedly for his inability to deal with the food crisis. In all, imports accounted for over 50 percent of Venezuela's food supply in 1976, a proportion unmatched in recent Venezuelan history.

The country's heavy dependence on food imports is not healthy, even for a nation with huge oil exports. Total imports, including a heavy, long-term commitment to capital goods, have already risen to outstrip the great increase in petroleum revenues. Venezuela is currently running its first trade deficit in recent history.

Economists, businessmen, and political leaders of all persuasions seem to unanimously predict, in private conversations, an economic downturn in the next few years. One leading member of Congress stated privately that whichever party wins the December 1978 election, the new administration will have to devalue the Bolívar. All this suggests that the country cannot sustain its current level of food imports in the coming years.

Yet the country's dependence on food imports is not likely to be reduced quickly. Despite the record breaking harvest of 1977, Venezuela was forced to import 42 percent of its food. An official of the National Agrarian Research Foundation (FONIAP) recently said it will take at least 20 years before the country can build up its rural infrastructure sufficiently to reduce food importation appreciably. President Pérez's brave words notwithstanding, his own actions betray his dissatisfaction with agrarian policies. In the first 3.5 years of his administration, he appointed 4 different Agriculture Ministers, 3 of them in a period of 18 months.

One question remains: Is the average Venezuelan eating better than five or ten years ago? The answer is undoubtedly "yes." Gradual increases in per capita food production, large jumps in food imports, and increased real income all indicate that average food consumption has risen. According to FAO statistics, per capita consumption of calories rose from 2,270 daily in 1965 to 2,416 in 1974.[44] Government experts speak of an average annual rate of increase in per capita calorie consumption of 1.4 percent in the 1960s, possibly slowing to one percent currently.[45] Protein levels have not been a significant problem for over a decade.

The caveat still applies, however, that average figures may simply reflect improved consumption by a portion of the population. Despite the gains, improvement in nutritional levels in Venezuela is apparently still a serious problem for both urban and rural poor. Production increases over the past 20 years, and the vast increase in food imports, have generally benefited the middle 40-50 percent of the income pyramid (the richest 10 percent had already achieved a high level of consumption by 1958). The poorest 40-50 percent of the population have apparently gained in some areas, most notably milk consumption. However, as government nutritional data show, the proportion of malnourished Venezuelans has decreased only slightly during the past decade and a half (approximately 55 to 45 percent).

Unfortunately, data on calorie consumption since 1974 do not exist. But indicators of malnutrition do not show any significant declines. Dr. José Bengoa, a leading nutrition expert for the government's Council on Science and Technology (CONOCIT), expressed the belief that the proportion of undernourished persons in Venezuela has remained fairly constant for the past four years or so. Indirect nutritional data from the National Institute of Nutrition suggest the same conclusion. Based on their measurement of over 560,000 Venezuelan children aged 1-14, conducted in 1976-77, approximately 46 percent were suffering from some level of calorie-protein deficiency, with nearly 10 percent suffering from severe deficiencies.[46] These proportions were essentially the same as those gathered by INN in 1971.

There is a strong case, then, to be made for a shift in policy toward more emphasis on improving the agricultural productivity of small farmers. Both from the standpoint of aggregate supply and from the standpoint of income and food distribution, more attention must be paid to directing agricultural investment to smaller farmers who can produce the basic food crops consumed by the lower income classes of the population and the feed crops required to sustain a growing domestic livestock and poultry industry. In this way Venezuela can enable its rural poor to earn a better living for themselves and contribute to the welfare of their urban compatriots.

NOTES

1. See UN Economic Commission for Latin America, *Estudio Económico de América Latina* (New York: 1968), Tables 1-10; Instituto Naciónal de Nutricion (Venezuela), *Consideraciones Sobre La Situación Nutricional en Venezuela* (Caracas: 1978), graph 5; A. Figueroa and R. Weisskoff, "Visión de las Pirámides Sociales: Distribución del Ingresos en América Latina," *Cuadernos de CISEPA* (March 1974).

2. *Resumen*, Caracas, June 23, 1974, p. 13.

3. Michel Chossudovsky, *La Miseria en Venezuela* (Valencia, Venezuela: Vadell Hermanos, 1977).

4. Victor E. Childers, *Human Resources Development: Venezuela* (Bloomington: International Development Research Centre, 1974); CONOCIT-CENDES, "Nutrición, Agricultura y Dependencia," *Cuadernos de la Sociedad Venezolana de Planificación* (Caracas: 1977).

5. Inter-American Development Bank, *Socio-Economic Progress in Latin America, 1971.* (Washington, 1972); United Nations World Food Conference, *Assessment of the World Food Situation*, E/Conf. 65/3, Rome, November 1974, p. 53.

6. Instituto Nacional de Nutrición, *Atlas Para Nutrición* (Caracas: 1974), *Consideraciones Sobre la Situación Nutricional en Venezuela* (Caracas: 1978), and unpublished data furnished to me by the Institute.

7. Childers, *op. cit.*, p. 98.

8. Franklin Tugwell, *The Politics of Oil in Venezuela* (Stanford: Stanford University Press, 1975).

9. Gustavo Pinto Cohen, *Agricultura y Desarrollo: El Caso Venezolano* (Caracas: CENDES, 1966), p. 2.

10. Mostafa F. Hassan, *Economic Growth and Employment Problems in Venezuela: An Analysis of an Oil-Based Economy.* (New York: Praeger, 1975), p. 5.

11. Defined as living in communities of under 1,500; Daniel Levine, *Conflict and Political Change in Venezuela* (Princeton: Princeton University Press, 1973), p. 17.

12. John Martz, *Acción Democrática* (Princeton: Princeton University Press, 1966), pp. 238-242; Acción Democrática, *Tésis Agraria* (Caracas Editorial, Antonio Pinto Salinas, 1958).

13. John D. Powell, *Political Mobilization of the Venezuelan Peasant* (Cambridge: Harvard University Press, 1971).

14. On the agrarian reform in general, see: David E. Blanc, *Politics in Venezuela* (Boston: Little Brown, 1973);

V.M. Jiménez Lández, *Reforma Agraria: Política y Programa, 1970* (Caracas: 1971); Norman Gall, "Oil and Democracy in Venezuela: Part I: Sowing the Petroleum" [NG-1-'73], *AUFS Reports*, East Coast South America Series, Vol. XVII, No. 1, 1973; Powell, *op. cit.*, pp. 162-181.

15. Theodore van der Pluijam, "An Analysis of the Agrarian Reform Process in Venezuela," in United Nations Food and Agricultural Organization, *Land Reform: Land Settlement and Cooperatives*, Rome, 1972, p. 6, and *Land Reform in Latin America: Bolivia, Chile, Mexico, Peru and Venezuela.* World Bank Staff Working Paper No. 275, April 1978, p. 88.

16. World Bank, *op. cit.*, p. 127.

17. World Bank, *op. cit.*, p. 88.

18. "Informe Final de la Comisión de Evaluación y Reestructuración de la Reforma Agraria" (Caracas, August 1975).

19. Julio Esteves, *et al.*, "Base Para La Planificación de los Sistemas de Riego en Venezuela" (Caracas: CENDES-Ministerio de Obras Públicas, 1976), p. 138. Almost all of this increased market concentration took place during the "reform" period of 1961-1971.

20. Esteves, *op. cit.*, p. 112.

21. Childers, *op. cit.*, p. 46.

22. See Norman Gall, "Los Indocumentados Colombianos" [NG-2-'72] *AUFS Reports*, East Coast South America Series, Vol. XVI, No. 2, 1972. The number of illegal Colombian aliens has continued to grow since Gall's article. Since most of the *indocumentados* are apparently not included in census figures, the per capita data cited may be overly optimistic.

23. Again, if Colombian illegal aliens were included in these calculations, the indices might actually fall slightly further.

24. *Resumen* (Caracas): April 28, 1974, p. 71; June 30, 1974, p. 50.

25. Banco Central de Venezuela, *La Economía Venezolana en los Ultimos 30 Años* (Caracas: 1971), p. 109; Ministerio de Agricultura y Cria, *Anuario Estadística Agropecuaria, 1974* (Caracas: 1975), p. 413.

26. Esteves, *op. cit.*, p. 20. Since a significant proportion of Venezuela's internal agricultural production consists of nonfood crops (sisal, cotton, tobacco, coffee), the proportion of food contributed by imports is actually somewhat higher than the proportion of agriculture.

27. Esteves, *op. cit*, p. 22.

28. *El Nacional* (Caracas, October 26, 1975).

29. *El Universal* (Caracas, April 29, 1974).

30. Esteves, *op. cit*., p. 198.

31. The other two were sisal and cotton.

32. In 1975, the proportion of the Venezuelan crop purchased by the CMA ranged from 19 percent of the potato harvest to 49 percent of corn and 85 percent of all rice. See CMA, *Informe Anual* (Caracas: 1975). Since then the proportion of the harvest purchased has risen.

33. It should be made clear that, despite these controls, Venezuelan food prices are very high—far higher in Caracas than in New York.

34. U.S. Agricultural Attache, *Situation in Report: 1977*, p. 18.

35. CMA, *Mercadeo Agricola* (December 1977).

36. José Luís Zapata, *et al.*, *CAP: Cero en Agricultura* (Maracaibo: IRFES, 1977).

37. Unpublished data from Ministry of Agriculture.

38. See Joseph Mann, "Frustration on the Farm," *Business Venezuela* (April 1975), p. 22.

39. *Financial Times* (London: September 30, 1977), p. 27, and personal conversations with Joseph Mann.

40. Esteves, *op. cit*., pp. 188-189.

41. Interview with Dr. Alfredo van Kesteren, CENDES.

42. René Dumont, "Informe Sobre La Agricultura en Venezuela," *Resumen* (May 11, 1975), pp. 22-29.

43. Caracas *Daily Journal* (June 2, 1978), p. 5.

44. FAO, *Provisional Food Balance Sheets: 1972-74* (Rome: 1977).

45. CONOCIT-CENDES, *Nutricíon*, p. 60 and interview with Dr. José Bengoa of the Council on Science and Technology (CONOCIT).

46. Instituto Nacional de Nutrición, *op. cit*.

Table 1

Deaths from Avitaminosis and Other Nutritional Deficiency States per 100,000 Population Among Children Under One Year and 1-4 Years of Age in Eight Countries, 1961-1963 and 1967

Country	1961-1963[a]		1967	
	under one year	1-4 years	under one year	1-4 years
Canada	1.8	0.4	1.3	0.1
Colombia	142.3	119.9	63.0	84.1
Costa Rica	10.9	19.5	3.2	21.0
El Salvador	1.8	49.0	5.7	37.8
Panama	5.2	12.9	2.0	25.6
Trinidad and Tobago	9.8	11.7	17.6	5.6
United States	0.5	0.5	0.3	0.2
Venezuela	14.9	23.2	3.9	23.1

a. Average annual rate.

Source: Pan American Health Organization, *Health Conditions in Latin America*, 1965-1968 (Washington: 1970), p. 31.

Table 2

Venezuela's Rural and Agricultural Sectors: 1950-1974

Year	Rural Population (%)	Agricultural Population (%)	Agricultural Share of GNP (%)
1950	52.0	43.0	8.5
1961	37.4	33.8	7.6
1974	25.9	21.9	6.6

Sources: Dirección General de Estadística, Censo de Población: *Resumen* (Caracas: 1971); Julio Estaves, *et al.*, "Base Para La Planificación de Los Sistemas de Riego en Venezuela" (Caracas: CENDES, Ministerio de Obras Públicas, 1976).

Table 3

Indices of Agricultural Production:
1952-56 through 1970 (1952-56 = 100)

Region	1952-56	1960	1970
North America	100	109	124
Western Europe	100	118	147
E. Europe-U.S.S.R.	100	132	177
Africa	100	120	149
Far East (Exclud. China)	100	121	161
Latin America	100	120	158
VENEZUELA	100	138	235

Source:FAO: *Monthly Bulletin of Economic and Agricultural Statistics*, Vol. 21, No. 1; Vol. 24, Nos. 7 and 8.

Table 4

Indices of Venezuelan Agricultural[a] and Food Production: 1964-1975
(1961-65 = 100)

	1964	1965	1966	1967	1968	1969	1970	1971	1972	1973	1974	1975
Total Agriculture	106	112	119	123	129	141	148	150	152	161	169	184
Per Capita Agriculture	103	105	108	109	111	117	120	118	116	119	121	129
Total Food	107	112	119	124	131	141	149	151	153	161	176	n.a.
Per Capita Food	103	105	109	109	112	116	119	116	114	116	122	n.a.
Population			110		117		125		133			

a. Includes production of food crops and livestock for human consumption (after deducting for agricultural commodities and imports used in agricultural production) as well as tobacco, industrial oilseeds, rubber, tea, coffee, and vegetable and animal fibers.

Source: *Statistical Abstract of Latin America*, Volume 18 (1977), James W. Wilkie, Ed., Los Angeles, UCLA Latin American Center Publications, 1977, pp. 39-41; Ministry of Agriculture figures drawn from *Venezuela: Situation Report—1976* (Caracas: Agricultural Attaché, U.S. Embassy, 1977). In 1977, the Ministry readjusted the basis of computing its food indices. This new calculation, presented in the 1977 *Situation Report*, alters previous indices and—not surprising in an election year—makes food production figures look better.

Table 5

Production of Major Food Crops, 1963-1976
('000 MT)

	1963	1964	1965	1966	1967	1968	1969	1970	1971	1972	1973	1974	1975	1976	Per Annum Growth Rates (percent)
Maize	430	475	521	557	633	661	670	710	720	506	454	554	653	532	1.0
Rice	131	166	200	210	223	245	244	226	240	165	302	297	363	277	5.0
Black Beans	38	40	42	47	50	46	46	46	58	30	25	33	37	31	-2.6
Yucca (cassava)	342	312	301	320	316	341	310	317	323	318	272	293	317	353	-0.1
Potato	111	124	136	126	133	113	124	125	115	109	124	152	152	131	0.9
Sugar [a]	3,814	3,959	4,491	4,585	4,052	4,217	4,416	4,900	5,152	5,476	5,623	5,895	5,482	5,500	3.1
Cattle [b]	6,936	7,155	7,380	7,612	7,852	8,102	8,289	8,499	8,485	8,549	8,730	8,843	9,089	9,404	2.1

a. Data for 1963-1970 refers to crop year rather than calendar year.
b. Thousand head.

Sources: FAO, *Production Yearbook*, various years.
OAS, *America en Cifras* (cattle, 1963-1970).

Table 6

Credit Activity in the Agrarian Sector: 1973-1975
('000 Bs.)

Source	1973	1974	1975
FCA[a]	--	64,800	1,750,279
BANDARGRO[b]	470,300	625,900	894,200
ICAP[b]	414,800	576,700	823,300
Private Banks[b]	922,285	1,167,550	1,383,653
Total	1,807,385	2,434,950	4,856,432

Source: Julio Estaves, *et al.,* "Base Para La Planificación de los Sistemas de Riego en Venezuela" (Caracas: CENDES-Ministerio de Obras Públicas, 1976), p. 196.

a. Most FCA funds are channeled through the other three sources.

b. Does not include FCA funds channeled through them.

Egyptian Agriculture Adrift

John Waterbury

Agricultural production in Egypt, like every other facet of economic performance, has followed a parabola from the early 1950s to the present time. From 1952 to 1965 there were increases in yields per acre, and in absolute quantities produced, for practically all crops. Thereafter production gains were uneven, some declines were registered, and the quantities harvested, with the exception of rice, generally stagnated. Beginning in the 1970s, per acre yields for a number of crops began to decline, as did the absolute amounts produced (see Table 1).

Most other economic indicators followed the same curve. Thus, it seems likely that some of the problem can be explained by factors outside agriculture itself (and also outside the purview of this paper). The early 1960s saw a combination of overambitious investment targets, inflated real wage rates in the public sector, uneven performance of state industries, a cooling of relations with the United States and the suspension of PL480 wheat shipments, and a costly involvement in the Yemeni civil war. Following the external payments crisis of 1965-66 and the June War of 1967, the economy as a whole ground to a halt. Despite President Sadat's advocacy of an economic open-door policy, the new direction has not been translated into a coherent set of programs and policies. A kind of strategic drift set in that has prevailed until today. Its effect on the rural poor is evident in the data compiled by Samir Radwan (Table 2), even if one disagrees with his placement of the poverty threshold, rate of inflation (12%/year), or the absolute numbers in each category.

The general slackness in the economy and the stagnation of cereals production has led to some deterioration in food consumption, although it should be emphasized that severe malnutrition appears not to be a major problem in Egypt. Calorie and protein intake levels are satisfactory as measured against international standards, even though they have fallen off since 1965. At that time daily per capita food intake averaged 3,021 calories and 86 grams of protein. By 1973 these averages had declined to 2,726 calories and 75 grams of protein.[1] Maintaining consumption levels in the future is, however, highly dependent on the government's willingness to import ever larger quantities of foodgrains and animal protein.

Dietary patterns and calorie availability differ between urban and rural areas. Whereas the rural diet consists primarily of cereals, legumes, and starchy roots, supplemented by small amounts of animal protein, urban consumers have higher wage incomes and tend to eat less grain and more meat, fish, eggs, milk, sugar, fruits and vegetables, and fats and oils. This gives the urban population (approximately 42 percent of the total) a somewhat higher per capita calorie intake, although average per capita calorie availability[2] is not seriously deficient for either group. Nutrition-related diseases do appear in lower income groups in both urban and rural areas, however, and in maize-eating rural areas there is also seasonal variation in the incidence of pellagra.

The government subsidizes the price of basic food staples consumed in urban areas, and the wheat bread subsidy in particular is considered politically necessary. The government's intention has been to pay for increasing food imports by expanding exports of cotton and rice. But the overall leveling off of agricultural production, and distortions in cropping patterns caused by inappropriate pricing policies, have caused a setback for this course of action.

Egyptian agriculture faces a peculiar problem. Production is not dependent on monsoons or rainfall. Except for severe infestations of cotton leafworm, neither is it subject to unpredictable natural calamities. Unlike India, Egypt does not move abruptly from feast to famine. At the same time, the country's agricultural output is not coming remotely close to feeding the growing population. Some of the factors limiting production are indirect but nonetheless significant. Illiteracy, for example, still prevails in the countryside. Debilitating diseases, especially bilharzia, afflict most of the peasantry. Production techniques for land preparation, lifting water, seeding, plowing, harvesting, threshing, transporting, and storing have changed little in the past century. Egyptian agriculture makes intensive use of animal and human energy, and is based on small, scattered plots not readily susceptible to mechanized cultivation. Even though per acre yields for some crops are relatively high, per cultivator yields for nearly all crops are relatively low. Thus the progress registered in the 1960s was really very modest: a 3.7 percent increase in annual value of production per feddan (one feddan = 1.038 acres) represented only a 1.2 percent increase in the value of production per worker.[3] Even these rates may have declined since 1970.

In recent years over two-thirds of the wheat consumed has been imported, and consistent deficits in maize, lentils, broad beans, sugar, and edible oils have also been registered. Rice represents the only food crop in which there is an exportable, albeit dwindling surplus. All these deficits are likely to grow, steadily and predictably, at a rate at least equivalent to that of the population (2.3 percent per annum). Dependence on international markets for basic food supplies means that there may well be years when international supply cannot accommodate Egyptian demand, or at least cannot do so at a hard currency cost Egypt can afford. While some Egyptian planners believe otherwise, the possibilities of substantially expanding Egyptian agricultural production to meet this challenge appear limited.

Macroeconomic Strategy

It is the contention of this paper that the administered pricing system applied in the agricultural sector must share a good deal of the blame for the poor production performance of recent years. The origins of that system are to be found in the broader macroeconomic development strategy which administered agricultural prices were designed to promote. It is generally accepted that Egypt has been following a strategy common to many developing countries of financing industrialization and economic growth by "taxing" the agricultural sector. The macroeconomic objectives of this strategy include: generation of foreign exchange receipts from the sale of export crops; generation of domestic investment resources for the government budget by buying cheap and selling dear to farmers; subsidization of urban food prices; and stabilization of real prices throughout the economy. In order to achieve these objectives, farm prices were kept at a lower level than international prices, and the rate of increase in crop prices was relatively lower than the rate of increase in costs of production, particularly costs associated with agricultural inputs supplied by the state.

This general strategy has been widely criticized elsewhere as counterproductive. It is argued that over the long run agricultural production languishes and, as a result, the state has less of a surplus to draw upon in financing further productive investment than would be the case were market forces allowed to operate. The validity of this criticism will be tested against Egyptian reality in the discussion that follows, but first it is important to determine whether or not Egypt has in fact pursued this strategy. It is certainly the strategy that Egypt's planners *intended* to pursue from 1960 on, if not before. However, what has actually transpired is open to more than one interpretation.[4]

Much depends, as in all other aspects of statistical accounting in Egypt, upon what rate of inflation one assumes and upon the exchange rate used for the Egyptian pound. Bent Hansen has stated flatly: "There has been a clear tendency to let the terms of the trade of agriculture deteriorate as a means of financing industrialization." A key element in his view was the policy of selling fertilizers to the peasantry at prices above those of the world market to protect the local fertilizer industry. Robert Mabro concurs in both his general assessment and in the specific case of fertilizers.[5] (It should be kept in mind, however, that since the leap in energy prices in 1973, fertilizer is now sold well below world market prices.) Abdel-Fadil contends that the net surplus squeezed out of agriculture for the period 1965-1970 represented 5 to 7 percent of total agricultural income.[6]

Other analysts have argued the opposite: that in fact the agricultural sector has been a net receiver of public investment and is by that token subsidized. For the period 1960-1971 Essam Muntasser estimated public financing of agriculture at LE 893.3 million,[7] including investment in irrigation and subsidized goods, plus the water storage component of the Aswan High Dam. Against this, the agricultural sector paid out LE 176.1 million in taxes, and the state realized net profits on the sale of cotton and rice abroad of LE 736 million. By this reckoning there was a slight tax of some LE 19 million on the agricultural sector. Muntasser feels this was more than offset by fertilizer subsidies and infrastructure maintenance costs, which were not included in his calculations.[8]

Despite this revisionist argument, conventional wisdom would still seem to prevail when government investment in developing new agricultural lands is taken into account. Over the period 1960 to 1970 total outlays for horizontal expansion, essentially land reclamation, reached LE 483.3 million. Investment in vertical expansion—that is, intensifying the use of land already under cultivation—reached LE 193 million. Yet it is precisely the old lands that generate practically all agricultural surplus and income. It is warranted therefore to conclude that the *existing* agricultural sector has been fairly heavily taxed to contribute to other sectors. In policy terms, Nasserist Egypt had established two basic priorities: horizontal expansion in agriculture and heavy industrialization. Administered prices and investments were ordered accordingly, and the traditional agricultural sector fell victim to them.

Surprisingly, taxation of land and water inputs has not figured in the government's management policies for the agricultural sector. Because of its desire to give land-starved peasants more equitable access to cultivable plots, the cost of these production factors has been held down. The effect of this policy has, however, given greater power to middle class farmers, despite the modest success of Egypt's land reform.

Land Tenure

Egypt's land reform acts of 1952, 1961, and 1969 reduced the ceiling on landholdings to 50 feddans per individual and 100 feddans per family. Land reform was accomplished by requisitioning land from large landowners and reselling it to peasants in small plots on concessional terms. Approximately 700,000 feddans had been redistributed in this way by 1970. In addition, the state also pursued a policy of reclaiming and developing new land in former desert areas. Land reclamation was administered separately from the land reform, however, and by 1975 only 200,000 feddans of reclaimed land has been distributed to smallholders.

Although there has been no agricultural census since 1961, we still have a fair idea of the distribution of landholdings. Table 3, prepared by the Ministry of Plan, shows the distribution of landholdings in 1961. It is clear from this table that the reform goal of equitable land distribution was only modestly served. Large landowners (over 50 feddans) saw their holdings drop as a proportion of all land owned to 21.5 percent, but middle-range owners (5-50 feddans), although proportionately reduced in number, saw their land share rise to over 40 percent of all holdings. Thus some 16 percent of all owners controlled 62 percent of the land, while 84 percent owned 38 percent of the cultivated surface. The middle-range landowners emerged not only unscathed but somewhat strengthened from these legislative reforms.

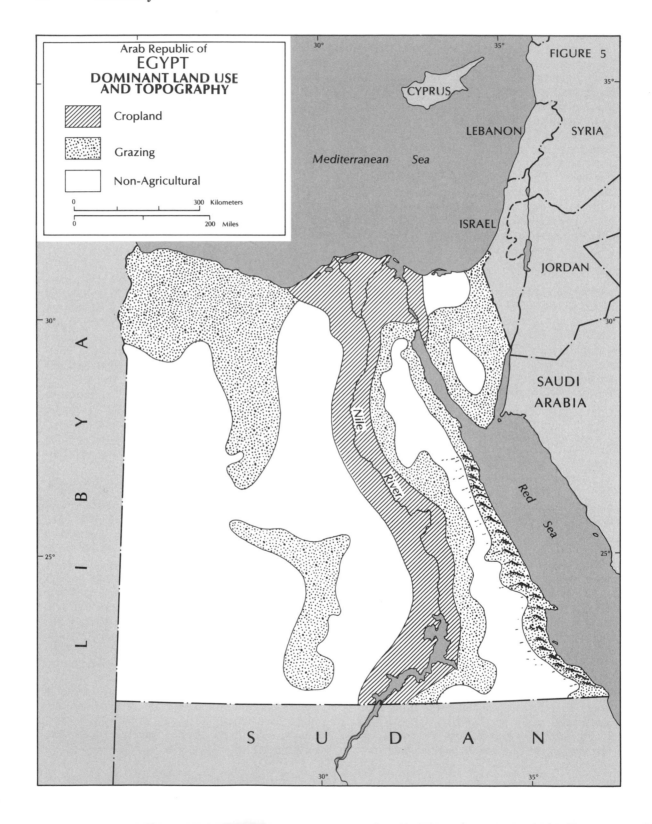

Arab Republic of
EGYPT
**DOMINANT LAND USE
AND TOPOGRAPHY**

Cropland

Grazing

Non-Agricultural

0   300 Kilometers

0   200 Miles

FIGURE 5

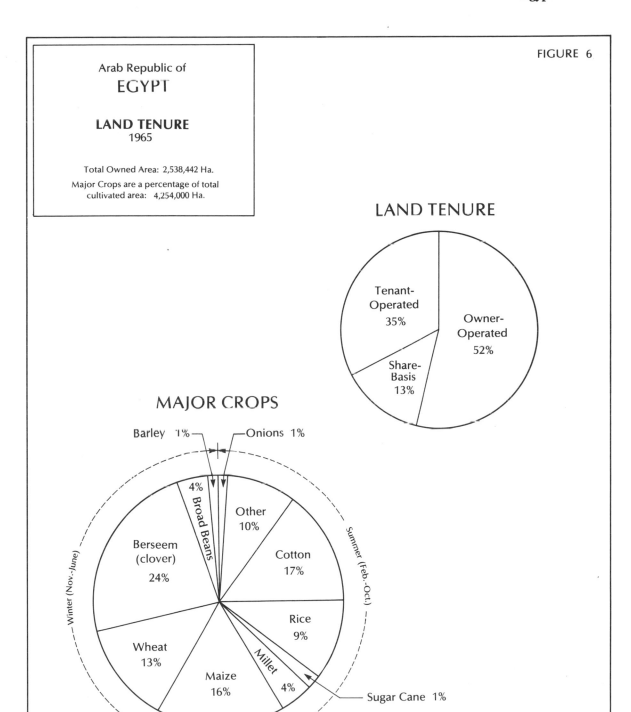

FIGURE 6

Arab Republic of
EGYPT

LAND TENURE
1965

Total Owned Area: 2,538,442 Ha.
Major Crops are a percentage of total
cultivated area: 4,254,000 Ha.

LAND TENURE

Tenant-
Operated
35%

Owner-
Operated
52%

Share-
Basis
13%

MAJOR CROPS

Barley 1%   Onions 1%

4%

Broad Beans

Other
10%

Berseem
(clover)
24%

Cotton
17%

Summer (Feb.-Oct.)

Winter (Nov.-June)

Rice
9%

Wheat
13%

Millet

Maize
16%

4%

Sugar Cane 1%

Flood (July-Nov.)

Abdel-Fadil believes that the group owning 20 or more feddans saw its real share of agricultural income rise from 25 to 32 percent over 20 years, while their numbers declined. Wage laborers and poor peasants also benefited from income redistribution, their share of agricultural income rising from 20 to 38 percent, but there may well have been no per capita increases because their numbers increased so rapidly.[9] Samir Radwan estimates that in 1972 the number of landless families was about the equivalent of the number of landed families, roughly 1.8 million.[10]

The most significant clauses of the land reform acts affected the large landless population and dealt with tenancy and rents. In this century most of Egypt's cultivated land has been rented out seasonally or annually, for cash or through share-cropping. In 1950, about 59 percent of the cultivated surface was rented, a fact reflecting substantial numbers of absentee landlords. Rents too reflected the scarcity of land, and payment frequently constituted upwards of 75 percent of income per feddan. On some estates, such as those of the Toussoun family, rents were pegged to cotton prices, and there was collective responsibility for rent payments by all tenants within a given bloc. It occasionally happened that rents exceeded real income, and violence at such times was not uncommon.[11]

Before 1952, the land tenure system led to serious abuses because of the combination of peasant land hunger and the rack-renting of this scarce factor. It was more profitable for landowners to earn rent income than to cultivate the land themselves and market its produce. From a per feddan average of LE 6.5 in 1938, rents rose by 1950 to levels of LE 20-60 according to the quality of the land and the crop grown.[12]

The credo of the new regime after 1952 was direct cultivation, suppressing absenteeism, and bolstering the ranks of smallholders through land reform and land reclamation. By 1961, however, pure tenancy still covered 1.2 million feddans or about 20 percent of the cultivated surface, and "mixed" holdings another 2.3 million feddans for a total of 57 percent of the 6.2 million feddans cultivated at that time. Due to urban sprawl and other forms of encroachment

on agricultural land, the cultivated surface has declined since 1961 to about 5.6 million feddans in 1976.) Since seasonal leasing is not always fully taken into account in official statistics, the extent of leasing is usually underestimated.

Even today, over 40 percent of Egypt's cultivated surface is rented, over 50 percent in Middle Egypt (Table 4). In seeking to explain Egyptian agricultural performance, therefore, it is still very important to understand the rental system. It is not easy, and Abdel-Fadil warns us of the ambiguities one confronts in this respect

. . . it is difficult in the Egyptian situation to draw any sharp distinction between owned *and* leased *land, as many owner-cultivators, who generally reserve the cash crops for themselves, often lease-out large areas, divided into small plots, to tenants or agricultural laborers on a* seasonal *basis.*[13]

After 1952, the Nasserist regime attempted to force rents to lower levels and introduced measures to protect the tenant. Rents were fixed at seven times the basic land tax, itself a function of the quality of the land and subject to adjustment every ten years. Average *legal* rents fell to LE 21 per feddan. Moreover, tenants were guaranteed contracts for a minimum of three years corresponding to the basic crop rotation period. Subsequently Law 52 of 1966 stipulated that contracts would be permanent unless the tenant failed to meet his obligations.

Sharecropping procedures were changed as well. Before 1952, a typical arrangement would be for the landowner to take five-sixths of the cotton crop, if he paid the land tax, supplied the inputs, and met half the cultivation costs. The cultivator would keep one-sixth of the cotton and all of what other crops (mainly *berseem*: clover) he produced. Since the revolution the practice is to split all costs 50-50 and net returns likewise. Labor costs and supply of organic fertilizer are borne by the sharecropper. Sharecropping, however, has seldom involved more than 10 percent of the cultivated surface.

Rent controls, had they been uniformly applied, should have meant a doubling of real income for tenants between 1952 and 1964. But they were not uniformly applied, and the middle-range landowners early on began to violate them.[14] A survey conducted in 1971 of three villages in Beni Suef province in Middle Egypt[15] found that 70-90 percent of all village families were landless, and that of the landowners 78-95 percent owned 5 feddans or less. The overwhelming majority of cases heard by village Disputes Committees between 1967 and 1971 involved rents. The single most important bone of contention was the widespread practice, imposed by the landowners, of unwritten, unregistered contracts. Tenants protested this practice, and it is indicative of the general mood that the second most frequent bone of contention consisted in complaints filed by owners for nonpayment of rents.

Over 80 percent of all registered contracts in the three villages were for cash rents. When asked, landowners judged that a "fair" rent would be LE 35-45 per feddan, and the survey director was confident that although the contracts were unwritten, most proprietors were receiving at least that much. He also noted a phenomenon in Beni Suef that is apparently widespread in Egypt, that of subletting. There is a group of unknown size whose sole function is to lease land from landowners and then sublet, thus further increasing the cost to the tenant.

Of the 141 landowners surveyed, 92 cultivated their own land, 45 cultivated part and leased part, while only 4 (of which 3 were large landowners) rented all their land. These landowners, most of whom owned 5 feddans or less, comprised less than 30 percent of all families in the 3 villages surveyed. Predictably, the main line of cleavage was not between large and small landholders, but between the relatively few landed families and the much larger number of landless. The haves regarded the have-nots as unreliable and negligent, while the have-nots saw the landed as rapacious and exploitative. Although absenteeism was rare, a discernible stratification of resources and attitudes was nonetheless present.[16]

In recent years the middle-range landowners of Egypt, above all those engaged in commercial farming (especially fruits and vegetables), have launched an assault on several facets of the tenurial legislation enacted since 1952. In contrast with the situation before 1952, rents no longer reflect land scarcity. With the skyrocketing value of several crops (especially *berseem*, vegetables, broad beans), it is more profitable for landowners either to cultivate the land directly or to resort to sharecropping. Through spokesmen in the parliament, these landowners were able to push through amendments to the basic agrarian reform laws that were approved, with little opposition, June 23, 1975. It was argued that because of rising per feddan productivity and the increased value of crops, rents were no longer realistic. The average return per feddan, so it was claimed, was LE 150, while the average rent was LE 17. Some statistical doctoring of the real situation was to be expected, and there was little mention of rising production costs, but the dubious claim that productivity has increased was skillfully used to disarm the left, which to refute the claim would have had to associate itself implicitly with the critics of Nasserist agricultural policy.[17] The claim stood and after only six hours' debate, several measures were passed.

First, it was agreed to reassess the value of agricultural land and hence the land tax. The survey process was completed by fall 1977, and it was expected that rents would go up 50-100 percent per feddan.[18] Delays in payment of rent would justify the landowner terminating the contract, as would the tenant's switching away from traditional government-assigned crops to more profitable alternatives. If both parties agreed, cash rents could be converted to sharecropping, a move likely to be resisted by tenants,[19] but without much effect.

Finally, the Village Disputes Committees were abolished and all litigation henceforth is to be referred to civil courts. Dib,[20] among others, saw this as a move to intimidate lessees from protesting unfair contracts, for to do so would involve traveling considerable distances to district courts and dealing with lawyers, judges, bureaucrats, and written forms. In sum, while there has yet been no modification of the ownership ceilings established since 1952, the protective legislation affecting rents has been considerably eroded. This has enlarged both the middle-range landowners' room to maneuver and the scope for continued polarization of agricultural assets.

Labor Costs

To the extent that the family is the primary production unit, labor inputs are assigned no cost in Egyptian agriculture.[21] Because of the large landless population and the number of sub-subsistence smallholders, however, there is an extensive rural market for wage labor. The Ministry of Plan put the total number of those actively employed in agriculture (presumably including women and children) in 1975 at 4,132,000. Of these, only about 9 percent are "permanent," working an average of 156 days per year. The total bill was estimated at LE 375 million in 1975, or LE 91 per capita per year, but the figure may be inflated.[22]

Be that as it may, rural wages have been rising rapidly in the past decade but especially since 1973. In 1952, the minimum daily wage for agricultural labor was set at 18 piastres (about 40 cents) for men and 10 piastres for women, but supply was so abundant, the minimum was seldom honored and real wages remained well below the legal floor. From the mid-'60s on, however, real wages rose above the legal minimum. Between 1971 and 1975 they jumped from 24 piastres to 41 piastres per day. More recent estimates indicate that during peak seasons (rice transplanting, cotton cultivating, and cotton harvest) wages for a 5-hour day range between 60 piastres and LE 1.50.[23]

Does this rise reflect labor scarcity? To some extent the answer is yes, for migration to the cities, and more recently to other Arab countries, has provoked seasonal shortages that are not geographically uniform. The most important reason, however, appears to be the even more rapid increase in the cost of living—the old 18 piastre floor is simply unrealistic under present circumstances. Real wages increasingly lagged behind the cost of living over the period 1952-1974.[24] While the growing wage burden has thus been a major factor in discouraging cultivators of specific labor-intensive crops such as cotton, other factors of production have increased as much or more than the cost of labor.

Agricultural Taxes

The direct tax burden upon Egyptian agriculture has been light and is becoming lighter. Agricultural incomes are not taxed but only the assessed value of the land.[25] The basic law still in force dates back to 1939 (#113). It set the tax rate at 16 percent of the assessed value of the land and fixed a ceiling of LE 1.64 per feddan. Each ten years village committees were to reassess land values and adjust the tax rate. Law 65 of 1949 reduced the tax rate to 14 percent of the assessed value of the land, but it also removed the absolute ceiling on the amount of tax per feddan. Despite decennial reassessments since 1949, no major change in assessed values or in the tax rate was introduced until 1977-78, when it was decided to increase sharply the assessed value of agricultural land. Some new taxes were imposed, however. An additional payment of 16 percent of assessed value to support local government councils was imposed on landowners in 1960. A defense tax of 3.5 percent, to be paid by all cultivators was instituted in 1956, and in 1965 the rate was raised to 10.5 percent. Cultivators were also required to pay a 3.5 percent national security tax after 1968. Finally, in 1973, a *jihad* (war) tax of 25 piastres per feddan on holdings of 3-5 feddans, 50 piastres on 5-10 feddans, and LE 1 on anything over 10 feddans, was instituted. These supplementary taxes notwithstanding, the fact that land assessments were not raised until last year has meant that the tax burden as a proportion of real income per feddan has declined over the years, from about 6 percent of income to about 2 percent now.

The real beneficiaries of this phenomenon are again the middle-range landowners, particularly those who are able to take advantage of the free market for the sale of highly valued produce not subject to administered prices (fodder, vegetables, fruits, beans, etc.). Perhaps in light of this visibly inequitable situation, by Law 51 of April 1973, President Sadat exempted all smallholders of three feddans or less from all taxes. Over two million peasants benefited from this measure.

The result of this policy has been that direct agricultural tax receipts dropped off from LE 13.8 million in 1952 to LE 8.9 million in 1964, rose to LE 21.7 million in 1972, and dropped off again to an estimated LE 14.5 million by 1978, a reflection of on-going land fragmentation as well as Law 51. (With the recent land reassessment completed, taxes as well as rents should once again increase.) It is difficult to know if these figures reflect real or expected receipts. Ahmad Yunis, a member of the parliamentary agricultural committee and a resolute enemy of the agricultural tax, made the astonishing claim that LE 63 million in agricultural tax "arrears" were not arrears at all, but had actually been collected and pocketed by local tax officials. All the more reason, he argued, to abolish the tax altogether.[26]

Middle-range landowners have been active in repulsing efforts to impose special taxes on highly profitable agricultural enterprises such as poultry, livestock, fruits, and vegetables. Ministry of Agriculture statistics show, for example, that the average income of one feddan of orchards is LE 100. Other estimates show that the gross income of a feddan of orange trees may be as high as LE 500-600. If, as is frequently the case, the orchards lie in reclaimed land, there is no tax on them at all, and, if the land is subject to taxation, the assessment does not reflect its true income-producing capacity.[27]

In 1959, taxes on poultry and livestock raisers were dropped in an effort to stimulate production and lower prices. Although the objective was not achieved, all attempts to reintroduce taxation of them have been thwarted. A draft law submitted to Parliament in 1972 to put a tax of LE 20 per feddan on all orchards was voted down by the agricultural committee 98-2.[28] In 1977, a new draft, supported by the Ministry of Finance, was submitted to Parliament. It proposed a profit tax on apiaries, orchards, truck farms, flowers, poultry, and livestock, and a tax on the renting of agricultural machinery. The interests opposed to this legislation cited the heavy initial investment and long lead time required before fruit trees produce, the fact that poultry and vegetable cultivation should be given positive incentives in order to fulfill Egypt's goal of "food security," and that new taxes would drive smallholders out of cultivation. Once again the legislation went down to defeat.

Water

Water is obviously the *sine qua non* of Egyptian agriculture, and none of it falls from the sky. Nor is it any longer delivered to Egypt's fields by the natural action of the annual flood. Instead it is conducted by thousands of kilometers of irrigation canals, in some instances pumped up considerable elevations, and the excess eliminated by a less extensive drainage network. Although it is difficult to know the real costs of water delivery and removal, one plausible estimate of recurrent outlays assumes a rate of 4 millemes per cubic meter delivered and drained, which results in total costs of about LE 90 million per year.[29] Whatever the costs, the Egyptian cultivator is not obliged to bear them. Water is supplied free of charge, and the only (ineffectual) deterrent to overirrigation is the structure of the delivery canals that oblige the cultivator to lift the water to his fields by means either of human or animal power. Electric and diesel pumps are wreaking havoc with this deterrent, and increased waterlogging and soil salinity are the result. Water is costless to the cultivator, but the policy is costly to society. There would be significant political and cultural resistance to the introduction of a direct charge for water, but delivery costs could be reflected in the assessment of land values and the agricultural tax.

Cooperatives, Prices, and Production

The mechanism by which Egypt's growth strategy and administered pricing system has been applied in the countryside is the rural cooperative. Initially, membership was required only for beneficiaries of the Agrarian Reform Act of 1952. The recipients of the redistributed land had to join a local cooperative and follow crop rotations prescribed by the Ministry of Agriculture. In 1961 the cooperative system was expanded beyond agrarian reform areas, and virtually all farmers now participate, as it is their only means of access to production inputs.[30] Minimum membership fees are 50 piastres per annum or LE 1 per feddan owned.

Local cooperatives provide credit to farmers for the purchase of seeds, fertilizers, insecticides, farm machinery, and feedstuffs at controlled prices.[31] Inputs are lent to a farmer in accordance with the norms for the number of acres he intends to plant to various crops. The state imposes delivery quotas for cotton and rice on all farmers, and these two crops, both cultivated in the summer, tie up nearly half of Egypt's acreage and determine the crops that precede and follow them. For cotton, rice, and some other crops, cash loans might also be made, but in any year upwards of 70 percent of all credit is in kind. Because average membership of individual cooperatives is low (622 per coop in 1972), as is average capital (LE 1,580), most coops rely on the General Authority for Agricultural Credit to help finance their activities (see Table 5).

Each year the state establishes the number of acres to be planted to cotton in each locality, and recommends acreage for other major field crops in accordance with a two- or three-year rotation cycle. In some areas farmers rotate crops on their own fields. In other areas, farmers join together to assemble larger land parcels, and the entire parcel is cultivated in accordance with the rotation cycle. Each June, when recommended rotations are announced by the Ministry of Agriculture, so too are the expected purchase prices of the major crops (Table 6). This announcement is supposed to act as an incentive to the peasant to follow the rotation, and in cotton zones the peasant has no choice. Control over the planting of cotton acres is exercised by the cooperative, which allocates inputs on the basis of the planting intentions of its members. At harvest time, the farmer is expected to sell to the cooperative, or to a state flour mill, cotton gin, or sugar cane crusher, at the announced prices, and to pay for his inputs from the proceeds.[32]

By fixing the price of inputs and the price of basic crops, and by regulating the acreage allotted to cotton, the state intends, through the mechanism of the cooperatives, to manage the agricultural sector to achieve its macroeconomic objectives. However, for a number of reasons, farmers prefer to avoid selling through the cooperatives whenever possible and the actual production and marketing performance of the agricultural sector frequently differs from the goals set by the government.

The original intent of the cooperatives, beyond the implementation of Egypt's macrostrategy for growth, was to provide the cultivator a full range of services and inputs to increase the quality of production. Extension services were to bolster skills in the utilization of state-supplied chemical fertilizers and standardized seeds, while agricultural supervisors were to assure that inputs were put to their intended use. On nearly every count the system has failed to perform as designed. Extension services exist more on paper than in the field, and the use of inputs is inadequately supervised. Tractor plowing has involved bureaucratic delays and maintenance problems, so that the peasant typically resorts to private owners of tractors, but at higher cost. Inputs have been on occasion in short supply (for example a 250,000 ton shortfall in fertilizers in fall 1976 when high-yielding variety wheat was being planted), or delivered at the wrong times.

One result is that there is a thriving black market, especially in fertilizers, where well-off farmers, coop officials, and smallholders can all profit. For instance, it may make financial sense for a peasant receiving his quota of fertilizer for a feddan of cotton to sell it to a neighboring truck farmer at black market rates. He may then shrug off a poor harvest on his own land, all the more easily if he is able to reap two or three snatch crops of winter clover (*berseem*), which he can sell on the free market at LE 40-60 per feddan and per cutting, before planting his cotton. This may further cut back cotton yield because cotton leaf worm pupae over-winter in *berseem* and its late spring cultivation means that hatched moths have immediate access to young cotton plants. In 1973 the Ministry of Agriculture threatened fines of LE 20 per feddan and six months in prison for anyone planting *berseem* beyond early April.

Another important factor in the malfunctioning of the cooperative system derives from the distinction between agrarian reform area cooperatives and those set up after 1961. In the former, new landowners were assigned land in three separate plots, each falling in a different crop area. Thus, in any one year the peasant could protect himself against the failure or unfavorable pricing of any given crop. Those who were obliged to accept fixed rotation schemes after 1961 in nonagrarian reform areas frequently found that all their land had to be planted to cotton in a given year, and that they would have to await the second or third years of the rotation to recoup losses, if then.[33]

Production of cotton, the crop on which government planners have pinned their hopes for export revenues, has suffered particularly from the distortions created by the rigid controls the state has attempted to exercise through the coop system. The crop is highly labor-intensive throughout most of its growing period, and rising labor costs make it unattractive to all but smallholders. Although there is a black market for short staple cotton needed by the private sector textile plants, these varieties are imported. Thus, the response to underpricing of state-purchased cotton is to neglect the "government crop" and literally tend to one's cucumbers. In 1975, for example, average production costs for cotton worked out to LE 165 per feddan while the purchase price for the average output from one feddan was LE 125.[34] The loss, as one source pointed out,[35] could only be compensated by illegal cuttings of *berseem* and by growing cucumbers under the cotton plants. In 1975 a feddan's worth of cucumbers could bring in LE 300.

The coops have also performed poorly because of the unequal benefits drawn from them by renters, smallholders, and middle landowners. This takes several forms. It is clear that well-off farmers have tended to monopolize agricultural credit, especially medium-term loans, cash loans, and loans for equipment and machinery (which, once acquired, they can rent to poorer farmers). Moreover, these same borrowers were most delinquent in repayments. In 1967 total arrears on coop loans totaled LE 80 million, of which LE 60 million was held by owners of 25 or more feddans.[36] Mustapha Gabali, the former Minister of Agriculture, issued a decree in June 1971 that forgave LE 9 million in arrears for peasants owning one feddan or less, and LE 6 million in back interest for owners of one to 5 feddans. By 1972-73 farmers still owed the agricultural credit banks LE 62 million in arrears.

The wealthier landowners are able to take advantage of the system in another way. Not only do they have the versatility inherent in larger surfaces which can be cropped in different ways,

but they generally achieve higher yields per feddan as well. For example, in rice areas the coop quota is set at 1.25 to 1.5 tons per feddan, reflecting *average* production levels. Large owners, however, are able to produce in excess of quota and sell the difference on the free market. Smallholders seldom have any excess. They do have animals to feed and may not have had the chance to grow their own fodder. Thus, they must buy fodder, freely priced or at black market rates, from the larger landholders who are able to grow it. With respect to rice, the result has been striking; peasants simply do not sell their rice to the coops and resort to the free market instead. Unlike cotton, there is a growing domestic market for rice at high prices. By contrast, in 1975 if the cultivator sold to the state, he received only about 20 percent of the net return received by the state from sales on the international market. Thus in 1974-75, of 2.2 million tons produced, only 800,000 were delivered to the government mills. This trend has in turn been reflected in declining rice exports. A decade ago Egypt could market upwards of a million tons abroad; now it is doing well to export 200,000 tons.[37]

Sugar production has also been affected. While the feddanage tied up by sugar cane is not great—some 200-250,000 feddans in Middle and Upper Egypt—its maturation period is so long (at least 11 months) that the cultivator can grow no other crops. Either he will make it with cane or go under. On the basis of average yields, the peasant would have been paid LE 122 per feddan for his cane in 1976 while his production costs would have amounted to LE 101 per feddan. Where poor drainage, salinity, and lack of fertilizers have led to declines in the sugar content of the cane, the state mills may reject or pay much lower prices for cane whose sugar content is less than 10.3 percent of its weight. Yet, despite having to supplement domestic production with raw sugar imports, the mills can market refined sugar and by-products (molasses, *bergasse*, etc.) for prices worth up to LE 1,500 per feddan. The result has been some flight from cane (fines are now LE 50 per feddan for violation of rotation), and, as with rice, resort to illegal selling to the private market where molasses manufacturers and cane-juice retailers will pay nearly five times the state purchase price per ton. In 1977 the state went halfway to meet the competition, but that incentive plus heavier fines will probably not deter the peasants from shunning the mills.[38]

A survey in Sharqia Province (a rice-producing area) found that only 19 percent of the peasants asked were willing to deal with the coops. The reasons most frequently cited were delays in payment for crops (88%), easier to deal with the private sector for rice sales (82%), because coop officials demanded "honoraria" for weighing and grading (72%), because cultivators must pay transportation costs of inputs and harvest (27%), and in order to avoid settling back debts (19%).[39]

Fathy Hamada is the owner of 16 *qayrot* (two-thirds feddan), and he rents another 10 *qayrot* in a cotton area of the Delta. His net annual income is about LE 45 ($90). On this he raises a family. He was asked the following questions by a reporter from *al-Tali'a*. T. "If they shut down the coop and sent all the employees away, what would happen?" H. "We'd need fertilizer." T. "Is that all the coop means to you?" H. "Yes." T. "There's no extension service or supervision?" H. "There are no services like that." T. "Doesn't the coop do anything with respect to animals and poultry?" H. "What could it do? There's nothing." T. "So all the coop means is fertilizers and seed." H. "That's it...and insecticides."[40]

Remedies?

Egypt's socialist experiment of the 1960s was mismanaged, and then battered insensate by war and balance of payments crises. A reassessment in the 1970s was inevitable. Theoretically at least a number of lessons could have been drawn from the crisis. One might have been that the real problem is to apply socialist policies more efficiently than in the past. In agriculture, this "more of the same, only better" approach would have meant strengthening the cooperatives, beefing up extension services, monitoring input utilization more closely, and making greater concessions to the peasants on price.

But the simple fact is that the rise in purchase prices has continued to lag behind the rise in the official prices of inputs (not to mention the black market prices), and even more so behind the increase in world market prices, of which the peasant is generally aware. Between 1964 and 1974 the purchase price of cotton rose 48 percent, rice by 122 percent, wheat by 79 percent, and sugar cane by 136 percent, whereas input prices (exclusive of rent) rose 158 percent, 119 percent, 231 percent, and 124 percent, respectively, over the same period (see Tables 6 and 7). Looking at crops which the peasant must or can sell to the coops, the drafters of Egypt's new five-year agricultural plan (1978-1982) found that in terms of world market prices the most profitable crops are cotton with a long growing season (LE 339 per feddan), wheat followed by rice (LE 213 per feddan), and wheat followed by corn (LE 137 per feddan). But in local prices the picture is as follows: permanent *berseem* followed by maize (LE 127 per feddan), cotton followed by snatch-crop *berseem* (LE 88 per feddan), wheat followed by rice (LE 52 per feddan), and wheat followed by corn (LE 49 per feddan).[41]

Fruits and vegetables, which are freely marketed, assure much higher returns for the cultivator. In 1972, the gross value of produce of a feddan of field crops was LE 122, that of fruit LE 208, and that of vegetables LE 500. The state's efforts to control retail prices for fruits and vegetables are largely ineffectual. As Cairo and Alexandria grow toward one another, the Delta heartland lying in between is increasingly given over to satisfying their demands, and by 1974 vegetable acreage had expanded to 76,000 feddans.[42] Ranking along with vegetables and fruits in profitability is *berseem*, which alone could provide a cultivator over LE 200 per feddan if he is able to grow a winter cutting and three spring snatch crops. One may reasonably assume that this combination of factors contributed to the declining yields per feddan for "government crops," as well as to the soaring number of violations of prescribed rotations: 1973, 43,000; 1974, 180,000; 1975, 289,000.[43] Peasants were willing to risk fines in order to plant other crops with higher returns.

In the face of this increasingly critical situation the government has raised purchase prices substantially in the past two years and has abandoned compulsory purchase of wheat. But this response has been largely reactive, with the government raising the purchase price and offering special input subsidies for crops whose production and marketing in preceding years did not meet state targets. These piecemeal government actions reflect little or no consideration of price relationships among crops produced domestically or between domestic and international markets.

One of the ironies of the current situation is that fertilizers, and to a lesser degree pesticides, which make up the bulk of the credit-in-kind to coop members, are, despite their rising cost to the cultivators, more and more heavily subsidized by the state. In recent years the annual subsidy has been running between LE 80 million and LE 119 million, a total in excess of all credit extended in any one year by the coops.[44]

However desirable rationalization of agricultural planning might be, there is little likelihood that Egypt will eliminate these anomalies in the near future. Responsibility for agriculture is divided among several government ministries, and each has a bureaucratic interest in retaining control over those policies which have been assigned to it. Further, the more well-to-do landowners are benefiting from the present confusion and drift. Thus, as in practically all sectors of the economy, the tendency has been to condemn all forms of state intervention in agriculture as counterproductive and to chalk up production declines to "collective dogma." By contrast, the market is re-emerging in Egypt as a kind of idol. Once again the agricultural committee of the parliament has led the charge. Ahmad Yunis, in May 1976, proposed that the coop marketing system for cotton be abolished and that the Alexandria futures market, closed since 1961, be reopened. Yunis' suggestion received some attention in an unexpected way. Not only was he an MP but also president of the Federation of Agricultural Cooperatives created in 1969 to promote cooperative spirit among peasants and to represent the Egyptian movement abroad. In summer 1976 Yunis was charged with misappropriating the Federation's funds and tolerating similar abuses at all levels of the cooperative hierarchy. With this as pretext more than cause, the government dissolved the Federation and along with it the General Authority for Agricul-

tural Cooperatives that supervised their actual operation.[45]

Having swept the board clean, the government could then begin to contemplate new arrangements. It has powerful external support for such an overhaul. A United States Department of Agriculture brief submitted to Congress in 1978 had this to say:

In their present form, most Egyptian cooperatives are an anachronism. Perhaps best left to its own decline, cooperative structure as it stands should be gradually replaced by modern, private business mechanisms, and, locally, by village banks and similar credit funds.

That indeed is what is actually happening. Fatallah Rifa'at, head of the 750 agricultural credit banks, described the new measures in an interview with the author. Henceforth, he said, the coops will have no role in the distribution of inputs or credit but instead will act as catalysts to local development projects, agro-industries, poultry farms, etc., contracting loans from outside sources, including the agricultural credit bank itself. The Village Banks, as they are now to be called, will deal directly with the cultivators. They will have their own storage facilities and will advance inputs according to the rotation inscribed in the peasant's card and as approved by the local agricultural overseer. The banks will either purchase the crops directly or collect repayment for their loans from the mills and gins. Failure to pay back loans on time will mean initially that the line of credit is severed, and ultimately that the bank will claim the collateral on its loans consisting in the peasant's crop and even his land. Simultaneously, the banks will try to encourage rural savings by offering 5 percent on local accounts, and with this they will make loans for local agro-industries at 9-10 percent. Rifa'at, who has been with the bank for 25 years, or well before its nationalization, said, "We are returning to our true mission as a commercial bank servicing the agricultural sector. Moreover we can now take equity positions in agro-industries and other projects, even with foreign partners."

The reintroduction of commercial criteria in the disbursement of credit will inevitably tend to favor the better-off farmers whose creditworthiness is greatest. To offset this, Egypt's planners recommend that Village Banks give priority to cultivators who fulfill government production targets and follow prescribed rotations. There should be no subsidized (i.e., 3% interest) credit for fruit and vegetable growers.[46] These may be more pious wishes than what is likely to transpire. The legal Egyptian left, for example, has warned that the fact the Village Banks will deal directly with the peasants *without their having to be members of a cooperative*, may mean that the entire cooperative structure will be dismantled.[47]

If the market once again is allowed to reign supreme and the owners of the means of production to develop their assets in the most profitable manner, several consequences can be anticipated. Acreage will gradually shift over to crops for which there are relatively high domestic prices. These will continue to be fruits, vegetables, and fodder, the latter to some extent a function of the soaring prices for meat in the cities. Indicative of the pressures at work is the fact that cultivators of cotton now have the option of planting soybeans instead of cotton. This new crop would then be put at the disposal of the nascent poultry feed industry and help meet urban demand for fowl.

The shift will be away from export crops, but to the extent that these are still cultivated, the amount actually exported will dwindle. Local demand for rice, cotton, and sugar is rising steadily so that the state will have to anticipate declining foreign exchange earnings from these crops. Consequently the entire strategy described at the beginning of this paper will be placed in jeopardy. Few contest that if Egypt is to survive as a viable economy, industrialization and industrial exports are essential. Yet the means to finance this process, partially derived in the past from the agricultural sector, are no longer secure. The alternative is near total reliance on external financing—bilateral or multilateral—and foreign private investment.

Finally, cleavages in the distribution of wealth in the countryside will be accentuated. This may be the price of increased production, but it would

be a steep one to pay politically. One would expect market forces to drive marginal producers out of cultivation with their land being acquired by the more efficient and the better-endowed. The basic line of cleavage may become that of the landless versus the landed with the latter made up eventually only of middle-range landowners.

It is easy enough to describe what went wrong with Egypt's administered pricing system in the 1960s, but far harder to prescribe remedies that would serve broader goals of equity, national sovereignty, and a diversified economy. The present regime has on occasion adumbrated three themes to cope with its agricultural crisis: food security, leaving the valley, and regional integration. The slogan of food security has been used frequently by President Sadat himself. It does not connote agricultural self-sufficiency but rather attaining a level of production that would allow Egypt to escape being at the mercy of international suppliers. The policy would require a combination of increased foodgrain production through the reduction of acreage given over to cotton and fodder crops; the introduction of mechanization, high-yielding varieties, and tile drainage, in addition to land reclamation; the cultivation of new crops such as soybeans and sugar beets; and a drastic increase in poultry production and fish farming. The Five-Year Plan for 1978-1982 fleshes out this policy, but notes that even though these goals might be achieved, the combination of population growth and income growth has created so much additional demand that even with all these modifications, Egypt would nonetheless be less self-sufficient in 1982 than it was in 1970.

The technocratic dream is to find in Egypt's deserts the agricultural miracle that has eluded the country in the ancient soils of the valley proper. Again, President Sadat has taken the lead in this direction, despite the very discouraging experience to date in the one million feddans under reclamation since 1960. In May 1977, before a "consultative group" of international financiers and creditors assembled by the I.B.R.D., Egypt's Minister of Plan spoke glowingly of cultivating three million feddans in the string of oases in Egypt's southwestern desert. The limiting factors here as elsewhere in "horizontal" expansion are available water and soil quality. The Ministry of Plan suggested that large amounts of water could be drawn off Lake Nasser and delivered to the oases to supplement groundwater supplies. The significant silence of the Ministry of Irrigation tends to confirm the view that Lake Nasser at present has no regular surplus to give away, and that the fossil deposits of the oases are being tapped at near optimal rates now. The soils of these areas are generally poor and would require enormous investment to sustain any crop. Finally, the oases are far from major areas of consumption as well as from ports.

The third option is to promote agricultural expansion in neighboring Arab countries and then seek barter deals to absorb part of that surplus: for example, Egyptian fertilizers against Sudanese sugar or Syrian wheat. The Sudan is clearly the logical partner for Egypt in this respect, although it is not likely to become a wheat exporter. On the other hand, within a decade it could have large exportable surpluses of maize, sorghum, edible oils, sugar, and beef. Likewise, Syria, Iraq, Algeria, and Morocco have the potential to generate wheat surpluses. Three problems stand in the way: at present, surpluses are merely potential while deficits prevail; political differences have consistently stymied any effective steps toward integration; and it seems likely that if any of these countries do market surpluses they will demand hard currency payment. In light of all these considerations it is reasonable to suppose that Egypt will remain a food-deficit country throughout the remainder of this century and one of the major grain importers in the world.

NOTES

1. See Faruq Shalaby and Muhammed Mustapha, "Nutritional Levels from the Point of View of Prices," Price Planning Agency Memo No. 12, June 1972; Ahmad Tawfiq al-Fil and Assam Abu Wafa, "Economic Problems of Food Production in Egypt and the Role of Arab Regional Integration in Overcoming Them," *L'Egypte Contemporaine*, Vol. 65, No. 355, January 1974, pp. 107-150, esp. p. 111; and H.A. el-Togby, *Contemporary Egyptian Agriculture*, 2nd edition, Ford Foundation, Cairo, 1976, p. 10.

2. See John Waterbury, "Aish: Egypt's Growing Food Crisis," *AUFS Reports*, Northeast Africa Series, Vol. XIX, No. 3, 1974.

3. M. Mohiey Nasrat and Ahmed Goueli, "The Productivity of the Human Workforce in Traditional Agriculture with special reference to Egypt," in *Proceedings of the World Food Conference of 1976*, Ames, Iowa, ISU Press, 1977, pp. 331-337.

4. For example, see Gilbert Brown, "Agricultural Pricing Policies and Economic Growth," *Finance and Development*, Vol. 14, No. 4, December 1977, pp. 42-45.

5. Bent Hansen, "Economic Development of Egypt" in Charles Cooper and Sidney Alexander, eds., *Economic Development and Population Growth in the Middle East*, Elsevier, New York, 1972, p. 83; and Robert Mabro, *The Egyptian Economy: 1952-1972*, Oxford, 1974, p. 78.

6. Mahmud Abdel-Fadil, *Development, Income Distribution and Social Change in Rural Egypt*, 1952-1970, Cambridge University Press, 1975, p. 120.

7. Exchange rates have varied over the time period covered in this paper, but the official rate has remained at LE 1 = $2.30. The so-called "incentive rate," more nearly reflecting the market value of the LE, is now at LE 1 = $1.70.

8. Essam Muntasser, "Agricultural Prices, Growth and Sectoral Terms of Trade in Egypt," FAO/SIDA Seminar on Agricultural Sector Analysis in the Near East and North Africa, Cairo, October 20-26, 1975.

9. Abdel-Fadil, p. 60.

10. Samir Radwan, *The Impact of Agrarian Reform on Rural Egypt* (1952-1975) World Employment Program Research, ILO WEP 10-6/WP-13, Geneva, January 1977.

11. Gabriel Saab, *The Egyptian Agrarian Reform 1952-1962*, Oxford University Press (1967), p. 11. Cf., James C. Scott, "Patronage or Exploitation" in E. Gellner & John Waterbury (eds.) *Patrons and Clients in Mediterranean Societies*, Duckworth, London (1977), pp. 21-40. Scott seeks to present a schema for understanding under what conditions peasants come to regard tenancy arrangements as exploitative.

12. Saab, *op. cit.*; Hamid Abd al-Gamid Draz, *Reform of the Agricultural Tax*. Mu'assassa Shabab al-Gama', Alexandria (1976), and Muhammed Anis, "A Study of the National Income of Egypt," *L'Egypte Contemporaine*, n. 261/62 (November-December 1950), p. 759, and Patrick O'Brien, *The Revolution in Egypt's Economic System*, Oxford, 1966, p. 9.

13. Abdel-Fadil, p. 17.

14. Saab, p. 145.

15. Abd al-Basit Abd al-Ma'ti, *Class Conflict in the Egyptian Village*, Dar al-Thiqafa al-Jadida, Cairo (1977).

16. *Ibid.*

17. "No to the People's Assembly," *al-Tali'a*, Vol. 11, No. 8, 1975, pp. 13-15 and in the same issue, Guma'Abduh Qassim, "Hands off the Egyptian Peasant," pp. 100 ff; "What is Happening to the Egyptian Peasant in the People's Assembly?", *Ruz al-Yussef*, No. 2455, June 30, 1975; *al-Ahram*, June 24, 1975; and Muhammed Abu Mandur Dib, "The Relation Between Owner and Renter in Egyptian Agriculture," *al-Tali'a*, Vol. 11, No. 6, June 1975, pp. 78-83.

18. *al-Ahram al-Iqtisadi*, No. 533, November 1, 1977.

19. Scott, *op. cit.*, pp. 31-34, argues that when fixed cash rents are high, reflecting land scarcity, then peasants may well prefer sharecropping where the share varies with the size of the crop.

20. Muhammed Abu Mandur Dib, "The Relation between Owner and Renter in Egyptian Agriculture, *al-Tali'a*, V. 11, No. 6 (June 1975), pp. 78-83.

21. For example, H.A. el-Togby calculates the value added in agriculture by deducting from the gross value of agricultural production the costs of seeds, fertilizers, pesticides, fuel, machine depreciation, but assigns no cost to labor or water, *op. cit.*, pp. 212-22.

22. ARE, Ministry of Plan, The Five Year Plan 1978-1982; Vol. IV, *The General Strategy for Agriculture, Irrigation and Food Scarcity*, Cairo, August 1977, p. 1974. At least one other source (Abdel-Fadil, *op. cit.* p. 64) estimated the wage bill for 1974 at LE 274 million. It is implausible that paid wages would have risen by LE 100 million in a single year.

23. *Ruz al-Yussef*, No. 2504 (June 7, 1976).

24. The Ministry of Plan forecasts an annual increase in agricultural wages over the period 1978-1982 of 3.3 percent, a rate greatly inferior to that of rural inflation.

25. The best treatment is Draz, *op. cit.* See also Jorgen Lotz, "Taxation in the UAR," *IMF Staff Papers*, Vol. XIII, No. 1, March 1966, pp. 121-153.

26. *The Egyptian Gazette*, May 5, 1976.

27. In 1974-75 the state purchase price for oranges was LE 60 per ton, and average yields were 8-9 tons per feddan, although many owners produced more. Thus, 50 feddans producing 10 tons per feddan might generate a gross income of LE 30,000 per year, conceivably tax free.

28. See Adil Abd al-Ghaffar, "The Problems Which Fruit-Growers Confront," *al-Ahram*, June 14, 1975.

29. The estimated costs are presented in Iz al-Din Kamil, *Mechanized Agriculture*, Dar al-Thiqafa al-Jadida, Cairo (1976), p. 123.

30. Muhammed Mahmud Abd al-Ra'uf, "Production Coops and the Evolution of Egyptian Agriculture," INP Memo 1007, February 1972; and Mustapha Gama', "Organizational Structure of Cooperatives and the Problem of Cooperation in the ARE," *L'Egypte Contemporaine*, Vol. 64, 352, April 1972, pp. 188-205. See also, Sayed Ahmed Marei, "Overturning the Pyramid," *Ceres*, 1969, No. 2, pp. 48-51.

31. N. Saad, "Socialist Transformation in UAR Agriculture," *L'Egypt Contemporaine*, Vol. 60, 1969; Food and Agricultural Organization of the United Nations, *Perspective Study of Agricultural Development for the Arab Republic of Egypt*, Rome, April 1973.

32. FAO, *op. cit.*, "Crop Production," ESP/PS/EGY/73/8; *Area Handbook for Egypt*, DA Pam 550-43, Washington, D.C., U.S. GPO, 1976, pp. 282-283.

33. el-Togby, *op. cit.*, pp. 57-58 explains the problem well; see also U.S. Department of Agriculture and USAID, *Egypt: Major Constraints to Increasing Agricultural Productivity*, Foreign Agricultural Economic Report No. 120, Washington, D.C., June 1976, pp. 36-37.

34. Izzat al-Sa'dni, "The Cotton Curse has Struck Egypt's Peasants," *al-Ahram al-Iqtisadi*, No. 486, November 15, 1975. Note that Sa'dni's production costs estimates are well above those of the Ministry of Agriculture's shown in Table 5B. See also James Mayfield, *Local Institutions and Egyptian Rural Development*, RDC, Cornell University 1974, esp. Table XXVII, p. 47.

35. "Who Killed King Cotton in Menufia?", *Akhbar al-Yom*, November 8, 1975. For other reasons the cotton harvest of 1978 was highly disappointing. Extraordinarily high temperatures in June, high rates of cotton leaf worm infestation, inadequate aerial spraying, and, allegedly, defective seed supplied by the Ministry of Agriculture in order to encourage an expansion in cotton acreage, all led to a drop-off in average yields, especially in Upper and Middle Egypt.

36. *al-Tali'a*, 1972, p. 25; and Abd al-Ma'ti, *op. cit.*, pp. 125-129 found in the three villages surveyed that the largest landowners dominated the coop boards, that they were the most indebted and most delinquent in repayment. In one village there was LE 25,000 in outstanding loans to the 525 coop members. Forty owners of 10-50 feddans held LE 16,000 of this debt.

37. *al-Ahram al-Iqtisadi*, No. 490, January 15, 1975; and Mustapha Fakry and Ahmad al-Fil, "Factors Responsible for the Major Proportional Decline of Rice in Egypt's

Cropping Pattern," *al-Magalla al-Zira'ia*, Vol. 17, No. 5, April 1975, pp. 150-160.

38. Izzat al-Sa'dni, "Cotton's Bitterness in the Cane Fields," *al-Ahram al-Iqtisadi*, No. 487, December 1, 1975; "Lentils are Sweeter than Sugar Cane," p. 44, *Akhbar al-Yom*, February 2, 1974; and *Ruz al-Yussef*, No. 2485, January 26, 1976.

39. See *al-Ahram al-Iqtisadi*, No. 483, October 1, 1975.

40. "The Pre-Occupations of the Fellah Fathy Hamada," *al-Tali'a*, Vol. 12, No. 4, April 1976, pp. 24-52.

41. ARE, Ministry of Plan, Vol. IV, *op. cit.*, p. 24.

42. Abderrahman 'Aql, "Human Development is the Essence of Economic Development, *al-Tali'a*, Vol. 13, No. 6, June 1977 and el-Togby, *op. cit.*, pp. 212-213.

43. *al-Ahram*, February 2, 1975 and Progressive Unionist Party, *Observations of the Deputies of the Progressive Unionist Party on the Prime Minister's Statement to Parliament*, Cairo, January 1977, p. 36.

44. Radwan, *op. cit.*, p. 62.

45. Yunis has not yet been convicted of anything. In summer 1976 he was stripped of his parliamentary immunity but then overwhelmingly re-elected to parliament in November 1976. See Ibrahim 'Amr, "Deviations of the Cooperative Federation and Set-Backs to Agricultural Coops," *al-Ahram al-Iqtisadi*, No. 540, February 15, 1978.

46. ARE, Ministry of Plan, Vol. IV, *op. cit.*, p. 78.

47. Progressive Unionist Party, *op. cit.*, p. 40.

TABLE 1

Evolution of Productivity of
Principal Crops, per Feddan

Crop	Unit of Measure	1971/72	1973	1974	1975	1976	% Change Annual
Wheat	Ardeb	8.68	9.82	9.17	9.72	9.36	+1.9
Shami Maize	Ardeb	11.00	10.82	10.75	10.85	11.51	+1.15
Rice	Ton	2.23	2.28	2.13	2.3	2.13	-1.1
Ful	Ardeb	6.92	6.51	6.20	6.14	6.32	-2.1
Lint Cotton	Metric Qantar	5.9	5.43	5.26	4.98	5.4	-2.1
Sugar Cane	Ton	38.9	38.00	33.7	36.25	38.3	-.38
Fruits	Ton	5.0	5.57	5.73	5.80	5.80	+4.1

Source: ARE, Ministry of Plan, The Five Year Plan 1978-82: Vol. IV, *The General
Strategy for Agriculture, Irrigation and Food Security*, Cairo, August 1977, p. 43.

*Measures	kilograms	pounds
1 Qantar unginned cotton	157.5 kgs.	346.5
1 Qantar ginned cotton or lint	50.0 kgs.	110.0
1 Qantar sugar	45.0 kgs.	99.0
1 Dariba unmilled rice	945.0 kgs.	2,079.0
1 Ardeb wheat	150.0 kgs.	330.0
1 Ardeb maize	140.0 kgs.	308.0
1 Ardeb berseem	157.0 kgs.	345.4
1 Feddan	1.038 acres	
1 Qayrot	1/24 feddan	

TABLE 2

An Estimate of the Rural Poor in Egypt: 1958-59 - 74-75

	1958-59	1964-65	1974-75
1. Household income corresponding to poverty line (LE)[a]	93	125	270
2. Total Population, '000	25,832	30,139	36,417
3. Rural Population, '000	15,968	17,754	20,830
4. No. of Rural Families, '000	3,224	3,345	4,166
5. Families below Poverty Line:			
% of rural families	35.0	26.8	44.0
number	1,161	903	1,833
6. Population below Poverty Line:			
% rural population	22.5	17.0	28.0
Number	3,593	3,018	5,832

a. LE 1 = US$2.30. See footnote 7.
Source: Samir Radwan, *The Impact of Agrarian Reform on Rural Egypt (1952-1975)*,
World Employment Program Research, ILO WEP 10-6/WP-13, Geneva,
January 1977.

TABLE 3
Results of Agricultural Censuses
1950 and 1961

Size of Holding	Number of Holders		Average Size of Holding		Proportion of Holders to Total Holders		Proportion of Cultivated Surface	
	1950	1961	1950	1961	1950	1961	1950	1961
	('000)		(feddan)		(percent)		(percent)	
Less than one feddan	214	434	.51	.49	21.3	26.4	1.8	3.4
All holdings of 5 feddans or less	787	1381	1.81	1.7	78.4	84.1	23.2	37.8
All holding 5 + feddans to 50	201	251	11.5	10.11	20.8	15.2	37.7	40.7
Over 50 feddans	15	10	161.5	128.6	1.5	.6	39.1	21.5
Total	1003	1642	6.13	3.79	100	100	100	100

Source: ARE, Ministry of Plan, The Five Year Plan 1978-82: Vol. IV, *The General Strategy for Agriculture, Irrigation and Food* Cairo, August 1977, Table 6, p. 46.

TABLE 4
Distribution of Rented Agricultural Land, 1975

Cash Rent Land Area			
Delta	1,015,410	**Average Rents per Feddan**	24.9
Middle Egypt	500,509	Delta	LE 24.9
Upper Egypt	438,006	Middle Egypt	LE 23.5
Total	1,953,925	Upper Egypt	LE 22.1
Sharecropping Land Area		**Rented Land as Percentage**	
Delta	310,755	**of all Cultivated Land Area**	
Middle Egypt	103,964	Delta	38.2%
Upper Egypt	29,545	Middle Egypt	51.2%
Total	444,264	Upper Egypt	46.1%
Grand Total Rented	2,398,189	Total	42.4%

Source: Arab Republic of Egypt, Ministry of Agriculture, Statistical Division, Unpublished figures.

TABLE 5
The expansion of the Cooperative System
1952-1972

	1952	1962	1965	1970	1972
Number of cooperatives	1,727	4,624	4,839	5,049	5,008
Number of members '000	499	1,777	2,369	2,830	3,118
Capital LE '000	661	2,178	2,653	7,415	7,915

Note: There are nearly as many coops as there are villages, but there are only 750 agricultural credit banks for all of Egypt, each bank serving a cluster of villages and coops.

Source: Samir Radwan,   *The Impact of Agrarian Reform on Rural Egypt (1952-1975)*, World Employment Program Research, ILO WEP 1;-6/WP-13, Geneva, January 1977, p. 53.

TABLE 6

Egypt: Announced Cooperative Purchase Prices and Average Ex-Farm Prices for Selected Agricultural Crops[a]

(In Egyptian pounds per unit stated)

Agricultural year ended October 31	Unit	1964	1969/70	1970/71	1971/72	1972/73	1973/74	1974/75	1977
Seed cotton (unginned) Average price	qantar (157.5 kg.)	16.8	18.19	18.24	19.86	19.51	23.00[b]	25.00[c]	35-45
Rice (paddy) Announced price	metric ton	18.09	27.00	27.00	27.00	27.00	31.23	40.00	50-57
Average price			28.41	27.54	26.83	28.09			
Wheat Announced price	ardeb (150 kg.)	4.4	5.00	5.00	5.00	5.00	6.50		7-8[d]
Average price			5.80	5.31	5.26	5.72	7.04		
Horse beans Announced price	ardeb (155 kg.)		7.00	8.00	8.00	8.00	9.00	13.00	16.27
Average price			7.37	8.92	8.47	8.35	13.33		
Sugar cane Announced price	metric ton		2.57	2.57	2.88	3.50	5.00	6.00	7-5
Average price			2.89	2.72	3.07	3.72			
Winter onions Announced price	metric ton		19.00		20.00	20.00	22.00		
Average price			14.00	15.78	13.63	19.47			
Groundnuts Announced price	ardeb (75 kg.)		7.00	7.00	7.00	7.00	7.00	12.00	
Average price			6.49	6.62	6.76	6.94			
Sesame Announced price	ardeb (120 kg.)		15.00	15.00	15.00	16.00	16.00	22.00	
Average price			14.85	14.97	15.00	16.03			

a. Covers major crops marketed cooperatively (or under contract to mills) in whole or in part. Announced prices are for first grade quality. Average prices reflect all grades sold to cooperatives and on the free market.

b. Preliminary estimate.

c. Projection.

d. The lower price is for Giza 155 and the higher price is for Mexican varieties.

Source: Arab Republic of Egypt, Ministry of Agriculture

TABLE 7A

Production Costs per Feddan
Wheat

	1964	1970	1976
Preparation of land	1.86	2.81	4.58
Seed	2.78	3.23	5.04
Irrigation	1.46	2.13	5.76
Fertilizers	5.05	6.84	10.93
Harvest and transport	5.30	8.95	19.10
Miscellaneous	.46	.71	1.54
Subtotal	14.2	24.6	46.8
Rent	13.9	15.1	18.2
- value of straw	-7.8	-14.3	-25.6
Net production cost	23.9	25.4	39.5
Average yield (ardeb/feddan)	7.7	7.7	9.2
Production cost per ardeb	2.99	3.28	4.23

TABLE 7B

Production Costs per Feddan
Cotton

	1964	1970	1976
Preparation of land	3.93	4.73	8.53
Seed	1.42	1.94	3.4
Irrigation	4.37	5.63	9.72
Fertilizer	6.05	11.83	17.7
Replacement of plants	2.98	4.66	12.4
Pest Control	7.56	12.59	12.68
Ginning	8.2	9.5	23.6
Miscellaneous	.62	.91	2.68
Subtotal	35.16	51.54	90.8
Rent	22.5	24.1	26.1
Total	57.6	75.6	122.8
Yield (qantar/feddan)	5.6	5.4	5.5
Production cost per qantar	6.2	9.4	16.4

TABLE 7C

Production Costs per Feddan
Sugar Cane

	1974	1970	1976
Preparation of land	2.87	3.39	4.52
Cultivation	1.18	1.06	1.80
Agricultural services	6.57	6.96	19.2
Harvest	12.2	15.2	36.9
Seeds	4.01	3.41	8.3
Baladi fertilizer	.64	.20	.54
Fertilizer	15.2	14.9	18.4
Irrigation	6.49	10.3	9.91
Miscellaneous	.94	1.39	1.94
Subtotal	45.4	57.4	101.5
Rent	24.8	21.8	25.6
Total	75.08	79.2	125.17
Yield (qantar/feddan)*	823	851	707
Production cost per qantar	.91	.93	1.21

*The figures appear to represent the actual weight of the cane per feddan (i.e., ca. 31-38 tons), as opposed to the sugar extracted (generally 10% of the cane weight).

TABLE 7D

Production Costs per Feddan
Summer Rice

	1964	1970	1976
Preparation of land	2.14	3.05	5.11
Seed	3.01	4.34	5.18
Transplanting	3.67	4.39	5.62
Irrigation	4.35	6.70	8.57
Fertilizer	4.96	9.03	11.8
Pest and weed control	1.74	2.12	4.01
Harvesting	5.06	6.61	14.6
Miscellaneous	.39	.56	2.0
Subtotal	25.3	36.8	55.3
Rents	9.69	11.7	14.8
Total	34.99	48.5	70.12
Yield (daribas/feddan)	2.25	2.42	2.44
Production cost per dariba	15.06	19.1	26.41

Source: Tables 7A-D, Arab Republic of Egypt, Ministry of Agriculture *al-Iqtisad al-Zira'i*, unpublished, various years.

Food and Small-Farm Strategies in the Philippines

Brewster Grace

Most of the food in the developing countries of Asia—of which the Philippines is a good example—is cultivated by small farmers, share tenants, and landless sharecroppers. Thus, the nutritional needs, economic incentives, and access to resources of this group are of critical significance to food production and consumption. In sharp contrast to the large, relatively profitable mechanized agriculture of North America, these financially marginal farmers work small plots of land for minimal returns, either in kind or in cash. Consequently, many of them suffer from malnutrition.

Seventy-one percent of the Philippines' population lives in rural areas, and nearly half of these do not earn or produce enough to provide themselves with adequate diets. Fifteen percent of the urban population is also very poor and malnourished.[1] As of 1976, the National Nutrition Council reported 24.8 percent and 5.8 percent of all Filipinos to be, respectively, moderately and seriously malnourished. Most of these were in the impoverished and rural areas of the Eastern and Western Visayas. Other areas of high malnourishment were shown to be the highly populated rural areas of central and northeastern Luzon.

Estimates of average per capita consumption in the Philippines vary, but one thing is clear—the calorie intake of the poorly nourished is significantly lower than that of their better-fed compatriots. A National Nutrition Council survey taken in 1974 showed, for example, that rice farmers throughout the Philippines had a mean intake of only 74.4 percent of required calories.[2]

Overall, consumption levels of the poorest third of the population are estimated to be at least 25 to 30 percent below standard.[3]

Assuming the present level of consumption to average approximately 2,050 to 2,100 calories and 53 to 54 grams of protein per person per day, recommended dietary allowance developed by the Philippine Food and Nutrition Research Center is more or less being met (see Chart A). But because of maldistribution, food supply might have to be as much as 50 percent greater in order to provide the entire population with at least the recommended minimum.[4] FAO estimates of the biologically necessary minimum are somewhat higher than those of the Philippine government, so that an adequate food supply might require that average per capita consumption amount to as much as 3,500 calories per day.[5]

Origins of Food Policy in the Philippines

Despite the implications of these data, the food problem in the Philippines is regarded primarily as a problem of production and distribution of resources and secondarily as a nutrition problem. During the disastrous harvest years of 1972 and 1973, the long lines of peasants waiting their turn to buy rice from mobile banks and retail outlets convinced the government of the importance of providing an adequate food supply to the country's poor. Yet at that critical time, traditional rice exporters in the Asian region were unable to supply the country's immediate requirements, even though foreign exchange was available to pay the high prices then prevailing. Thus by early 1974 the government had decided to launch a major effort to increase rice production, and make the country self-sufficient in staple cereals at least at current consumption levels.[6]

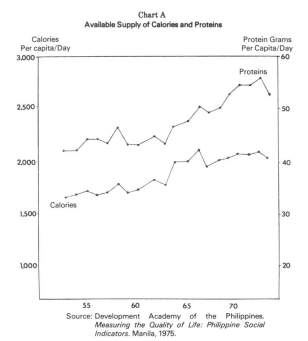

Chart A
Available Supply of Calories and Proteins

Source: Development Academy of the Philippines. *Measuring the Quality of Life: Philippine Social Indicators.* Manila, 1975.

Most developing Asian nations desire to achieve food self-sufficiency and eliminate hunger, and in order to do this, the importance of small-farmer productivity is increasingly perceived. In addition, there is growing concern among the international development community and domestic policy makers for the economic equity of these producers—both in terms of equal access to critical inputs such as land, capital, and markets, and in terms of equitable pricing policies for food crops vis-à-vis export crops.

In traditional, patronage societies, no matter how many formal democratic institutions may exist, economic equity depends on the political determination of national leaders to make financial, technical, and natural resources accessible to the small producer, and to pursue remunerative price policies. Too often in the past large landowners controlled access to inputs and favorable price policies, at the expense of the small farmer. Equity also depends on the willingness of political leadership to undertake financial

risk and to allow mobilization of the small producers to organize and cooperate collectively. Such mobilization could have positive economic effects, but it also generates opposition to existing political leadership and to conservative investment policies which limit the access of small producers to necessary production resources. This conflict lies at the heart of the politics of food in the Philippines.

A few efforts were made before 1972—prior to imposition of martial law by President Marcos—to direct financial and other resources to the small farmers, tenants, and landless workers cultivating staple crops. Since 1952, the government had established or promoted several credit facilities—most notably the Agricultural Credit Administration (ACA), the Farmers Cooperative Marketing Associations (FACOMA), and the privately owned rural banks. The former two were directly under government administration even though they sought to serve a cooperative movement. The latter, the rural banks, were a product of Central Bank incentives; largely through rediscounting, opportunities were afforded to provincial entrepreneurs and wealthy landowners to establish banks to serve the credit needs of the small farmers. Finally, a halfheartedly implemented land reform sought to restructure the basic ownership of land and control rents.

None of these efforts to confront the problem of rural poverty had any significant effect. The rural banks' lending policies largely favored those wealthier farmers with collateral assets. The small producers without collateral remained unrecognized. In fact, most agricultural lending, including commercial banks, by-passed the production of food staples to a very large extent in favor of export crop production and marketing—most notably sugar.

Other efforts at providing credit through ACA and the FACOMAs ran into a host of administrative, financial, social, and political problems. As a result, the first two decades of ACA and the FACOMAs were, at best, a learning experience, and, at worst, a disaster. Including the rural banks, these institutions represented the major mechanism for agrarian policies of the Philippines until martial law. Consideration of reasons for their failure is therefore appropriate.

First, the ACA program never began to reach the level required by the rural economy. Annual lending to and through the FACOMAs to small producers rarely exceeded ₱50 million or less than 7 million current (1978) dollars. This could only scratch the surface of the need. A disproportionate share (approximately 18 percent) normally went to the one province of Nueva Ecija.[7] Other Central Luzon provinces received most of the remainder. And the loans themselves averaged only ₱300, hardly enough to finance any significant change in production technology and affect the productivity of individual small farmers.

Second, the FACOMAs—the farmers' cooperatives through which the ACA credit operated—were subject to a number of problems. Some FACOMAs had memberships of 5,000 which made effective individual participation impossible. Membership meetings were unwieldy and ineffective. Moreover, FACOMA membership was open to any farmer. It was not unusual to find in many instances that the rich powerful farmers in the community dominated the cooperative, thus it often failed to reflect the interest of the economically powerless. In political terms, this meant that the landowners and patrons were able to use the ACA/FACOMA establishments to further their own interests. ACA credit, if not simply mismanaged, often became political dole with subsequent repayment problems. By 1971, only two-thirds of all matured loans had been collected.[8] Entrenched economic and political interests had so intervened in the administration of credit and cooperatives that the FACOMAs and ACA by 1971 had become an insignificant effort to support the small food producer.

Given these failures in rural reforms and institutions throughout the 1960s and early 1970s, political resistance to the regimes which failed to implement change grew at a rate inversely proportional to their failure. The radical Hukbalahap movement flourished in the 1950s; but the "Huks" succumbed as much to their own internal dissension as to the Magsaysay regime's repression and half-hearted reforms. Their suc-

cessor, the New People's Army (NPA) of the Communist Party of the Philippines, has yet to be adequately assessed in its efforts to mobilize financially marginal farmers in revolutionary resistance to administration policies. The NPA is, nonetheless, a constant threat to the national authorities in many local communities throughout Luzon and in a few localities on other islands.

A more persistent and widespread political mobilization on behalf of the small farmer—especially the tenant—came from the Federation of Free Farmers (FFF). Founded originally to organize tenant farmers to press for land reform as well as to counter the Huk movement, the FFF throughout the 1960s mobilized tenant farmers on land issues. It did not participate significantly in the cooperative movement except to support some small farmers in the FACOMAs. By the late 1960s its membership reputedly reached more than 750,000. But it also became increasingly divided between the less militant faction under its founder, Jeremiah Montemayor, and a more militant faction led from a Mindanao base of organizers who campaigned initially against the incursion of large plantations on small-holder agriculture and ultimately fought to mobilize a political lobby which would pressure for general land reform. Many of the more militant, anti-mainstream, anti-Montemayor leaders were increasingly disenchanted with the promised land reforms, and the small-farmer credit and cooperative efforts of the 1960s; as they turned to Catholic liberation social doctrine, they became increasingly Marxist.

By 1972, the rural Philippines was at a point of social combustion. The FFF and a few smaller peasant movements had mobilized a potent political movement of tenant farmers, even though the FFF was deeply split. The Huks had lost their grip on the radical revolutionary movement and had been pushed aside by the more ideologically pure and the better organized Maoist NPA. On the other hand, most landed and capital interests remained intact as land reform and government credit programs proved ineffective. All this contention, kindled with political promises of institutional reform and economic policy promises to the small producer, along with economic decay, bad harvests in 1971

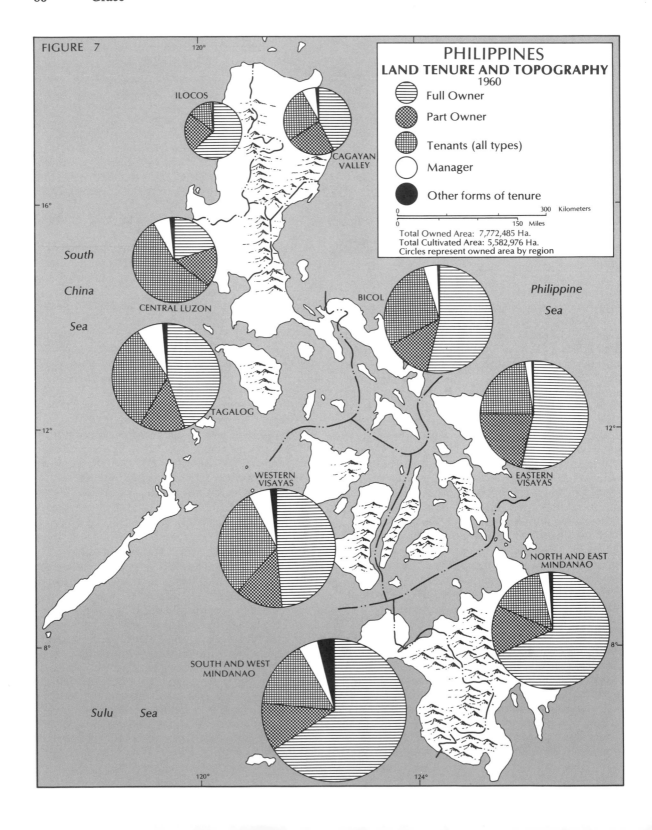

FIGURE 7

PHILIPPINES
LAND TENURE AND TOPOGRAPHY
1960

Full Owner

Part Owner

Tenants (all types)

Manager

Other forms of tenure

300 Kilometers
150 Miles

Total Owned Area: 7,772,485 Ha.
Total Cultivated Area: 5,582,976 Ha.
Circles represent owned area by region

ILOCOS

CAGAYAN VALLEY

South

China

Sea

CENTRAL LUZON

BICOL

Philippine

Sea

TAGALOG

WESTERN VISAYAS

EASTERN VISAYAS

NORTH AND EAST MINDANAO

SOUTH AND WEST MINDANAO

Sulu   Sea

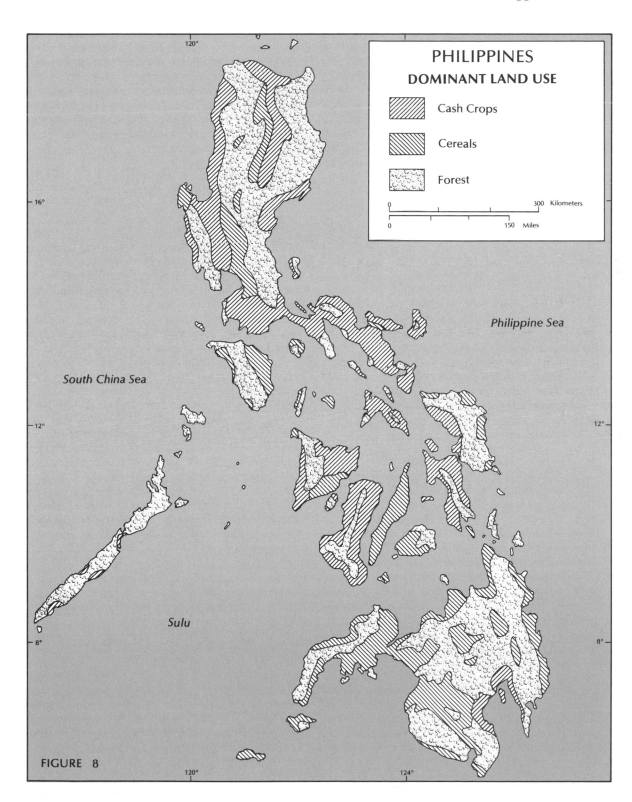

PHILIPPINES
DOMINANT LAND USE

Cash Crops

Cereals

Forest

0   300   Kilometers

0   150   Miles

Philippine Sea

South China Sea

Sulu

FIGURE 8

due to heavy monsoon rains and floods, and political strife in other sectors, brought on Marcos' decision to declare martial law and stridently proclaim the "new society." The economic situation was so severe that according to some sources the country at one point had only a three-day supply of rice. His solution to rural discontent consisted of land reform, along with credit and cooperative programs, serving the productivity and nutritional needs of tenant and financially marginal farmers.

Structure and Performance of Philippine Agriculture

Compared to many other developing countries Philippine agriculture has performed well. The production growth rate for staple food crops (cereals, pulses, and root crops) averaged 3.9 percent per year from 1960 through 1975, more than keeping pace with population growth. Yet, because average per capita consumption is not adequate, keeping pace is not enough to eliminate malnutrition. The International Food Policy Research Institute estimates that a production growth rate of nearly 6 percent per year is needed to provide adequate nutrition to the poor and satisfy increasing demand among higher income classes.[9]

In considering what strategy the Philippines must follow in order to achieve this objective, it is important to recognize that until the mid-1960s the availability of unused lands permitted farmers to increase production by expanding crop acreage without increasing yield. Thus, in terms of yield per hectare, Philippine agriculture has performed very poorly, despite its relatively high production growth rate. Further, because of the increasing importance of the land constraint and the relatively poor yields, the agricultural production growth rate has been declining steadily[10] (see Table 1).

Some new land is still being brought into production, primarily by clearing forests, but in the future, significant improvements in farmer productivity can only come about through yield increases. Increasing production on the many small farms which supply the country's two major food crops—rice and corn—will require irrigation, multiple cropping, and increased use

of fertilizer and chemical pest and weed controls, along with the introduction of improved plant varieties. Although the Philippine rice farmer's yield is still very low compared with other countries of South and Southeast Asia, some improvement in productivity has already taken place in response to introduction of high-yielding varieties and related technology associated with the Green Revolution (see Table 2).

Small farmers, cultivating less than 5 hectares each, make up nearly 85 percent of the farm population of the Philippines; 57 percent work less than 1 hectare.[11] Although estimates as to the number of families engaged in farming vary, the figure of 2.3 million obtained by the World Bank for 1971 is probably fairly accurate (see Table 3). Before imposition of martial law, nearly one million of them did not own the land they tilled.[12]

Altogether, including landless laborers along with farm operators, about three million families engage in agriculture as their primary source of income. These families comprise roughly two-thirds of the country's rural population. Other activities that provide employment to the rural population include fishing, forestry, mining, trade, and transport. Many small farmers do not depend solely on agriculture for their income, but seek supplementary nonagricultural employment for themselves or their family members. Eighty-two percent of all rural families receive incomes of less than 4,000 pesos per year. Average family income for this group is less than half that amount, and many of these poor families are heavily indebted.[13]

The majority of the rural poor are engaged in agriculture as small and tenant farmers, many of them eking out little more than a subsistence living for themselves and their families. This is the group for which malnutrition is a serious problem, and which could most benefit from a shift in government policy favoring distribution of more production resources to small farm operations. Rice and corn are by far the most important crops grown on these small farms, accounting for 62 percent of the country's total harvested acreage in 1970. Coconuts, the other major small farm crop, occupied another 21 percent. Mixed farming is not uncommon, and some sugar may be grown as a secondary crop on small farms, although more than half the country's total sugar output comes from large estates. Despite its importance as an export crop, sugar uses less than 5 percent of the country's cropland. Specialty items such as hogs, poultry, and fruits are raised on very small farms—many of them less than one hectare[14] (see Table 4).

Philippine agriculture is dualistic in nature—whereas the traditional domestic food-producing sector is characterized by small landholding with little access to credit and other services, a more developed commercial export sector exists side by side with it. Since colonial times, when much of the best agricultural land was put into sugar and coconut production for the American market, the export sector has been heavily favored. In the past, this sector has received a great deal of the development expenditure for agriculture, and has been the primary beneficiary of institutional credit. It is dominated by powerful families, who also control much of the rice and corn land farmed by tenants in the traditional sector. As long as food production could be increased by expanding acreage, the channeling of capital resources into agricultural export growth seemed to many development strategists as well as Philippine officials a sound strategy. But the combination of increasing rural demand for food and the disappearance of the land frontier have forced a change in approach.

Production and trade data for the food and export sectors bears out the importance of this change (see Tables 5 and 6). The government has, at various times, tried to use price policy to achieve production and food distribution objectives, but without too much success. Therefore, the current policy focus is on institutional reform and direct assistance to staple food crop producers.[15]

Agriculture Under Martial Law

When President Marcos established martial law in 1972, his first decree was to declare the entire nation under land reform. Subsequent decrees limited land reform programs to the rice and corn lands leased or sharecropped in small parcels on behalf of a relatively few wealthy landlords.

Extensive administrative infrastructure under the Department of Agrarian Reform has been established to redistribute these lands to a reported one million tenant farmers. As of early 1978, however, only 46,000 of these have actually entered into formal land transfer amortization procedures while 258,000 have been given certificates of transfer conditional on the crucial agreement with the landowner on the financial terms of the transfer. Tenanted holdings of seven hectares or less (about half of the total) have been excluded from the land transfer operation. Under previous land reforms a leasehold system intended to assure security of tenure and a legally fixed rent was established. The degree to which it is effective is uncertain.

Whether the land reform is succeeding or failing at this time is a matter of substantial, often heated, debate. But for the purposes of this paper, the issue must be set aside.

Of more importance is whether Philippine government policies can establish a credit and cooperative structure to serve the small producers—particularly the declared million new landowners if and when they become commercial, independent producers. Under the previous system, landlords played an important role by providing credit, seeds, and other inputs to their tenants. Now the government must provide and improve upon these necessary services if the social and economic objectives of the land reform are to be achieved.[15] Without the successful functioning of new structures and institutions to provide these services, agricultural productivity will not improve, economic frustration in the rural areas will continue to foster unrest, and the social fabric of Philippine rural society may again become as unsettled as before martial law.

In the Philippines, there are two general views of Marcos administration's rule by martial law. One view sees local, independent political mobilization either carefully controlled from the center or virtually absent. Consequently, economic institutional reform in favor of the small producer frequently appears to be from the top down rather than bottom up, highly dependent on centrally administered projects and programs rather than on local self-reliance, and consequently risk-averse. Also in this view, the marginal farmers who are critical to the nation's food economy appear more often as recipients of the benefits of development rather than as actors in the process. They are "target" groups for greater access to whatever the central administration passes down to them through "bureaucratic patronage," but they do not participate actively in the political decision-making process upon which national policies are based.

The other view sees the Philippines as more complex. It recognizes the top-down quality of the development programs, the still dominant emphasis on growth and risk-minimization, and the political factors constraining small producers. At the same time, however, it also sees more opportunities for participation—at least economic participation—through the new national policies declared by presidential decree, and aimed more directly at the basic needs of the small producer than those of past administrations.

Whichever is the case is of enormous debate. Yet whatever is ultimately concluded, it is increasingly clear in the Philippines and elsewhere in Southeast Asia that without effective participation from the bottom-up, top-down administration of development programs and policies will not be sufficient to meet the basic needs and welfare of the small food producers.

Philippine development under martial law has attempted several economic and social institutional reforms with real potential for helping the small producers. Socially and politically, the land reform is the most critical effort. It is essentially a top-down effort as all successful land reform efforts in Asia have been. But in other ways, the credit and cooperative efforts may be the critical test for the land reform since its success may depend less on its implementation than on the economic viability of the new land-owning small farmers supported by cooperatives and credit. Without genuine participation and initiative by the intended beneficiaries in the cooperative and credit institutions being created, the reform is unlikely to take hold.

Success depends on much more than good planning, good administration, good projects,

and comfortable offices in departments and ministries. It involves the intricate participation of the small producers in many areas of economic and political life. It often involves allowing the small producer to make mistakes and learn from them. This requires administrative and political leadership willing to take greater risks with credit and tolerate increased political opposition.

In the words of an Indonesian planner:

The Basic Needs Model, with its emphasis on development from the bottom up, community participation and initiative, and autonomy and village self-reliance, puts a premium on the development of the organizational and management capacity of rural communities, as well as on the development of cooperatives and other forms of organization, often derived from traditional institutions—with the right to run them under their own leaders.

It means, in short, the adjustment of traditional hierarchical and patron client relationships to more modern, more democratic forms of social organization, capable of addressing new problems. All of this runs directly counter to the conventional bureaucratic approach to the village which tended to strengthen those traditional structures. It means, in effect, a quantum jump, from paternalism to emancipation, requiring fundamental changes in attitude on the part of administrators, and in prevailing, deeply rooted concepts of the relationship between the governing and the governed....

The absolute necessity that our institutions be given the opportunity to make their own mistakes is likely to be considered a waste of time. Still it is only in freedom that these institutions can learn and can develop skills, and also the self-discipline that is essential to their further development.[16]

How well has the Philippines done under Marcos? The remainder of this paper will assess the strengths and weaknesses of the programs aimed at small farmer development and suggest ways in which these programs could become an effective strategy for feeding the country's rural poor.

Two important programs the Marcos government has implemented to meet credit and cooperative needs of the small producers are the Masagana-99 small farmer credit program and the village level associations called Samahang Nayon (or "pre-cooperatives"), which serve as bases for cooperative rural banks and area marketing cooperatives.

Masagana-99 Credit

Masagana-99 is intended to provide an extensive line of unsecured but supervised credit to small farmers, regardless of tenurial status.[17] It has been a unique and largely successful credit program, viewed from three perspectives. Since its introduction in 1973, yields and production have been raised to the politically desirable level of self-sufficiency in rice—even to a minimal but highly symbolic export capacity. Second, it did so under all of the risks inherent in unsecured loans to small and often tenant farmers of US$365,000,000. Third, while repayment losses have not been negligible, repayment has been much better than previous small farmer credit through ACA and the FACOMAs prior to martial law. These achievements command considerable respect.

The Central Bank of the Philippines has been ultimately responsible for this money through its rediscounting to the rural banks, the government-owned Philippine National Bank and, to a much lesser extent, to the still functioning Agricultural Credit Administration (ACA). The bulk of the funds has gone through the rural banks.

The technique of rediscounting is critical to understanding the process of how this small farmer credit gets to the small farmer and the crucial relationship between the rural banks and the Central Bank—most notably its Department of Rural Banks and Savings and Loan Associations. The Central Bank, in effect, makes deposits in the form of "special time deposits" (STDs) in rural bank accounts at 3 percent interest per annum, payable by the rural bank. With this seed money, the rural bankers through the government or their own technicians and their more than 600 independent, privately owned banks throughout the country, seek farmers requiring credit. After the farmers have signed

promissory notes for production loans worth double the amount of the STDs, the rural banks bring the promissory notes to the Central Bank and borrow again on the full value of the notes. They immediately pay off the STDs and are given another loan at an interest rate of one percent per annum on the basis of the promissory note. If the initial STD was worth ₱500,000, the rural banks are, in effect, in control of Central Bank funds of ₱1,000,000 to be loaned to farmers. The small farmers' interest rates are one percent a month or 12 percent per annum, while the rural bank's interest due to the Central Bank will vary between one and three percent per annum—depending upon the time they take to gather the promissory notes and rediscount the second loan at one percent. The incentive for the rural banks to avail themselves of this Masagana-99 credit is thus substantial.

In spite of the apparent success and the unique, risk-taking commitment of the Central Bank on behalf of the small farmer, there are many political and economic issues at stake and subject to hot debate.

First and foremost is the problem of repayment and whether the rural bankers want to avail themselves of this credit opportunity in the future in light of repayment problems. Tables 7 and 8 give some indication of these difficulties.

It should be noted at the outset that Phase IX is still in the collection process so that the 83 percent repayment is not a final percentage figure.[18] There is no reason to expect, according to Central Bank sources, for it to be much above the average of 77 percent for the previous 3 or 4 Phases. Phase X is in process at time of writing, so final repayment figures are not now available.

Repayment, of course, is the central issue in the Masagana-99 controversy. Central Bank repayment rate data are subject to questioning. They may be too high. Rural bankers, in order to avail themselves of rediscounting, must show good repayment. They have a number of ways to conceal bad loans. First, they can draw on other accounts, since most of them have in-family retail operations, to cover for losses. Or they can make private deals with overdue farmer-borrowers to reschedule while carrying current account payments on their books. Or, third, they can create fictitious borrowers, both to inflate their rediscounting availabilities as well as to cushion losses. To a greater or lesser degree, all three ways are used.

Rural bankers, of course, deny this. They claim they are bearing a major risk and need protection from bad repayment. Others argue they have served the rural small farmer production needs well for the past 25 years and the Central Bank should be grateful. Losses should be appreciated and tolerated by the Central Bank. Finally, rural bankers recognize, although it is not stated openly, that the Central Bank has a substantial amount of credit out through their institutional participation in Masagana-99 and therefore they have some leverage over the Central Bank because of their liabilities. If, in other words, a bank loans a client $100, the bank controls the client; but if the bank loans a client $1,000,000, the client controls the bank. The Central Bank, as of December 1976, was owed ₱1.16 billion by rural banks. This is a relatively small share of the total Central Bank liabilities of ₱32 billion. But most of this was in sectors other than food-crop production, and the majority of lending to small farmers was dependent on the rural bankers. Given the increased political importance of the small farmer in the Philippines, this liability has important political as well as economic significance.[19]

Another reason for concern about the present Central Bank relationship with the rural banks is that Masagana-99 credit has become the major source of rural bank finance—to the extent of being alarmingly disproportionate to other motivation for the mobilization of savings. At present, over 50 percent of rural bank assets are through borrowings (largely Masagana-99) and not more than 25 percent through deposits and savings. In effect, Masagana-99 has bloated the liability of rural banks to a potential crisis level.[20] If serious repayment problems develop in Masagana-99 from the farmers to the rural banks, much of the financial apparatus for small farmer production credit could collapse. The bubble could burst on any one of a number of pinpoints—including market prices or natural calamities.

The Central Bank seems to be out on a delicate limb. While having risked much for the small farmer, it has promoted the rural banks to the point where negative effects are beginning to be felt. The rural banks, in order to protect their liabilities from the farmers, have begun to find ways and means of making more selective lending. Consequently, they are increasingly lending to proven productive farmers. More often than not, this means farmers with irrigation and in regions where irrigation is more developed. Thus, wealthier farmers in Central Luzon get much more production credit than, for example, poorer coconut farmers on other islands where malnutrition is most prevalent. Upland rice farms—probably 85 percent of all rice production and with only single crops dependent on rains—are getting relatively, if not absolutely, less. Here, too, malnutrition is more noticeable.

The dangers are therefore twofold. First, there is a major fear that Masagana-99 has benefited the rural banks more than anyone else (their total resources have grown from ₱105 million in 1961 to ₱2.75 billion in 1975). Second, while the rural banks may play an important role in Masagana-99 lending, by introducing creditworthiness as a criterion they are contributing to the more privileged farmers and thwarting the risk-taking objective of the program. Traditionally, more than half, and among small farmers virtually all production credit has come from noninstitutional sources—landlords, relatives, merchants, and moneylenders—at very high interest rates. While rural banks have accounted for three-fourths of the recent increase in institutional credit, this is still a relatively small portion of the total. Further, most of it is still lent on a short-term basis to cover seasonal credit needs rather than to finance investment in new production technologies. A growth rate of 6 to 8 percent per year in institutional credit to agriculture will have to be maintained over the next decade to meet production objectives.[21] This rate of growth cannot be achieved unless Masagana-99 is made available to the many poor farmers as intended.

The Cooperative Movement

The cooperative movement was intended to create a democratic, participatory base of support for the credit program and other agricultural policies designed to help the small farmer, but in practice the Samahang Nayon have so far been largely controlled from the top down, with policies and procedures determined by the central government. Under the land reform program a farmer cannot qualify for land ownership without being a member of a Samahang Nayon. The Samahang Nayon are called "pre-cooperatives" because the Bureau of Cooperatives in the Department of Local Government and Community Development sees the need for education, discipline, and savings before true cooperative enterprises with business functions are established. Past history (namely the FACOMAs) have convinced the Undersecretary of the Department of Local Government and Community Development, Orlando Sacay, that village-based Samahang Nayon should include not more than 200 members and these should receive extensive discipline, training, and education in the meaning, spirit, and functions of cooperatives and learn how to save.[22] In addition to overseeing implementation of the land reform and disseminating information on credit, markets, and technology, the Samahang Nayon are expected to perform the functions demanded of earlier cooperatives—to promote modern farm practices and to engage in the collective purchasing of inputs and the marketing of output. By limiting size of membership and promoting a "sense of belonging," however, it is hoped to avoid the nonrepayment problems and corrupt practices of earlier associations (FACOMA).

It was intended that Masagana-99 would be used in part to serve the needs of the Samahang Nayon. As part of the Samahang Nayon "forced savings" program, each member of a Samahang Nayon who borrows Masagana-99 funds through the rural banks or the Philippine National Bank must place 3 percent of the value of the loan (formerly 5 percent) in a special savings fund deposited in the lending institution by the Samahang Nayon. These "forced savings" are to be used for financing the cooperative institutions. Second, and more important, the cooperative rural banks—at least the four that currently exist, can receive Masagana-99 loan funds from the Central Bank.[23]

As of December 1977, 17,555 Samahang Nayon had been registered with the Bureau of Cooperatives, involving 896,708 members. The vast majority of these were small, often tenant farmers who had little collateral for commercial non-Masagana-99 loans and were therefore willing to participate in the "forced savings." Through the saving programs, these Samahang Nayon had saved ₱84,171,000. Obviously, some have done much better than others in achieving the discipline, educational, and saving requirements to participate in cooperative activity. For example, only 3,226 Samahang Nayon were members of the cooperative rural banks. Many of these would be the same 2,168 Samahang Nayon which were members of the 29 operating area marketing cooperatives.[24]

The fact that there are only four cooperative rural banks attests to the slow pace of cooperative development in the Philippines as well as to the general complexity and difficulty of establishing viable banking institutions. Not only must the bank rely on farmer savings for the base of its capitalization, it must also find adequate management. In fact, the cooperative rural banks have had to contract professional management. Both capital and management are in short supply.

The same has been true of the area marketing cooperatives, although perhaps less so in light of the larger number organized and operating, as well as the existence of management trained during the FACOMA era. The area marketing cooperatives supply farmers with inputs, and buy and sell Samahang Nayon members' produce. Marketing cooperatives do not make loans; however, funds for inputs supplied to members are borrowed from the cooperative rural banks. Because the banks do the lending, they have the ultimate responsibility for supervising the use of production credit. This supervision is the critical test as it determines repayment rates.

Still, the area marketing cooperatives also depend on good management. Profit margins can be thin and there is competition from private traders and the government's National Grains Authority—which also buys rice. As of December 31, 1976, only 8 of the then existing area marketing cooperatives had net profits—totaling ₱351,465. The remaining 5 had lost a total of ₱379,000.[25]

The ultimate objectives of the cooperative banks and marketing systems—to provide established small farmers and new land owners with a savings mechanism, access to credit, and assured markets—should remove the present domination of trade, credit, and marketing by the usually usurious private trader, supplier, and money-lender. Much remains to be done, however, to achieve these ends.

Some of the problems are external to any faults within the cooperative movement and extremely difficult for the young movement to solve. First, the Bureau of Cooperatives recognizes as a problem "the proliferation of functionally overlapping and sometimes conflicting organizations at the *barangay* (village) and other levels."[26] It is not a question of too much assistance, but a matter of lack of integration among government agencies involved in the agricultural sector at village level. This is a clear manifestation of smothering, top-down development.

Second, and possibly the bitterest of all disputes in rural finance and cooperatives, has been the reluctance of the privately owned rural banks to allow withdrawal of Samahang Nayon funds for redeposit in the new cooperative banks. There are a number of reasons for their reluctance. First, many of these funds represent the savings deposits required of each Samahang Nayon member when he obtains a Masagana-99 loan. Since the repayment rate of these loans has not been good, the rural bankers claim the right to hold this money as a kind of protection against default. Nonetheless, withholding of these deposits is illegal and it remains for someone to challenge the rural banks in court. Unfortunately, the Bureau of Cooperatives' legal advisers cannot practice in court; thus the Justice Department bureaucracy must represent the small farmers. Given the rural bankers' enormous strength, combined with the bureaucratic red tape involved in legal action, it is unlikely the government will challenge them.

Another problem the cooperatives cannot easily solve is the outright competition the rural banks are giving to the cooperative rural banks. Withholding cooperative members' savings is just one tactic. The rural bankers quite naturally fear cooperative banking and, it appears, have used their influence on the Central Bank to act on their behalf. For example: the Central Bank at first allowed the cooperative rural bank to use 100 percent of Samahang Nayon savings funds usually deposited in the private rural banks as capitalization for cooperative business ventures. This has since been lowered to only 25 percent, with another 25 percent earmarked for guaranteeing the loans of defaulting Samahang Nayon members. This further supports the rural banks withholding of the savings funds. The Central Bank has directed the release of these deposits—except where individual rural banks' liquidity is threatened—but rural banks are still refusing to comply with this directive.

A fourth problem arises because of obstacles preventing cooperative rural banks from merging effectively with the rural banks, as intended by the original savings fund policy. Supposedly rural bankers were to give equity positions to the savings deposit holders—up to 50 percent of common shares—and in this way allow, in effect, a cooperative rural banking system to be built on an already established, efficient, private rural banking system. But rural banks are usually the financial domains of wealthy families and are not about to give up very much control to small farmer interests. They see their private affairs potentially subject to incompetent meddling through small farmer shareholders. It is a bitter dispute; and again the cooperatives are losing.

Taking the best from the past has been a tactic used in creating the area marketing cooperatives. Here, these new area marketing cooperatives have often been built on the surviving FACOMAs and their management, some of which have done quite well. The latter are able to supply experience. Had this been able to work with the rural banks, the cooperative movement might be moving much more rapidly in building the financial institutions upon which introduction of improved production technology to small farmers must depend. That it has not worked testifies to the continuing strength of rural banks' interests.

Management skills—or the lack of them—is the final critical problem. It takes a generation of education to build good management and at present there is little of it available for the Samahang Nayon movement. To a certain extent this is a result of the top-down administration of the Samahang Nayon. Also, in launching the cooperative system, the Department of Local Government and Community Development required all cooperatives already established in the country (some by private, secular groups, some by church organizations) to re-register—a long and complete process often setting back their programs. This alienated much of the private cooperative management experience there was in the Philippines in 1972.

The most notable and acrimonious debate came between Orlando Sacay and the Mindanao Cooperative Alliance with its 40,000 members and highly competent staff. The latter's alienation and decision to operate as a nonprofit organization rather than join the Samahang Nayon was a loss of talent. It was also symbolic of the reaction of many of the private cooperatives and socially conscious rural workers to martial law. This has, to an important degree, hurt the Samahang Nayon movement by depriving it of experienced leadership.

Although they are central to the success of the government's agrarian reform policy, the Samahang Nayon are not the only form of agricultural association open to the small Filipino farmer. A different approach is that being tried by the Farm Systems Development Corporation, which is encouraging the formation of Irrigators' Service Associations (ISA). These associations are being organized to own, operate, and manage small-scale irrigation systems averaging 100 hectares each. However, their scope is not limited to the use of water. They will provide production credit, sometimes absorbing the loss of Masagana-99 farmers with bad debts, regrouping them, and refinancing their loans through the Agricultural Credit Administration (ACA). They provide an integrated program for the purchase and resale of production inputs to association members; some are even producing their own seeds based on local experience as to which varieties would give the highest yields. Although a permanent field worker supervises each ISA program, the farmers themselves participate in the decision-making process as to the kinds of

enterprises for which financial and technical assistance should be provided. As yet, however, this program can service no more than 25,000 members.[27]

It is difficult and perhaps foolhardy to make a general assessment of the Samahang Nayon only six years after they have been launched. Historically, cooperative movements in other countries (e.g., Holland, Scandinavia), have taken decades, if not generations, to build. New attitudes must be formed—something which Orlando Sacay reiterates constantly in his speeches and writings on the Samahang Nayon. Enormously complex institutions must then be built—bottom up—on these new attitudes. The question is constantly present: to what extent are the disciplining, attitude-changing efforts by a central administration necessary or desirable? Does this not imply an imposing of behavior and structure by a central administration through a bureaucracy which has all the problems government bureaucracies suffer throughout developing countries? Is not the spirit of cooperatives ultimately dependent on private efforts by individuals to build their organizations in light of their perceived needs? The Bureau of Cooperatives repeatedly maintains that the Samahang Nayon are private—and are only government-assisted. But still, the bureaucratic weight and control mechanisms appear top heavy and individual Samahang Nayons are more passive than active.

In its report to the President the Bureau of Cooperatives in early 1978 noted the need "...to bolster the sagging morale of the farmer cooperatives belonging to the Samahang Nayon movement."[28] One solution is to give strong support to the cooperative rural banks in their struggle with the rural banks by encouraging greater mobilization and participation at the local level. Yet an institutional framework of greater freedom and less centrally administered discipline might open the door for the abuse of some of the cooperative efforts prior to martial law—as in the case of some private cooperatives used for tax havens, and the political use of cooperative loans to buy votes.

Another solution might be to tighten martial law, force the rural banks to cooperate, and totally restructure economic ownership with further loss of established economic privileges. Politics and political interests suggest this is impractical.

Cooperatives have worked well in Japan under democratic political regimes because of strong grassroots participation, private mobilization, and firm national support. In China, communes appear to have worked well because of strong leadership, restriction of many economic freedoms, and a good response from the poorest farmers. The Philippine formula is yet to be found.

Conclusions

The small producer in the Philippines has been the object of cooperative mobilization to instill savings habits and to foster a credit program while promoting savings. This effort is an expression of the political desire of the Marcos administration to increase rice production—especially since the bad crop years of 1972 and 1973 and the 1972 declaration of martial law. But it may not fully reflect the needs and potentials of the poorer farmers.

Discipline, education, and savings affect all farmers, but increased loan selectivity does not benefit all equally. This raises the question whether Philippine agricultural development directed toward productivity must be at the expense of equity. Masagana-99 has proved successful for many small farmers with assets—especially irrigation. But the poorest group—those recently converted from tenancy to landownership and others tilling very small plots—are the least creditworthy. With a land reform only barely implemented and with the majority still without the critical infrastructure of irrigation, forced savings are not meeting their needs. They remain unable or unwilling to repay easy loans. And rural banks are not cooperating for obvious reasons of self-interest. The lessons of the past are self-evident, but whether the solutions now available will work is a more important concern.

A critical issue is whether the present tightly controlled and oligopoly-based rural bank financial structure and the centrally controlled Samahang Nayon cooperative movement can provide the right institutional structure for encouraging full participation by small farmers in the economic and political life of the country. Can the Department of Local Government and Community Development administer cooperative development by disciplining a small farmer who lacks an economic incentive to save? Can Masagana-99 take the risks and meet the needs of these small farmers when the economic interests of the rural banks and their owners are so fundamentally at stake?

Many producers with very small holdings earn part of their income from nonfarm employment. As irrigation becomes more widespread, there will be increased opportunities for underemployed farmers to make a living as agricultural laborers. Yet one must still wonder about the fate of many of the million or so small farmers whose welfare depends on the equitable implementation of current agricultural policies in the Philippines. It would seem that greater, not lesser, financial risk-taking in providing credit and lesser, not greater, control of cooperative efforts (in spite of their political potential) are required to meet both the production and the food needs of new Filipino landowners.

The author wishes to gratefully acknowledge the many perceptive comments and helpful advice given by Mrs. Meliza Agabin, of the Technical Board for Agricultural Credit, on the complex problems related to credit, land reform, and cooperatives in the Philippines. In addition, the Department of Local Government and Community Development, the Central Bank, and the Rural Bankers' Association were generous with their time and made an invaluable contribution to the author's examination of the problem.

1. World Bank, *The Philippines: Priorities and Prospects for Development*, A Country Economic Report, Washington, D.C., 1976, pp. 95-96.

2. See: *The Philippine Nutrition Program: 1978-1982*, National Nutrition Council (Manila, 1977), p. 60.

3. USAID/Philippines, *Development Assistance Program for the Philippines*, Vol. I, June 1975, p. II-2.1.

4. Jose Encarnacion, Jr. and others, *Philippine Economic Problems in Perspective*, Institute of Economic Development and Research, School of Economics, University of the Philippines, 1976, pp. 95-99.

5. *Ibid.*

6. Meliza Agabin, "Origin and Implementation of Masagana-99." Comments at AUFS Seminar on the Politics of Food, Rome, 1978.

7. Rocomoa and Panganiban, *Rural Development Strategies: The Philipine Case* (Manila: The Institute of Philippine Culture, 1975), p. 77.

8. *Ibid.*, p. 76.

9. International Food Policy Research Institute, *Food Needs of Developing Countries: Projections of Production and Consumption to 1990*, Research Report No. 3, December 1977, p. 78.

10. Encarnacion, *op. cit.*, pp. 107-121.

11. Food and Agriculture Organization of the United Nations, *State of Food and Agriculture*, 1976, p. 46.

12. International Labour Office, *Sharing in Development: A Programme of Employment, Equity, and Growth for the Philippines*, Geneva, 1974, p. 91. Brewster Grace, "The Politics of Income Distribution in the Philippines," [BG-3-'77], *AUFS Reports*, Southeast Asia Series, Vol. XXV, No. 8, 1977.

13. USAID/Philippines, *op. cit.*, p. IV-7.1.

14. World Bank, *op. cit.*, pp. 100-105; ILO, *op. cit.*, pp. 55-64.

15. World Bank, *op. cit.*, pp. 110-113; 475-489.

16. Soedjatmoko, "National Policy Implications of the Basic Needs Model," mimeographed, Jakarta, 1978, pp. 17-18.

17. The Masagana-99 program offers supervised credit to rice farmers; a similar program, Masaganang Maisan, is available for corn farmers but is not discussed here.

18. Phases are based on six-month cropping seasons and interest on one percent per month. Collateral is based on sale of crop.

19. Central Bank of the Philippines, *Statistical Bulletin* (Manila: Department of Economic Research, 1976), p. 98.

20. Technical Board for Agricultural Credit, *Financing Agricultural Development: The Action Program*, Manila: The Presidential Committee on Agricultural Credit, 1977, p. 19.

21. *Ibid.*, p. 19; World Bank, *op. cit.*, pp. 173-176; Orlando Sacay, "Small Farmer Credit in the Philippines," USAID Country Paper No. 113, February 1973.

22. Sacay, Orlando, *Samahang Nayon: A New Concept in Cooperative Development* (Manila: National Publishing Cooperative, Inc., 1974), p. 142.

23. ILO, *op. cit.*, pp. 481-482.

24. See Bureau of Cooperatives *Report on Cooperatives: Calendar Year 1977* (Manila Department of Local Government and Community Development, 1978), p. 16.

25. Bureau of Cooperatives, *Report on Cooperatives Development*, *FY 1975-76* (Manila: Department of Local Government and Cooperative Development, 1977), Appendix A.

26. *Ibid.*, p. 14.

27. Agabin, *op. cit.*; USAID/Philippines, *op. cit.*, pp. II-3.10ff.

28. Bureau of Cooperatives, *Report on Cooperatives Development, FY 1975-1976, op. cit.*

Table 1

**Contributions of Area and Yield per Hectare to Agricultural
Growth Rates, 1948-52 to 1958-62 and 1958-62 to 1968-72**

	Annual Growth Rate			Relative Contribution		
	Output	Area	Yield	Output	Area	Yield
			(percent)			
1948-52 to 1958-62						
Rice	3.5	3.5	− 0.04	100	101	−1
Corn	6.4	7.4	− 1.0	100	116	−16
Sugar	6.2	4.6	1.5	100	75	23
Total Agriculture	4.1	3.4	0.7	100	83	17
1958-62 to 1968-72						
Rice	2.9	− 0.1	3.0	100	− 3	103
Corn	5.2	2.0	3.2	100	39	61
Sugar	3.3	4.7	−1.4	100	142	− 42
Total Agriculture	3.6	1.8	1.8	100	50	50

Source: Crisostomo and Barker, IRRI Report No. 75-14, *Agricultural Growth against Land Constraint: the Philippine Experience*, IRRI, November 1975, Tables 1 and 2.

Table 2

Rice Yields and Annual Compound Growth Rate of Paddy Area and Yields in Selected DMCs[a]

Country	Paddy Yield (tons/hectare)[b] 1955	1965	1973	Annual Growth Rate (percent) 1955-65 Area	Yield	1965-73 Area	Yield
Pakistan	1.3	1.5	2.4	3.25	1.21	1.11	6.44
Indonesia	2.0	2.1	2.7	0.90	0.51	1.84	2.76
Philippines	1.2	1.3	1.6	1.24	1.10	0.86	2.52
Sri Lanka	1.6	1.9	2.3[c]	2.88	2.10	3.16[d]	2.37[d]
India	1.3	1.5	1.7	1.26	1.30	0.61	1.86
Korea	2.6	4.3	4.9	1.08	4.90	−0.12	1.82
Malaysia (West)	2.1	2.5	2.9	3.42	1.97	4.67	1.72
Burma	1.5	1.6	1.7	1.93	0.94	0.13	0.71
China, Republic of	2.8	3.9	4.0	−0.03	3.53	−0.30	0.45
Bangladesh	1.4	1.7	1.7	1.10	1.98	0.60	0.45
Thailand	1.6	1.9	1.9	1.73	1.73	1.84	0.23
Nepal	0.9	1.9	1.7	1.71	8.24	3.02	−1.42
South and Southeast Asia[a]	1.4	1.6	1.9	1.28	1.41	0.91	1.71

a. Countries included in South and Southeast Asia are Bangladesh, India, Nepal, Pakistan, Sri Lanka, Burma, Indonesia, West Malaysia, Philippines, and Thailand.

b. Five-year average centered on the years shown.

c. Average for the period 1970-74.

d. Annual compound growth rate for 1965-72.

Source: Asian Development Bank, *Rural Asia: Challenge and Opportunity*, Praeger Special Studies, 1977, p. 67.

Table 3

Rural Families Classified by Level and Main Source of Income, 1971

Main Source of Income	Families in Lower 40 Percent		Families in Upper 60 Percent		Total Families		Total Population	
	Thousands	Percent	Thousands	Percent	Thousands	Percent	Thousands	Percent
Farming	1,756	64.8	1,208	31.2	2,964	45.1	18,440	48.5
Self-employed	1,409	52.0	852	22.1	2,261	34.4		
Wage Labor	347	12.8	356	9.1	703	10.7		
Forestry and Fishing	165	6.1	117	3.0	282	4.3	1,635	4.3
Other Occupations	388	14.3	900	23.4	1,288	19.6	7,280	19.2
Self-employed	190	7.0	231	5.9	421	6.4		
Wage Labor	198	7.3	669	17.5	867	13.2		
Other Sources	130	4.8	107	2.9	237	3.6		
Agricultural Rents	54	2.0	31	0.9	85	1.3		
Other	76	2.8	76	2.0	152	2.3		
Total Rural Families	2,439	90.0	2,332	60.5	4,771	72.6	27,355	72.1
Total Urban and Rural Families	2,710	100.0	3,862	100.0	6,572	100.0	37,901	100.0

Note: The data presented here were adjusted in two ways. First, all urban household reporting their main earnings from agriculture, forestry, and fishing were shifted into the rural category. Second, to allow for the fact that the surveys underestimate the national population, the number of families in each group was increased using the following ratios: for 1961, 1.0879; for 1965, 1.0403; and for 1971, 1.0355.

Source: World Bank, *The Philippines: Priorities and Prospects for Development*, Washington, D.C., 1976, pp. 93 and 96.

Table 4
Actual Harvested Area of Crops

Crop	Actual[a] 1950	1960	1970
	('000 hectares)		
Food crops			
Rice	2,210	3,278	3,186
Corn	909	2,000	2,350
Other	485	882	855
Subtotal	3,604	6,160	6,397
Export and Other Crops			
Coconuts	979	1,088	1,926
Sugarcane	143	242	384
Other	353	291	280
Subtotal	1,475	1,621	2,590
Total	5,079	7,791	8,987

a. Based on three-year averages of 1949-51, 1959-61, and 1969-71, respectively.

Source: World Bank, *op. cit.*, p. 130.

Table 5
Cereals Production and Imports, 1965-1975
('000 metric tons)

Calendar year	Milled Rice Domestic Production	Net Imports	Import Dependence[a]	Corn Domestic Production	Net Imports	Import Dependence[a]	Wheat Net Imports	All Cereals Domestic Production	Net Imports	Import Dependence[a]
1965	2,690	569	17.5	1,346	6	...	506	4,036	1,081	21.1
1966	2,747	108	3.8	1,407	2	...	495	4,154	605	12.7
1967	2,844	237	7.7	1,481	50	3.3	476	4,325	763	15.0
1968	3,289	− 41	...	1,537	3	...	525	4,826	487	9.2
1969	3,264	...	...	1,870	29	1.5	505	5,134	534	9.4
1970	3,582	...	...	2,007	...	...	449	5,589	449	7.4
1971	3,496	370	9.6	2,002	83	4.0	485	5,518	936	14.5
1972	3,149	451	12.5	1,920	168	8.0	490	5,069	1,109	18.0
1973	2,870	310	9.7	1,830	100	5.2	504	4,700	914	19.4
1974	3,279	168	4.9	2,289	110	4.8	...	5,568	278	4.8
1975	3,861[b]	152[b]	3.8	2,568	121[b]	4.5	557	6,429	830	12.9

... Zero or negligible.

a. Import dependence is the ratio of imports to total supply.

b. Projected as of November 1, 1975.

Source: World Bank, *op. cit.*, p. 132.

Table 6

Production and Exports of Sugar and Coconuts
('000 Metric Tons)

Crop Year [a]	Sugar Production	Exports	Calendar Year	Copra Production	Exports
1970	1,927	1,178	1970	1,356	1,036
1971	2,056	1,444	1971	1,756	1,456
1972	1,816	1,299	1972	2,174	1,820
1973	2,245	1,359	1973	1,871	1,514
1974	2,446	1,587	1974	1,424	1,085
1975	2,394	1,065	1975	2,217	1,867
1976	2,875	1,466	1976[b]	2,742	2,338

a. The crop year for sugar begins September 1 and ends August 31.
b. Preliminary.

Sources: Philippine Sugar Institute. Export data is provided by the Sugar
Administration and is by crop year. United Coconut Association
of the Philippines, based on information provided by its members.

Table 7

Loans Granted by Rural Banks of January 31, 1978
(Amount in million ₱)

	Number of rural banks	Number of borrowers	Amount	Fallen Due	Repayment	Percent of Repayment Fallen Due
Phase I	443	168,001	152.9	152.9	150.1	98.2
Phase II	415	118,490	117.2	117.2	114.1	97.3
Phase III	416	237,997	303.6	303.6	284.6	93.7
Phase IV	484	217,020	333.3	333.3	281.6	84.5
Phase V	517	132,403	235.4	235.4	186.8	79.3
Phase VI	397	86,637	127.2	127.2	99.5	78.2
Phase VII	401	75,942	139.1	139.1	105.2	75.6
Phase VIII	300	43,675	78.5	78.5	59.9	76.3
Phase IX	331	61,898	114.1	65.4	54.9	83.9
Phase X	224	28,146	53.4	--	--	--

Source: Central Bank of the Philippines

Table 8

Status of STD Releases to Rural Banks
Under the "Masagana-99" Rice-Financing Program as of
March 17, 1978 (in million-₱)

	Gross Releases	Repay-ment	Outstanding Balance	Percent of Repayment to Gross Releases
Phase I	84.0	83.7	0.3	99
Phase II	50.0	49.0	1.0	98
Phase III	102.5	99.5	3.0	97
Phase IV	103.3	100.2	3.1	97
Phase V	115.7	110.2	5.4	95
Phase VI	66.2	60.7	5.5	91
Phase VII	76.7	72.8	3.9	94

Source: Central Bank of the Philippines

Indian farmer in the Punjab.

The Dynamics of Indian Food Policy

Marcus Franda

For the past three years India has enjoyed some of the largest foodgrain surpluses in its history. As of June 30, 1978—the end of the agricultural year—stocks amounted to around 20 million tons, with most of that surplus being stored in government warehouses and other facilities. Increased foodgrains production has become a source of considerable optimism about the future for many Indians, as indicated by the five minute standing ovation received by the Agricultural Minister in Parliament when he announced an expected 125 million ton harvest in late April 1978. And yet, any talk of "surplus" when so many people are still undernourished and malnourished must necessarily be meant only in a special, provisional sense.

The existence of surplus amidst poverty is one of many pointers to the political dynamics that lie at the heart of India's food problem. The crux of that the problem is what Dr. V.M. Rao has called "the latent hunger of the poor," which, as he points out, "does not impinge on the market as effective demand for food."[1]

Average per capita consumption equals approximately 2,050 calories per day, of which about three-fourths are accounted for by foodgrains (see Table 1). This is sufficient to meet the minimum physical requirements of the average Indian, but Sanderson and Roy estimate that 30 to 40 percent of the country's population consume less than this amount, with more of the urban population eating inadequately than of the rural population.[2]

Because of the existence of this widespread "latent hunger" it is possible for government leaders and international development officials to say that India's food needs are currently being met, when, what is really meant is that present *effective demands* for food are being met. The tragedy of India's food situation is that demands for nutritious food for the entire population are infrequently made because under present circumstances, they could not be met, even with a so-called foodgrains surplus.

In an effort to get at the problem of India's food requirements during the rest of this century, and assuming the desirability of the goal of a nutritious food supply to all, Dr. Rao has identified four different population categories based on their per capita consumption: (1) the "lower poor" (about 30 percent), whose diet is severely inadequate; (2) the "poor" (30-35 percent), which are subject to malnutrition; (3) a "middle class," consisting of the remaining population with the exception of the uppermost 3 percent (Dr. Rao assumes that this "middle class" enjoys "adequate diets, given the prevailing food habits and preferences, without being able to indulge in excessive consumption of food"); and (4) the upper 3 percent who have sufficient income to rule out any need to economize on food. Food consumption among the wealthiest, Dr. Rao points out, "contains an element of excessive indulgence in the richer varieties."[3]

From a political perspective, the food problem in India has ramifications for society that go far beyond the malnourishment of the lower classes. If food deficiencies are going to be dealt with in any meaningful manner, purchasing power must be created among the mass of the people so that they can buy increasingly larger portions of nutritious foods. Granted that there will be more than 5 million new entrants into the Indian labor force each year for at least the next 20 years, mass purchasing power can be created only if jobs become available in unprecedented numbers. Unemployment at levels found in India today leads not only to a lack of earnings, but also to frustration and human degradation. Both malnutrition and unemployment, therefore, hang like depressing weights on the whole of the economy at the same time that they demoralize society in myriad different ways. Moreover, there is now overwhelming evidence that a stagnating agriculture and inadequate food supplies in the rural areas will eventually produce large-scale migration to the cities, with the consequence that gaps between rich and poor will widen further, producing ever more difficult food distribution and employment problems.[4]

In this atmosphere, the political challenge confronting Indian politicians involves not only an increase in food supplies; it also involves the provision of additional jobs in the rural areas and, ultimately, a whole series of measures that will make rural life sufficiently attractive that the incentive for large numbers of people to drift into the towns is mitigated. This political challenge becomes the more intense in India because it must, at least for the present, be met within the confines of a democratic federal framework, with all the constraints and opportunities this implies.

Past Approaches to Agricultural Production and Food Distribution Policies

It would be impossible to speak of a single national food policy that has been in effect for all of India. In India's federal Constitution, most matters having to do with agricultural production and food distribution are *state* or *concurrent* subjects, meaning that powers to legislate and administrate over them are reserved either to the states exclusively or to the state and central governments concurrently. For example, the Constitution specifically lists as state subjects: agriculture, including agricultural education and research; protection against pests and prevention of plant diseases; preservation, protection and

improvement of stock and prevention of animal diseases; veterinary training and practice; protection of wild animals and birds; land and land tenure systems; moneylending and moneylenders; relief of agricultural indebtedness; cooperatives; forests and fisheries; and the supply of water. The Concurrent List includes powers over the production, supply and distribution of foodstuffs; the bringing under cultivation of any waste or arable land; adulteration of foodstuffs and other goods; and the prevention of the extension from one state to another of infectious or contagious diseases or pests affecting men, animals, or plants.

The central government becomes involved in agricultural and food matters primarily through its powers from the Concurrent List, the considerable financial powers that it has acquired since 1947, and in its role as chief planner of the economy. In addition, the federal government (or, as it is more commonly known in India, the Union) has powers over trade and commerce, formation of trading and other corporations with objects not confined to one state, scientific and technical education and research, the production and marketing of certain agricultural commodities (including tea, coffee, and cardamom), the development of interstate rivers and river valleys, interstate water disputes, interstate quarantines on fishing beyond territorial waters, banking and insurance, standards of quality of agricultural goods, and health standards for food products. Each of these items impinge substantively on food and agriculture, thereby allowing the central government considerable involvement. However, control over only these subjects does not confer sufficient powers to allow for federal domination in policymaking.

Because constitutional powers over agriculture and food are divided, policies have to be evolved through long processes of bargaining and negotiation between central and state governments. Initiatives may come from central or state ministries, or from private individuals, but decisions are made only after extensive debates in Parliament and the state legislative assemblies, periodic national meetings that bring state Agricultural Ministers and Chief Ministers together with their central counterparts, and, occasionally, meetings of special national or state commissions appointed to sort out varying viewpoints on particular issues. In the 1950s and 1960s most state legislatures contained powerful lobbies representing the interests of the better-off landed rural interests. In the 1970s a more broad-based agricultural lobby has gained a tenacious foothold at the national level, as the proportion of agriculturalists in Parliament has risen from 14.7 percent in 1951 to 33.8 percent in 1971 and to over 40 percent in the 1977 elections. Stanley Kochanek has recently pointed out that, "These members of Parliament have come to act as a commodity lobby to reinforce the substantial voice already enjoyed by the Chief Ministers of the states as spokesmen for agrarian interests."[5]

Both central and state government initiatives in agricultural matters have occasionally led to center-state or state-state tensions and stalemates (in 1978, for example, there were around 120 unresolved interstate water disputes, many of them pending for a decade or more). On balance, however, problems in devising and implementing effective food policies have resulted not so much from center-state conflicts as from a general lack of organizational strength and cohesion among poorer sections of the Indian population and weak administrative organization and management in the rural areas on matters relative to food.[6]

In a country where universal adult franchise (over the age of 21) is meaningful, and where more than 80 percent of the population lives in rural areas, most Indian politicians have found it necessary to at least assume a rhetorical public posture in which considerable importance is attached to rural development and the upliftment of the most poverty-stricken groups and areas. However, in practice the major accomplishment of the Congress Party over the first three decades of independence (Congress was finally defeated at the central level in March 1977) was the building of a political patronage network that was essentially dependent on urban interests and rural influentials, including leaders of a select few lower castes and minority communities. In his major work on the Congress Party, Myron Weiner has shown how the party organiz-

ation usually adapted to local political power structures without trying to change them, often bringing into its fold aspiring elites who might otherwise effectively oppose the party. "In rural areas," he points out, "the party has sought and won the support of those who own land, have wealth, control village panchayats (village councils), manage the local cooperatives, and can lead large numbers of persons." In Weiner's view, the Congress was concerned primarily with the maintenance of its own organization, rather than the achievement of national goals; "it is doubtful," he concludes, "that the party would have succeeded had the leadership acted in any other way."[7]

While this situation has often been described by outside observers as tending toward stagnation, from the point of view of people in India there have been very important changes. The old Maharajahs and absentee landlords have been dispossessed of much of the land they held under the British, even though large landholders have often been generously compensated with non-landed forms of wealth. Some degree of land redistribution has taken place, permitting about 20 million tenants to become direct landowners while making available for redistribution about 14 million acres.[8] The resulting situation is still skewed in most states in favor of those who own 10 to 30 acres of good land, but this is quite a different situation than that existing in 1947 when landed estates of 10 and 20 thousand acres were common. Perhaps most important, some previously poor castes and local communities have risen in status and in political power, to the point where they now either dominate or have significant influence in government at the state and national levels.

Thirty years of Congress rule has produced considerable debate within India about the degree to which agriculture has received its fair share of attention. Urban economists like Ashok Mitra have suggested that the most favored people in India are those with the most sizable amounts of land, constituting no more than 10 percent of the agricultural population. In an analysis that is still relevant today, Mitra pointed out as early as 1963 that this privileged rural minority

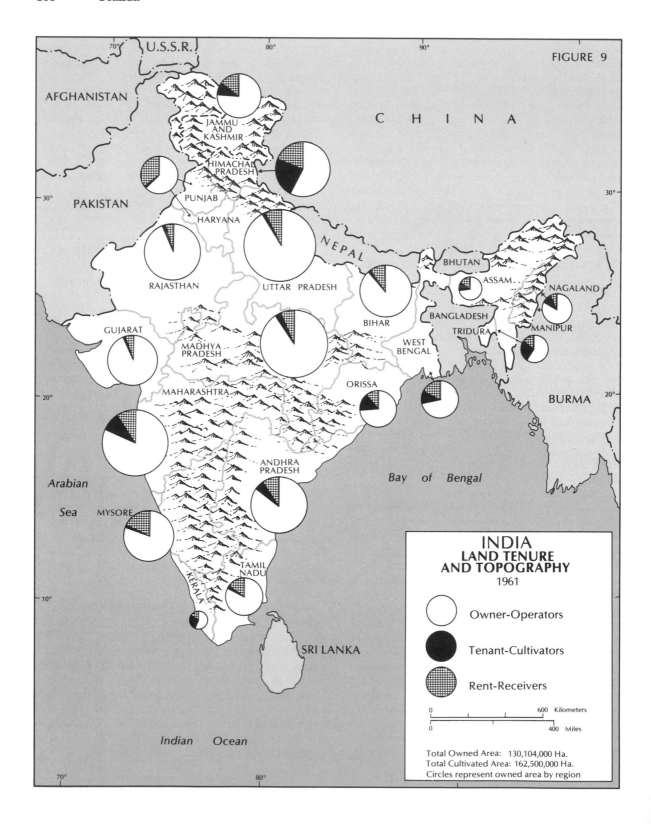

FIGURE 9

INDIA
LAND TENURE
AND TOPOGRAPHY
1961

○ Owner-Operators

● Tenant-Cultivators

⊞ Rent-Receivers

0		600	Kilometers
0		400	Miles

Total Owned Area:	130,104,000 Ha.
Total Cultivated Area: 162,500,000 Ha.
Circles represent owned area by region

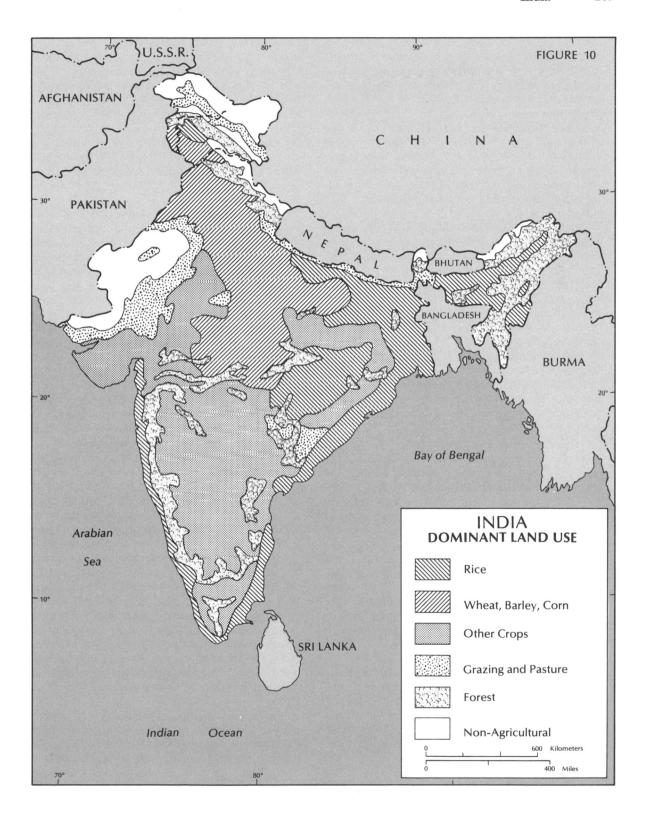

FIGURE 10

INDIA
DOMINANT LAND USE

Rice

Wheat, Barley, Corn

Other Crops

Grazing and Pasture

Forest

Non-Agricultural

0   600 Kilometers

0   400 Miles

owns land which is more than half the total culti-vated area, their per capita income is signifi-cantly higher than even in the major segments of organized industry and commerce, yet they are among the least taxed groups in the country. Even assuming that this minority contributes as much as four-fifths of the total revenue at present collected from agriculture, the tax burden is merely 5 percent of their income. With a per capita income which is apparently 40 percent lower, the nonagricultural population is carrying a tax burden which is twice this proportion.[9]

Further evidence that the agricultural sector has benefited from Indian development policies is provided by Lawrence Veit, who has found that the terms of trade between agriculture and industry, when measured as a ratio of farm to industrial prices, shifted noticeably in favor of agriculture in the late 1960s.[10] John Mellor also points out that "Government expenditures on agriculture have consistently exceeded tax reve-nues from agriculture...credit institutions have transferred funds into it; and the nature of industrial growth has encouraged little net in-vestment by rural people, while urban workers have made net remittances back to the agricul-tural sector."[11]

Without denying that landed wealth remains a major source of privilege in modern India, it is still clear that the agricultural sector *as a whole* has not kept pace with industry and defense. Indeed, the percentage contribution of agricul-ture, forestry, and fishing to net domestic product declined from 56.1 percent in 1950-51 to 41.7 percent in 1973-74.[12] Moreover, the changes in the terms of trade that Veit has iden-tified do not stem from a particularly buoyant position for agriculture relative to industry; Veit himself suggests that such changes simply reflect the inflationary impact on food prices of scarcity conditions.[13]

The key decision affecting the roles of agricul-ture and industry in the Indian economy was made in 1955, when the Second Five-Year Plan development strategy was evolved by P.C. Mahalanobis and Jawaharlal Nehru. The crux of the Mahalanobis strategy was to turn attention away from labor mobilization and small-scale

production while emphasizing instead the acquisition of capital goods and modern indus-trial power. As Mellor has pointed out, "There was no place in these theories for accelerating growth by mobilizing labor, and they led in practice to a capital intensive, low-employment strategy that had little role for investment in a dynamic agriculture. The bulk of resources were channeled into the set of large-scale industries—most notably steel and machine building—generally identified with modern world power."[14]

During the years when Jawaharlal Nehru was Prime Minister (1947-1964), the employment and food production deficiencies of a heavy industry strategy were widely recognized, but these were not considered significant enough to override the political compulsions—both domestic and inter-national—that were pushing India toward rapid industrialization. In the Second Five-Year Plan, employment deficiencies were to be met "by a set of policies for agricultural and cottage industry development that were parallel to, but not an integral part of, the strategy of growth."[15] The Mahalanobis strategy, as Mellor has observed, is analagous to Mao's strategy of "walking on two legs"; its appeal—particularly to a large and socially segmented country seeking a major place in world affairs—cannot be overestimated.

Indeed, most Indians, rich or poor, exhibit considerable pride in the fact that India has built an industrial infrastructure that makes it the seventh, eighth, or ninth ranking industrial nation in the world, depending on the indicators used for ranking. There is also a remarkable consensus among its citizenry that India must have a large defense force (its 1.2 million person military is now the third largest in the world) and that nuclear power must be exploited for both commercial and security purposes.[16] Critics of the Congress regime continue to argue that the poorest of the Indian poor have suffered because of an undue emphasis on industry and defense, but no major political party in India has yet called for a reduction in defense spending.

The successful functioning of a heavy industry strategy required a large-scale distribution system for supplying food to urban areas during times of scarcity and for controlling the price of food. The divided jurisdictions of India's federal system prevented the federal government from devising a single distribution network with a clear overall set of goals, but state and central governments did cooperate (with varying degrees of effectiveness from time to time) to set distribution policies in four areas. These included restrictions on private movement of foodgrains between zones, procurement of supplies for government foodstocks, direct intervention in the foodgrains trade to prevent hoarding and speculation, and the operation of some 240,000 fair price or rationing shops. Policies have varied from time to time and from state to state, alternating between complete control, complete decontrol, and partial control. The last two of these three choices have generally been pursued during periods of relative abundance.

On the basis of his studies of India's public food distribution systems, Arvind Gupta has concluded that they have not been as successful as is often assumed, either in controlling urban prices or in protecting the economically vulnerable sections of the rural and urban populations. Instead, Gupta singled out the widespread import and public sale of foreign foodgrains as the most significant factor in containing price rises throughout the 1950s and 1960s. As Table 2 makes clear, food aid flows accounted for virtually all of India's grain imports through 1971. Concessionally priced cereals began to be imported, primarily from the United States, in 1956, with most of them being paid for in rupees under the terms of the Food For Peace (PL480) programs. By 1977, the U.S. government estimated that more than 60 million tons of foodgrains had been shipped to India under Title 1 of Public Law 480, with a total value of about $5 billion.[17] Since lower expenditure classes tend to consume more coarse grain, but the crisis orientation of the public distribution system has made it more successful in containing price increases for fine cereals, these classes benefited least from the food aid.[18]

Often crucial in mitigating hunger, preventing famine, and providing some modicum of political stability, these grains nevertheless became, according to one school of thought, "an opiate on India's resource-scarce, development-minded leaders who could not easily resist allowing imports to substitute for domestic food production."[19] Veit argues that "incremental food supplies from abroad reduced the incentive for India to adopt production-increasing policies and, by enabling Delhi to hold the price of grain below what it otherwise would have been, tended to discourage agricultural investments by private farmers." In addition, since foodgrains were acquired on long-term credits but sold almost immediately to Indian citizens through government-run fair price shops and private traders, Indian leaders often used the imported grains to supplement budget revenue, thereby diminishing the pressures on them to levy and collect domestic taxes.[20]

Not all experts agree that food aid has had such a deleterious effect. In a recent survey article on the disincentive effects of food aid, Isenmann and Singer point out that food aid eases a major constraint on growth in output and employment. As new jobs are created, demand for food by the newly employed increases rapidly. Without food aid as a stopgap source of supply, inflationary price rises would prevent this new demand from being realized and producers would find no market for their increased output.

With respect to India, the authors found that "food aid did cause a decline in relative foodgrain prices, but only during a fairly short part (1960-1962) of the food aid period (1956-1971). The depressing effect on prices was much less than some analysts had expected, partly because the food aid was used to increase government food distribution, which, being subsidized, added to net foodgrain demand."[21] In another more comprehensive study, Rogers, Srivastava, and Heady found the net loss in domestic production to be only 3 percent of the food aid provided.[22]

The New Janata Government

While the March 1977 election of India's first non-Congress government at the national level opened up several possibilities for change in food and agricultural policies, much of the discussion about directions and objectives during the first year of Janata rule is understandable only in light of a series of basic questions about the party's future constituencies. The Janata is still essentially a collection of five smaller political parties that banded together in early 1977 to oppose the Emergency regime of Indira Gandhi. None of these smaller parties previously had anything resembling a national political base.[23] The Jan Sangh, the largest of the constituent parties, was associated in the minds of most people with militant Hinduism; its electoral strength was greatest in the urban areas and in some small rural pockets of the Hindi-speaking portions of India. Two other constituent parties in the Janata—the Bharatiya Lok Dal and the Organization Congress—were heavily influenced by rural landed interests that were anathema to many members of the Socialists, a fourth constituent. The fifth constituent, the Congress for Democracy, was dominated by Jagjivan Ram, leader of a major portion of India's Untouchable community.

Granted the diversity of interests represented in the Janata government, it is not surprising that it has pursued an essentially aggregative political strategy during its first two years in office. Trying to appeal to all points on the political ideological spectrum, the party even entered into some limited political agreements with the Communist Party of India-Marxist and a number of regionally based parties.

Two common goals of all of the Janata constituent parties have been the desire to rid the Indian policy of excessive degrees of centralism and some authoritarian constitutional provisions, and to change the focus of economic activities from the urban to the rural areas. Both of these goals became firmly established during the 1977 electoral campaigns, as features that distinguished the Janata Party from Mrs. Gandhi's Congress; both have since provided some minimal points of agreements for a party that is obviously struggling to achieve a degree of unity that will make it possible for it to last out its full five-year term in office.

Not only did the government come to power on the basis of a political platform that promised an entirely new economic strategy, focused on the rural areas and oriented heavily toward employment, its ascendancy to power also coincided with a period when a number of economic indicators have been on the upswing simultaneously. In addition to record food crops and a record food surplus during its first year in office, the Janata government has also witnessed the burgeoning of India's foreign exchange reserves to unprecedented levels (more than $6 billion in May 1978) and, for a temporary period during its first year in office, the elimination of India's chronic trade deficit. To be sure, much of this good news is a result of long-term economic trends that were set in motion before the Janata Party came into office, but Janata leaders have been heartened by their continuance.

Nevertheless, because of a lack of purchasing power in the domestic market, food, foreign exchange, and trade surpluses have been accompanied by a very sluggish demand for industrial and consumer goods and credit has been so tight that neither private entrepreneurs nor governments seem able to accumulate sufficient resources to step up industrial growth rates. Indian businessmen, therefore, have put enormous pressures on Janata leaders to boost industrial investments and provide tax breaks for industry, at precisely that moment when the government has been trying to pay more attention to agriculture. To complicate matters even further, a mild inflation for some food items (particularly edible oils and pulses, both staples of the Indian diet) has produced a number of political demonstrations and movements in the cities, reminding Janata leaders of the need to protect the interests of middle-class urban constituents if the party plans to obtain support outside the rural areas at the next elections.

Janata Agricultural Policy: The Sixth Five-Year Plan

At the core of the Janata government's new economic strategy is the Sixth Five-Year Plan, which has already been accepted by the federal Cabinet and is now waiting approval and adjustments by the states. More than 40 percent of the Sixth Plan ($60 billion of $145 billion) is allocated to agriculture and rural development. This represents an increase in investment in agriculture of more than 100 percent over the Fifth Five-Year Plan, as compared with an increase for organized industry of only 30 percent. Even more important than the amount of additional investment in agriculture, however, are changes that have now been set in motion to reorient investments toward rural development, small-scale industry in the countryside, and employment-intensive rather than capital-intensive production.

Aside from their public rhetoric on the food and poverty issues, Janata leaders are generally agreed on two broad goals. First, they would like to increase food production to the point where they can meet effective demands for food and still have sufficient surplus to tide the nation over at least two years of bad weather. To do this, the government estimates it needs at least 12 million tons of foodgrains in storage (in autumn 1978 it had 16 million tons with an additional 4 million in private hands). Excess foodgrains are considered undesirable because of the large amounts of money and credit that must be tied up in storing them, and because stored grains are subject to rot, pilferage, and rodents. Second, the government would like, in the words of one of its spokesmen, "to build a floor below which the poverty of any given individual would not drop, rather than construct a ceiling above which the wealth of any given individual could not soar." In the words of a Planning Commission member, this would involve "raising the purchasing power and consumption levels of the bottom portions of society, but not chopping the top."

On the production side, it is entirely possible that India could witness dramatic gains in foodgrains production during the next few years. As the past record indicates, scope for vast improvement exists.

India has succeeded in building a solid scientific capability and an increasing ability to get ideas about scientific farming out to the villages. Price incentives, subsidies for key agricultural inputs, investments in irrigation and power, and substantial increases in supplies of credit—all of these would seem to be pushing India in the direction of bigger and bigger harvests in the years ahead. That the Janata emphasis on a rural-oriented development strategy is solidly grounded in political realities adds to the probability that such inputs will be continued at significant levels.

The introduction of Green Revolution technology for wheat and rice has led to impressive increases in production since the mid-1960s (see Table 3). Adoption of new rice varieties and improvements in yield spread rapidly in North India, but in most waterlogged areas of eastern India growth in yield has been low during the wet season and local varieties still predominate. Many farmers in these regions adopt new varieties and modern inputs during the dry season, but switch back to traditional varieties during the wet season, emphasizing the importance of the physical environment in the farmer's behavior.

The remarkable increase in wheat production was associated with a rapid increase in yield and expansion of the area planted with new varieties. Unlike rice, which encountered a land constraint, growth in wheat output has been made possible by expansion of the wheat growing area as well as a growth in yield. After taking hold in Punjab and other parts of North India, the new varieties spread rapidly to the southeast down the Gangetic plain into eastern Uttar Pradesh and the northern portions of Bihar, West Bengal, and Bangladesh—wherever water was available. In some cases, wheat replaced inferior grains such as maize, sorghum, millet, or to a lesser extent, pulses. In other areas, it was possible to grow two crops, wheat followed by rice, where only one had been grown before. There have been no comparable breakthroughs in the production of coarse grains. Sorghum and millet production is, in aggregate, more important than maize production in India, and was greater than wheat production in the mid-1960s. Since then area planted to these crops has declined. Both output and average yields fluctuate widely because crops are grown in areas of low and uncertain rainfall.[24]

Irrigation

The first priorities of the Sixth Plan will be irrigation, power, and other key inputs in the rural areas, with irrigation facilities being extended to more than 17 million hectares of land in the next five years, at a cost of more than $9 billion. Of this 17 million hectares, 8 million will be accounted for by major and minor irrigation schemes consisting primarily of canals, and 9 million will be covered by minor irrigation schemes consisting primarily of tubewells and pumps. Much of this additional irrigation is planned as part of integrated schemes for the development of entire river valleys, under the terms of what is known as Command Area Development. While some observers doubt India's ability to construct irrigation channels at this projected rate, the Planning Commission has been heartened by the sustained pace of construction at the projected rate during the first year of Janata rule, with no sign of a slowdown for the second year.

The scope of such an increase in irrigated acreage is revealed by the fact that eight million hectares is more than the entire area covered by large and medium irrigation schemes in 1950, a hundred years after the construction of major canals began. It is also about one and a half times the total new area covered by such schemes between 1950 and 1970. As Pran Chopra has noted, expenditure on major and medium irrigation schemes during the next five years is now projected to be more than twice as much as in the past five years and more than five times as much as in the five years before that.[25]

For a variety of reasons, major and medium irrigation schemes have tended to benefit poorer farmers in India while minor schemes have disproportionately helped the more affluent. Since the major schemes consist essentially of hand-dug canals, they employ large numbers of workers, all of whom come from the poorer sections of the population. Once the canals are constructed, anyone within a certain distance can draw water upon payment of a relatively small fee. Tubewell irrigation, on the other hand, tends to be biased in favor of large farmers, on two counts. Not only is their construction and maintenance not labor-intensive, they also tend to be placed in locations convenient to those farmers who either have the money to build their own wells or to influence the government's selection of sites. By spending much more money than before on canal projects, in areas that have been neglected during the past three decades, the new government hopes to create employment and boost agricultural output in relatively underdeveloped regions.

The principal reason for the strong emphasis on extending irrigation networks is the overwhelming consensus in the Planning Commission on the empirical proposition that two to three times as many cultivators are employed on an irrigated hectare as on an unirrigated one. Moreover, the irrigated land is usually far more productive. Irrigation results in increased use of hybrid seeds and fertilizers, demands for farm machinery and multiple cropping, possibilities for growing cash crops, and greater feasibility for the development of cooperative societies. While the Planning Commission is somewhat biased against use of big farm machinery (like combines and tractors) it has been particularly impressed by the increased output levels associated with irrigation and the potential doubling and tripling of rural employment.

Credit

In addition to massive increases in investment in agriculture, the Indian government hopes to undertake a host of other measures designed to promote the interests of what Professor Raj Krishna calls "the small man." Krishna, a prominent member of the Planning Commission, would like to reserve all "official credit"—i.e., all credit that comes from government agencies, cooperatives that are financed by government, and the nationalized banks—to those farmers owning less than 2.5 hectares of land.[26] At present, Krishna estimates, 70 percent of India's farmers own less than 2.5 hectares. Official credit accounts for 34 percent of total credit, with the other 66 percent being provided by private moneylenders and private banks. If implemented, Krishna's proposal would mean that the 70 percent of farmers owning the smallest plots of land would receive about a third of total credit while the remaining 30 percent would have access to two-thirds. At present, according to Planning Commission estimates, farmers with less than 2.5 hectares receive less than this amount, with most being forced to resort to private moneylenders for loans.

India already has a number of highly successful cooperative and credit societies that have been able to bring about increases in agricultural production and distribute resources more widely than in the past. Some idea of the importance the

Indian government attaches to the building of cooperatives and credit societies can be gained by viewing the growth of such societies over the past three decades. In 1951, for example, only 6 percent of borrowing by cultivators came from cooperatives and government sources. By the early 1970s such borrowing had expanded to 40 percent of total borrowing and in 1978 the figure went over 50 percent for the first time.

It is still the case that most cooperative and credit societies are dominated by rich and middle peasants who tend to structure local institutions in a manner that works to the relative disadvantage of the poor. In that sense, institutions like the Kaira District Cooperative Milk Producers Union in Anand, Gujarat, which operates in such a way as to keep both cattle and people in rural areas while providing the landless with a steady source of income from the sale of milk, or the Agricultural Refinance Corporation (ARC) which specializes in loans to small farmers for minor irrigation projects, stand out as exceptional.[27] However, a study by John Mellor has found that even cooperative and credit societies dominated by the relatively affluent represent significant improvements over traditional moneylenders and other credit sources.[28] Moreover, to the extent that it becomes politically possible for state governments to effect laws and policies for cooperatives and credit societies that favor the relatively disadvantaged, both the Anand Dairy Cooperative and the ARC can provide extremely valuable models of what might be possible on a larger scale in India in the future.

Public Works

Consistent with its emphasis on "the small man," both the Planning Commission and the Janata government have been encouraging a series of massive rural public works programs designed to provide employment for the landless. In addition to the building of irrigation channels, these include road construction, electrification projects, land development, social conservation measures, the building of schools and hospitals, market yards and storage facilities, and a variety of other projects requiring large amounts of manual labor. Many states have been using excess foodgrains from current bumper harvests to pay manual laborers, either in full or in part,

in a variety of different food-for-work schemes. Dr. Krishna has been advocating the nationwide adoption of an Employment Guarantee Scheme (EGS) such as has been tried in the state of Maharashtra since 1971. Under the EGS, employment must be provided within 15 days and within 5 kilometers of the residence of any 50 villagers who register for employment with local authorities.

Local Planning

One way the Planning Commission hopes to introduce a guaranteed employment scheme, small-scale irrigation projects, and more official credit to small farmers is by devolving planning down to the most local level. Over the course of the next 2 years the commission hopes to fund more than 500 plans at the rural block level (each block is an administrative unit containing approximately 100 villages and 100,000 people). If these 500 block plans are successfully drafted, local plans will be funded in approximately 2,000 blocks by 1984-85 and in the remaining 3,500 blocks by 1989-90. Block-level plans are now being drawn up by both government and private agencies that have been active in local areas.

Locally based planning has been introduced in part to narrow the gap between theory and implementation (and in most cases block-level planning agencies will also play a major role in the plan's implementation). It is also considered important because of its potential for facilitating the introduction to small farmers of such allied agricultural activities as forestry and conservation, fisheries, animal husbandry, horticulture, and cottage-like industries (what has come to be known in India as the "tiny sector"). Encouragement of locally based planning by the new government has bolstered the spirits of large numbers of voluntary agencies throughout India that have for years been advocating such a focus.[29]

Research

India's major institutional advantage in agriculture is its scientific agricultural establishment—centered in 21 universities and 30 research institutes—often described as the third largest in the world. During the past three decades, Indian scientists have been blamed for being highly theoretical and failing to get their laboratory and office results out to extension workers and peasants. In recent years, however, agricultural authorities like Norman Borlaug have argued that Indian food production is on the verge of substantial breakthroughs, precisely because of the way farmers have begun to have access to, and respect for, Indian science. The record-breaking harvests of 1977-78 are especially important in this regard because they were chalked up despite unfavorable weather conditions in many parts of the country.

Indian officials have argued that the reason for the 10-12 percent increase in foodgrains production this year—the highest increase for any single year since Independence—has to do with the increasingly widespread application of Green Revolution technology. The creation of additional irrigation, a 26 percent increase in fertilizer use, better distribution of high-yielding drought-resistant seeds, and better dissemination to farmers of information about seeds and pesticides have all helped improve yields per hectare.

Price Policy

Fairly high government procurement prices have also contributed to the remarkable growth of Indian wheat production since 1968-69. In 1978, pressure from India's surplus-producing wheat states (particularly Haryana and Punjab) influenced the Janata government to raise the procurement price for wheat even further, from 110 to 112.50 rupees per quintal (1 quintal = 100 kilograms) or $138 per ton on-farm. This is considerably more than the American on-farm income support price of about $110 per ton and approximately equivalent to the c.i.f. import price for 1976-77. A comparison of the procurement price for wheat with the average price of wheat to Indian consumers in mid-1978 indicates that wheat farming is being government subsidized at the rate of about 23 rupees per quintal.

Proposals now being discussed within the Agricultural Ministry would use both the price mechanism and supplies of credit to attempt a more rational use of land and better crop planning by encouraging the planting of particular crops in areas where soils and other ecological conditions are most favorable. For 1978-79 the government is using price incentives

to try and jack up production of pulses (i.e., lentils, or what is known in India as *dal*). The procurement price of pulses has been raised from 80 rupees (approximately $10) per quintal to 125 rupees per quintal, a more than 50 percent jump. This means that production of pulses will now be subsidized at rates comparable to those for wheat, with the result that many agricultural observers are now expecting that production of lentils over the next ten years might increase at a pace comparable to that for wheat during the past decade. If this does happen, it could be a most welcome development since lentils are the principal source of protein for India's largely vegetarian population.

Because of local and regional political factors, price incentives for rice have not been used to nearly the same extent as they have for wheat. The on-farm price of milled rice in India today is only $165 per ton, far less than the $335 paid for comparable rice in the United States and the international price of $370-$380. In mid-1978 government subsidies for rice (again, measured by comparing procurement prices with average consumer prices) amounted to less than a rupee per quintal. Price incentives to farmers have not been characteristic of India's rice-producing areas because of the dominance there of urban-based political parties that have gained their support from middle-class consumers who have an interest in keeping rice prices low.[30] India's rice-producing areas, which are generally also deficit in food production, have been opposed to free movement of foodgrains between states; two deficit states—Bihar and West Bengal—adamantly objected to increases in the procurement price for wheat, rice, and pulses in 1978.

Consistent with its employment-oriented strategy, the Planning Commission has recommended that there be a "drastic reduction in the incidence of explicit and implicit (farmer) subsidies" and that food distribution networks be restructured to favor the poorest of the poor. This is because the principal beneficiaries of agricultural subsidies in the past have been that 10 percent or so of India's wealthiest farmers who have a marketable surplus, rather than the small producer and the rural landless. In addition, as

Balraj Mehta makes clear, the fair price shops that have been established to distribute subsidized foodgrains

tend always to get located, first of all, in areas of high effective demand. It is those, generally speaking, living in slums, the migrant laborer, the destitute or the people without any settled living or regular incomes in the cities and the landless and the underemployed in the rural areas who have no access to the benefits of subsidized production and distribution by public agencies. Those with small incomes or purchasing power are, in any case, in no position to command the consumption of goods and services which have price tags on them.[31]

Despite the admonitions and ideas of the Planning Commission it seems doubtful that the Janata government will be able either to reduce or rationalize subsidies within the Indian economy to any significant degree. Subsidies are not only routinely paid by state and central governments to farmers—for using such things as fertilizer, electricity, and water or for producing wheat, sugar cane, and milk—they are also paid to others for manufacturing such diverse items as cloth and aluminum or for building transport, housing, educational, and medical facilities.[32] In a country where the largess of patrons is still viewed as both legitimate and good, where more than two-thirds of the population sees itself as being poor, and where government is often viewed as the chief patron responsible for the poor, no political leader is going to speak too strongly against the principle of subsidization. So long as one cannot abolish subsidies for one segment of the population it becomes difficult to abolish them for another, particularly when large numbers of groups have at least some degree of influence in both the administration of subsidy programs and the decision-making apparatus that governs such programs.

Problems of Implementation

The attempt to build a national political base by concentrating heavily on "small men" in the rural areas is considered by Janata Party leaders to be both politically realistic and essential at this juncture in India's development.[33] Nevertheless, reactions to the Planning Commission's emphasis on employment for the "small man" points up the enormous difficulties facing any Indian government that seeks to effectively implement an employment-oriented development strategy with a rural focus. No one in India will publicly disagree with the proposition that most of the government's attention should be focused on the poorest of the rural poor, but, in fact, a number of powerful interests are working to dilute or "readjust" plan priorities. Primary among these are private businessmen and industrialists in the urban areas, the government's own industrial establishment, other urban interests (especially urban consumers), and the wealthier segments of the rural population.

Private and public industrialists are principally concerned about the possibilities that large-scale investments might now be denied to industry, and that big industry might in the future be even more heavily taxed for resources than it is at present. The government has tried to allay some of these fears by providing for easier credit to private industrialists, simplifying some licensing procedures, and pointing out to businessmen that their relative inefficiency in the past has led to considerable excess capacity, thereby making it possible for many of them to increase their own production rates without enormous new investments. The Planning Commission has also tried to reassure urban businessmen by suggesting that additional resource mobilization over the next five years should come from agricultural taxation, increases in irrigation and electricity rates to farmers, and other forms of cesses and surcharges that could be collected from the better-off segments of the rural population.[34]

Prospects for industrial expansion in the Sixth Plan have been confined largely to exploration of sophisticated and capital-intensive technologies that cannot be rationally pursued in the small-scale sector, as well as various forms of encouragement to private businessmen to get involved in the development of small-scale industries. For example, it is now clear that large-scale consumer businesses will be sanctioned in the future only if they agree to buy or develop major portions of their components or products from small-scale units. The classic case of such a business is the national shoe company that designs and markets shoes manufactured essentially by hand, in thousands of small cottage industries spread across the face of India. To insure that small-scale units are not exploited by large marketing organizations under such arrangements, considerable government supervision is expected to become necessary.

Within the public sector itself, the Janata government is in the process of establishing district centers for the promotion of small-scale industries in the countryside, in all of India's 460 districts. These centers will not be staffed by civil servants, as in the past, but will instead be run by locally based boards, like the successful Khadi and Village Industries Board, with representatives from local banks and voluntary organizations being provided with incentives to become heavily involved in their activities. One of the major problems confronting the national government in this endeavor is the constitutional provision requiring that such bodies must be delegated their powers by state governments.

Big business reactions to the Sixth Plan have been mixed, but, on the whole, negative. Many Indian businessmen can accept the arguments of the Planning Commission that big industry in India has required more capital for creating jobs than the country can afford, that it has produced less output per unit of capital than the small-scale sector, and that it has perpetuated an urban consumer bias in the economy. Nonetheless, private Indian businessmen are understandably concerned about the degree of government control that the Sixth Plan could conceivably introduce, and both public and private sector industrialists are leery of the government's true ability to shift the attention of the entire nation to new priorities.

Pran Chopra has suggested that these attitudes will present the Janata government with two rather formidable challenges, either of which could ultimately be fatal. In Chopra's words:

The first challenge is that, while imposing all the restrictions that it needs to impose upon the private sector, the government must nevertheless carry the leaders of the private sector with it. If

the private sector were to be discouraged out of existence, or if out of sullenness it were to withhold cooperation, production would plummet and the economy would collapse.

The second and bigger challenge is the organization of an adequate small-scale sector—adequate in efficiency to be an economic source of consumer goods and adequate in size to fulfill the hopes aroused by the new economic policy.[35]

Perhaps an even greater challenge for the Janata government in the urban areas is to secure the acceptance of its rural-oriented strategy among urban laborers and members of the urban middle class. This the Planning Commission hopes to promote by insuring that a considerable amount of funding is available for urban housing, health, and education, as well as other items that significantly affect India's city dwellers. The Janata government is also committed to a "regime of price stability," particularly on essential consumer food items, in large part because it realizes that Indian urban voters have been quick to desert ruling political parties during periods of inflation.

With both foreign exchange and food surpluses, the Janata government has thus far had little difficulty in holding inflation rates for food below those experienced during the scarcity years toward the end of Indira Gandhi's regime. Janata leaders also argue they will not hesitate to use large-scale imports and price subsidies to reduce the price of such essential items as foodgrains, sugar, kerosene, cheap cloth, salt, matches, tea, soap, common drugs, exercise books for schoolchildren and standard footwear through an expanded network of fair price shops. The government has rejected a series of proposals from the communist and socialist parties for the government to establish a nationwide procurement system for the eight or so most essential commodities, to be distributed on a monopoly or near-monopoly basis in fair price and rationing shops. Similar efforts in the past—in West Bengal in 1966 or during Indira Gandhi's 1972 takeover of the wholesale trade in wheat—were political fiascoes for their architects. Moreover, the present government is unlikely to make a serious effort in this direction, if only because the Janata

Party contains a number of local trading interests who would feel threatened.

The most vociferous opposition to Janata government food and agricultural policies thus far has come from rural-based interests in the Janata Party. One particularly powerful faction is headed by Home Minister Charan Singh. The 76-year-old Singh is a firm believer in the argument that India can only escape excessive "statism" by securing private ownership of land for a broad section of the rural population.[36] His power in the central Cabinet stems from the fact that he has the unquestioned political support of the Jats, a large caste of farmers spread across northern India, as well as millions of other owner-cultivators from other "middle castes" who have benefited from agrarian reform measures that have provided them with secure ownership of land, particularly in India's largest state of Uttar Pradesh. Singh also possesses considerable political stature because of his reputation for personal honesty and his ability to convince others of interpersonal contacts.

Charan Singh has criticized the Sixth Five-Year Plan because it does not invest as much in agriculture as he would wish. He argues that the Planning Commission should allocate 40 percent of planned investment to agriculture proper, meaning, in his terms, only agriculture, irrigation, and flood control. Instead, the Planning Commission has allocated 43.1 percent of public investment to "rural development," but this category includes such things as small-scale industries, tribal development, roads, and public health and education, in addition to agriculture and irrigation. Using the Planning Commission's categories, Charan Singh contends that planned public investment in "rural development" should be far greater than 43.1 percent.

Members of the Planning Commission point out that they have already increased allocations to "rural development" from 37.5 percent in the Fifth Plan to 43.1 percent in the Sixth Plan, an increase greater than for any other item in the Plan. To spend more, they contend, would be unrealistic and impolitic, primarily because it would severely tax the capability of the rural sector to absorb additional public spending and diminish planned investments in industrial and urban sectors. Indeed, the Planning Commission is already being criticized by urban journalists for its "idealism" in thinking that it could meaningfully enhance plan allocations to India's rural areas to the extent it has projected.

Because of his emphasis on orienting government expenditures in rural areas toward the needs of owner-cultivators, it is frequently alleged that Charan Singh is a defender of rich peasants. Many urban leaders and socialists argue that Charan Singh is not only anti-urban and anti-industrial, but that he is also anti-Untouchable and anti-low caste. These charges do not fairly represent Charan Singh's position. In his extensive writings on agriculture, he has advocated ceilings on land far smaller than any that exist at present; he has also indicated a decided preference for nonmechanized agriculture. He argues strenuously that the new technology in agriculture is "neutral as to size of holdings." In his view, the anti-Untouchable label has been unfairly pinned on him by Indira Gandhi (his long-standing archfoe) and by rival leaders within his own party.

In the Janata government, Charan Singh championed policies very much like those he enacted into law in Uttar Pradesh in the 1960s. As Paul Brass described it, his stance consists of "opposition to large-scale mechanized farming and explicit support for an agricultural policy favoring the middle cultivating owners, appealing specifically and with considerable success to the class interests of the self-sufficient and the better-off peasantry.[37] Perhaps the fairest assessment of Charan Singh is that his thinking goes beyond strictly caste terms, being concerned primarily with insuring private ownership of land to farmers of all caste groupings as a means of building purchasing power among the rural poor. Since many of the castes that have benefited most from his agrarian reform measures are of low status, the charge that he is anti-low caste can hardly be sustained.

Charan Singh's political position differs considerably from that of India's "Green Revolution" farmers—who depend on mechanization and other modern inputs—and larger landowners, the two accounting at best for 5 to 10 percent of the rural population. The leading spokesman for mechanized farming is Dr. M.S. Randhawa, former Vice-Chancellor of Punjab Agricultural University, who argues that dramatic increases in agricultural production of the kind necessary for India to progress are possible only with mechanized agriculture and fairly large landholdings. In Randhawa's words:

An efficient farmer must have a tractor and tubewell. Without a tractor, multiple-cropping and timely sowing is not a political possibility. If a farmer has a tractor and a tubewell powered by an electric motor or diesel engine, he must have a minimum economic holding of 20-25 acres of irrigated land. This in itself explodes the myth that the new technology of production is neutral to the size of the holdings. Perhaps this cliche was invented by those who wanted to promote a low ceiling for landholdings, ignoring its evil effects on production.[38]

Randhawa objects particularly to price increases for fertilizer (from Rs. 840 per ton of urea in 1967 to Rs. 1850 in 1977) and diesel oil (from Rs. 0.86 per liter in 1967 to Rs. 1.40 in 1976), and to central government taxes that have caused the price of tractors to double and tubewell pumps to increase by more than 75 percent during the past decade. In Randhawa's view, the Janata government's major failing has been its insistence on increasing taxes on some agricultural items and its unwillingness to reduce them for others. He has also come out strongly against the Janata government's unwillingness to raise significantly the price government pays to farmers for procuring wheat for its public distribution system.

Supporters of the Planning Commission and Charan Singh counter Randhawa's arguments by insisting that high taxes on tractors will encourage labor-intensive farm practices and small holding technologies. They also point out that the tax on fertilizer, which they see as being conducive to modern, scientific farming on any size holding, is actually lower under the Janata than it was under the previous government. On the question of agricultural prices, a number of Janata government theoreticians, especially in the Planning Commission, suggest that high prices for farm crops may well hurt both rural and urban poor by changing the terms of trade against industry and slowing down the kinds of industrial development that would lead to high employment. According to Radha Sinha:

High grain prices in many developing countries simply enhance the economic power of the richer peasants, traders, and grain speculators. With their increased resources the latter groups are able to extend their activities. This adds to inflationary pressures and consequently, to the hardship and misery of the poor. If governments were able to siphon off inflationary profits from the rich farmers, traders, and speculators and use these funds for capital formation, the sacrifices of the poor would not be in vain. In the absence of any meaningful taxation of the rural rich, guaranteeing high prices for grains is morally indefensible and economically wasteful. Much of the inflationary profits of the rich farmers and traders go into property speculation, luxury housing construction, and conspicuous consumption. These activities divert scarce resources into nonproductive uses (e.g., steel and cement in luxury housing rather than in dams and reservoirs).[39]

The militancy and potential for violence by farmers who have already invested heavily in mechanization was indicated in Tamilnadu in early April 1978, when 8 people died and more than 500 were injured in a clash between farmers and police. Police fired on the farmers when they resorted to numerous acts of sabotage, arson, and vandalism, including the use of gelatine-packed explosives.[40] In this case, as in a number of nonviolent demonstrations throughout India in 1978, farmers were demanding lower rates for electricity and water in rural areas, reduced prices for fertilizer and other agricultural inputs, postponement of recovery of short and medium-term loans, and higher procurement prices for foodgrains, sugar cane, and other farm products. The widespread nature and intensity of such demonstrations indicate that government policies in favor of the smaller, nonmechanized cultivation are being viewed as threatening by larger farmers in the mechanized sector.

The Janata Party has also sided frequently with low-caste landless laborers and sharecroppers, and this too has produced a violent reaction, in this case from some middle caste groups who feel threatened. The most clearcut case is in Bihar, where Janata Chief Minister Karpoori Thakur has clearly based his regime on appeals to the so-called "Backward Castes," who together make up 47.14 percent of Bihar's population. Not only has Thakur (who is himself from a "backward" caste) reserved 26 percent of government jobs for "Backward Classes," he has also initiated a series of measures that promise to put some teeth into land reform laws in Bihar's most feudal districts.[41] While none of the opposition parties in Bihar have come out officially against Thakur's moves, middle class students in the towns have been leading a statewide violent agitation in support of the demand that "relief be provided for the weaker sections of the elite castes." As P.C. Gandhi has pointed out, the "advanced castes" feel that "their interests will be better served if the current turmoil continues and things come to such a pass that the machinery of law and order visibly breaks down beyond retrieve."[42]

To prevent the breakdown of governmental machinery, the Planning Commission has argued that the poor must themselves become organized at the local level. In the words of one Plan document:

...critical for the success of all redistributive laws, policies and programmes is that the poor be organized and made conscious of the benefits intended for them. Organized tenants have to see that the tenancy laws are implemented. Organizations of the landless have to see that surplus lands are identified and distributed to them in accordance with the law. Local leaders of the poor have to ensure that all area plans and sectoral plans designed for the benefit of their localities and target groups are effectively administered. [43]

As Pran Chopra has noted, such statements are highly unusual for the Planning Commission, which has always in the past shied away from questions of political organization. Granted that both the protest of the poor and the resistance of

the rich are becoming more and more violent, in an atmosphere where the Janata Party has created high expectations that significant change is in the offing, a number of observers in India are looking for some kind of upheaval to occur in the next few years. Chopra, for example, argues that:

It can be taken for granted that one of two kinds of upheavals is in the offing, and it will not take five years to come. Either the upheaval will come when the promises begin to be implemented, or it will come when it begins to be clear that they are not going to be implemented. In either event the upheaval will be a powerful one. There is mounting evidence that agrarian militancy is growing in large parts of the country, especially those parts comprising Bihar, Uttar Pradesh and Madhya Pradesh, in which rural society was quiet to the point of being stagnant until recently. [44]

Chopra's observations contrast markedly with the widespread notion in the Western world that very little is happening in Indian agriculture. In Western journals the Indian rural scene is usually described as static, much is made of the widening gap between rich and poor, and potential political instability is often attributed to sporadic and anomic retributive acts of violence directed against high caste oppressive moneylenders and landlords by low caste and Untouchable landless sharecroppers and tenants. The usual Western news article focuses on such things as traditionalism and lethargy among the poor as the principal constraints detracting from the ability of government to increase food production and to distribute food harvests more equitably.

This perception is not shared by most Indian politicians now active in the Indian countryside. From their point of view, the most formidable challenge of the 1970s and 1980s is not so much the breaking of *stasis* as it is to control a pace of change that increasingly threatens to get out of hand. While no one disputes the widening gap between the richest and poorest segments of the Indian population, the worst problems have been caused by the increasing politicization of the vast middle sections of the population, portions of which are low caste and Untouchable. In this sense, political change does not and is not likely to stem from the imminent threat of unorganized attacks on India's "haves" by the most wretched "have-nots." Rather, political stability or instability will depend on the capacity of India's leadership to evolve institutional arrangements that will provide for the orderly participation of newly politicized rural beneficiaries of agricultural reform.

Prospects for the Future

India's Agricultural Minister, Mr. Surjit Singh Barnala, told the Indian Parliament on April 29, 1978 that dramatic increases in food production in 1977-78, despite poor weather, indicate that Indian agriculture has "come of age."[45] With increased irrigation and fertilizer use, better dryland farming techniques, and plant protection measures, Barnala is convinced that Indian agriculture should not be "too badly affected by bad weather in the future." Pointing out that India is currently exporting 70,000 tons of wheat to Vietnam, 50,000 of wheat to Afghanistan, 50,000 of rice to Indonesia, repaying previous wheat loans from Russia in kind, and contemplating the sale of wheat to Iran on a continuing long-term basis, Barnala suggested that "there is no reason to doubt our capacity to ensure self-sufficiency in foodgrains."

It is a measure of differing international perspectives on the food problem that perhaps most outside observers doubt the ability of India to achieve self-sufficiency in foodgrains, at least on a sustained basis. In most cases, such arguments are linked to overall population growth figures, which, in the Indian case, are declining in some states but are still above 2 percent for the nation as a whole. Even if India can achieve its goal in some years, most economists find it difficult to imagine that India could avoid massive and crippling food deficits in years of adverse weather.

By far the most demoralizing statistic to be published recently was the projection of a 14-17 million ton cereal deficit for India by 1985-86, contained in a study carried out by the International Food Policy Research Institute (IFPRI) of Washington. Most Indians find the projection

unbelievable in light of their current successes. Indeed, if the production performance of recent years were to continue unchecked, India could well attain at least the 3.3 percent average annual rate of growth needed to meet the country's food needs at existing levels of consumption, if not better. However, the lower average annual growth rate of 2.5 percent used by IFPRI in projecting a future food deficit takes into account the possibility that in due course the weather cycle will cause another sharp decline in production such as India experienced in 1965-66 and 1966-67. Should this occur, the country could experience a very serious food deficit in certain years, despite a generally satisfactory production performance.[46]

Even with a continuation of current rates of growth in Indian foodgrains production, most Western observers are chary about the government's efforts to narrow significantly the gap between rich and poor. One prominent Indian official told me in mid-1978 of his conviction that any future food "surplus" in India, no matter how large, would be viewed in the West as the result of a failure to raise nutritional levels fast enough or to boost incomes for the bottom portions of the population. Echoing somewhat the same sentiment, two prominent American scientists have recently argued that "The current mood of pessimism, following so closely on a period of optimism when it was widely held that the Green Revolution was bringing about dramatic changes and that India was on the way to becoming a net exporter of foodgrains, clearly calls for a re-evaluation of the situation and what it implies for the future of India, and, indirectly, the rest of the world."[47]

One of the great ironies of the present food situation in India is that Western pessimism about India's capability to produce and distribute food might well be precisely the kind of incentive needed by a highly nationalistic people to goad them on to good harvests. It is a matter of great national pride, among Indians of all political suasions, that the country is no longer importing foreign foodgrains. Indeed, because self-reliance is so highly valued, failures on the food front tend to be viewed as the most calamitous that can befall an Indian government; they invariably promote an acrimonious factionalism centered around the charge that the nation's future is being imperiled. In this atmosphere, one of the major variables affecting the ability of the government to implement the Sixth Plan will inevitably be the time frame within which the government can work before pressures for quick and dramatic results begin to mount.

In the eyes of its own leaders, success for the Janata government will depend largely on the party's ability to build a political base and to begin to tackle bottom-end poverty during the remaining three years of a five-year term in office. Granted the massiveness of India's economic problems, the depths of Indian poverty, and the complexity of its social and political systems, improvement of the economic position of low status groups is necessarily a long-term proposition, even under the most favorable circumstances.[48] Should the expectations of the Indian people outstrip the ability of politicians to bring about improvement, any number of factors could intervene to thwart the Janata's political aims, either toppling the government or rendering it ineffective in the process. These include: (1) various degrees of political instability breaking out as a consequence of chronic factionalism or party splits; or (2) the reassertion of a dominant position by the urban and heavy industries sectors, either through the use of highly authoritarian measures, or, much more likely, by manipulation of national or regional political symbols like linguistic demands, a nationwide reorganization of state boundaries, or other federal rearrangements.

Indira Gandhi plays a crucial role in all this because she has been staging a remarkable political comeback by using her consummate political skills and knowledge, learned during the almost three decades she was associated with the Prime Minister's office. Sumanta Banerjee has shown how her appeal to the Indian poor during this comeback has been based on many of the same kinds of millennarian promises and political manipulations that she used during her 11 years as Prime Minister.[49] Nevertheless, she won a number of important by-elections, was returned to Parliament in a close election in a southern constituency, and had many of her old allies (in-

cluding some pro-Moscow communists) realigning with her.

Mrs. Gandhi again promised that she would, if brought back to power, create a new political and economic order in which poverty will either be eradicated or greatly reduced. She also publicly apologized to voters for "excesses" that she and her partymen committed during the 21 months of the Emergency in 1975-1977. The usual explanation for the success of Mrs. Gandhi's party in 1978, among the same voters who had decisively rejected her less than a year before, has less to do with the gullibility of the Indian electorate than with the susceptibility of large sections of the Indian poor to change sides in electoral contests. Frequent alternations in voting loyalties reflect a desire to reap whatever little temporary advantage might be available and, in many cases, simply an urge to protest. In Banerjee's words, "So long as the mass of the electorate remains frustrated with the surrounding reality and continues to be vulnerable to demagogic promise, ruthless and cunning politicians like Indira Gandhi will find a convenient base among them.[50] It need hardly be pointed out that the very presence of a millennarian leader like Indira Gandhi, who has the capability of making the most outrageous promises seem believable, by itself places tremendous strains on the timetables within which the Janata Party is expected to perform.

Most observers agree, however, that so long as buffer stocks of foodgrains and foreign exchange exist, the government will have some time to deal with the Indira Gandhi phenomenon. This is so in large part because such "surpluses" provide a cushion with which to soften the impact of the numerous conflicting interests that become involved with the food issue. With food and foreign exchange reserves, the government can afford to invest in both industry and agriculture, in experiments that promise to promote manual labor and full employment, and in projects designed to increase agricultural productivity. This does not mean that conflict will be absent. Indeed, the existence of the already wide gap between the better- and worse-off portions of the Indian populace almost guarantees perpetual conflict between rich and poor, in a variety of different contexts.

The crunch for the government is likely to come when food stocks or foreign exchange reserves (or both) dwindle, a situation that can be prevented only by a rapidly accelerating rate of food production and the continuing growth of India's exports. The dynamics of this relationship between food and politics is perhaps best summarized by Indian economist K.N. Raj's concluding statement at a seminar in New Delhi in August 1977:

The fact that today we have large buffer stocks of foreign exchange, of foodgrains and so on, may provide us with some maneuverability and some insulation from the impact of...fundamental conflicts. But this may well be temporary.

The foreign exchange reserves could fall. There may be an outward movement of capital instead of an inward one. Similarly, one poor harvest can have disastrous effects on our stocks of foodgrains. Once food stocks start falling they have their own effect on prices, especially in the rural areas, because our public distribution system does not extend that far. Therefore, the general point I wish to make is an obvious one; unless agricultural growth can be really accelerated, and unless there is a breakthrough in exports, the conflicts to which I have referred may set in more deeply and, because they have other dimensions, these conflicts may become extremely serious.[51]

NOTES

1. V.M. Rao, *Second India Studies: Food* (New Delhi: The Macmillan Company, 1975), p. 3.

2. Fred H. Sanderson and Shyamal Roy, *Food Trends and Prospects in India* (Washington, D.C.: The Brookings Institution, forthcoming).

3. Rao, *op. cit.*, pp. 4-5.

4. Radha Sinha, *Food and Poverty* (London: Croom Helm Limited, 1976), see especially pp. 45-47.

5. Stanley Kochanek, "India," in *Politics and Modernization in South and Southeast Asia*, ed. Robert N. Kearney (New York: John Wiley and Sons, 1975), pp. 83-85.

6. An interesting study of the problem is M.S. Krishnaswamy, *A Report on the Problem of Delay in Agricultural Administration in Gujarat State* (Ahmedabad: Indian Institute of Management, 1971); and B.S. Minhas, "Key Note Address," in *Rural Development for Weaker Sections: A Seminar*, ed. Shreekant Sambrani (Ahmedabad: Indian Institute of Management, 1974), pp. 8ff.

7. Myron Weiner, *Party Building in a New Nation: The Indian National Congress* (Chicago: University of Chicago Press, 1967), p. 481.

8. Lawrence A. Veit, *India's Second Revolution: The Dimensions of Development* (New York: McGraw-Hill for the Council on Foreign Relations, 1976), p. 245.

9. Ashok Mitra, "Tax Burden for Indian Agriculture," in Ralph Braibanti and Joseph J. Spengler, eds., *Administration and Economic Development in India* (Durham, N.C.: Duke University Press, 1963), p. 303. Quoted in Veit, p. 241.

10. Veit, *op. cit.*, p. 241.

11. John Mellor, *The New Economics of Growth: A Strategy for India and the Developing World* (Ithaca, N.Y.: Cornell University Press, 1976), pp. 178-179.

12. National Commission on Agriculture, *Report, Part II, Policy and Strategy* (New Delhi: Government of India, 1976), p. 3.

13. Veit, *op. cit.*, p. 241.

14. Mellor, *op. cit.*, p. 3.

15. *Ibid.*

16. The role of industrialization and security matters in the Indian polity is explored in detail in Baldev Raj Nayar, *The Modernization Imperative and Indian Planning* (New Delhi: Vikas Publishers, 1972), see especially pp. 3ff.

17. Ivan Johnson, *Brief on Indian Agriculture, 1977* (New Delhi: U.S. Embassy, 1977), pp. 46-47.

18. Arvind Gupta, *Public Distribution of Foodgrains in India* (Ahmedabad: Indian Institute of Management, 1977), see especially pp. 188-192.

19. Veit, *op. cit.*, p. 241.

20. This issue is explored in B.M. Bhatia, *India's Food Problem and Policy Since Independence* (Bombay: Samaiya Publishers, 1970), pp. 129ff. See also Veit, *op. cit.*, pp. 241-242.

21. Paul J. Isenman and H.W. Singer, "Food Aid: Disincentive Effects and their Policy Implications," *Economic Development and Cultural Change*, Vol. 25, No. 2, January 1977.

22. Uma K. Srivastava, Earl O. Heady, Keith D. Rogers, Leo V. Mayer, *Food Aid and International Economic Growth*," Ames, Iowa: Iowa State University Press, 1975, p. 49.

23. An excellent analysis of the Janata Party appears in Lloyd I. Rudolph and Susanne Hoeber Rudolph, "India's Election: Backing into the Future," *Foreign Affairs*, 55:4 (July 1977), pp. 836-854.

24. *Rural Asia, Challenge and Opportunity*, Asian Development Bank, Praeger Special Studies, New York, 1977, pp. 67-71.

25. Pran Chopra, "The New Economics of Water," *The Tribune* (Chandigarh), January 20, 1978.

26. A more detailed analysis of Raj Krishna's position on development issues is provided in my "India's Planning Commission Shifts Course" [MF-1-'78], *AUFS Reports*, No. 2, 1978.

27. An excellent short description of the Anand project appears in David Moller and Ashok Mahadevan, "The Miracle Worker of Kaira," *Reader's Digest* (October 1977), pp. 35-40. See also Pranab Bardhan and Ashok Rudra, "Interlinkage of Land, Labour and Credit Relations," *The Economic and Political Weekly* (Bombay), XIII: 6-7 (February 1978), pp. 367-384.

28. Mellor, *op. cit.*, pp. 36-37.

29. See my forthcoming volume, *India's Rural Development: an Assessment of Alternatives* (Bloomington, Indiana: Indiana University Press and AUFS, 1979).

30. Donald Zagoria, "The Ecology of Peasant Communism in India," *The American Political Science Review*, 65:1 (March 1971), pp. 145ff.

31. Balraj Mehta, "Prices and Public Distribution," *Indian Express*, May 5, 1978.

32. An especially interesting discussion of the subsidies issue is N.S. Jagannathan, "That Thing Called Subsidies," *The Statesman* (Calcutta), April 7, 1978.

33. See, for example, James Manor, "Structural Changes in Karnataka Politics," *The Economic and Political Weekly* (Bombay), XII:44 (October 29, 1977), p. 1868.

34. See, for example, the statement by Dr. D.T. Lakdawala, Deputy Chairman of the Planning Commission, in the *Indian Express* (New Delhi), April 9, 1978.

35. Pran Chopra, "An Exceptional Challenge," *The Tribune* (Chandigarh), March 10, 1978.

36. For a systematic exposition of Charan Singh's position, see Charan Singh, *India's Economic Policy: The Gandhian Blueprint* (New Delhi: Vikas Publishers, 1977). For a critique of this position by an eminent economist and former Minister under Indira Gandhi, see V.K.R.V. Rao, "Charan Singh's Blueprint for India," *The Illustrated Weekly of India*, XCIX:1 (January 1, 1978), pp. 18-21.

37. Paul R. Brass, "The Politicization of the Peasantry in a North Indian State," unpublished paper, September 10, 1977, p. 104.

38. M.S. Randhawa, "Is There Enough Food for All?" *The Illustrated Weekly of India*, XCVIII:32 (August 7, 1977), p. 12.

39. Radha Sinha, *op. cit.*, p. 76.

40. *The Hindu*(Madras), April 17, 1978. See also *India Today*, III:9 (May 1-15, 1978), pp. 42ff.

41. See my "Agrarian Reform in North Bihar: Operation Kosi Kranti" [MF-3-'78], *AUFS Reports*, No. 6, 1978.

42. P.C. Gandhi, "Job Reservations in Bihar: Playing for High Stakes," *Times of India* (New Delhi), April 20, 1978.

43. Quoted in Pran Chopra, "The Sixth Plan's Time Bomb," *The Tribune* (Chandigarh), March 24, 1978.

44. *Ibid.*

45. *Indian Express*, April 30, 1978.

46. See *Meeting Food Needs in the Developing World: The Location and Magnitude of the Task in the Next Decade* (Washington: IFPRI, February 1976), p. 3.

47. James D. Gavan and John A. Dixon, "India: A Perspective on the Food Situation," in *Food: Politics, Economics, Nutrition and Research*, ed. Philip H. Abelson (Washington: American Association for the Advancement of Science, 1975), p. 49.

48. V.M. Rao calculates that chronic malnutrition and undernutrition could be eliminated from India by the year 2000 if one could assume an annual economic growth rate of 6 percent per year, a sharp reduction in overall population growth rates, income distribution with only modest disparities and considerable changes in patterns of food production and consumption. See Rao, pp. 20ff.

49. Sumanta Banerjee, "If the System Changeth Not, Mrs. Gandhi May Well Return to Power," *Perspective* (Calcutta Monthly), I:10 (May 1978), p. 12.

50. *Ibid.*

51. K.N. Raj, "The Economic Outlook," *India International Centre Quarterly*, IV:3 (July 1977), p. 274.

Table 1

**The Indian Diet (1970)
Calories and Proteins
Derived from the Principal Foods**

Foodstuffs	Calories per day	Proteins (grams per day)
Rice	645	12.0
Wheat	327	9.8
Coarse grains	381	10.5
Total cereals	1,353	32.3
Pulses	162	9.8
Total foodgrains	1,515	42.1
Starch roots	39	0.5
Sugar and products	203	0.5
Nuts, oilseeds, and vegetable oils	125	0.7
Vegetables, fruits, and miscellaneous	81	2.8
Total vegetable foods	1,963	46.6
Meat	7	0.5
Eggs	0	0
Fish	5	0.8
Dairy products	92	4.4
Total animal food	104	5.7
Total	2,067	52.3

Source: FAO Food Balance Sheets, *Food Production Trends and Prospects in India*, Fred H. Sanderson and Shymal Roy, the Brookings Institution, forthcoming.

Table 2			Production and Use of Grains[a] and Pulses, 1960/61-1977/78						
Crop Year	Beginning Stocks	Production	Imports	Cereals Food Aid	Exports	Ending Stocks	Domestic Consump- tion	Change in Production	Change in Domestic Consumption
1960/61	7.3	82.2	3.4	3.9	.1	7.2	85.1		
1961/62	7.2	83.0	4.0	2.7		8.2	86.0	+0.8	+0.9
1962/63	8.2	80.3	4.9	3.9		8.2	85.2	-2.7	-0.8
1963/64	8.2	80.7	6.7	5.0		7.4	88.2	+0.4	+3.0
1964/65	7.4	89.3	8.1	6.7		8.8	96.0	+8.6	+7.8
1965/66	8.8	72.3	10.0	8.8		13.4	77.7	-17.0	-18.3
1966/67	13.4	74.2	9.1	7.4		12.8	83.9	+1.9	+6.2
1967/68	12.8	95.1	6.1	6.7		16.6	97.4	+20.9	+13.5
1968/69	16.6	94.0	3.7	3.0	.1	15.4	98.8	-1.1	+1.4
1969/70	15.4	99.5	3.4	3.1	.1	14.5	103.7	+5.5	+4.9
1970/71	14.5	108.4	2.1	2.4		16.0	109.0	+8.9	+5.3
1971/72	16.0	105.2	.6	1.6	.8	15.2	105.8	-3.2	-3.2
1972/73	15.2	96.5	4.1	.4		10.2	105.6	-9.7	-0.2
1973/74	10.2	104.7	5.9	.1		11.3	109.5	+8.2	+3.9
1974/75	11.3	99.8	7.3	.9		11.4	107.0	-4.9	-2.5
1975/76	11.4	120.8	6.1	.5	1.0	23.3	115.0	+21.0	+8.0
1976/77	23.3	109.0	.5		2.1	17.8	114.0	-11.8	-1.0
1977/78	17.8	120.0				20.0	115.7	+11.0	+1.7

a.Includes barley, corn, millet, rice, sorghum, and wheat

Source: *Developments in the Grain Sector of India*, Foreign Agricultural Circular, Foreign Agricultural Service, U.S. Department of Agriculture, Washington, D.C., September 1977. Schnittker Associates estimates for 1977/78. Food aid data
from donor country sources assembled by the International Food Policy Research Institute.

Table 3

Growth in Production and Yields of Major Grains since 1955

	Yield[a] (MT/ha)			Growth in Area		Growth in Yield (percent)	
	1955	1965	1973	1955-65	1965-73	1955-65	1965-73
Wheat	0.7	0.9	1.3	1.36	4.68	2.67	4.91
Paddy Rice	1.3	1.5	1.7	1.26	0.61	1.30	1.86
Maize	0.8	1.0	1.0	2.56	2.18	2.78	-0.65
Total grains and pulses	n.a.	0.7	0.8	n.a.	.67	n.a.	3.77

	Growth in Production (percent)	
	1965-1973	1973-1978
Total grains and pulses	3.72	3.61

a.Five-year average centered on the years shown.

Sources: *Rural Asia, Challenge and Opportunity*, Asian Development Bank, New York:
Praeger Special Studies, 1977, pp. 67, 69, 71; Developments in the Grain Sector of
Indian Agriculture, U.S. Department of Agriculture, Foreign Agriculture Circular,
FG-15-77, September 1977, p. 6.

Labor teams on the North China Plain harvest potatoes and prepare for sowing a winter crop.

Whose Good Earth?
Observations on Chinese Agriculture

Albert Ravenholt

Over the past decade or so, China has imported on the average four to seven million tons of wheat a year—some 10 percent of its consumption, a little less than 10 percent of the global wheat trade. It has been a net exporter of rice. Its potential impact on world markets, should there be a significant shift in its degree of self-sufficiency, is obviously momentous. Outsiders have been in a poor position to appraise China's agricultural performance, although that is to some extent changing because of the regime's increasing openness, its entry into FAO (of which the Soviet Union is still not a member), and, perhaps, Landsat imagery.

In the atmosphere of mystery long associated with China and compounded by her relative isolation from the international community during the past three decades, it has been difficult to gain a factual understanding of affairs in the Chinese countryside. Chinese villages, with their weathered houses and earthen walls, crooked lanes, and partially cobbled streets, looked as drab in 1978 as they did in 1943,[1] although the graves, clan shrines, and temples are virtually all gone. But there is a fundamental change; in the same communities one feels there now must be about twice as many people as before. This is the result of the greatest single physical achievement of the new Communist order which has truly revolutionized public health and sanitation.

Health and Population Growth

Human excrement, or "night soil" as it is more politely known, has been critical for maintaining fertility of Chinese fields throughout recorded time. The *mao fang* or open pit latrine was almost omnipresent in the countryside; here the feces accumulated to the delight of some very healthy flies until the season when the farmer chose to haul the night soil to his field in wooden tubs. In the cities with their surrounding "green circles" this was a continuing routine. On the canals the sampans that carried fresh vegetables into Shanghai and other cities hauled back the night soil to the farmers. In Chengtu, capital of the most populous province of Szechuan, men pulled "honey carts" through the streets early in the morning, stopping at each house to ladle out from the *mao fang* the night soil to be sold later that day to surrounding farmers who were expert at detecting any dilution. A partial list of the fecal-borne diseases suggests the implications; bacillary and amoebic dysentery, typhoid and paratyphoid, enteritis and diarrhea, cholera, schistosomiasis, ascariasis and the hookworm, ancylostomiasis. Nearly 80 percent of the population of Canton alone were estimated to be infected with clonorchiasis, due in part to the marvelously economical planning of fishpond owners who placed public toilets conveniently to feed their carp, which then were often served raw as a delicacy.

Improved toilets appear to be almost everywhere in China today. Naturally, these are not flushing facilities in the countryside, nor in the cities except at a few hotels and modern buildings. Rather, they are concrete lined troughs and pits, often with screen over the window openings. In a city such as Sian, every evening families place their excrement-filled wooden buckets on the pavement in two or three locations per block. After daytime traffic has left the streets, tank trucks collect the contents. Use of trucks allows hauling to greater distances from the cities—at intervals along the roads concrete and covered cisterns are used to store night soil until it is needed on the land. In smaller communities night soil still may be hauled by humans pulling wooden tubs on carts, but nearly everywhere it appears to be accumulated in covered concrete pits.[2]

Provision of piped water into the villages and enforcement of sanitation regulations inhibiting contamination of wells has been as vital for public health as the improved management of human excrement. Widespread use of DDT, which was the preferred insecticide in agriculture although it is now being replaced with organophosphates and other chemicals, also has helped reduce the fly population as well as control malaria by killing the mosquitoes. This in part may explain a noticeable reduction in the bird population, which also was curbed by the mass campaign to kill the sparrows. Cats always were rare in China and more so now. Dogs have been eliminated, with a few exceptions, and thus are not available to spread rabies or any of the other 65 diseases they share with man. (It was not possible to get a clear account of whether dogs were eaten in a time of food shortage or merely a luxury no longer to be tolerated.)

Rats were omnipresent in the Old China and sometimes so bold they would gnaw through a mosquito net at night to disturb the sleeper at an inn. Even during World War II, rats following movement of grain after the harvest carried the lice and fleas that brought plague. The Communists have organized several mass campaigns to kill rats—presumably these were not sabotaged as before by enterprising individuals who then bred rats to sell the tails. Although reliable statistics are not available, examination of granaries and other buildings on communes suggests there has been a significant reduction in the rodent population.

The massive organization of street committees in the cities and production teams in the countryside that facilitates political control of the population has also provided an efficient means to vaccinate against smallpox and some other communicable diseases and to curb schistoso-miasis in Central and South China. Paramedics, many of them middle school students, were mobilized and trained to carry out this national program soon after the new authorities established power in 1949.

Continuing this preventive health program in the villages has become the responsibility of the barefoot doctors, who administer first aid and treat simple illnesses with both modern and traditional medical methods. One of the most obvious improvements has been a great reduction in skin disease, especially among children. Rural folk have access to a network of common clinics and provincial hospitals that commonly utilize acupuncture for anesthesia and otherwise capitalize upon indigenous resources. Production teams are proud of the member-financed health insurance that enables farm families to pay for such services. Although some modern types of antibiotics are in short supply and hospital facilities may appear crude by Western standards, they are a marked improvement over the medical facilities that existed in pre-Communist China and rarely were available in the rural areas. For the peasants it is important that similarly effective measures appear to have curbed epizootics of rinderpest, hog cholera, and other communicable livestock diseases.

The demographic revolution inaugurated by this effective and massive improvement in sanitation and preventive medicine combined with rudimentary clinical care is on a scale difficult to visualize and assess. Morbidity and mortality statistics in the Old China were at best available in sample surveys.[3] Typhoid, dysentery, and cholera ranked with smallpox, tuberculosis, and measles as the leading causes of death in the north.

As is the case in much of the nonmodern world, infants and children were the most frequent victims of this mortality pattern, making it necessary for a family to have many babies in order to insure that a few survived to adulthood. Since male children were so essential to the Confucian concept of immortality through the family, this further fortified emphasis upon procreation—the original grounds for taking a concubine was to provide descendants for one's uncle. However, in times of critical food shortage or among the most impoverished families drastic measures were taken to curb the number of mouths to be fed. In the fertile Chengtu Plain of Szechuan, where an irrigation system has functioned almost without interruption for some 2,300 years, when a family had all the children it could feed, a newborn infant might be destroyed by one of the grandmothers who hit its head on a stone, smothered, or drowned the baby. In Shanghai such infants were abandoned in the streets and in Kwangtung they often were left in a basket in the markets, where the mother hoped someone would take the child, in effect, for adoption.

After establishment of the People's Republic the new Marriage Law in 1950 gave legal equality to women, abolished concubinage, and led to rapid elimination of infanticide as the young enthusiastic Communist cadres preached the benefits of the New China where there would be enough for all to eat. Similar fervor fortified their early mass efforts to enforce the initial sanitation and vaccination programs. When expedient, popular compliance with essentially sound public health measures was prompted by all the persuasive methods an authoritarian state can command. Between 1951 and 1953 the "anti-U.S. germ warfare campaign," triggered by charges that the United States was resorting to bacteriological means in the Korean conflict, was made the occasion for galvanizing the entire populace into killing flies and other insects. As the death rate, especially infant mortality, dropped drastically, a few independent-minded Chinese leaders warned of the danger of population pressure, but these warnings were brushed aside in the heady atmosphere of the early years of Communist triumph. Socialism, they evidently assumed, would rapidly solve China's problems of food production. During the early and mid-1950s, moreover, performance by Chinese peasants tilling their own fields with improved irrigation and under conditions of peace and order fortified these expectations with bountiful crops. The pronatalist Confucian value system was reinforced by a conviction prevalent in the minds of important Chinese leaders of this century, like Sun Yat-sen, who argued China must make up with numbers of people for what she lacked in industrialization. It was in this context that Mao Tse-tung, with the immense authority of a successful revolution and

civil war behind him, evolved the principle that "people are capital" and the more you have the faster you can develop the country, provided they are effectively organized. It was a short step intellectually to inaugurating the "Great Leap Forward" in 1957, when tens of millions were marched to massive public works and much else, and the following year to the momentous decision creating the "Peoples' Communes."

The population growth spurred by these public health achievements is as yet only partially perceived. The best available base figure is the national census conducted during the 24-hour period between midnight June 30 and midnight July 1, 1953, for which some 2.5 million officials, students, party cadres, and other personnel had been recruited and trained to carry out this task. While purists sometimes argue that there are mistakes in the management of the census, the evidence indicates it was the most complete and accurate the new government could accomplish. The tally, rounded to 583 million, corresponded to the estimates of some of the most experienced China observers.

The growth in population since 1953 has often been a subject for speculation and dispute. Nikita Khrushchev in his recollections reported that in 1959 Mao Tse-tung told him China's population numbered 700 million. Actually, I believe it only passed this mark in summer 1962; the terrible food shortages following creation of the Peoples' Communes meant that from the winter of 1958-59 to the summer of 1962 many women stopped menstruating, and mortality increased greatly, especially among infants. With importation of grain to feed coastal cities and restoration of agricultural production, the most radical features of the communes were moderated. Incentives were restored in part for the peasants through private garden plots and free markets. The rate of population increase moved up to where it had been in the 1950s, or about 2.5 percent annually. Pragmatic policies of the time under the leadership of Chairman Liu Shao-chi, Premier Chou En-lai, and Communist Party Secretary General Teng Hsiao-ping had just begun to show results in birth control by 1966, when China became embroiled in the Great Proletarian Cultural Revolution.

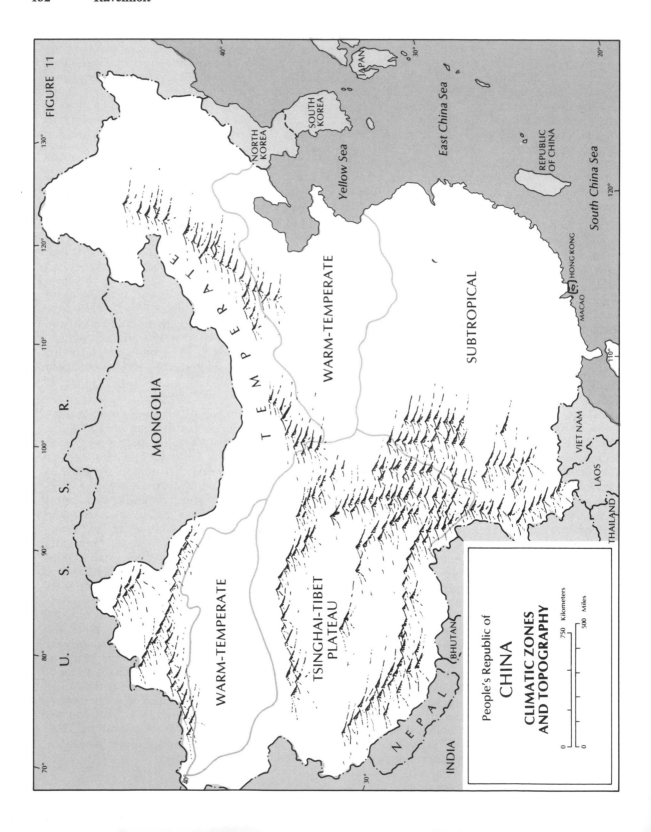

FIGURE 11

People's Republic of
CHINA

CLIMATIC ZONES
AND TOPOGRAPHY

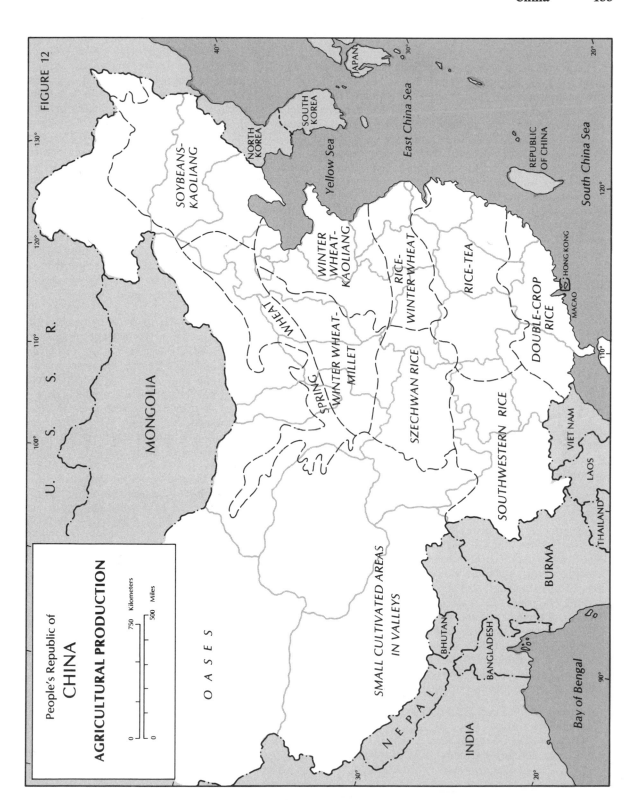

FIGURE 12

People's Republic of
CHINA

AGRICULTURAL PRODUCTION

These political events had important consequences for China's population policy and action. The birth control program begun earlier slackened during the Cultural Revolution while the cadres were preoccupied with political infighting and peasants returned to older ways, including desire for more children to provide security in old age. A lack of consensus on population policy was evident among the senior Communists until Chairman Hua Kuo-feng's leadership was assured. Even today visitors to Peking are given widely varying figures for China's total population. Some are told it is 800 million, some are informed it is 900 million and others that it is 950 million; my own calculations put it somewhere between the last two estimates.

During the past six years, as the necessity for more drastic food rationing became increasingly apparent, government officials at all levels have recognized the urgency of birth control. Measures now being enforced would be judged draconian in any other society. Women are forbidden to marry before the age of 24 or 25, depending upon local option, and men before the age of 28. When we questioned doctors, as in Honan, about premarital sex and illegitimate births they were aghast; such activities are not tolerated in the New China where a marriage must be sanctioned by the local Revolutionary Committee. Tubal ligation is recommended for a woman who has had three children, and often two. We observed two such operations done under acupuncture anaesthesia. Contraceptives appear to be nearly universally available and knowledge of their use effectively disseminated. In 1973, the then Minister of Health, Li Hsu-hsien, stated privately at an international conference that she believed China's birthrate was 25 per thousand and the death rate 7/1,000, a rate of increase of 1.8 percent. Two years later a leading Chinese official of the World Health Organization estimated China's birthrate had dropped to 16/1,000. Clearly, the present Chinese leadership recognizes the demographic implications of an immense population of which well over one-half is under the age of 21.

"For the People Food Equals Heaven": Diet and Nutrition

This classical Chinese proverb, *min yi shih wei t'ien*, is as compelling for the Communist rulers of today as it was for the mandarins of old who jealously sought to retain the "mandate of heaven." Probably no society on earth historically has been so occupied with insuring this most basic of human needs, nor so zestfully devoted to enjoying eating and measuring the quality of life by this yardstick.

Chinese think of food in two categories. *Fan* is usually prepared from wheat, millet, sorghum, or buckwheat, possibly with ground corn mixed in the north, and rice, frequently cooked with sweet potatoes, especially in Central China and the south. *Ts'ai* refers to the almost innumerable variations in cooking vegetables—China has the world's greatest variety—often blended with bean curd, bits of meat, pickles, and possibly seafood. In addition, soybean products—a major source of protein—are considered *Ts'ai*.

In the Old China, only the rich and powerful ate dishes of pure meat or fish, except on special occasions like Chinese New Year when ordinary folk might feast. This reflected the basic nutritional fact of China, that 98 percent of food eaten came direct from the vegetable kingdom. Popular awareness of this was expressed in the phrase "mandarins eat meat." For the less affluent, there were inexpensive options for sampling a small bit of meat or seafood along inland waterways and in the coastal communities. They were chopped and mixed with the vegetable fillings in the boiled dumplings called *chiao tzu* or pan fried to become *kuo t'ieh*. A similar stuffing might be covered by a ball of dough and steamed to become *pao tzu*, or a bit of meat or seafood blended with vegetables and noodles and fried to become *ts'ao mien* or cooked with soup stock to become *t'ang mien*. For the abstemious or less affluent these could be eaten either as snacks or an entire meal at noon or in the evening, the flavor enlivened with selections of chopped ginger, chopped garlic, shredded radish, soya sauce, hot oil made with chili peppers, sesame, or peanut oil, and numerous other seasonings.

Of necessity because of burgeoning population pressure the People's Republic has concentrated upon providing the *fan*, or staple component of the diet. The model production brigades we visited were quick to emphasize that they are growing enough to supply the basic ration for their members, plus meeting their quota for state grain purchases. They were less definite about revealing what proportion of the ration was provided by grain and how much was supplied by the less desirable sweet potatoes, potatoes, and other tubers (four kilos of tubers are the equivalent of one kilo of grain in the ration).

Economies in the use of grain are apparent in North China. Only the favored elite and visitors eat white *man t'ou* or steamed bread. The general population must make do with a staple that is dark brown, and rather heavy and may include ground bran, barley, sorghum, and other rough grains. In Central and South China all the rice we saw was rough milled; the bran had been removed and the grains were lightly polished. Brown rice, with its greater protein and vitamin content, generally is not eaten, although this may reflect the methods of milling.[4]

Inferior *ts'ai*, however, is now the most critical food problem for the Chinese. *Tou fu*, which is the curd, was traditionally the most important single source of protein in the diet. Along with other foods made from soybeans in the Old World, it was normally abundant and cheap. Poor people especially relied much upon the curd, which might be dried (*tou fu kan*) or fermented. They also drank soy milk (*tou chang*), and ate bean sprouts (*tou ya*), cooked green immature seeds as a vegetable and seasoned with soy sauce (*chang yu*). Mature seeds were pressed to produce oil used for cooking, lighting, and industrial manufacture, while the residual bean cake was returned as feed for animals or applied directly as fertilizer. (Growing of this legume also augmented nitrogen in the fields.)

No vegetable is more important in China than soybeans, yet production problems appear to be growing. During the mid-1950s, China's total soybean crop fluctuated between 11 and 14 million tons. Exports went from 950,000 tons in 1955 to 1,343,000 tons in 1959 and then began to drop off until 1974, when China purchased 376 thousand tons on the world market, chiefly from the United States. Since that time, the country has been a net importer of soybeans. The available data lead the most knowledgable agricultural observers to conclude that the 1977 soybean crop totaled about seven million tons.

This decline in China's soybean harvests at a time when a growing population needs greater nourishment reflects both policy confusion at the center in planning and purchasing and peasant resistance in the production brigades to growing a crop with comparatively low yields. Some of these decisions are only dimly perceived from the scanty evidence available, yet they suggest a pattern. Until 1956, soybeans were included with grains and potatoes in statistics and in the Five Year Plan. From 1957 until 1974, soybeans were excluded and placed in a separate category. Then, officials in Peking said they again were counting them into total grain production, which in China is a sensitive and consequential figure in major decisions. This reflected an apparent national tendency to give a low priority to soybeans.

The production decline is also contributing to an equally serious shortage in China today—that of cooking oils, both those of vegetable origin and lard. The average annual ration when it is available is 2.75 liquid quarts, a daily allowance of one-fifth ounce (less than one teaspoonful). During the grim years of the Sino-Japanese War from 1937 to 1945, refugee Chinese professors and students who had retreated into Western and Southwestern China subsisted on meager salaries and allowances. For them at the time eight kilos each annually of lard or equivalent of cooking oil seemed hardly enough to manage. Poorer families in the eastern Indian state of West Bengal will use 10 to 11 kilos of cooking oil, including ghee or clarified butter, per capita annually.

A hint of what this means is provided by the *ta chung shih pu*, or "cook book for the masses." The 264 recipes include scrupulous measurements for as little as one-tenth of an ounce of lard or oil, although a number of dishes call for one-half an ounce of oil or more. Generally, the recipes for North China allow less oil in contrast with the recipes for South China, where pigs and thus lard are more abundant and where deep-fat frying was more commonly employed. Stir-frying, which allowed rapid cooking and thus an economy in the use of fuel, also was fundamental to the Chinese culinary genius in conserving to the maximum vitamins and other nutrients in vegetables. Now, housewives are compelled to rely far more on steaming and boiling, which have significant nutritional implications.

Although meat provides a tiny fraction of the Chinese diet, it is also important symbolically as a popular measure of well-being. The figures vary with the regimes, but it appears that in some communes of South China the meat ration is six ounces per capita per month and the fish ration is one-third this amount.

Producing Food: Progress, Problems, and Prospects

Providing the basic *fan* requirement for an adequate diet of one-half a kilo daily for 900 million persons necessitates China producing annually 153 million tons net of milled rice or its equivalent in other grains or tubers. Allowance must be made of course for seed, plus losses in storage, transport, milling, and cooking. This figure must be increased to 230 million tons rough grain equivalents to allow for milling losses alone, even when harvest weights are determined in grain dried to 13 percent moisture. Thus it is evident that China's recent harvests, fluctuating between 250 and 285 million tons of rice, wheat, and other staples according to the most experienced and knowledgeable observers, leave little for accumulation of reserves.

The model production brigades we visited were proud of their granaries, which were usually constructed of tamped earth or brick. Clearly, this communal food reserve also has important psychological significance. It is the only real guarantee that brigade members will receive their ration of 256 kilos annually of rough paddy rice or its equivalent. With a 60 percent milling recovery this would allow an annual per capita grain or equivalent consumption of 153.6 kilograms, or a bit less than the optimum of one-half a kilogram daily. Provincial authorities retain the option of providing food assistance to communes that fail to grow enough to provide the ration for their members and meet state grain deliveries. However, the overwhelming emphasis is upon self-sufficiency within each production brigade,

commune, county (*hsien*), and province, and there is no guarantee that a deficit will be made up from outside.

Much is made of Tachai, the model commune in Shensi Province where mobilization of manpower, terraced mountain slopes, and resources were mustered to maximize production and publicize an example of achievements by politically motivated peasants. A United Nations report mentions corn harvests at Tachai of 8 to 10 tons per hectare (one hectare equals 2.47 acres), which is equivalent to 125 to 158 bushels per acre. This certainly is an achievable yield. However, it is misleading as a general indication of farm production in North China. According to responsible Chinese Communist officials, average corn yields in neighboring Shensi Province, which has generally better soils, are equal to 76 bushels per acre, or about 5 tons per hectare. (It is a bit like suggesting that Michigan farmer Roy Linn, Jr.'s 1977 harvest of 352 bushels of corn on one acre, or the equivalent of about 22 tons per hectare, is indicative of the crops grown by most American midwestern farmers, when they would be more than happy with a crop approaching one-half of this yield.) That average corn production in Shensi Province from 1937-1945 was 280 *shih chin* per *mou* or equivalent to 2,100 kilos or a little over 2 tons per hectare—less than one-half the present average yield—puts the Tachai commune achievement in even clearer perspective.

Supplying this ration of *fan*, whether of grain or tuber equivalent, has been the overriding production objective of agricultural programs in the People's Republic and both notable achievements and mistakes are evident. The greatest single area of effort has been in expansion of the classical Chinese concern with water control. Just as the emperors of old mobilized corvée labor by the millions for such massive construction projects as diking the Yellow River to hold "China's sorrow" from wreaking havoc as the bed of this most silt-laden of all streams rose ever higher, so the Communists have acted on an even grander scale. Almost every production brigade, and commune for larger projects, appears to have its heroic account of mobilized man- and woman-power using hoes, baskets, wheelbarrows, and other simple equipment to move water to where it is needed and away from where it was not wanted. Certainly there are more dams and canals than before.

An insight into what this can mean for farming is provided by a model production brigade south of Chengchow in Honan; the Wang Hu T'ai Brigade of the Shih Pa Li Ho Commune. The brigade is composed of 10 production teams that correspond roughly to former villages including 576 families with a total population of 3,400 (they report that 41 families died during the 1942-43 famine). The total land area is 5,400 *mou*, or 360 hectares, of which 100 *mou* are planted to apples, 1,600 *mou* are devoted to raising vegetables for sale in Chengchow, and the balance of the fields are used for growing grain. The brigade owns 207 draft animals, 31 carts, 6 tractors, including the small hand tillers, 4 trucks of various models and ancient vintage, and 3 diesel generators. Although they have terraced 9 hills during the past 20 years, their greatest accomplishment has been in irrigation; instead of the 9 wells that 30 years ago belonged to a landlord, they now have 67 plus a 4-kilometer cement-lined canal. Such water control has been the chief means to increasing grain production by 225 kilos per *mou*, mainly from the combination of the winter wheat crop and the summer corn crop. Their yields now are 255 kilos of winter wheat per *mou*, equal to 56 bushels per acre, and 230 kilos of corn per *mou*, or 54 bushels per acre. Their state grain deliveries quota is 560,000 kilos, for which the brigade is paid Yo.14 per kilo, or the equivalent of US$75 per metric ton. Provided this quota is met, the brigade is then relatively free to decide what to grow on the remaining roughly two-thirds of their fields from which their members must be fed.

Setting aside the political verbiage about how drops in grain production were related to the "crimes of Liu Shao-ch'i" or others, it becomes apparent that progress has been primarily a product of mobilizing labor. In addition to water control, this has allowed leveling land, planting trees for windbreaks, and some simple house construction so that they can claim to "nearly live like factory workers." The brigade includes a small brick kiln, a simple flour mill, a shop for making noodles and bean curd, a repair shop with two lathes, a blacksmith forge, and a small hog raising farm.[5] Although their orchard never would make a living for a fruit grower in New Zealand, Japan, or the United States, they were growing good millet and sorghum, called *kaoliang*. Their excellent horse and mule farm reflects the exceptional leadership of this brigade.[6]

China is more abundantly endowed with varieties of vegetables than any other country and traditional skills—cutting, seasoning, and cooking them—probably are without peer. The art of growing these many vegetables is a distinguishing feature of the East Asian civilizations; an equivalent capacity for cultivating intensively and productively small plots of land to yield a maximum of edibles is largely lacking in Southeast and South Asia. Much of the traditional physical vigor and sustained working endurance of Japanese, Koreans, and Chinese must be due to their diets which combine an abundance of cheap protein with this wealth of vegetables. Significantly, in Northern and Western China where corn is grown, failure to utilize lye or lime in its preparation evidently restricts its nutritional value. When China's peasants were dispossessed of their property with creation of the People's Communes two decades ago, food shortages that overtook the land resulted partly from peasants abandoning cultivation of their gardens and slaughtering the pigs since they had become the property of the state. Recovery of agricultural production after 1961-62 also resulted in part from the then pragmatic decisions of Liu Shao-ch'i, Teng Hsiao-p'ing, and their associates to restore use of private garden plots to peasant families and encourage free markets where they could sell their produce.

As the Great Proletarian Cultural Revolution gathered momentum after 1966, Mao Tse-tung, as part of his campaign to recapture power, charged that this pragmatic policy in the countryside betrayed the revolution and was a step toward bourgeois capitalism. With Mao's consolidation of control and political power accorded the radicals, free markets largely were abolished—this happened only gradually in some regions because political infighting between factions left the peasants scope to barter with the people in towns until the new authority was firmly in place. Most serious was reduction in the land allotted for private garden plots. Formerly, in most areas of China, private gardens were allowed about 5 percent of the cultivated area. After the Cultural Revolution these ideas for growing family food were drastically reduced. In Kwangtung, we were informed that private plots now are allowed one-half of one percent of the cultivated area of the production brigade. The intensive crowding of these plots, creating a multistoried effect with numerous vines, vegetables, spices, and medicinal plants, suggests the pressure farmers feel in augmenting their food supplies.

In the fields, peasants were simultaneously finding it less advantageous to grow more soybeans than needed for their own immediate consumption, even in the North China and Manchurian regions where the plant does well. Officially, the state insisted upon purchases of oil rather than beans in most instances. This was intended in part to avoid transporting beans to the cities from which the residue oil cake then must be shipped back to the countryside. After farmers were corralled into People's Communes in 1958, the private enterprise incentives that had encouraged them to grow soybeans for sale through free markets to towns and villages ceased to operate. Meanwhile, during the following years of desperate food shortages all emphasis was focused upon inducing the radical new mechanism of the production teams and brigades to grow just enough of the basic grains and tubers people needed to fill their stomachs. As China recovered in the 1960s and began expanding agricultural production, a pattern had been set. Instead of raising soybeans as a single crop, which was the practice formerly in the main growing areas, soybeans became an interplanted crop. This is how we saw most of them growing in North China in 1977; a row or two of soybeans were grown between corn rows or interplanted with other crops, while crops like cotton retained their single field dominance. Although the soybean originated in China supposedly some 26 centuries ago and has had a vital dietary role, the People's Republic has accorded it only limited attention in research and plant breeding and without the incentive of a free market farmers show scant interest in expanding production.

In addition to soybeans, the other chief sources of cooking oil in the past were rape seed, sesame, peanuts, cotton seed oil, miscellaneous crops such as sunflower, plus lard, a little tallow, and limited use of fish oils along the coast. It appears that commune production brigades, in order to meet the state purchase quotas of grain and cotton, hemp or ramie, where these are designated to be grown, have given these crops priority in allocation of available fields. The compulsion to grow sufficient staple grains and tubers to provide the rations for their members also has been important. As a result, these other oil crops also now are chiefly planted as an intercrop and their yield is subordinated to the staples. As with the soybean, so with most of these oil crops, problems of where and how to extract the oil have hindered production in this era of drastic social and economic remaking of the countryside. The seed cake remaining after extracting the oil is considered useful only for feeding livestock or use as fertilizer. China so far has not developed the modern oil extraction, packaging, and transportation facilities for managing large-scale distribution of a perishable commodity like cooking oil.

Irrigation

Standing on the dikes of the Yellow River at Hua Yuan K'ou, 15 kilometers northeast of Chengchow, the provincial capital of Honan, one gains a sense of the enormous stakes. Here, in 1938, the dikes were breached and the river changed course shifting its mouth some 600 kilometers to the south of the Shantung Peninsula as part of a deliberate effort to slow the southward march of the Japanese armies coming from Manchuria and North China. An estimated three million peasants were flooded out with an inestimable loss of life. In 1946-47 the return of the Yellow River to its old northerly course became a major concern of the United Nations rehabilitation efforts, and today it remains a challenge as female labor teams unload boulders from railway boxcars atop the dike and energetic young cadres explain the mistakes in the 106 meter high San Men Dam built with Russian assistance between 1957 and 1960. One-half the storage capacity of the vast reservoir already has silted up and there are schemes to correct this by tunneling through rock on the north side and opening gates for sluicing out the silt. On a smaller scale the Huai River and other drainage basins have been similarly made over, and the Grand Canal has again been tied into a complex water conservancy network. The main stream of the Yangtze has yet to be controlled, except chiefly for diking and water storage in the T'ungt'ing Lake region of Central China. Otherwise, wherever earth and rock can be moved to harness water the Communists have capitalized upon their mustering of human labor to enlarge and refine China's ancient engineering enterprises.

In irrigation the new dimension is mechanization. Old China utilized the giant wheels turned by the streams from which they lifted water up to 60 feet to supply flumes. Low lifting of water frequently was by foot-powered treadle pumps; small diesel powered centrifugal pumps, often mounted on sampans, began appearing only after World War II. Now such pumping is mechanized and has been the chief stimulant to extending electrification from the cities into the surrounding countryside. On communes not linked into a grid, power is provided by small generators or directly by diesel engines. These are especially important in exploiting the aquifers delineated during the past 28 years, which have become a major source of supplemental irrigation in regions of marginal rainfall. A huge aquifer has been delineated under the Wei River Valley in Shensi. Several very large underground water reservoirs are being exploited on the North China Plain. The one in Honan, presumably recharged from the Yellow River, proved invaluable in winter, spring, and early summer 1977 when the region experienced 203 days of drought. The net result of these efforts has brought water control either by gravity and supplemental pump irrigation or drainage to approximately one-half China's 114 million hectares of cultivated land.

Such improvement of water control has allowed two major changes in Chinese agriculture; shifting north the areas where rice can be grown and improved double-cropping. Especially in North China, this has been combined with field consolidation and planting of windbreaks that reduce problems with the wind deposited loess soil and rapid evaporation of moisture. Where the necessary water to provide 11,000 cubic meters per hectare per crop can be delivered on the North China Plain and South Central Manchuria, rice now is being grown. This allows the Chinese to benefit from the advantages of anaerobic cultivation which releases a larger portion of nutrients locked in the soil, especially in more acidic regions. The model commune that has reclaimed land from the 1938 to 1947 bed of the Yellow River at historically memorable Hua Yuan K'ou reports a yield now of 385 kilos of paddy rice per *mou*, equivalent to 5,775 kilos per hectare. In addition they claim that on most of their land they can harvest, with the benefit of irrigation, 265 kilos of winter wheat per *mou*, equal to 3,975 kilos per hectare, or 58 bushels per acre.

Related to this northward shift of staple grain crops has been much of the plant breeding program. Between 85 and 90 percent of China's annual wheat production is winter wheat grown roughly between the Yangtze River to just beyond the Great Wall—the spring wheat belt reaches further north into Manchuria, Inner Mongolia, and irrigated oases in Central Asia. In addition to seeking disease resistance and dwarfing characteristics, which shift utilization of nutrients from stalk growth to grain production, plant breeders have sought spring wheats with a shorter growing season and winter wheats with greater temperature hardiness. Yields still are modest, especially on the nonirrigated fields, and are variously reported from scattered communes to be ranging from 1,058 kilos per hectare, equal to 15 bushels per acre, up to 2,500 kilos per hectare, or about 36 bushels per acre. Since 1962, China has supplemented its domestic wheat production by importing up to five million tons annually.

It was a pleasure to see some of the fine sorghum and millet varieties developed. A field of Chengchow Green Number One near the Yellow River was expected to yield 300 kilos of millet grain per *mou*, or 4,500 kilos per hectare. A new variety of sweet potato, the *Hung Tsu*, was reported to be yielding 4,500 kilos per irrigated *mou* in 4 months, or about 67 tons per hectare. In Central and South China there is a similar emphasis upon multiple-cropping and breeding rice varieties with a shorter growing season, plus other desirable characteristics. In Hunan

Province, the heart of the immense Yangtze Valley and one of the most fertile regions in China, a special effort has been made because this was the birthplace of the late Chairman Mao Tse-tung. Moreover, the new Chairman, Hua Kuo-feng, made his mark from 1949 to 1972 as the political boss of Hunan. The average yield for the province is reported by officials to total 400 kilos per *mou* from 2 crops, or about 3,000 kilos of paddy rice per hectare per crop.

Fertilizer

Fertilizer has been and remains the greatest single physical input problem for China's agriculture. Conservation and return of nutrients to the soil has been fundamental throughout history to the maintenance of agricultural productivity in China. The best available calculations indicate China may now be returning to the fields better than two million tons of true nitrogen annually, or the equivalent of about ten million tons of ammonium nitrate. The potassium content in human excrement is about 35 percent that of true nitrogen and the phosphorus content roughly 16 percent. Aside from conserving nutrients, night soil has the advantage over chemical fertilizer of not requiring transport over long distances since it is utilized locally and farmers are accustomed to its application.

Yet chemical fertilizers are also needed, and the slowness to develop production capacity illustrates the curious amateurishness that periodically has dominated decisions about agriculture within the *chung yang*, or "central authority," of the Chinese Communist Party and the government of the People's Republic. When the outline of the First Five Year Plan was made public in 1953, providing for the construction of only about 200,000 tons of annual fertilizer production capacity, it was apparent that someone has miscalculated. Evidently, the political leaders, without technical experience themselves, overrated what could be accomplished with mobilization of manpower and simple improvements, reflecting largely the ideas that gained dominance during the years of hibernating in Yenan from 1937 to 1945. It was only after three years of terrible food shortages when, in 1962, the late Liu Shao-ch'i, as Chairman of the government, and his political partner, the tough-minded Teng Hsiao p'ing, as Secretary General of the Party, restored some incentives to farmers that the value of chemical fertilizer was officially acknowledged. Unfortunately, the government chose an unconventional solution that proved a disastrous failure; they would build "backyard" fertilizer plants in each county, utilizing natural gas in the few communities where available and otherwise coal. These appear to have been intended to employ an ammonium carbamate process. Producing nitrogenous fertilizer like urea from coal is a sophisticated chemical engineering task. It proved impractical with the crude equipment and limited skills available in most *hsien*. But by 1966, when this was becoming manifest, China was embroiled in the Great Proletarian Cultural Revolution. It was not until the early 1970s, therefore, that scientists and engineers won full acceptance for their view that China must build modern chemical fertilizer plants, much as is done in the rest of the world. But two decades of time had been largely lost, while China's population continued to grow.

Although for most years in this decade China has imported between 4 and 6 million tons of chemical fertilizer (calculated on a 20 percent nitrogen basis), it is necessarily a small factor. Contracts for building major fertilizer complexes have been negotiated with the French, the British, Japanese, Dutch, and, most recently, the Americans. The largest single contract is with Pullman Kellogg of Houston and their Dutch associates for building eight urea plants each designed to produce half a million tons of fertilizer annually. On a 20 percent nitrogen basis China appears now to be producing annually approximately 30 million tons—ammonium nitrate has 20 percent nitrogen, whereas urea contains about 46 percent nitrogen. Included in this total figure also are limited quantities of phosphate, which the Chinese have been slow to develop, and potash. Most of these plants are located deep in the interior, chiefly near natural gas deposits in West, Northwest, and North China, and Manchuria. Foreign engineers who have worked on construction report several problems. Aside from difficulties of securing parts and tools and the language problem, they have been compelled to contend with local political struggles over whether "red or expert" is best and even with some Chinese technicians who insisted the

"Thought of Mao Tse-tung" would allow them to operate equipment faster than the rated speed.

Once a fertilizer factory is in production, the greatest problem is transportation. The Communists have extended and improved China's rail network, as with the double-tracking of the Pinghan. Road construction into the countryside, however, is rudimentary. While there are more trucks in rural China now than after World War II, most transport still is by animal- and human-drawn cart. Even the limited number of tractors introduced especially in North China for plowing appear to be used at least as much for hauling wagons. This very limited construction of a rural road system is in keeping with the Communist philosophy of emphasizing local self-sufficiency. However, it creates major problems of distribution—some chemical fertilizer plants have had to close down while waiting to move out accumulated production. Experience in Japan, Taiwan, and the Philippines indicates that for intensive multicropping such as China is attempting, annual chemical fertilizer requirements are of the order of 1.5 tons per hectare on a 20 percent nitrogen basis. For China to produce and distribute approximately six times the chemical fertilizer now available will require a technological revolution of major proportions plus a commitment for many years of national resources to agriculture on a scale not in sight.

The chemical fertilizer problem becomes even more acute when exploring options for expanding China's cultivation. Officials now say that 12 percent of the land area is cultivated and use the figures of 106 or 107 million hectares. This writer believes the actual cultivated area is about 114 million hectares. Theoretically, the largest available area for reclamation where rainfall is sufficient is in Southwestern China. Those most knowledgeable about these soils estimate that perhaps up to 20 million hectares could be added to the cultivated area here with massive terracing of mountain slopes and construction of irrigation systems. The second most promising area is in Manchuria where several million additional hectares possibly can be brought under plow. But these soils will require very heavy applications of nitrogen, phosphates, and potash to make them productive even for wet culture rice. While the Chinese aver they will provide an important part of this with pig manure, their present hog population of 260 million is still far short of the announced goal of the 2 billion needed, at the ratio of one for every *mou*, which is still not adequate for supplying the required soil nutrients.

Farmer Motivation

Ironically, restraint upon the Chinese farmers' skills and initiative in service of a political theory creates the greatest handicap crippling agriculture and also offers the new leaders their most available opportunity for expanding production. Time wasted in production teams arguing about whether a family's night soil had been devoted to their private plot or gone to the brigades' fields could be better employed. Peasants are forbidden to leave their production brigade or even travel away from the commune without the permission of the revolutionary committee. Once this is granted, it is still extremely difficult to secure the special ration tickets needed to eat anywhere else. The lethargy observed among production teams in the fields contrasts oddly with the traditional physical vigor of work style in the China of old. While this may partly reflect dietary deficiencies, the national work-to-rule attitude evident also in so many factories that are obviously inefficient and overstaffed now has become a concern of officials at the highest level. It is questionable whether only raising wages in this land of comparatively stable prices will prove an adequate remedy. The tortuous ideological circuses, when everyone condemned first one deposed national leader and then the next for setbacks in agriculture due to entirely different causes, are no longer creditable. even among the cadres. China's leadership has a renewed opportunity to evolve a genuinely scientific and productive method of solving problems in the countryside. Meanwhile, China's best hope of feeding herself even meagerly resides in the traditional skills and wit of her extraordinary farmers.

NOTES

1. The author, a writer and farmer who first began observing Chinese agriculture in 1941, was a correspondent in China during and after World War II. In 1977, he returned to China as a member of the International Dwarf Fruit Tree Association.

2. Although we did not see this, we were informed that in several of the larger cities, including Shanghai and Peking, the sewage system is designed to pump human excrement into the rural areas for distribution.

3. In his classic *Land Utilization in China*, J. Lossing Buck includes a table indicating the role of fecal-borne disease in relation to other selected causes of mortality—the figures are chiefly indicative of conditions in North China and would be different in the south and southwest where malaria and schistosomiasis were much more prevalent.

4. China appears not to have introduced rubber roller rice hullers in substantial numbers. These are manufactured mainly in Japan and their use is spreading rapidly throughout Southeast Asia because they permit recovery of at least another 20 percent of edible grain from the paddy rice, even when the bran is removed.

5. Rural emphasis today is upon inducing every family to raise two pigs annually to capitalize upon table scraps and to produce manure for the fields. Usually the hogs are sold to state agencies; the export of trainloads of live pigs to Hong Kong provides an important part of China's annual earnings of US$1.7 billion from the British Crown Colony. In the regions of China we visited, better boars are being used for breeding. Occasionally, one sees an old type swaybacked Chinese sow with her teats dragging on the ground. These native pigs were prolific and, at the present state of China's development of agricultural science, gradual upbreeding indigenous stock is probably a sounder strategy than replacing them with foreign breeds that offer more efficient feed conversion ratios.

Chickens appear to command a low priority and there is little evidence of either improved egg and meat breeds or a modern feed industry; they are still raised chiefly as scavengers. Ducks, and to a lesser extent geese, have rated attention both in breeding and feeding. Again, they are a valuable export item to Hong Kong where they go live and dried, smoked, salted, or canned to overseas Chinese communities in Southeast Asia. Beef, mutton, and dairy products have been important in China's diet chiefly in the North and Northwest, which has been influenced by the nomadic Mongols and other minorities. Limited quantities are shipped to the cities and a few special herds are maintained there to supply this largely hotel demand. Although China's wastelands offer potential for livestock raising, it is alien to their Han cultural tradition.

6. Chinese in general always have abused their draft animals and fed them miserably, and this was as true in the Old China as in the New. At this production brigade, however, the mares being bred to an ass for producing mules were in splendid flesh and the young colts were quick and healthy.

A Statistical Assessment of China's 1985 Foodgrain Production Targets

Bruce Stone

The principal purpose of the paper is to provide those interested in the study of Chinese agriculture with a range of estimates of outputs and inputs to the foodgrain production process covering the three decades of history of the People's Republic of China. Hence the core of the work is the Appendix and the explanatory section which places that material in some perspective. The estimates in the Appendix are either "official" series, ones that are particularly reliable or particularly well-known, or a combination of the two. Most of the series are original estimates of the cited authors or at least their own compilations based on official material. Notable exceptions are the Tang estimates. Tang's series have been included whether they have been independently developed or adopted from works of other scholars inasmuch as they are part of a recent draft specifically addressing the issues of projected supply and demand for foodgrains in the PRC. Occasionally my own series has been included where works of other scholars predate or have neglected important material bearing on the subject. In general, the aim is not to resolve statistical debates or add yet another set of estimates to those available, but rather to provide the reader with some basic tools to place other articles or opinions on China in some sort of perspective by enabling him to gain a quick impression of (1) whether the author in question is using especially high or especially low statistical values to support his arguments; (2) how wide the range of well-known, reputable, and official estimates actually is for particular categories of data; and (3) other information which might reflect on the strength of arguments being made, or otherwise help guard the reader from coming to misinformed conclusions on the basis of the selected articles or books with which he has come in contact.

In addition to this material, it may be useful to highlight a number of issues that bear upon the significance of the production targets and the likelihood of their fulfillment.

The 1985 Output Targets in the Perspective of China's Structure of Consumption

China has set a foodgrain production target for 1985 of 400 million metric tons (mmt). The goal was already an ambitious one when it was formulated in 1975 prior to two years of output stagnation. Although production recovered impressively in 1978, rising to 295 mmt despite poor weather, the prospects of achieving the full target by 1985 appear slight. Yet there is good reason for believing the goal may not be too far from the mark, so it seems reasonable to investigate what the Chinese might do with the extra grain production, particularly inasmuch as no explicit and comprehensive official statements about planned grain use have been made.

Most of China's domestic production is currently devoted to direct consumption by the world's largest population. However, one should not be unduly alarmed to note that average foodgrain consumption per capita in contemporary China seems to exceed prewar levels by fairly small margins.

First of all, although prewar estimates are not too reliable,[1] the average foodgrain consumption was already high in the 1930s, and today China ranks above almost all other countries in this respect (see Chart A, page   ).

Second, China's population has roughly doubled since that time. It is thus a considerable achievement that China's foodgrain production has more than kept pace with the rapid population growth rate of the past quarter-century. Population growth now appears to be coming under better control, and the percentage of total grain production going for direct consumption appears to be declining. This could mean that future increases in foodgrain production would not all be needed for direct human consumption.

Third, the distribution of income and of available foodgrain supplies is considerably more equitable than in the prewar period, and is now one of the most egalitarian in the developing world.[2] The variety of foodstuffs consumed by middle income brackets in many areas may be more restricted than for good years in the prewar era, but this does not negate the Chinese government's accomplishment in meeting their guarantees of minimum allocations of oils, cloth, shelter, basic medical treatment, and rudimentary education for all, along with providing generally ample quantities of foodgrains and vegetables.[3]

Although harvest fluctuations remain a problem throughout China, extreme losses, especially those resulting in famine, are no longer a threat. Moreover, a variety of redistributive policies, infrastructure development, and other activities assist backward provinces and localities to maintain subsistence and insure all areas against extreme harvest loss.[4] A fundamental policy in this regard is the government's guarantee to each citizen of a subsistence ration of several different commodities, including foodgrains. The average grain ration had been increased to 165.6 kilograms per year by 1957 and was probably raised subsequently.[5] Although we should take care not to overemphasize the egalitarian nature of Chinese society and the redistributive impact of government policies, the high average level of grain consumption in China and the ample rationing program indicate that a relatively small increase in aggregate supply, perhaps as little as 10 mmt, would be required to meet unsatisfied demand for direct consumption of grain among poorer citizens.

The same cannot be said for many other food items, however. Of the 105 mmt increase over current output necessary to achieve China's ambitious 1985 foodgrain production target of 400 mmt, about 20-25 mmt will be required to keep pace with population growth. If, indeed, around 10 mmt or less is used to improve direct consumption levels, and 10-15 mmt is slated to build stocks (currently estimated at around 50 mmt)[6] then over half the 105 mmt targeted increase would still be available for other uses. A large portion of this remainder, if achieved, would be devoted to improvements in diet quality.

Reports of pent-up demand for animal products, fruits, oils, and a greater variety of vegetables, together with public pledges by party and government officials to pursue policies to meet that demand,[7] are entirely consistent with the relatively low proportion of nonfoodgrains in the current diet, the apparent increase in per capita income in both rural and urban areas, recent policy changes which will further raise money income,[8] and the high income elasticities of demand for livestock products, sugar, fats and oils, and fruits and vegetables observed elsewhere in the developing world.[9] The most important food in this respect is undoubtedly pork. The Chinese have focused on increasing the pig population in view of its relatively short maturation time, its omnivorous and hence less immediately competitive consumption habits, its importance in traditional Chinese diets, and its relative efficiency as a fertilizer producer. Further, recent Chinese policy is moving away from grain-saving techniques in hog raising.[10] If the entire nutritional requirements of the Chinese hog stock were supplied by grains and millings, it would necessitate the allocation of 80 mmt. This, of course, will not occur but current policies could add over 100 million pigs to the 1977 stocks by 1985. This could easily necessitate an extra 30 mmt, due to planned development of suburban hog farms requiring concentrated use of feedgrains[11] and a slight upward drift in the unusually low fine feed consumption rates among private and collective pigs.

One might suppose that greater numbers of oxen, cattle, horses, mules, and so forth might similarly present a claim on future increases in grain production. But the large animal population has registered little growth since the mid-1950s, and the central authorities are evidently neither expecting nor encouraging the expansion of large livestock in China's current farming regions. The government is considering a program of cattle herd development in the sparsely populated and generally uncultivated areas of the north and west, but it is hoped that suitable feedgrasses can be adapted and grown extensively in those areas, thus avoiding additional grain demand.[12]

China's participation in international grain markets is expanding and rice exports will probably grow slowly, helping to offset the foreign exchange costs of the recently increased grain import bill. But even the current imports of around ten million metric tons per year will not significantly alter per capita consumption. Rather, they should be seen as part of a coordinated program of investment in peasant incentives allowing more grain to be left in rural areas for private and collective livestock feeding, while easing bottlenecks in transport facilities, increasing urban reserves, and supplying the new suburban pig farms.

In order to achieve the 1985 foodgrain production target, output must grow at a rate of 4.5 percent per year for the next 7 years, a level not only exceeding that of any period in the history of the People's Republic but also one which has rarely been achieved by any major producer for such a sustained period of time.[13]

While this ambitious target gives rise to justifiable skepticism, both technical developments and recent policy changes could make it possible for China to better its average growth rate in foodgrain output—around 2.5 percent per year from 1952-1978. To do so would involve one or more of the following: a radical increase in the rate of application of key production inputs; a significant improvement in the quality of these inputs; a major change in the efficiency of allocation or manner of combining these inputs; and technical innovations capable of effecting

significant production increases. Although problems persist, there is convincing evidence that China is in a favorable position to improve its performance in each of these categories of change.

Quantity and Quality of Agricultural Production Inputs

A cursory glance through the Appendix will yield a strong impression of long-term trend increase in the application of industrial inputs to agriculture. However, that this effort has resulted in a relatively modest average growth rate over the past two and a half decades, culminating in an alarming stall in foodgrain output expansion in 1976 and 1977, does not justify a pessimistic view of output prospects over the immediate future. China's experiment with the modernization of its farm sector did not really begin until 1962,[14] after the severe natural calamities of 1960 and 1961 and policies associated with the Great Leap Forward had combined to produce some of the worst nationwide agricultural failures in Chinese history. Before that time, a development strategy emphasizing concentration of resources on the expansion of industrial producers' goods, a central focus of attention on national security, and preoccupation with organizational reform in both farm and industrial sectors coalesced to give a low priority to agriculture's transformation.

Even after 1962, central investment allocations to develop rural infrastructure—an important constraint—were still inadequate to the task of achieving high and sustained growth. But the application of industrial inputs to agriculture—farm machinery, fertilizer, pesticides, and so forth—began expanding at a rapid rate and resulted in impressive foodgrain output growth (over 52% per year) through 1967. The Cultural Revolution brought on a decline in output, despite average weather conditions, owing to the competition of political activities with farming tasks in many rural areas and the adverse impact on the growth rate in the application of inputs caused by work slowdowns in the industrial sector.

The scenario was repeated in the 1970s. A rededication to agriculture followed the Cultural

Revolution, resulting in an average growth rate in agricultural production of close to 4 percent per year (including the poor weather year of 1972). This lasted until industrial slowdowns during the Gang of Four period caused another stall in the growth rate of industrial inputs to agriculture. Combined with poor weather and rural unrest, this brought aggregate agricultural output growth to a halt.

In 1977, China again embarked on a recommitment to agriculture, calling for accelerated production and delivery of industrial inputs at growth rates exceeding average levels over 1962-1977 and far exceeding those achieved during the Gang of Four period.[15] Following the advent of the new policy, output grew by 3.5 percent in 1978 despite poor weather. The new program pledges annual investment in agriculture in quantities equal to the sum for the previous 28 years of PRC history.[16] It also twists the sales prices of industrial inputs to agriculture and purchase prices of farm goods in a manner benefiting the rural sector as never before.[17]

Improvement in the quality of production inputs is also a major plank of the new agricultural policy. Large discrepancies exist between reconstructed official figures for "tractors produced" and "tractors in use." This indicates either that large numbers of tractors are being produced but not purchased by local production teams, brigades, and communes, or that there is a very high rate of mechanical and repair failure, or both. Forty percent of installed tubewells are evidently inoperative, and irrigation dams have shown a high rate of collapse.[18] The current shift away from small- and medium-sized domestic fertilizer plants toward new centralized plants constructed by American, European, and Japanese corporations will raise the nutrient content and reduce the volatility of this production input. That existing production inputs have apparently been functioning well below capacity has often eluded analysts who then underestimate the past, and hence future productive impact of inputs that function satisfactorily. Improvement in this area could significantly affect agricultural production growth rates. Thus, the commitment by central authorities to provide better repair and maintenance services, and improve input quality,

may be a source of better than average growth in foodgrain output.

Farm Labor Incentives

Three kinds of recent central policy changes should raise farm labor incentives and hence contribute to a higher effective labor input in rural areas. One is embodied in the government's greater concentration upon the agricultural sector in terms of administrative priorities and central budget allocations for agricultural infrastructure and investment in industries with strong demand linkages to agriculture. These will tend to raise the long-term rewards available to peasants for applying extra effort to agricultural development.

A second category includes such measures as (1) the 20 percent increase in government purchase price of within-quota grain; (2) the additional 50 percent price increase for delivery of surplus grain; (3) the decision not to raise the quotas of grain that must be delivered at the lower, within-quota price; (4) the 10 to 15 percent decrease in the sales price of industrial inputs to agriculture;[19] (5) encouragement of rural fairs for the inter-rural exchange and sale of produce from private plots and sideline production.[20] These changes will raise the immediate rewards to extra productive effort in the rural sector.

A final approach is embodied in the government and party repudiation of "commandism"— a dictatorial tendency that often leads to the application of production team labor and savings, without team approval, to projects that benefit larger organizational units, or are otherwise unpopular. Commandism of course not only alienates peasants from expropriating and dictatorial authorities, but results in labor productivity declines as well. Repudiation of commandism should tend to reverse that decline as should the other incentive measures. But these policies are not without potential drawbacks.

Resource Allocation Within and Among Collectives and Income Distribution among Productive Units

Within collective units these drawbacks may not prove serious. In fact, recent changes in relative prices could improve the efficiency of resource allocation within collective units. Previously the purchase price of private and sideline products has been high relative to foodgrains. The amount of land sown to foodgrain is officially determined and virtually impossible to divert to other uses. But the price differential created an incentive for both the individual and the fairly successful collective unit to concentrate variable inputs like labor and fertilizer on nonfoodgrain production. This price structure resulted in a relatively land-abundant, capital-scarce production system for foodgrains. The recent price changes may be sufficient to affect allocational decisions at the margin, however. If individuals and collectives shift variable inputs from other farm production to foodgrains, this could have a fairly significant impact on grain production.

Rural fairs previously operated as an outlet for the sale of private plot sideline produce at prices frequently exceeding those offered by the state. Falling prices for sideline produce and increased opportunity to sell surplus foodgrains at the fairs should redress this imbalance, however. A survey of 206 such markets showed that total sales in the last quarter of 1978 increased 30 percent over the corresponding 1977 period and that prices of the 10 principal product groups had declined by 7.3 percent.[21] The closing of price differentials between the state purchasing organs and the rural fairs and a more generally competitive purchase price for grain may also be sufficient to neutralize the potential adverse impact on grain production caused by greater peasant autonomy over their private plots.[22]

The impact of the price changes on resource allocation among collective units is less clear. Quite possibly these changes will not produce the most efficient allocation of resources and could widen income differentials among collective units. In raising the grain purchase prices and lowering prices of industrial inputs, the state obviously wanted to encourage collective units to acquire the necessary inputs. But is this tactic an efficient one?

With respect to fertilizer, for example, Narain demonstrates for Indian agriculture that the price level is in general a rather ineffective policy instrument; fertilizer becomes a very profitable investment, fairly irrespective of price, only when all other yield-increasing conditions have been met for the adoption of an improved seed technology.[23] Despite a low production response rate where other inputs are missing, Wiens cites cases for China in which some additional purchases have been made when fertilizer prices are low, regardless of the relatively poor yield effects.[24]

The price twist seems justified in view of the frequent cases of production units in which output has increased, but income has fallen.[25] But there are at least two adverse results of addressing the problem in this fashion. Two broad categories of localities will be able to purchase extra industrial inputs: (1) those which have recently resolved other growth constraints and for which the yield impact will be large; and (2) those which have previously been successful at raising production or have generated additional cash income in some other way but have recently run into new constraints limiting growth beyond their current production level and are experiencing sharply diminishing marginal effects of additional fertilizer applications. The first group, which did not need the price twist to begin with, will receive a large windfall income from their success, further exacerbating income differentials among localities. The second group will be able to continue applying some extra fertilizer without experiencing income loss, but the scarce input will be inefficiently allocated. There remains another category of localities, in addition to the first category, for which the incremental yield effect of additional fertilizer may be reasonably great.

This group of relatively poor localities has a long history of slow growth. Some fundamental constraints to growth for this category may be a deficiency in rural infrastructure and organizational support, or the lack of an improved seed technology suitably adapted to local conditions. These areas are strongly subsistence-oriented and state purchase prices have not appreciably increased cash income because quotas, of necessity, are set at very low levels and little surplus is produced. Grain, for the most part, is eaten or paid as tax, not sold to the state; hence, purchase price increases have a much smaller impact.

While this group of rather impoverished localities probably cannot currently use extensive additional applications of fertilizer efficiently, relatively modest additional allocations may here have a greater productive impact than elsewhere, and would serve to raise yields in the very poorest localities. Yet, the constraint limiting rapid expansion in output is not merely a lack of fertilizer, but a more general discrimination by central authorities against poor areas with respect to the sheer physical allocation of scarce inputs, skilled manpower, and investment in developing infrastructure (e.g., transport, water control, and hydroelectric power facilities). Owing to this more general constraint, and because these peasants are too cash poor or too risk averse to purchase or produce fertilizer, the most needy areas may not be disposed to undertake even modest increases in fertilizer application although it would result in respectable if not spectacular increases in output. A program favoring price incentives over local infrastructural or organizational work therefore discriminates against the development of such areas. The redistributive policies of the state have aided backward and calamity stricken areas to maintain subsistence, but have been less effective in redressing fundamental self-perpetuating differences in income and welfare.

The large planned increases in centrally allocated investment in rural infrastructure have the potential of resolving this difficulty, but there are two possible snags: (1) there is likely to be little impact of these major allocational increases in the current planning period; (2) it is not clear whether the distribution of allocations will emphasize backward areas or again concentrate on more successful regions. Without compensatory allocations of capital and skilled manpower from the state, "commandism," now in disrepute, may represent the only means of relieving constraints to increased production in backward areas that require investments of size and duration too great for a production team to handle.

Prospects for Technological Progress

Recent policy changes may have a favorable impact upon output by increasing the growth rate of input applications, improving the quality of inputs, and improving the allocation of resources within the collective. They will also clearly widen income disparities among collectives, at least within the current plan period. In the past, this has often resulted in political disturbances which stall growth. Whatever the theoretical and political dialectics of periods such as the Cultural Revolution and the "Gang of Four" crisis, it is clear that the popular response resulting in reduced labor inputs is principally concerned with distributional issues. The policies may also lead to further deterioration in the efficiency of resource allocations among collectives brought about by excessive concentration on areas that are already doing well, but are currently encountering steeply rising marginal costs. However, this depends upon the exact nature of technology that will be used to increase production.

Fortunately, the outlook in this area is bright since China appears to be on the brink of a breakthrough in rice production, although current yields are already high by world standards.[26] China's natively developed male sterile F1 rice hybrid was grown successfully in 1977 and 1978 on 5 percent and 15 percent of China's rice acreage.[27] In 1977, it yielded about 20 to 30 percent more than conventional dwarf rice hybrids. Normally, the seed propagation process for such a strain requires hand-pollination and gives low seed sets. But the F1 hybrid is a variety requiring only 7.5 to 15 kilograms of seed per hectare, offsetting the low seed yield.[28] Wiens suggests that replacement of the current F1 hybrids with a cross with IRRI varieties of equal or better yield could add 2 percent or more to yields while saving labor. Furthermore, China is now actively participating in seed institute exchanges and will be exposed to a wider range of genetic variation, with auspicious potential for increased disease and pest resistance and decreased need for chemical insecticide and fungicide application. Finally, China has evolved a "streamlined" system permitting simultaneous stabilization, selection for local adaptability, evaluation and seed multiplication, all within about three or four years rather than the more customary eight to ten. Hence as yet undiscovered, seed-related technological developments could further raise yields, even with the current economic plan. The F1 hybrid may noticeably augment aggregate yields as early as this year and is well suited to localities with histories of successful well-integrated development. Thus policy concentration on these areas may in fact be advantageous to output growth.

Improvement of average wheat yields progressed rapidly from 1973-1977 throughout the main winter-wheat producing provinces due to proliferation of high-yielding semidwarf varieties,[30] but further progress in average wheat yields is dependent upon the status of the water control projects on the North China Plain. A few of these projects may actually have some impact within the current Plan period, but organization for rapid output expansion by 1985 would require

regions without a strong history of experience in technical transformation to do a variety of things correctly, simultaneously, and immediately—an unlikely achievement.

In summary, although the foodgrain targets for 1985 are probably too ambitious to be achieved, technical developments and policy changes point to higher than average growth over the next 7 years culminating somewhere between 350 and 380 mmt. Periods of temporary stagnation, however, cannot be ruled out, owing to the probably unavoidable prospect of future administrative failures and political unrest fueled by at least a short-term deterioration in income distribution.

NOTES

1. T.C. Liu and K.C. Yeh, *Economy of the Chinese Mainland* (Princeton: Princeton University Press), 1965; T.B.Wiens, "Agricultural Statistics in the PRC" in A. Eckstein (ed.), *Quantitative Measures of China's Economic Output* (Ann Arbor: University of Michigan Press), forthcoming, first presented as a draft in 1975.

2. C.R.Roll, "Incentives and Motivation in China" (a paper prepared for presentation at the American Economics Association Meeting, December 28, 1975), p. 36.

3. T.B.Wiens, "The Economics of Municipal Vegetable Supply in the PRC" (paper prepared for the Vegetable Farming Systems Delegation, National Academy of Sciences, *Vegetable Farming Systems in the PRC*, December 1977).

4. N. Lardy, *Economic Growth and Distribution in China* (Cambridge: Cambridge University Press), 1978.

5. Chu Ching-chih in *Liang-shih* (August 2, 1957) and *Hsin-hua Pan-yueh-K'an* (October 27, 1959) cited in D.H. Perkins, *Market Control and Planning in Communist China* (Cambridge: Harvard University Press), 1966, p. 187.

6. National stocks in the early 1970s were at 40 mmt with long-range target of 80 mmt. Vice Premier Li Hsien-nien cited in S. Ishikawa, "China's Food and Agriculture" in *Food Policy* 2:2 (May 1977), p. 90.

7. E.G., Chou En-lai's statement (1971) to the Japanese delegation reported in Nogyo to Keizai, 38:4 (March 1972), p. 20, cited in Ishikawa, *op. cit.*, p. 95; see also more recent statements by Chairman Hua Kuo-feng.

8. C. Howe, "Labor Organization and Incentives in Industry" in Stuart Schram (ed.), *Authority, Participation and Cultural Change in China* (Cambridge: Cambridge University Press, 1974), pp. 233-235. Schram,

"China's Price Stability: Its Meaning and Distributive Consequences" (unpublished paper, 1976). A. Eckstein, "The Chinese Development Model," in Joint Economic Committee of the U.S. Congress, *Chinese Economy Post-Mao*, Vol. 1 (Washington: GPO, 1978). Communiqué of the Third Plenary Session of the 11th Central Committee of the Communist Party of China," adopted December 22, 1978, in *Peking Review*, 21:52 (December 29, 1978), p. 13.

9. FAO figures cited in J.W. Mellor, *The Economics of Agricultural Development* (Ithaca: Cornell University Press), 1966, p. 66.

10. T.B.Wiens, "Animal Husbandry in the PRC" (unpublished paper), August 1978, and D. Stolte (U.S. Feedgrains Council Pres.) at news conference (March 30, 1979) following U.S. Agricultural Trade Mission to PRC.

11. "Mechanized Pig and Chicken Farms," *Peking Review*, 21:42 (October 20, 1978), p. 30; G. Gunset, "China's Grain Push Could Alter Markets" in *Chicago Tribune* (February 8, 1979).

12. D. Stolte, *op. cit.*

13. Robert F. Dernberger and David Fasenfast, "China's Post-Mao Economic Future," in JEC, *op. cit.*, pp. 3-47. International Food Policy Research Institute, *Food Needs of Developing Countries: Projections of Production and Consumption to 1990*, Research Report #3, December 1977, pp. 137-146.

14. "Communiqué of the 10th Plenary Session of the 8th Central Committee of the CCP" cited in B. Stavis, "Making Green Revolution" (Ithaca: Rural Development Committee, Cornell University), 1974, p. 95.

15. See Appendix and "Farm Mechanization Targets for 1980" in *Peking Review*, 21:8 (February 24, 1978), p. 10.

16. A. Tang, "Food and Agriculture in China: Trends and Projections," (unpublished draft presented at the Inter-

national Food Policy Research Institute, December 1978), p. 24.

17. "Communiquē of the 3rd Plenary Session of the 11th Central Committee of the CCP" in *Peking Review*, 21:52 (December 29, 1978), pp. 6-16.

18. Foreign Broadcast Information Service, May 4, 1978, p. K1. See also T.B. Wiens, "The Evolution of Policy and Capabilities in China's Agricultural Technology" in *JEC, op. cit.*, p. 689.

19. See note 17.

20. "Rural Fairs" in *Beijing Review*, 22:12 (March 23, 1979), p. 8.

21. *Ibid.*

22. D. Bonavia, "A Revolution in the Communes" in *Far Eastern Economic Review*, 103:13 (March 30, 1979), pp. 8-9.

23. Dharm Narain, "Growth of Productivity in Indian Agriculture," Technological Change in Agriculture Project, Cornell University Department of Agricultural Economics, Occasional Paper No. 93 (June 1976).

24. Unpublished presentation by Li Ching-hsiung, maize breeder from the Chinese Academy of Agriculture and Forestry Sciences, to CIMMYT staff (August 26, 1977) cited in T.B. Wiens, "China's Agricultural Targets" in *Contemporary China* (1978), p. 8.

25. Ishikawa, *op. cit.*, p. 100.

26. For further discussion see Wiens, *ibid.*, and Wiens, "The Evolution of Policy," *op. cit.*

27. FBIS (March 24, 1978), p. E19.

28. *Peking Review*, 21:9 (March 3, 1978), p. 30.

29. Wiens, "The Evolution of Policy," *op. cit.*, p. 677.

30. FBIS, February 10, 1978, p. E10; February 24, 1978, p. J3; BBC, SWB, January 25, 1978, p. A6; and Wiens, "The Evolution of Policy," *op. cit.*, p. 672.

Chart A
International Cross-Section Relationship Between Per Capita Grain Consumption[a]
Per Year and Per Capita Calorie Intake Per Day of All Food

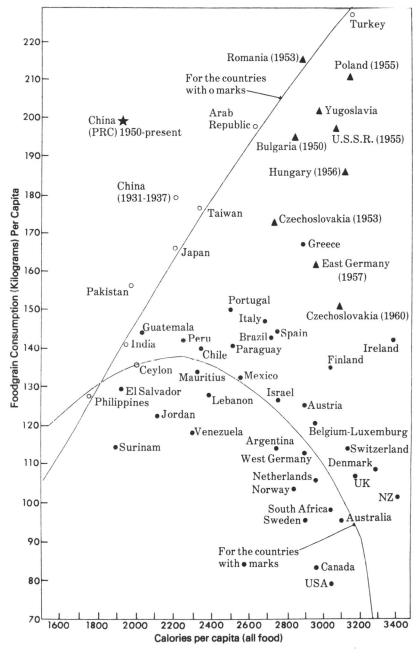

a. The figures for per capita foodgrain consumption are calculated as the sum of the weight of processed foodgrains and one-quarter of the weight of tubers.

Source: S. Ishikawa, "China's Food and Agriculture: A Turning Point: in *Food Policy*, Vol. 2, #3 (May 1977), p. 93. Ishikawa used data for the socialist countries for the dates indicates; where the date is not given, figures are taken from the FAO Production Yearbook for 1965. PRC has been added to indicate the general position of the People's Republic of China (1950 to present).

Table 1

Total Population and Annual Rates of Increase, 1949-2000 (projected) (millions)[a]

	OFFICIAL		AIRD[b]		U.N. (Adjusted)		ORLEANS	
	Total	Growth Rate	Total	Growth Rate	Total	Growth Rate	Total	Growth Rate
1949	542				529	2.0		
1950	552	1.8			540	2.0		
1951	563	2.0			551	2.0		
1952	575	2.1			562	2.0		
1953	587	2.1	583		573	2.0		
1954	602	2.6	596	2.2	584	2.1	588	
1955	615	2.2	610	2.3	597	2.1	600	2.0
1956	628	2.1	625/626	2.3/2.6	609	2.1	613	2.2
1957	657	4.6	639/641	2.4	622	2.1	626	2.1
1958			654/657	2.3/2.5	635	2.0	638	1.9
1959			667/672	2.0/2.3	647	1.8	651	2.0
1960			680/686	1.9/2.1	658	1.7	663	1.8
1961			692/696	1.8/1.4	669	1.7	674	1.7
1962			705/708	1.9/1.7	681	1.8	686	1.8
1963	(680/690)		720/723	2.1	694	1.8	698	1.7
1964			734/740	1.9/2.4	706	1.7	710	1.7
1965			749/758	2.0/2.4	718	1.7	723	1.8
1966	(700)		765/776	2.1/2.4	730	1.6	736	1.8
1967			781/795	2.1/2.4	742	1.6	749	1.8
1968			798/815	2.2/2.5	754	1.5	762	1.7
1969			816/836	2.2/2.6	765	1.5	774	1.6
1970			834/858	2.2/2.6	776	1.4	788	1.8
1971	(750/830)		852/880	2.2/2.6	787	1.4	800	1.5
1972			869/902	2.0/2.5	798	1.3	813	1.6
1973			885/924	1.8/2.4	808	1.2	825	1.5
1974			900/946	1.7/2.4	817	1.1	838	1.6
1975	(800)		915/968	1.7/2.3	826	1.1	850	1.4
1976			930/991	1.6/2.4	835		863	1.5
1977			947/1014	1.8/2.3			875	1.4
1978			964/1039	1.8/2.5			887	1.4
1979			980/1062	1.6/2.2			899	1.4
1980			994/1084	1.4/2.1			911	1.3
1985			1058/1177	1.3/1.7				
1990			1119/1265	1.1/1.5				
1995			1186/1368	1.2/1.6				
2000			1255/1488	1.1/1.7				

a. All estimates rounded and given at mid-year.
b. Aird gives low, intermediate, and high estimates, of which

Table 1

Population

Population statistics for the People's Republic of China involve greater discrepancies than most other economic indicators. It is now widely believed that the Chinese themselves have had no source of information that they feel is genuinely reliable, though greater efforts are evidently being made at present to develop better statistical machinery. Officially published statistics for the 1950s depend heavily upon a single national census conducted over a 24-hour period in 1953 and occupying upward of a million workers. Since then scattered official statements refer to rounded figures of a very general and, many believe, increasingly inaccurate, nature.

John Aird of the United States Department of Commerce has pursued independent estimates of the Chinese population more intensively and extensively than any other individual or group. Leo Orleans of the U.S. Library of Congress provides another set of serious estimates based on broadly plausible alternative assumptions. United Nations figures in their raw form include Taiwan, appear subject to some political constraints, and in any event are not as thoroughly documented, especially for recent years. Estimates by the Soviet demographers Konovalov, Petrov, and Molodtsova assume extremely high levels of mortality following the Great Leap Forward, essentially ignore any discussion of China's family planning policies, and show more drastic annual fluctua-tions in the rate of natural increases than is common in the West. There is, moreover, some confusion over an appropriate series for the Soviet demographer Konovalov. A series reconstructed by Suzanne Paine and ostensibly including Taiwan is actually lower from 1968 onward than another Konovalov series apparently excluding Taiwan, published in the same year and cited by Orleans. These estimates, and those of Petrov and Molodtsova, have been omitted from the table since they appear to be less persuasively documented than those of Aird and Orleans, and less well known than the UN series. From 1965 onward the Konovalov/Paine series assumes net population growth rates which are lower than those the Chinese do not officially expect to achieve until 1985. This result is apparently produced by comparing population data for the 1950s, which are substantially higher than any Western estimates, with the relatively low official figure of 800 million for the mid 1970s. In the aggregate, the other two Soviet series conform fairly closely to one or another of the Western estimates, but the disaggregated birth and mortality rates diverge quite sharply.

All sources agree on rising population growth rates at least through the middle 1950s, decline due to decreased fertility during the agricultural failures of the early 1960s, at least a partial recovery by the mid-1960s, followed by a gradual decline to the present. According to the more conservative and more scholarly works of Aird and Orleans, the official goal of one percent per year by 1985 is ambitious, but not a radical distortion of what appears possible.

Table 1 References

Official. For 1949-1957 see Chen Nai-Ruenn, *Chinese Economic Statistics*, Chicago: Aldine, 1957.
For 1963, 1966, 1970-71, and 1975, government estimates not generally accepted by Western scholars are cited in Suzanna Paine, "Development with Growth: A Quarter Century of Socialist Transition in China," in *Economic and Political Weekly*, Special Number (August 1976), pp. 1349-78.

John S. Aird, "Population Growth in the People's Republic of China," Joint Economic Committee of the Congress, *Chinese Economy Post-Mao*, Vol. 1, Washington: GPO, 1978, p. 465.
United Nations Population Division (adjusted to exclude Taiwan), cited in Paine, *op. cit.*
Leo A. Orleans, "China's Population: Can the Contradictions be Resolved?" Joint Economic Committee of the Congress, *China: A Reassessment of the Economy*, Washington: GPO, 1975.

Table 2

Total Foodgrains Production,[a] 1949-1978
(million metric tons)

| | OFFICIAL | | | USDA | | CIA | | FIELD & KILPATRICK | | SWAMY & BURKI | | ISHIKAWA |
	Total with soybeans	Total without soybeans	Growth Rate	Total	Growth Rate	Total	Growth Rate	Total	Growth Rate	Total	Growth Rate	Total
1949	113	108				108		111				
1950	132	125	16.8/15.7			125	15.7	130	17.1			
1951		135	8.0			135	8.0	141	8.5			
1952	164	154	14.1			154	14.1	161	14.2			164
1953	167	157	1.8/1.9			157	1.9	164	1.9			
1954	170	160	1.8/1.9			160	1.9	166	1.2			
1955	184	175	8.2/9.3	175		175	9.4	180	8.4	175		
1956	193	182	4.9/4.0	182	4.0	182	4.0	188	4.4	183	4.6	193
1957	195	185	1.0/1.6	185	2.2	185	2.2	191	1.6	186	1.6	
1958	(260)[b]	(250)[b]	?	200	8.1	200	8.1	206	7.9	215	15.6	
1959	(282)[b]	(270)[b]	?	165	-17.5	165	-17.5	171	-17.0	193	-10.2	
1960	150		?	150	-9.1	160	-4.0	156	-8.8	161	-16.6	
1961	160		6.7	162	8.0	160	0.0	168	7.7	189	17.4	
1962	170		6.3	174	7.4	180	12.5	180	7.1	204	7.9	
1963	183		7.6	183	5.2	185	2.8	190	5.6	219	7.4	
1964	195	2.6	6.6	200	9.3	195	5.4	194	2.1	238	8.7	
1965	200		2.6	200	0.0	210	7.7	194	0.0	240/258	0.8/8.4	208
1966	220		10.0	215	7.5	215	2.4	215	10.8	220	14.7/-8.3	
1967	230		4.5	230	7.0	230	7.0	225	4.7	231	5.0	
1968			?	215	-6.5	215	-6.5	210	-6.7		?	
1969			?	220	2.3	220	2.3	215	2.4	230	?	
1970	243		?	240	9.1	240	9.1	243	13.0	240	4.3	
1971	246		1.2	246	2.5	246	2.5	246	1.2	246	2.5	
1972	240		2.4	240	-2.4	240	-2.4	240	-2.4	240	-2.4	
1973	257		7.1	250	4.2	250	4.2	266	10.8	250	4.2	
1974	275		7.0	265	6.0	255	2.0	275	3.4			260/275
1975	285		3.6	270	1.9	284	11.4	284	3.3			
1976	285		0.0	272	0.7	285	0.4	285	0.4			
1977	286		.4	270	0.7	286	0.4	285	0.0			
1978	295		3.1			295	3.1					

a. Foodgrains include rice, wheat, coarse grains, soybeans and tubers (normally assumed to be valued at 1/4 natural weight). The "official" series probably values them at 1/5 natural weight from 1965 on. The Field and Kilpatrick series values them at 1/5 weight throughout. Some of the series (e.g., at least portions of the USDA and CIA series) exclude soybean production of 5-10 mmt. Coarse grains include: millet, corn kaoliang, barley, buckwheat, mung beans, oats, proso-millet, small beans, green beans, broad beans, peas and others. Soybeans include: green, yellow, and black soybeans (often called black beans).
b. Generally regarded as unreliable estimates.

Table 2

Foodgrain Production (Paddy rice, wheat, coarse grains, soybeans, and tubers)

The "official" series is a combination of figures taken verbatim from officially published materials and the estimates of scholars based on published growth rates for various periods. The numbers in this series have come to be accepted, within a few million metric tons, by most Western scholars who use "official" figures. Exceptions to this statement are 1974 and 1976, for which the total range of contemporary "official" estimates exceeds 5-6 million metric tons, and the recent effort by Field and Kilpatrick, who have attempted to recalculate a consistent "official" series on the basis of recent and still somewhat ambiguous information regarding the exact years in which soybeans were included in "official" foodgrains figures and in which potatoes were valued at one-fifth rather than one-fourth their natural weight in these statistics. U.S. Department of Agriculture and the Central Intelligence Agency have regularly produced independent estimates less critically dependent upon literal implications of official statements. Over time, however, and with the clear exception of 1958 and 1959, these agencies have come to accept figures increasingly close to "official" ones. The most recent (1978) CIA estimates use Field and Kilpatrick's effort which is essentially an "official" series, and it would not be surprising to find that the USDA will eventually reconcile its estimates for the mid-1970s with those given as "official."

The core of the Swamy and Burki series is from figures through 1965 given to a Pakistani delegation to the PRC. They are substantially higher than all other estimates for 1958-1965, except for 1960 and the "official" figures for 1958 and 1959. Most Western scholars have come to disregard these figures and Swamy himself seems to repudiate them implicitly in his more recent works. The 1958 and 1959 figures, however, may be as good as any estimates for those chaotic years.

Ishikawa is probably the most authoritative non-Western, non-Chinese scholar addressing questions of Chinese agriculture. He has performed painstaking resolutions of official statistics based on extensive familiarity with PRC methodology and utilizing complex econometric projections and analyses. He has now almost discontinued the latter, due to a decreasing confidence in their reliability when applied to current and future output, and due to increased confidence in the former approach based on official materials.

All sources imply rising production through 1958 followed by large declines (1959-1961) due to extremely poor weather and the disastrous policies of the Great Leap Forward. A dedication to agriculture and to the technical transformation of that sector in 1962 coincided with recovery and progress through 1967; 1968 and 1969 suffered, in part due to the chaos of the Cultural Revolution, and 1972 also registered a drop, primarily because of poor weather. The period 1975-1977 was essentially stagnant owing again to poor weather, a sharp decline in the growth rate of industrial inputs supplied to agriculture, and to political conflicts related to "commandism" and the "Gang of Four." Otherwise, production has expanded consistently and well in excess of population increases—especially just after each renewal of attention to agriculture by the central authorities in 1962, the early 1970s, and 1977.

Table 2 References

Official. For 1949-1959 see Chen, *op. cit.*, pp. 338-39. Revised for 1957 to conform to *Ten Great Years*.
For 1960-1965 see Chao Kang, *Agricultural Production in Communist China*, Madison: University of Wisconsin Press, 1970, p. 246.
For 1966 and 1967 see Han and Strong, cited in Benedict Stavis, *Making Green Revolution: The Politics of Agricultural Development in China*, Rural Development Monograph #1, Ithaca: Rural Development Committee, Cornell University, 1974, pp. 12-14.
For 1970 see Maxwell Neville, "Recent Chinese Grain Figures," *China Quarterly* #68, December 1976, p. 817.
For 1971-1973 see Thomas B. Wiens, "Agricultural Statistics in the People's Republic of China," in Alexander Eckstein (ed.), *Quantitative Measures of China's Economic Outlook*, Ann Arbor: University of Michigan Press, forthcoming; first presented as a draft in 1975.
For 1974 see Vice Minister of Agriculture Yang Li-Kung's 1975 FAO General Assembly presentation (a lower estimate is given in Chou En-lai's report to the National Congress in January 1975).
For 1975 see R.M. Field and J.A. Kilpatrick, "Chinese Grain Production: An Interpretation of the Data," *China Quarterly* #74, June 1978, p. 373. For 1976-1978, estimates derived from official statements in *Beijing Review*, Vol. 22, #2, January 12, 1979, p. 7 and *Summary of World Broadcasts*, FE Weekly Report #985, June 21, 1978, p. 87.

USDA. Estimated by Economics, Statistics, and Cooperative Service, U.S. Department of Agriculture in *PRC Agricultural Situation*, May 1978, p. 29.

CIA. Estimated by Office of Economic Research, Central Intelligence Agency, "People's Republic of China: Handbook of Economic Indicators," Research Aid: A(ER) 75-72, August 1975. For 1975-1978 the agency accepted figures supplied by J.A. Kilpatrick.

R.M. Field and J.A. Kilpatrick, "Chinese Grain Production," *op. cit.*, have attempted to recalculate a consistent "official" series on the basis of recent information regarding the exact years in which soybeans were included in "official" foodgrains figures and in which potatoes were valued at one-fifth rather than one-fourth of their natural weight in these statistics. Their work, based to some extent on that of other scholars, leads them to conclude that: (1) 1964 was the first year since 1949-1955 that soybeans were included in "offi-

Table 3
Livestock Population, 1949-1977

	OFFICIAL			GROEN & KILPATRICK			WIENS			TANG			FAO/UN		
	Hogs	Large Animals[b]	Sheep & Goats	Hogs	Large Animals[b]	Sheep & Goats	Hogs	Large Animals[b]	Sheep & Goats	Hogs	Large Animals[b]	Sheep & Goats	Hogs	Large Animals[b]	Sheep & Goats
1949	58	60	42	58	60	42	58	60	42						
1950				64	65	47									
1951				74	70	53									
1952	90	76	62	90	76	62	90	76	62	93	78	67			
1953	96	80	72	96	80	72				99	83	77			
1954	102	85	81	102	85	81				95	86	83			
1955	88	87	84	88	87	84				88	87	88			
1956	84	87	92	84	87	92				98	86	94			
1957[a]	115			115	83	99	115	84	99	115	84	99			
1957[a]	146	83	99	128	85	108									
1958	160	85	109							160	85	109			
1959	180	85								136	82	82			
1960										106	80	78			
1961										102	73	78	190	109	116
1962							122	71	113	116	71	100	195	110	118
1963										137	77	97	198	111	120
1964										148	83	104	202	112	121
1965				160			167			168	91	116	206	114	124
1966										183	92	119	210	114	126
1967					85					199	86	131	213	113	126
1968										198	84	119	215	113	126
1969										191	87	123	220	114	128
1970				196						210	88	138	223	114	129
1971				218						231	92	130	226	114	129
1972				248	95	147	260	95	148	260	95	148	231	114	129
1973				242			260			233	98	146	236	114	131
1974				260						253	101	158	234	116	133
1975										268	104	161	233	116	134
1976							280			272	107	162	238	117	135
1977				280		160	290	96	160	274	110	161			

a. In 1957 the official annual date of reference was shifted from July to December 31 (from articles by Huang Mengfan and Liao Hsien-Lao in Chen, p. 63.

b. Includes oxen, buffalo, horses, asses, mules, and camels.

Table 3
Livestock Numbers

The first three series of livestock numbers are based either upon absolute official figures or official statements of growth rates over previous years. Tang's series is a combination of such official statements and a least squares regression analysis of the relationship between the livestock series and a complete series for livestock exports and grain production. The FAO/UN series is of unknown derivation and, at least for most of the 1970s, includes Taiwan.

Hog numbers grew through 1954, then declined due to pricing inconsistencies and a lack of fodder following upon overzealous compulsory grain delivery requirements. Correction of these policy errors led to rapid growth, which was only reversed by more fodder shortages during the agricultural failures of the early 1960s. Growth has continued steadily since then, averaging 3.5 percent per year over the entire 1957-1977 period, and almost 6 percent per year from 1962 through 1977. Only in 1973 did hog numbers drop off, probably due to poor foodgrain production in 1972. Fine feed availability appears to have a lot to do with hog population growth rates, and the high level of the latter suggests that foodgrain production is more than sufficient to accommodate demand for direct human consumption in rural areas.

The populations of large animals, and of sheep and goats, rose more steadily in the 1950s, although the former appears to have suffered somewhat from the fodder shortage following the advent of compulsory grain deliveries in the mid-1950s and from expropriation during the cooperativization and communization movements of the late 1950s. These animal populations declined during the agricultural failures of the early 1960s, but recovered by the mid-1960s and have grown very slowly but more or less steadily since then (though it is possible that they may have stagnated or declined somewhat during the latter years of the Cultural Revolution [1968-69]). Sheep and goats have continued their slow rates of expansion of a few percent a year into the 1970s. Despite increased government interest in pastoral areas, however, these animals seem to be in greater direct competition for grain-producing land than was previously believed. Large animal populations have stagnated recently and may continue to do so. Their role as draft animals is diminishing, their consumption of grain is more directly competitive with that of humans, they mature more slowly, and they are less efficient producers of fertilizer than hogs.

Table 3 References

Official. The figures are all given as absolute magnitudes in official Chinese publications. See Chen, *op. cit.*, p. 340.

H.J. Groen and J.A. Kilpatrick, "China's Agricultural Production," JEC, *op. cit.*, 1978, p. 649. This series is derived from officially quoted figures and the authors' estimates, based on officially published or broadcasted growth rates and other materials.

Anthony Tang, "Food and Agriculture in China: Trends and Projections" (draft), a paper for the International Food Policy Research Institute (1978-79). All data are year-end estimates on available official figures, increments over previous years given in official statements, and least squares regression analysis of the relationship between the livestock series and a complete series for livestock exports and grain production.

From selected FAO Production Yearbooks (1967, 1971, 1974, and 1976). All figures based on fragmentary official information and other qualified nonofficial sources.

Table 2 References Continued

cial" foodgrains figures and that most figures released since then have included them; and (2) potatoes have been included on a grain-equivalent basis of five to one since 1970. More recently, an informed Chinese source has indicated that 1958 and 1963 are in fact the relevant dates respectively, implying that a recomputation is in order.

Subramanian Swamy and Shahid Burki, "Foodgrain Output in the PRC, 1958-65," *China Quarterly*, January-March 1970, p. 62; Swamy, "Economic Growth in China and India, 1952-70," *Economic Development and Cultural Change*, Vol. 21, #4, July 1973, p. 29; and Dwight H. Perkins, "Constraints Influencing China's Agricultural Performance," JEC, *op. cit.*, 1975, cited in Swamy, "The Economic Distance between China and India, 1955-73," a paper presented at Cornell University, November 1, 1975.

Ishikawa Shigeru, "China's Food and Agriculture: A Turning Point," *Food Policy*, Vol. 2, #2, May 1977, p. 2.

Table 4

Foodgrain Production and Per Capita Availability,[a] Selected Years

				WIENS/STONE					FIELD AND		
	(low)	(best)	(high)	(Aird)	(Orleans)	(UN)	(Chou)	DONITHORNE	KILPATRICK	DAWSON	ISHIKAWA[c]
Output (million metric tons)											
1930s	131	149	166						161	175	164
1952		168						154	191	185	193
1957		197		186	186		186	185	194	207	208
1965				200	200	200	200	210			260/275
1974									275		
Population (millions)											
1930s		503									
1952		571						570 575	576	578	570
1957		646		633	627		590	641 647	648	637	631
1965				741	722	694	680	747	763	728	711
1974									934		878/800
Per Capita Availability (kilograms)[b]											
1930s	169	188	213								
1952		190						(168-172) (167-171)	(173-185)	192	185
1957		195		188	190		201	(174-186) (172-184)	(178-196)	191	191-194
1965				(170-183)	(174-188)	(181-195)	(185-199)	177	(160-172)	190	191
1974									(182-192)		192/213

a. Per capita availability of foodgrain calculated as total availability per capita (production plus imports) minus losses due to processing and nonfood uses. Foodgrains as defined in Table 2.

b. Range of per capita availability estimates indicates range in estimate of percentage of total grain supply used for food, and/or of amount of loss due to processing; computed by Stone from author's data.

c. 1957 estimates are for 1956-1959; population and per capita availability figures computed by Stone.

Table 4
Per Capita Foodgrain Consumption

Discrepancies among estimates of per capita foodgrain consumption derive from the authors' choices of statistics for foodgrain production, population, processing loss, percentage of foodgrain used for food and, very occasionally, net foreign trade (which in any event is quite minor). Increases over the levels of the 1930s appear slight, but average annual foodgrain consumption was already quite high by world standards (around 180 kilograms per person); current availability apparently exceeds by a comfortable margin the minimum ration of 165.6 kilograms fixed in 1957.

The Chinese citizens' most immediate need is more meat and a greater variety (not quantity) of vegetables; thus the estimates assume a decline in the percentage of grain used directly for food from 80 percent to 75 percent, and a doubling of average pork consumption from the 1950s to the present. Because the distribution of income is more equitable now than it was in the 1930s, and because availability per capita is higher, a much larger proportion of the population has the option of consuming the average per capita quantity of foodgrains than previously. Further, because of China's policy of imposing compulsory delivery quotas on all regions, grain deficit regions are assured of receiving at least enough grain to supply all their citizens with the minimum subsistence ration. Thus the Chinese people are now protected to a far greater extent against temporal and local fluctuations in foodgrain production which ravaged rural China in prewar years.

Outside China there is a general paucity of information on stockpiling activities within the PRC. We do know that reserves were accumulated in the 1950s and were probably nearly depleted in the early 1960s, by which time net accumulation began again. By the early 1970s Chinese official statements claimed reserves of 40 million metric tons, with a long-range official target of 80 million metric tons. Most probably, national stockpiles have been accumulating over the past 15 years at around 1.5 percent of production per year, and probably now stand at around 50 million metric tons. These figures denote national stockpiles and do not include local or perhaps even provincial reserves. Visitors and refugees attest to reserves at several local levels, while provinces have substantial incentive to maintain reserves in order to avoid the designation of "grain deficit province" and consequent loss of leverage in the competition for nationally allocated production inputs in scarce supply. The full extent of reserve accumulation is probably not accounted for in these estimates of net foodgrain availability for current consumption.

Table 4 References

Thomas B. Wiens, "Agricultural Statistics" in Eckstein, *op. cit.* For 1957 and 1965 Wiens uses four population estimates besides his selected estimate: Aird, Orleans, UN, and Chou.

Audrey Donnithorne, *U.S.-China Business Review*, Vol. 1, #2, March-April 1974, p. 33, and "Per Capita Grain Output in China and India," *Food Policy*, Vol. 2, #1, February 1977, pp. 60-66.

R.M. Field and J.A. Kilpatrick, "Chinese Grain Production," *op. cit.*, pp. 369-384.

Owen L. Dawson, *Communist China's Agriculture*, New York: Praeger, 1970.

Ishikawa Shigeru, "China's Food and Agriculture, *op. cit.*, pp. 90-102, and "Factors Affecting China's Agriculture in the Coming Decade," Tokyo: Institute of Developing Economies, mimeographed, 1967.

Table 5

Daily Calorie Intake per Capita,
Total and Percent Derived from Foodgrains,
Selected Years

	Buck (1929-33)	Shen (1931-37)	Liu & Yeh (1933)	Low Est.	Wiens Best Est. (1930s)	High Est.	Wiens (1952)	Dawson (1952/53)	Wiens (1957)	Dawson (1957)	Dawson (1965)	Groen and Kilpatrick (1977)
Total Calories	2,537	2,226			1,998		2,000	2,187	2,053	2,059	2,064	2,099
Foodgrain[a] Calories	2,362	1,913	2,020	1,613	1,789	2,036	1,802	1,815	1,848	1,709	1,713	1,750
Percent of Total	93.1	85.9			90		90	83	90	83	83	83

a. Foodgrains as defined in Table 2.

Table 5
Daily Caloric Intake

Estimates of the percentage of per capita calorie intake attributable to foodgrains have traditionally been used to derive estimates of total daily per capita calorie intake in China. However, these estimates are highly suspect.

The wide discrepancy among prewar estimates is indicative of the unreliability of any one of the figures included. Unfortunately, the postwar material is, if anything, worse. The foodgrain production figures are undoubtedly more accurate than for the 1930s, but the population figures after the 1950s exhibit a much wider range, and the percentage of calories supplied by foodgrain and nonfoodgrain sources may have no statistical basis at all.

Wiens adopts 90 percent by rounding down Buck's figure for the 1930s. Dawson adopts 83 percent by averaging the prewar figures of 87 percent from Buck and 79 percent from Shen. In arriving at this figure he is clearly ignoring the role of legumes, which are unmistakably included in the Communist definition of coarse grains and hence foodgrains. An average of the two percentages, adjusted for legumes, should yield 88.5 percent. Groen and Kilpatrick present no sources for their data and may simply have adopted Dawson's figure based on his inaccurate compilation of prewar data of probably biased origin.

The apparent drop in total calories consumed from 1952 to 1957 in the Dawson statistics is partly due to his assumption that the percentage of foodgrains in total calories consumed remains constant, and partly due to a bias in the pair of production figures he uses. His 1952 figure is by far the highest estimate for that year, whereas his 1957 figure is the lowest (see Table 4). Dawson's 1965 estimates do not suffer from this bias, but the assumed lack of change in the percentage of foodgrains in total consumption is arbitrary. Groen and Kilpatrick's production figure is probably correct, but they apparently adopt Aird's higher population figures which are at the far upper end of the spectrum of estimates, and their foodgrains percentage may be totally arbitrary.

Without polluting the page with an additional arbitrary estimate, it seems reasonable to conclude that: there is no reliable evidence to indicate complete stagnancy in total calories consumed (1957-1977). In fact, due to slight increases in foodgrains consumed per capita and recent progress in per capita supply of vegetables and pork, there has surely been progress at least during the 1970s; the consistency of the foodgrains percentage in total calories is merely assumed and may be entirely false; the relationship to prewar consumption is really unknown and Dawson's implied decline in total consumption per capita over 1952-1957 is almost certainly incorrect.

Table 5 References

John L. Buck, *Land Utilization in China* (3 Volumes) Nanking: University of Nanking Press, 1937 and Chicago: University of Chicago Press, 1937, Stat. Vol., pp. 407-413.

T.H. Shen, *Agricultural Resources of China*, Ithaca: Cornell University Press, 1951, pp. 378-381.

Ta-Chung Liu and Kung-chia Yeh, *The Economy of the Chinese Mainland*, Princeton: Princeton University Press, 1965, p. 29.

Thomas B. Wiens, "Agricultural Statistics" in Eckstein, *op. cit.*

Owen L. Dawson, *op. cit.*, p. 187.

H.J. Groen and J.A. Kilpatrick, "China's Agricultural Production," JEC, *op. cit.*, 1978.

Table 6

Exports and Imports of Foodgrains,[a] 1949-1977
(millions of metric tons)

	OFFICIAL	USDA		TANG		KIRBY		CIA	
	Foodgrain Exports	Wheat Imports	Rice Exports	Grain Imports	Grain Exports	Grain Imports	Grain Exports	Net Imports[b]	Grain Imports
1949									
1950									
1951									
1952					0.6	0.02	0.3	(0.3)	
1953	1.6				0.8	0.04	0.3	(0.3)	
1954	2.2				0.9	0.02	0.3	(0.3)	
1955	2.2				1.1	0.2	0.6	(0.5)	
1956	2.3				1.2	0.01	1.1	(1.0)	
1957					1.2	0.01	0.5	(0.4)	
1958					1.2	0.2	1.3	(1.1)	
1959					1.2	0.01	1.9	(1.9)	
1960		1.9			1.2	0.03	1.5	(1.4)	
1961		4.9	0.4	6.2	0.4	5.6	0.6	5.0	5.7
1962		4.9	0.6	5.3	0.6	5.1	0.7	4.4	4.5
1963		5.2	0.6	5.7	0.7	5.6	0.9	4.8	5.5
1964		5.0	0.8	6.8	0.7	6.3	1.1	5.2	6.3
1965		6.3	0.8	5.7	0.7	6.0	1.0	5.0	5.9
1966		5.0	1.3	5.6	0.9	5.8	1.5	4.3	5.6
1967		4.2	1.2	4.1	0.7	4.4	1.3	3.0	4.1
1968		3.5	1.0	4.4	0.7	4.4	1.0	3.4	4.4
1969		5.1	0.8	3.9	0.8	4.0	0.8	3.1	3.9
1970		3.7	1.0	4.6	0.9	5.0	1.0	3.9	4.6
1971		3.0	0.9	3.1	0.9	3.1	1.0	2.1	3.0
1972		5.3	0.9	4.6	0.9	4.6	1.0	3.6	4.8
1973		5.6	2.1	7.6	2.1	7.6	2.2	5.4	7.7
1974		5.7	2.0	6.8	2.0	6.8	2.1	4.6	7.0
1975		2.2	1.4	3.5	1.4	3.4	1.6	1.8	3.3
1976		3.1	0.9	2.1	0.9	2.1	1.1	1.0	1.9
1977		9.5	0.7	6.9	0.7	6.9	0.8	6.1	6.9

a. Foodgrains includes soybeans in official series. All other series exclude soybeans.
b. Parenthesis indicates net exports.

Table 6
Exports and Imports of Major Foodgrains

Discrepancies in this series often hinge upon the year under which particular trade contracts are entered. Moreover, the years are not strictly comparable. Kirby's work for the U.S. Department of Agriculture, supplemented by Surls' estimates, are in calendar years. The "official" series and the CIA series also appear to be in calendar years. The USDA series is based on the USDA supply tape, which is in fiscal years with the exception of rice, which is in calendar years. Tang's series is based on a combination of estimates by USDA, the CIA, Eckstein, official sources, and some linear interpolations. It is not immediately clear if Tang's work is entirely in calendar years, or if some fiscal year data are included. The interpolations are an additional source of difference from other series.

The table indicates that China has exported rice for the entire three decades of PRC history. Recent econometric work on China's rice trading shows the international price level as a strong determinant of the quantity exported. Although China imported wheat and other foodgrains in the 1950s, the quantities imported increased substantially in 1961, owing to the agricultural failures of 1960-61. Since then, imports have continued at a high level, ranging from 3.9 - 7.6 million metric tons each year except 1971 and the foreign exchange conservation years of 1975 and 1976. Total grain imports in 1977 amounted to 6.9 million metric tons and 1978 imports may be even greater.

Although China's imports since 1961 must be viewed as large in the context of world grain trade, the grain import policy does not have a particularly significant impact on average availability per capita in China, providing in the neighborhood of 4 kilograms out of about 191 kilograms consumed per capita in 1977. Increases in imports have generally followed, not coincided with, poor harvest years and have more to do with the government's investment in rural incentives, its stockpiling goals, and the easing of domestic transportation bottlenecks than with the adequacy or inadequacy of domestic production.

The total value of China's trade has increased steadily from about $1.2 billion in 1950 to $13.2 billion in 1977, with exports and imports roughly balancing in most years. Whereas grain imports as a percent of total imports have been declining fairly steadily, averaging around 10 percent for the past 6 years, grain exports as a percent of total exports have fluctuated around an average of nearly 7 percent over the entire period since 1961. Current policy has recently exhibited unprecedented flexibility toward credit mechanisms which would foster trade expansion. These include direct longer-term borrowing, barter agreements, product payback schemes for imports, importation of raw materials and semifinished products to be reprocessed for export, and even joint ventures with foreign firms. Thus it seems likely that China's trade will continue to grow, permitting Chinese authorities to pursue whatever grain import policy best fits their overall objectives for the rural sector.

Table 6 References

Official. Chen, *op. cit.*, p. 408. Derived by multiplying total output by percentage exported.

USDA. USDA Supply Tape, 1977. Data Library of the International Food Policy Research Institute, Washington, D.C. All data cited from USDA sources are in fiscal years, except for rice, which is in calendar years.

Tang, *op. cit.*, Table 1A.

Riley H. Kirby, "Agricultural Trade of the People's Republic of China, 1935-69," *Foreign Agricultural Economic Report* 83, U.S. Department of Agriculture, ERS, August 1972, cited in Frederic M. Surls, "China's Grain Trade," JEC, *op. cit.*, 1978, p. 655. Data are in calendar years.

CIA. For 1961-1965 see Central Intelligence Agency, National Foreign Assessment Center, "China-Economic Indicators," ER-77-10508, October 1977, Table 32, p. 7.
For 1966-1977 see Central Intelligence Agency, "China International Trade 1977-78, ER-78-10721, December 1978, Table A-9, p. 18.

Table 7

Cultivated Area (millions of hectares)[a]

	NARB	Buck	Liu & Yeh			
Prewar	93.1	(104.7-110.8)	102.2			
	Official	Chao	Wiens	Tang	Dawson	Perkins
1949	97.9	111.1	99.9			
1950	100.4	111.1	102.4			
1951	103.7	111.0	105.7			
1952	107.9	110.9	109.9	107.9		
1953	108.5	110.9	110.5	108.5		
1954	109.4	110.8	110.4	109.3		
1955	110.2	111.5	111.2	110.1		
1956	111.8	112.4	111.8	111.8		
1957	111.8	111.8	111.8	111.8	112.0	111.9 (or 110.2-113.5)
1958	107.8			107.8		
1959				107.3		
1960				107.2		
1961				107.1		
1962				107.0		
1963				107.0		
1964				107.0		
1965				107.0		
1966				107.0		
1967				107.0	110.3	
1968				107.0		
1969				107.0		
1970				107.0		
1971				107.0		
1972				107.0		
1973				107.0		
1974				107.0		
1975				107.0		
1976				107.0		
1977	(107-114)					

a. Since the official data appears to have used a conversion ratio of 15 mou = 1ha., for better comparability, data from other sources given in Chinese units have been converted at that ratio, although the actual ratio is slightly higher.

Food 7
Cultivated Area

There are only two truly independent well-documented sources of data on cultivated acreage during the Nationalist period in China: The National Agricultural Research Bureau's *Crop Reports* (1933-1937), based on field worker reports of from 900-1,200 of China's 1,680 *hsien*; and J.L. Buck's *Land Utilization in China*, containing results of a carefully planned sample survey of 16,786 farms and 38,256 farm families in 168 localities in 22 provinces (1929-1933). Buck discovered that official data were unreliable because landowners had underreported landholdings to evade taxes. NARB estimates, the basis of which, though unexplained, are thought to be farmland registration records of the Nationalist government, almost surely suffer from this defect. Whereas the NARB estimates that cultivated acreage amounted to 93.1 million hectares in the prewar period, Buck's work indicates that the figure fell more nearly within the range of 105 to 111 million hectares. Liu and Yeh have also made a judgmental estimate of 102.2 million hectares, based on choice among a variety of estimates for each province and supplemented by Shen's estimates for Manchuria, Sinkiang, and Sikang, which were not considered part of China proper during the Nationalist era.

These discrepancies in estimates of cultivated acreage carry over into the first half decade or so of PRC history. Official figures during the early years suffer from the underreporting of landholdings which affected the prewar NARB estimates. Wiens and Chao explore alternative hypotheses for correcting this deficiency. Wiens' analysis of prewar data leads him to believe that cultivated acreage before the war was not as great as previously thought. He also believes that two million hectares of unregistered land had been under cultivation at least since 1949, but were not discovered and added to the "official" series until the mid-50s. His analysis of provincial data and other Chinese material lead him to conclude that most of the increase in actual cultivated acreage claimed by the Chinese was more real than statistical. Basing his estimates on an analysis of a variety of provincial data, prewar and postwar, and a consistent figure of 1.1 million hectares for

Tibet, Peking, and Shanghai, Chao concludes that the 1949 figure was substantially higher than the official estimate, and that very little acreage was added to total cultivated area during the 1950s.

Tang adopts official figures through 1958, a CIA estimate for 1959, interpolates for 1960 and 1961, and arbitrarily adopts 107 million hectares as roughly correct through 1977 on the basis of odd official statements referring to cultivated acreage at about that level beginning around 1962. Dawson suggests that acreage may have recovered somewhat from the effects of the ill-considered policies of the Great Leap Forward (1959-1961), the naive application of which led to considerable economic destruction of farmland; but additions of recovered or frontier land may be largely offset by forced retirement of depleted or destroyed land. His estimates are based on official figures plus .2 million hectares for Tibet in 1957-58 and .266 million in 1967.

The Chinese themselves have not given a precise estimate of the amount of acreage currently under cultivation. They have announced plans to reclaim 13 million hectares of frontier wasteland by 1985, primarily in the northeast, and have stated that this will equal about two-thirds of total land reclaimed in the past 28 years. This would mean that the gross amount of land reclaimed since 1949 would be approximately 20 million hectares. Due to the loss of at least 4 million hectares during the Great Leap Forward, and the necessity of recovering it a second time, the 20 million figure overestimates the net amount of land reclaimed by at least that much and probably more. Deducting only the 4 million hectares destroyed in the early 1960s, the net figure for new land brought under cultivation would be 16 million hectares. Adding this amount to the 1949 official estimate of 98 million hectares gives a figure of 114 million hectares as the probable maximum estimate of current cultivated acreage. If the Chinese statement that new reclamation will expand the country's cultivated land area by one-eighth is taken at face value, the current area could be as low as 104 million hectares. The true figure is, however, probably no lower than Tang's estimate of 107 million hectares.

Table 7 References

Official. State Statistical Bureau, *Ten Great Years*, Peking, 1960, p. 128. Cited in Chen, *op. cit.* and Leslie T.C. Kuo, *Agriculture in the People's Republic of China*, New York: Praeger, 1976.
Chao, *op. cit.*, p. 207.
Wiens, "Agricultural Statistics," in Eckstein, *op. cit.*, Table 11A-4.
Tang, *op. cit.*, Table 4, "Land Input."
Dawson, *op. cit.*, p. 50.
Dwight H. Perkins, *Agricultural Production in China*, Chicago: Aldine, 1969, p. 240.

Table 8

Sown Area as Percent of Cultivated Area (multiple cropping index)

Year	Official	Wiens	Chao	Tang	Tang (modified multiple cropping index)
1949		127.1			
1950					
1951					
1952	130.9	133.5	134.3	130.9	115.45
1953	132.7	134.8	135.6	132.7	116.35
1954	135.3	136.8	138.7	135.3	117.65
1955	137.2	137.6	137.6	137.2	118.60
1956	142.3	139.7	142.6	142.3	121.15
1957	140.6	140.6	139.7	140.6	120.30
1958	145.0			145.0	122.50
1959				141.2	120.60
1960				137.0	118.50
1961				132.8	116.50
1962				136.1	118.05
1963				139.4	119.70
1964				142.6	121.30
1965				145.8	122.90
1966				145.4	122.70
1967				145.6	122.80
1968				145.9	122.95
1969				146.4	123.20
1970				147.2	123.60
1971				148.9	124.45
1972				149.9	124.95
1973				151.6	125.80
1974				153.2	127.60
1975				154.9	127.45
1976				156.4	128.20
1977				157.9	128.95

Table 8
Sown Area

Throughout much of Asia sown area exceeds cultivated area because some localities plant more than one crop per year on a given plot of land. This practice is particularly common in rice-growing areas, where two and sometimes three crops can be harvested each year. Thus the percentage by which sown area exceeds cultivated area indicates the extent of this multiple cropping.

In their interpretations of Chinese production statistics for the 1950s, official statements have been criticized by Wiens and Chao as underreporting the extent of multiple cropping and overreporting the extent of yield improvement. Tang, however, has synthesized a complete series. He adopts official statistics through 1958, then uses estimates based on fragmentary official material for 1961 and 1965 compiled by Edwin Jones, with interpolations for intervening years; for 1966-1972 he uses CIA material based on scattered official information for particular crops, and then assumes the same growth rate for the 1973-1977 period as that implied for 1966-1972. Whether this growth rate has actually been maintained in the recent period has been questioned by Wiens. It is clear that many localities have had trouble shifting to more intensive cropping patterns. Some areas of Western Szechuan, for example, have recently gone back to a single crop of mid-season rice to avoid net losses occurring under double-cropping as a result of the low output of late rice caused by long spells of autumn rain and severe shortages of manpower and fertilizer in the late rice transplanting season.

Principal requirements for shifting profitably to a more intensive cropping system include: improved water control; a suitably adapted early maturing seed strain; resolution of overlapping peak period demands for labor (normally through mechanization); and sheer availability of additional fertilizer. Since progress appears to be forthcoming in all these areas, China should be able to increase sown area significantly. For broad regions in China, however, ultimate resolution of water control problems is over a decade away at best; and it is not clear that financing and resource allocations are being extended to risk averse peasants in subsistence areas with fair water control in sufficient amounts to induce mechanization and fertilizer application which would permit more intensive cropping.

Tang includes a modified multiple cropping index designed as a rough means of correcting for the fact that double cropped land does not yield under the same state of the art twice as much as the same land under a single crop.

Most of China's sown area is planted to foodgrains. All estimates roughly agree that foodgrains (including soybeans and potatoes) have occupied 80 to 90 percent of total sown area throughout PRC history. A minor exception may have been in the mid-60s, when the lowest estimates place the figure at just under 80 percent.

The most extensively planted nonfoodgrain is undoubtedly cotton, which attained a high of almost 4 percent in 1956; peanuts and rapeseed apparently took around 1-2 percent in the 1950s and sesame somewhat less than one percent. Acreage sown to cotton grew over the 1950s, but had already begun to decline by 1957, then plummeted with the unavoidable concentration on foodgrains during the agricultural failures of the early 1960s, reaching a low of around 2.4 percent of total sown area in 1962. Recovery followed thereafter, but cotton's share of sown area never regained the levels of 1951-1959, although acreage losses have been more than counterbalanced by yield increases.

It is clear that China does not have large areas sown to nonfood grains that could readily be converted to foodgrain production. The elimination of all industrial and luxury crops, as well as nongrain food crops, would only add in the neighborhood of 30 million metric tons to foodgrain production, at a ridiculous cost. Yields of several nonfoodgrain crops seem to have improved in recent years, as cotton did in the late 1950s and 1960s. It appears unlikely that there will be large fluctuations in area sown to such crops, though a modest continuation of the extremely gradual declining trend of the late 1960s and 1970s is quite possible.

Table 8 References

Official. Computed from data given in *Ten Great Years*, *op. cit.*, p. 128.
Wiens, "Agricultural Statistics," in Eckstein, *op. cit.*, Table IIB-9.
Chao, *op. cit.*, p. 213.
Tang, *op. cit.*, Table 4, "Land Input."

Table 9

Average Foodgrain Yields
(tons per hectare)

	Rice	Wheat	Corn	Soybeans
Prewar				
Buck	3.35	1.06	1.33	.84
Buck (Liu and Yeh)	3.27	1.01	1.43	.92
Buck (Wiens)	2.72	.81	1.13	.68
Statistical Monthly	2.91	1.10	1.35	1.07
Statistical Monthly (Wiens)	2.01	.69	.86	.64
NARB (Wiens)	2.48	1.07	1.38	1.17
NARB (Perkins)	2.57	1.08	1.38	1.16
NARB (Liu and Yeh)	2.77	1.08	1.37	1.16
Liu and Yeh	2.77	1.04	1.40	1.04
1949 Official (Wiens)	1.89	.64		.61 (.78)
1950 Official	2.11	.56		
1951 Official	2.25	.75		
1952 Official (Wiens)	2.41	.53	1.34	.82 (1.01)
1953 Official	2.52	.71	1.27	.80
1954 Official	2.47	.87	1.30	.72
1955 Official (Wiens)	2.67	.86	1.39	.80 (.88)
1956 Official (Wiens)	2.48	.91	1.31	.85 (1.06)
1957 Official (Wiens)	2.69	.86	1.43	.79 (.95)
1958 Official	3.47	1.09		
1965 Official (Wiens)		1.05		
1967 Official (Dawson)	2.92	.93		
1969 Official (Wiens)		1.11		
1971 Official (Stavis)	3.2	1.5	2.8	
(FAO adj.)	3.1	1.1		
1972 Official (Wiens)		1.40		
1971 Egypt	5.4	2.8	4.1	
India	1.7	1.3	1.2	
Mexico	2.6	2.7	1.2	2.0
Philippines	1.7		0.8	0.8
South Korea	4.6	2.3	1.4	0.8
Thailand	2.0		2.5	1.0
Japan	5.3	2.7	3.0	1.2
U.S.	5.2	2.3	5.5	1.9

Table 9
Average Foodgrain Yields

Although there is some disagreement among scholars, it appears that average yields of many crops did not reach prewar levels until the late 1950s. Thereafter rice yields made strong progress with the introduction of dwarf rice varieties beginning around 1964; today yields are high by world standards. The recent development of a male sterile dwarf hybrid provides a further opportunity for yield increases, which more or less stalled in the 1970s. It was planted to 15 percent of rice acreage in 1978 and its use is likely to spread.

Wheat yields in China have never been high by world standards, but significant progress was achieved in the 1970s with the introduction of semidwarf varieties obtained through crosses of Chinese and Mexican strains. Further progress in wheat yields seems to depend upon resolution of water availability and control problems in North China.

Maize breeding work has been reasonably successful and accounts for its increasing dominance in acreage over sorghum and other summer grains in the North. Yields of other coarse grains are not particularly high by world standards and even without the resolution of the water control problem, they could probably be improved at relatively low cost.

Little information is available about current soybean yields. China was once one of the world's leading producers of soybeans with a large export market, but production has actually declined somewhat since the late 1950s. Soybean acreage was probably squeezed out by other high-yielding foodcrops, though total production recovered in the late 1960s and stabilized in the 1970s. Today soybeans are primarily intercropped and planted at the edges of fields. The value of soybeans as a protein source and their prominent role in traditional Chinese diets, the increasing demand for fine feed concentrates, and the pent-up demand for vegetable oils have all contributed to a renewed government interest in soybean production and a somewhat improved seed technology has been developed. But the high land costs involved in producing them domestically may lead Chinese authorities to import soybean products over and above planned increases in domestic output.

Table 9 References

Buck, *op. cit.*, Statistical Volume, p. 209, for 1929-1933 average.
Statistical Monthly, Directorate of Statistics, May 1933, cited in Wiens, "Agricultural Statistics," in Eckstein, *op. cit.* (Hereinafter Wiens, 1975), Table IIC-1.
National Agricultural Research Bureau (NARB), Chang Yu-i, *Chung-kuo Chin-tai: Nung-yeh Shih Tzu-liao (Materials on Modern Chinese Agricultural History)*, Vol. 3, Peking, 1977, p. 926, cited in Wiens, 1975, Table IIC-1. Chang reweighted the figures to include Manchuria.
Chinese Ministry of Information, *China Handbook, 1937-1943*, pp. 561-73, converted by Perkins and presented in Perkins, *op. cit.*, p. 267, Appendix D, Table D-1. Rice is a national average figure; corn and soybeans are for 22 provinces only; period covered is 1931-1937.
NARB, *Agricultural Estimates*, 1933, Liu and Yeh, *op. cit.*, pp. 300-302, Table A-9, Col. 4. All figures are for 22 provinces only.
Wiens revisions of Buck and *Statistical Monthly*, Wiens, 1975, Table IIC-3.
Liu and Yeh revision of Buck, Liu and Yeh, *op. cit.*, pp. 130 and 300-301. Soybean figure clearly excludes black soybeans.
Liu and Yeh, *op. cit.*, p. 300, Table A-9, Col. 6. Estimates for 1933 by the authors are an average of their presentation of Buck's data and the NARB estimates for China Proper. Soybean figure clearly excludes black soybeans.
Official. For 1949-1958 see Chen, *op. cit.*, pp. 318-319. Wiens revisions for soybeans are weighted averages of incomplete yield figures derived from provincial data. See Wiens, 1975, Table IID-6. Wiens also presents foodgrain yield figures disaggregated by province in Table IIC-5.
Wiens, 1975, Table II-15 for 1965, 1969, and 1972. These calculations for wheat are based on official sources.
Dawson, *op. cit.*, p. 199 for 1967. See pp. 199-260 for discussion of derivation of estimates calculated as percentages over official 1957 figures.
Stavis, *Making Green Revolution, op. cit.*, pp. 4 5, based on field surveys of Chinese agricultural scientists and economists.
FAO *Production Yearbooks*, 1971 and 1972, adjusted by Stavis to exclude Taiwan, cited in Stavis, *op. cit.*, p. 5.
FAO *Production Yearbook*, 1971 for other country data.

Table 10

Irrigated Area
(million hectares)[a]

	Statistical Bureau	OFFICIAL Hydro-electric Generation	Provincial Data	Chao	Perkins	Kuo	Groen and Kilpatrick	Tang
1949	16.0	20.3	14.8			16.0	16.0	
1950	16.7	20.8	15.3			16.7	16.7	
1951	18.7	21.8	16.9			18.7	18.7	
1952	21.3	23.4	19.1		21.3	21.3	21.3	21.3
1953	22.0	24.0	20.6			22.0	22.0	22.0
1954	23.3	24.8	21.8			23.3	23.3	23.3
1955	24.7	26.1	23.4		24.7	24.7	24.7	24.7
1956	32.0	36.0	28.9			32.0	32.0	32.0
1957	34.7		35.7		34.7	34.7	34.7	34.7
1958	66.7[b]					66.7[b]		34.7
1959				71.3[b]		73.3[c]		33.8
1960				46.7		54.7		32.9
1961								32.1
1962						36.7		33.0
1963				36.7	37.3	34.0	(30-33)[d]	34.0
1964				32.0	(33)[d]	33.3		33.3
1965				33.3		34.7		34.7
1966						37.3		37.3
1967								38.0
1968								38.7
1969								39.4
1970								40.3
1971								41.5
1972					42.6		43.3	42.5
1973					44.0		45.3	44.0
1974								45.3
1975								48.0
1976								48.0
1977							(50)[d]	48.0

a. Converted at 1 HA = 15 mou
b. May be substantially exaggerated
c. Planned
d. Parenthesis indicate approximate

Table 10

Irrigated Area

The extent to which China has brought a controlled supply of water to its farming regions can be measured by the expansion in irrigated area which has taken place since 1949, and by the increase in the rural stock of powered irrigation equipment. With respect to irrigated area, most scholars use an official series given in the State Statistical Bureau's publication *Ten Great Years* as the basis for estimating the increases achieved in the 1950s. Chao, using material found in the official publication *Sywe-li Fa-dyan* (Hydroelectric Generation) and by aggregating official provincial data, showed there is room for substantial disagreement as to the true 1949 starting base. By 1957, however, all three official sources seem agreed on an estimate of irrigated area of approximately 35-36 million hectares. No really solid information is available for the years 1958-1960. In any event, damage to irrigation networks and land destruction resulting from ill-advised local engineering projects of the Great Leap Forward undoubtedly brought about a fall in irrigated acreage, a decline which continued through 1964. Recovery and expansion proceeded thereafter.

Table 10 References

Official. *Ten Great Years, op. cit.*, p. 130.

Sywe-li Fa-dyan *(Hydroelectric Generation)* #7, 1957, cited in Chao, *op. cit.*, p. 121.

Chao, *op. cit.*, p. 121, summation of official provincial data.

Chao, *op. cit.*, p. 121, based on official statements.

Perkins, "Constraints," in JEC, *op. cit.*, 1975, p. 360, except for 1963, for which the estimate is presented in Perkins, *Agricultural Production, op. cit.*, p. 64.

Kuo, *op. cit.*, p. 124.

Groen and Kilpatrick, "China's Agricultural Production" in JEC, *op. cit.*, 1978, p. 65.

Tang, *op. cit.*, Table 4, "Land Input."

Tang's estimates for 1958-1962 and 1967-1971 are derived from interpolation. The 1976-77 estimates are his own and 1964 is from a Hong Kong publication. The remainder of his series is based on official statements regarding absolute area of land under irrigation or the rate at which irrigated area has been expanding. All other estimates are based directly on official materials. By 1966 total irrigated area had clearly surpassed 1957 levels and the expansion growth rate to the present has been about 3 percent per year, with the largest documented increments occurring in the 1964-1966 period and in 1973.

Table 11

Irrigation and Drainage Equipment Capacity and Number of Tubewells

Year	Irrigation and Drainage Equipment (10,000 hp.)						Number of Tubewells (1,000 units with pumps)	
	Chao	Dawson	Perkins	Wiens	CIA	Tang	Perkins	Kuo
1949					97			
1950								
1951					118			
1952						153		
1953						200		
1954	176					260		
1955	220				338	338		
1956	390				508	508		
1957	560	560	560	560	560	560		
1958	1,610		690		1,280	1,280		
1959	3,380		900		2,535	2,535		
1960	5,900		1,200	1,200	4,145	4,145		
1961	4,500		2,230	2,230	4,845	4,845		
1962	4,000		3,600	3,600	5,800	5,800		
1963	6,000		5,200	5,200	6,440	6,440		
1964	7,300		7,000	7,280	7,300	7,300		
1965	8,570		7,500	8,570	8,450	8,450	100	200
1966	10,400				9,980	9,980		
1967		9,000			10,695	10,695		
1968					12,742	12,742		
1969					14,790	14,790		
1970				20,000	16,911	16,911		
1971			20,000	20,000	20,000	20,000	600	
1972					24,016	24,016	800	900
1973			30,000		30,000	30,000		1,200
1974					36,000	36,000	1,300	
1975				40,000	43,000	40,000		
1976						43,500		
1977					47,000	47,000		

Table 11
Powered Irrigation Equipment Capacity

Except for a portion of the CIA and Tang series, all sources base their estimates of powered irrigation equipment capacity directly on official statements. Early discrepancies often have to do with imprecision in the Chinese source material indicating whether electrical and fuel injection equipment have both been included. The higher official estimates seem more probable, with the exception, of course, of 1958-1960. The Perkins and Wiens series are consistent with official statements for the 1960-1965 period, but if officially announced growth rates are applied to this base period, they yield figures for the 1970s that are inconsistent with absolute magnitudes given in official sources. Therefore, either the 1960 figures are greater than those given by Perkins and Wiens (as the CIA evidently concludes), or the officially stated absolute magnitudes for the 1970s are in error (as no one seems prepared to believe), or the manner of interpolating officially stated increases for the 1960s is in error. The program of conflict among official statements may again reduce itself to one of noncomparability among categories of equipment included in the various Chinese sources.

Table 11 References

Chao, *op. cit.*, p. 141.
Dawson, *op. cit.*, p. 165.
Perkins, "Constraints," in JEC, *op. cit.*, 1975, p. 360.
Wiens, "Agricultural Statistics," in Eckstein, *op. cit.*, Table II-17.
CIA. National Foreign Assessment Center, "China: Economic Indicators," ER77-10508.
Tang, *op. cit.*, Table 6, "Farm Machinery."
Kuo, *op. cit.*, pp. 128-129.

In any event, it is clear that this input to agriculture was largely neglected in the 1950s, not only due to an inability or unwillingness to allocate more resources to the production of the equipment, but also to the absence of hydroelectric infrastructure and an apparent unwillingness to allocate hydrocarbon fuels to the agricultural sector during this period. Growth in the 1960s and 70s, however, has been rapid.

Tubewell construction began in the mid-1960s to relieve the constraint on multicropping due to insufficient surface water, and proceeded at a good pace. However, it has recently been revealed that 40 percent of the existing tubewells are inoperative. Several possible causes suggest themselves: (1) inadequate repair and maintenance, possibly exacerbated by poor quality original materials or installation; (2) insufficient allocation of fuel, coupled with a lack of hydroelectric power to operate the pumps; (3) an aversion to using limited local financial resources to maintain tubewells perceived to be of poor quality.

Table 12

Stock of Tractors (1,000 standard units)[a]

	Official	Chao	Wiens	Dawson	Kuo	CIA	Tang
1949	.4				.4	.4	
1950	1.3				1.3	1.3	
1951	1.4				1.4	1.4	
1952	2.0	2.0			2.0	2.0	2.0
1953	2.7	2.7			2.7	2.7	2.7
1954	5.1	5.1			5.1	5.1	5.1
1955	8.1	8.1			8.1	8.1	8.1
1956	19.4	19.4			19.4	19.4	19.4
1957	24.6	24.6	24.6	24.6	24.6	24.6	24.6
1958	45.3	45.3		45.3	45.3	45.3	45.3
1959		59.0		59.0	59.0	59.0	59.0
1960		79.0	79.0	79.0	79.0	79.0	79.0
1961		90.0	99.0	95.0	99.0	95.0	95.0
1962		103.4	103.4	110.0	100.0	103.0	103.0
1963		115.0	115.0	115.0	115.0	113.0	115.0
1964		123.0	123.0	123.1	123.0	138.4	123.0
1965		130.5	130.5	134.8	154.2		134.4
1966				145.0		153.6	153.6
1967				150.0			178.1
1968							195.4
1969							216.1
1970					308.3	320.1	293.0
1971			(200-300)		700.7		352.7
1972					770.8	397.0	484.1
1973						506.0	639.5
1974							836.2
1975			613.2			784.5	971.8
1976							1,187.3
1977							1,300.0

a. 1 Standard unit = 15 horsepower

Table 12
Stock of Tractors

The best measure of the extent of mechanization in agriculture is frequently considered to be the stock of tractors. As with the irrigation data, most scholars accept data given by the Chinese State Statistical Bureau in *Ten Great Years* for 1949-1958, and consensus on the appropriate official figure extends through 1960. For later years there are conflicts over the exact meaning of particular statistics. Do they refer to numbers of tractors of any size, or only to standard 15 horsepower units? Does the growth rate refer to tractors in use, tractors produced, or tractors supplied to agricultural areas? Do "in use" figures fully include depreciation and retirement of inoperable machines, and by what method of calculation?

All the series verify large increases in supply of tractors to rural areas in the 1970s, though the timing of the transition seems to be in dispute. The purchase of tractors has sometimes been hampered because the expense is often too great for the production team (about 30 families) to handle, yet several teams sometimes seem unwilling to cooperate on a purchase owing to mistrust and ambiguities about the benefits. To some extent this problem was addressed in 1964 with the introduction of small garden tractors. Growth in supply of these units has been high, owing in part to the fact that it began from a very small base in the mid-60s, and in part to the rededication to agriculture in the early 1970s.

Rural stock of all tractors has grown at an average rate of 19 percent per year since 1962, but slowed down considerably in 1975-1977 as a result of the impact of the "Gang of Four" on the industrial sector. By contrast plans for 1980 call for a resumption of the 1962-1977 growth rate with emphasis on large and medium-sized tractors.

Inasmuch as transportation is a major bottleneck and source of considerable labor drain in many localities, the widespread use of tractors for transport in rural areas, often criticized by central authorities, should not be so readily viewed as inefficient.

Table 12 References

Official. *Ten Great Years, op. cit.*, p. 135.
Chao, *op. cit.*, p. 170.
Wiens, "Agricultural Statistics," in Eckstein, *op. cit.*, Table II-17.
Dawson, *op. cit.*, p. 139.
Kuo, *op. cit.*, p. 229.
CIA.   National Foreign Assessment Center, "China: Economic Indicators," ER78-10750, December 1978, Table 10B, p. 15.
Tang, *op. cit.*, Table 6, "Farm Machinery."

Table 13

Pest and Disease Control

	Supply of Chemical Pesticides Herbicides and Fungicides (thousand metric tons)		Number of Varieties of Chemical Pesticides	Percentage of Total Cultivated Area Under Biological Pest and Disease Control
	Tang	"Official"		
1949		.064	1	
1950				
1951				
1952	15	15		
1953	19	19		
1954	41	41		
1955	67	67		
1956	159	159		
1957	149	149	20	
1958	246	478[a]		
1959	326		30	
1960	405			
1961	256			
1962	283			
1963	312		60	
1964	345	447		
1965	380	494		
1966	420			
1967	464			
1968	512			
1969	565			
1970	624			
1971	689			
1972	761	998		.08
1973	859	1,117	120	
1974	970			
1975	1,095			
1976	1,236			3.24
1977	1,395			

a. May be substantially exaggerated.

Table 13
Pest and Disease Control

Only three factories produced chemical pesticide prior to World War II and the total production in 1949 was only 64 tons of copper sulphate. Production expanded to 149,000 tons of 20 different varieties by 1957, but this represented only about 20 percent of the pesticides used. The remainder were "native pesticides" produced from more than 500 varieties of plants and minerals in 240 factories. These are far less concentrated and amounted to 17 million tons of gross weight in 1958.

The official figure for 1958 chemical pesticide production cannot be taken as reliable, owing to the distortion of statistics during the Great Leap Forward. Otherwise the official series is consistent with the hypothesis that production of industrial inputs to agriculture grew rapidly just after the period of dedication and rededication to agri-culture in 1962 and the early 1970s. Tang's series is also consistent with this hypothesis, although it shows lower absolute figures. His series assumes constant growth rates of 10.41 percent for 1965-1972 and 12.88 percent for 1973-1977 on the basis of official statements that production in 1972 was over twice that of 1965 and that 1973 production was 2.26 times the 1965 level.

The progress of "native pesticide" production is not known in the aggregate. But it is clear that a large share of production is decentralized and many hundreds of localities produce their own native pesticides. These products are cheap to produce except that the labor required to manufacture and apply them is considerably greater than for chemical pesticides. They are generally less dangerous than the latter, but the supply of many is locally restricted or seasonal. Biological and environmental methods of pest and disease control have been pursued much more actively since the early 1970s.

Table 13 References

Tang, *op. cit.*, Table 7, "Current Inputs."

Official. For 1949, see Fei Yu-ch'um (ed.), *Nung-yao Wen-ta* (Questions and Answers on Agricultural Chemicals) rev. ed., Peking: Fuel Chemical Industry Press, 1975, cited in Kuo, *op. cit.*

For 1952-1958 see *Ten Great Years*, *op. cit.*, p. 17 cited in Chen, *op. cit.*, p. 401.

For 1964 see *Chung-Kuo Nung-pao* (*China Agricultural Journal*), February 1965, p. 2 cited in Wiens, "Agricultural Statistics," in Eckstein, *op. cit.*, Table II-17.

For 1965, 1972, and 1973 see Foreign Broadcast Information Service, *Peoples Republic of China Daily Report*, January 11, 1974 and "All Round Rich Harvests in China," *Peking Review* Vol. 17, #1.

January 4, 1974 and *Peking Review*, Vol. 16, #45, November 2, 1973 for growth rates applied to 1964 estimate.

NCNA (New China News Agency), Peking, October 9, 1973, cited in Kuo, *op. cit.*, p. 212.

Peking Review, "Biological Control of Plant Diseases and Insect Pests," Vol. 20, #30, July 22, 1977, p. 32.

Table 14

Supply of Chemical Fertilizers
(thousand metric tons of nutrients)

	Liu	Liu/CIA[a]	CIA	Chao (approx.)	Ishikawa	Stavis	Tang[b]
1949		(6)	5				
1950		(34)	34				
1951		(68)	67				
1952		(79)	79	50			90
1953	79	(134)	133	116			140
1954	95	(206)	205	150			190
1955	182	(230)	243	251			280
1956	313	(390)	401	320			360
1957	401	(458)	429	403	384		490
1958	628	(688)	626	566			560
1959	615	(663)	639	640			660
1960	620	(658)	710	634			650
1961	510	(546)	589	640			700
1962	704	(720)	788	853			890
1963	1,102	1,205)	1,297	1,242			1,190
1964	1,318	(1,355)	1,485	1,441			1,630
1965	2,199	(2,337)	2,120	2,208	1,922		2,060
1966			2,604				2,490
1967			2,763				2,830
1968			3,128				3,150
1969			3,558				3,650
1970			4,266				4,220
1971			4,820				4,860
1972			5,494			4,520	5,580
1973			6,434				5,960
1974			6,106				6,370
1975			6,935				6,650
1976			5,851				6,500
1977			9,088				8,500

a. Parenthesis indicates domestic production plus imports.
b. Three years moving average.

Table 14

Supply of Chemical Fertilizers (nutrient weight)

Figures on chemical fertilizer supply differ due not only to conflicting estimates of domestic production and imports, but because of imprecise knowledge of the composition of these quantities. Official data are normally given in gross weight, aggregating a variety of nitrogenous, phosphatic, and potassic fertilizers, tne nutrient content of which ranges from a few percent for liquid ammonia produced in "native method" fertilizer plants to 65 percent or more for some kinds of concentrated superphosphates. The proximity of the estimates, despite this source of extreme variation, reflects the relative precision of the data, as well as some overlapping of source material.

The Liu/CIA series includes domestic production figures from Jung-chao Liu (1970) and imports from CIA (1978). Since no easily comparable figures were given directly in Chao (1970), and since Chao's method for computing total nutrients was somewhat ambiguous, approximate figures were calculated by Stone from Chao's data. Estimates of the amount of chemical fertilizer nutrients applied per unit of land were multiplied by estimates of the amount of land under cultivation. Since Chao published his data in rounded form, this calculation for the first few years may result in substantial differences from his actual but unpublished figures. Tang's data base is essentially the same as the CIA series with the exception of 1976-77, but it is a three-year moving average, computed for the purpose of minimizing year-to-year discrepancies between consumption and available supply arising from inventory changes.

All sources point to gradual growth in the 1950s and rapid acceleration beginning in 1963, the year after the dedication to technical transformation of agriculture. The CIA series shows that growth slowed a bit in 1967, during the Cultural Revolution, but picked up thereafter. There was a large leap in 1973 shortly after the rededication to agriculture following the Cultural Revolution, but an absolute decline in 1974 and again in 1976 due to the impact of the "Gang of Four" upon the industrial sector and a foreign exchange conservation program which reduced imports. In 1977, however, rededication to the goal of agricultural expansion resulted in full recovery and rapid acceleration in the quantity of chemical fertilizer nutrients supplied.

Table 14 References

Jung-chao Liu, *China's Fertilizer Economy*, Chicago: Aldine, 1970, Table 4.2, p. 50.

Liu/CIA For nutrients supplied from domestic production, see Liu, *op. cit.*, Table 2.2, pp. 12-13.
For nutrients supplied from imports, see CIA, "China: Economic Indicators," ER78-10750, December 1978, Table 10A, p. 14.

CIA. See CIA, *ibid.*, and Groen and Kilpatrick, "China's Agricultural Production," JEC, *op. cit*, 1978, p. 650, which gives identical series except for 1976.

Chao, *op. cit.*, derived from data given in Table 6.5, pp. 156-57, Table 8.5, p. 207, and Appendix Table 15, pp. 306-309.

Shigeru Ishikawa, "Mainland China: Changes in Production" in W.A. Douglas Jackson (ed.), *Agrarian Policies and Problems in Communist and Noncommunist Countries*, Seattle: University of Washington Press, 1971, pp. 368-371, estimated from Chinese and Japanese sources.

Stavis, *Making Green Revolution*, *op. cit.*, p. 43, high estimate only.

Tang, *op. cit*, Table 7, "Current Inputs."

Table 15

Supply of Organic Fertilizer
(Million metric tons of nutrient weight)

	Chao	Chao (adjusted)	Tang	Wiens	Ishikawa	Dawson
1949						
1950						
1951						
1952	2.8	9.7	10.1			
1953	3.0	10.7	10.9			
1954	3.3	11.8	11.4			
1955	3.4	12.2	11.7			
1956	3.6	12.7	12.4			8.8
1957	4.1	14.6	13.0	12.4	12.5	
1958	4.2	15.2	14.2			10.1
1959	4.4	15.8	13.5			
1960	3.8	12.5	12.5			
1961	3.1	9.2	12.0			
1962	3.3	9.9	12.2	12.0		
1963	3.5	10.8	13.7			
1964	3.7	11.8	15.2			
1965	4.0	12.7	17.0	14.0	12.9	
1966	4.2	13.7	17.6			
1967			17.6			
1968			17.5			
1969			17.7			
1970	Stavis		18.4		Stavis	
1971			19.5	17.4		
1972	6.1		20.6		14.8	
1973			20.4			
1974			21.2			
1975			22.1			
1976			22.5			
1977			23.0			

Table 15

Supply of Organic Fertilizers (nutrient weight)

Organic fertilizers include such items as compost, green manure crops, draft animal and hog manures, various oilseed cakes, night soil, river and pond mud, and so forth. Estimation of the aggregate supply involves estimating gross weights available and actually applied in each category, and multiplying by average nutrient content factors. This process is subject to relatively large errors, but a number of scholars have made serious attempts for particular years. Chao, Ishikawa, and Dawson have employed relatively independent methods and distinct data sources. Stavis' high estimate is based on Ishikawa's computation for 1965, assuming a 2 percent annual growth rate in gross weight supplied by each of the components of organic fertilizer.

Wien's figures are also based on Ishikawa, but incorporate Wiens' own more recent estimate of human and animal populations for 1957 and 1965, and assume rising rates of pig manure utilization for fertilizer. These assumptions result in a change in the relative weight of hog manure vis à-vis other sources of organic fertilizer, and the increased importance of hog manure in the total is reflected in Wiens' estimates for 1962 and 1971. However, since hog numbers were down in 1962 due to the effects of the agricultural failures of the early 1960s, the actual weight of nutrients supplied by organic fertilizer in 1962 was down slightly from 1957. Tang's method of estimation was not included in his draft.

Chao's estimates are significantly lower than those of other scholars due to his procedure of calculating the quantity of nutrients actually absorbed by plants, rather than the total quantity supplied from each fertilizer source. In order to render this series more comparable with other data, an "adjusted" series has been calculated on the basis of Chao's table of nutrient content and absorption rates; this calculation yields total nutrients supplied rather than total nutrients absorbed. Stavis' low estimate is computed on the basis of Chao's method. If this procedure had not been used, making Stavis' low estimate

more comparable with scholars other than Chao, it would probably be above his high estimate (perhaps as much as 18 to 19 million metric tons), but he does not present disaggregated figures which would enable a recomputation.

The important things to note from this table are that organic manure application is still increasing and that the absolute magnitudes involved are still large relative to nutrients supplied by chemical fertilizers. For 1965 estimates of the percentage of plant nutrients supplied from organic sources include 85.4 percent (Chao, adjusted), 86.5 percent (Ishikawa), 87.1 percent (Wiens), and 89.2 percent (Tang). Despite significant increases in the use of chemical fertilizers in the 1960s and 1970s, percentages supplied from organic sources are still high: 80.1 percent in 1971 (Wiens), 77 percent in 1972 (Ishikawa/Stavis), and 80 percent in 1971 declining to 73 percent in 1977 (Tang).

The largest sources of increase still available are human and hog excrement. Improved facilities for collecting, treating, and transporting the former and the sheer growth in supply of the latter have coalesced to keep organic fertilizers in a dominant position. Little more can probably be gained from river and pond mud; oilseed cakes are land consumptive, require more expensive processing, and may be more efficiently used as livestock feed. Growth possibilities for compost and plant residues are limited and green manure is land consumptive.

The principal difficulties with organic fertilizers are the relatively low growth possibilities and the considerable labor requirements. Human and hog excreta have considerable growth potential, but the labor costs are substantial for collecting and moving them, treating them, and mixing them with leftover plant materials, weeds and soil, storing them and transporting them to the field. One 1965 report cited by Ishikawa indicated that the cost of farmyard manures containing 100 kilograms of nitrogen nutrient is 35-45 human labor days and 20-25 animal labor days. With shifts to more intensive cropping patterns, these large drains on available human and animal labor can become a serious limitation.

Table 15 References

Chao, *op. cit.*, pp. 144-150, 310-314.

Tang, *op. cit.*, Appendix.

Stavis, *Making Green Revolution, op. cit.*, p. 43.

Wiens, "Agricultural Statistics" in Eckstein, *op. cit.*, Table II-18.

Ishikawa, "Mainland China" in Jackson, *op. cit.*, pp. 368-371.

Owen L. Dawson, "Fertilizer Supply and Food Requirements" in Buck, Dawson Wu, *Food and Agriculture in Communist China*, New York: Praeger, 1966, pp. 138-148.

Table 16

Indexes of Agriculture-related Prices[a], 1949-1980 (projected)

Year	State purchase prices of agricultural products	Retail prices of industrial goods sold in rural areas	Prices of industrial inputs to agriculture	State purchase prices of foodgrains[b]
1949				
1950	82.2	91.2		82.7
1951	98.4	100.5		(91.4)
1952	100.0	100.0	100.0	100.0
1953	110.1	98.5		
1954	113.8	100.2		
1955	113.2	101.4		(104.2)
1956	116.6	100.4		115.7
1957	122.4	101.6		116.5
1958	125.1	101.0		119.1
1959	129.0			(128.6)
1960				
1961				
1962				
1963	154.7	114.3	135	(147.5)
1964				
1965	100.0	100.0		
1966				
1967				
1968				
1969				
1970				
1971	156.2	103.9		(161.3)
1972				
1973	167.0	99.3	50	(183.6)
1974	108.4	92.6		
1975				
1976				
1977				
1978				
1979-1980	(200-250)		(42.5-45)	(220-275)

a. 1952 = 100.
b. Parenthesis indicates derived from direct information on prices, or market survey results, or from interpolation, rather than from official statements about price indices.

Table 16

Aggregate Price Incentives

From 1949 to 1959 the official purchase price for agricultural commodities, including foodgrains, rose steadily, whereas the aggregated prices of industrial goods sold in rural areas remained fairly steady. These conclusions are based on indexes of agriculture-related prices given in Joe Hart's unpublished draft "China: Comparison of State Purchase Prices of Agricultural Products in 1952 and 1957," which is in turn based both on official statements about indexes and about individual prices.

Little is known about the aggregation methods employed in deriving these indexes after the 1950s and their changes over time. However, they seem broadly consistent with other available data, although they may not fully reflect quality changes and could distort the impact of industrial goods not available during the early years of the PRC. Excessive reliance upon the exact numbers in the table does not seem well-advised, but the existence of several broad trends seems undeniable: (1) state purchase prices of agricultural goods have risen steadily and substantially; (2) retail prices of industrial goods sold in rural areas have remained roughly constant in the aggregate and may be broken down into two components: (a) prices of industrial inputs to agriculture which may have risen somewhat in the 1950s and early 1960s but had fallen dramatically at least by the early 1970s; (b) prices of other industrial goods sold in rural areas, which rose less rapidly than prices of inputs to agriculture during the first decade or so, but did not experience the dramatic drop with the latter over the past 10 to 15 years.

The work of some scholars indicates that the official indices have somewhat exaggerated the twist in prices in favor of rural areas during the first decade of the PRC's history. Also, it seems clear that the early price structure of the PRC discriminated against rural areas compared with prewar years. By the Communist's own calculations, purchase prices of agricultural goods relative to sales prices of industrial goods in rural areas were about 22 percent higher in 1930-1936 than they were in 1952. This bias, however, was redressed by around 1957.

Table 16 References

Derived largely from Joe W. Hart, "China: Comparison of State Purchase Prices of Agricultural Products in 1952 and 1957," unpublished draft, December 1978; and from "Communique of the Third Plenary Session of the 11th Central Committee of the CCP" (December 22, 1978) in *Peking Review*, Vol. 21, #52, December 29, 1978. For derivations, see Bruce Stone, *Agricultural Purchase Price Policy in the People's Republic of China*, Washington, D.C.: International Food Policy Research Institute, forthcoming.

A nori (*seaweed*) *farm on Japan's coast.* Photo by Joseph A. Massey).

A terraced rice farm in Japan. (Photo by Joseph A. Massey).

The Political Economy of Food in Japan

Michael W. Donnelly

Japan is essentially a "follower" nation in world politics and economics. This does not mean that the country is without policies or merely the passive agent of external pressures. Quite the contrary. One study has recently concluded that "Japan has utilized foreign economic policy to bolster its overall economic growth with more autonomy, sovereignty, coherence, and macro-level success than any other major industrial power."[1] But as Chalmers Johnson has written, "Japan's processes of policy formation begin with concrete problems, often created by other actors in the international system, and then go forward to generalized principles and grand strategy, not vice-versa."[2] Japan's response to the international food crisis is a good example of this style of behavior. The purpose of this paper is to determine what, if any, principles and grand strategies Japan is following in light of the world food crisis. The paper will first discuss the country's political economy of agriculture, then summarize recent efforts in Japan to boost domestic food production. The final sections will review recent trends in foreign trade and aid policies, with particular reference to the ASEAN countries of Southeast Asia (Indonesia, Malaysia, the Philippines, Thailand, and Singapore).

A Decline in Food Power

Japan is a crowded country, poor in almost all natural resources and with less than 16 percent of total land area suitable for agricultural cultivation.

It is often said the nation's dependence on imports of raw materials, energy and food for survival fosters a collective feeling of being "defenseless on all sides" (*happo-yabure*).[3] During the 1960s, however, there was no major concern among most of the country's economic, political, and administrative elite about secure, reliable sources of food. In a period when the international market provided sufficient food, stable or declining prices, and large grain stocks, it was forgotten that food can be a weapon of war and a tool of diplomacy. The inability of Japan's farmers to satisfy rising demand led to a rapid growth in imports of food and animal feeds. The import policy seemed rational for a government-business elite pursuing with great determination the goal of rapid growth based on capital-intensive industrialization and unhindered access to world markets and technology. As late as 1972 government planners and private research organizations were calmly projecting continuing rapid decline in the agricultural economy as a consequence of official programs of rationalization and liberalization.[4]

A country's self-sufficiency in food can be measured in various ways. Table 1 indicates Japan's self-sufficiency ratio during the period 1960-1972.

However measured, Japan's self-sufficiency ratio declined dramatically. Fred H. Sanderson has measured Japan's self-sufficiency in terms of original food energy. According to his calculations, self-sufficiency was 80 percent in 1955 and 51 percent in 1972. He notes that even these figures overstate the country's real position since food production depends heavily on fertilizer produced from imported petroleum.[5]

By the early 1970s Japan was claiming close to 10 percent of total world agricultural imports; for commodities like grain sorghum, soybeans, maize, and raw sugar the percentage was higher. Altogether, food commodities were accounting for about 15 percent of total Japanese annual imports.[6]

No country is self-sufficient in all agricultural commodities. Nonetheless, such a rapid overall drop in a nation's food position is uncommon, if not unprecedented. An eminent agricultural economist in Japan declared that such a rapid decline in self-sufficiency had not happened since the final days of the Roman empire! Overall domestic production in agriculture grew at about 2.2 percent per annum. Production of vegetables and fruit improved, the livestock industry grew impressively and the dairy industry exceeded a growth rate of 10 percent each year during the 1960s. But the fall in self-sufficiency of wheat (from 39% to 4%), barley and naked barley (from 107% to 10%), and soybeans (from 28% to 3%) was startling.[7] Such a decline in food power must certainly give pause to foreign critics of Japan's "highly protectionist" policies toward agriculture.[8]

The reasons for this rapid deterioration in the country's food position are complex and can only be suggested here. Per capita income rose by 8.5 percent per annum during the 1960s. An increase in income reinforced changes in taste patterns. Consumption of rice, barley, and potatoes declined significantly while consumption of meat, eggs, dairy products, fruit, vegetables, sugar, and fish rose as the country moved toward more "westernized" consumption patterns. Structural change in agriculture is never easily accomplished, however, and Japan's small-scale, family-farm system simply could not respond to rapid changes in the food demands of a more affluent and growing population. Moreover, Japan's agricultural land has never been sufficient to provide food for the entire population. The country is especially poor in land needed for grass-eating livestock such as dairy and beef cattle. The cost of producing grain rose during the 1960s and trade liberalization of feed grains (1951) and soybeans (1961) provided more efficient farmers in countries like the United States with a growing market. Price incentives were not forthcoming from the government to encourage Japanese farmers to grow wheat or barley.[9]

Government action in connection with private ownership of agricultural land, farm scale, price policies, and fiscal spending for agriculture might have prevented some of the decline. As early as 1960 it was widely recognized that a new "modernization" program was necessary to alter the basic structure of agriculture by enlarging farms, adjusting output to changing consumption patterns, and by raising labor productivity and income. But politics and rural income standards took precedence over agricultural "modernization." For example, subsidized rice prices doubled in less than a decade; almost half the total budget for the Ministry of Agriculture and Forestry was used to encourage production of a food for which total and per capita demand was declining.[10]

After 1968 various problems connected with rice abundance forced the government to proclaim once again its intention to move away from a rice-centered to a more "integrated" agricultural policy. But it was the disturbing suddenness with which food problems developed in 1972 that prompted doubt about international transactions based on theories of comparative advantage of production and free markets. International shortages, the U.S. government's temporary embargo on soybean exports, and the oil crisis awakened the primeval fear that Japan was defenseless and vulnerable in an uncertain world. The Ministry of Agriculture and Forestry, farm groups, all the political parties and even some businessmen began to call for higher levels of self-sufficiency in the name of national security. More attention was given by government officials to ways to diversify the source of supply of imported agricultural products. New concern was also paid to foreign aid programs that might help improve the agricultural situation in Asian and other countries. Government-determined rice prices rose by a whopping 37 percent in 1974.

Japan's Current Food Position

Japan's external sources of food are relatively concentrated. The United States, Australia and Canada accounted for about half of Japan's total imports in 1976.[11] The United States provides about 29 percent of total food supplies including wheat (56%), corn (74%), and soybeans (91%). Japan is thus America's most important food customer; officials in Washington claim there are more Americans producing food for Japan than there are Japanese producing food for Japan. Australia supplies about 13 percent of total imports including beef, mutton, lamb, wheat, grain sorghum, and raw sugar. Japan is also Australia's largest single export market for agricultural products. Canada's major exports include wheat, barley, rapeseed, and pork. The Canadians have also made Japan their biggest agricultural customer. All three countries are eager to expand their exports to Japan.

Although Japan is not dependent on any single Asian country in the sense that there is a dependence on the United States for food commodities and on the Middle East for oil, altogether, Asia (including South Asia) accounts for almost 25 percent of Japan's total food imports. Viewed from an Asian perspective, over half of all exports to Japan from Thailand and the Philippines are foodstuffs. Food commodities from Taiwan are about 43 percent of total exports to Japan. Several other resources come from Asian countries in significant amounts (e.g., oil, bauxite, and timber from Indonesia).

Japan is thus an economic giant in Asia whose capacity to exercise "food power" derives from its position as a major food importer. The country is self-sufficient in only a few important foods: rice, potatoes, vegetables, eggs, and some seafoods. Japan derives about half its nonvegetable proteins from the sea. In this category also, the country is potentially vulnerable. In 1976 Japanese fishermen harvested about 10.8 million metric tons of seafood from the world's waters. However, about half of this was taken within 200 miles of another nation's shores. Food exports have been limited to frozen and chilled tuna, canned fish, mandarin oranges, and dried mushrooms (accounting for 1.3% of total exports in 1976).

Clearly, the food crisis in the early 1970s tapped reasonable fears in Japan, even if the reaction was a bit exaggerated. There are many reasons why officials in Japan continue to be concerned about external food supplies.

- A declining self-sufficiency ratio is synonymous with a greater dependency on foreign countries. Moreover, many projections for future international supplies are gloomy, world population is growing, weather is becoming more uncertain, costs of food production are rising and agricultural lands in export countries like Canada are increasingly being used for industrial and other nonfarm purposes.

- The United Kingdom, Italy, and West Germany all have serious food deficits. But Japan is the only large importer among industrial nations not integrated into a regional group. Therefore, the effects of international market changes may have a more direct impact on Japan than on other importing countries.

- The United States government has to worry about consumers as well as about farmers. A good deal of food policy in America seems to be more concerned with consumer welfare and farm equity than with international trade. Policies might be adopted to reduce production in the interest of maintaining farm incomes.

- GATT agreements make it difficult for countries to restrict imports. However, there is no international frame of reference to regulate the use of export controls. Since it is not an age of global food surplus, the United States might be tempted to use food as a weapon of diplomacy in the same manner that oil is used by the world's major exporters.

- Food imports are not a balance of payments for Japan. But in a time of food scarcity and distorted distribution, the suspicion can easily develop that Japan is using its powerful economic position in the world to take too much food.

- The worldwide trend toward establishing a 200-mile fishing zone is a direct threat to needed food supplies; at a minimum, new fishing zones will force Japan to bargain for its share of the world's seafood. The prime minister of New Zealand has hinted already that he would like to obtain food trade concessions in Japan in exchange for fishing rights in New Zealand waters.

Not all these anxieties are shared equally among politicians, bureaucrats, professional economists, and other informed elites. But while the shock of the international food crisis has abated, there is still concern about the future. Officials in Japan's Ministry of Agriculture and Forestry have projected that without food imports nutrition standards would drop in their country to perhaps 1,500 calories a day.[12]

The Political Economy of Agriculture

Japan's response to the world food crisis has been shaped by a delicate interplay of politics and economics. Agricultural policy in any country is enormously complicated because of the wide variety of economic and political goals connected with most government decisions. In the case of Japan, major farm policies are affected by such considerations as adequate production, national security, farm incomes, consumer welfare, government fiscal resources, stable prices, orderly markets, private profit, foreign trade, foreign aid, and political power. Different actions affect different individuals and groups associated with these considerations in different ways. There are no uniform patterns of decision nor are all decisions made in the same way. Matters become more complicated because international actors must also be taken into account. A brief review of some of the major domestic "actors" in Japanese agricultural policy can show why there is conflict in politics and inconsistency in government action.

Political Parties - During the Allied Occupation period the Liberal and Democratic Parties built their electoral strength in rural Japan. Following amalgamation in 1955, the new Liberal-Democratic Party (LDP) adopted policies of rapid industrialization that seemed to undermine their rural voters. Nonetheless, a substantial "rural voice" is still heard in party deliberations. Japan's electoral districts can be divided into four categories: metropolitan, urban, semi-rural, and rural. LDP support has declined considerably in metropolitan and urban districts. It has remained at about 61 percent in semi-rural districts and 70 percent in rural districts.[13] Excessive malapportionment provides even more advantage to rural voters. The political implications are clear to a ruling party desperately trying to hold on to political power: keep farmers reasonably happy.

Rural politicians become party leaders and Cabinet officials. Rice farmers can easily muster 200 or more LDP members in their marvelously flamboyant "rice-pricing" struggle each year. Dairy farmers, beef farmers, fruit farmers, and other cultivators of specialty crops heavily concentrated in key political districts, all have considerable support within the LDP. During recent trade negotiations with the United States, 100 members of the Diet opposed further liberalization of the beef trade. Over 200 members supporting fruit farmers joined together to oppose further imports of oranges and grapefruit. The Minister of Agriculture and Forestry warned that U.S. demands on agricultural imports were too high; the Minister of External Economic Affairs declared that Japan was not ready to accept "cheap, foreign products." None of the nation's opposition parties will dissent; at times, they are even more enthusiastic than the conservatives in their support of farmers.

There is no denying widespread concern among politicians about the welfare of rural Japan. And there is sufficient veto power within the LDP to protect farm constituents. But the political strength of rural Japan must not be exaggerated. For the most part, foreign economic policy has been dominated by the priorities set by a coalition of growth-oriented officials within the bureaucracy, large federations and trade associations of big business, major financial institutions (especially the government-dominated banks) and by successive LDP Cabinets eager to facilitate rapid industrialization. Thus Ohkawa and Rosovsky observe that "Since the 1950s, Japan has been not only a businessman's economic paradise—it has been an economic and political paradise...."[14] Considerations of foreign trade, consumer welfare, balanced budgets and private profit still find their way into agricultural policies.

Interest Groups - Farmers are well organized. For example, the Association of Agricultural

Cooperatives has maintained access to top political leaders in all parties, developed effective mass-lobbying techniques, contributed organizational and financial support to political parties, sponsored its own candidates to Parliament, maintained access to the Ministry of Agriculture and Forestry, provided extremely professional proposals concerning all aspects of agricultural policy, retained the membership of almost all farm families, and retained a key role in agricultural administration. A delegation led by the president of the Central Union of Agricultural Cooperatives visited Washington to explain their views concerning trade liberalization directly to Congressmen and officials of the government. There are also several farmers' unions and the semiofficial Chamber of Agriculture which lend their support to rural producers.[15]

But farmers have increasingly become divided along commodity and geographical lines. In the 1960s it was reasonably easy to mobilize the cooperative movement behind the annual rice-pricing struggle since a majority of farmers throughout the country produced at least some rice. Rice production has become more regionally concentrated in recent years. Farmers in the livestock industry or producers of vegetables, fruit, and other commodities are now anxious to seek their own advantages. Intra-crop competition has become a part of agrarian politics and the parliamentary form of decision-making is permitting government officials and politicians to play off different groups. This has divided the farm movement to some extent.

Equally important, there are other major interest groups, which might not be able to command as many troops as the farm organizations, but which are nonetheless quite effective. As in other countries, interest groups in Japan tend to form very close links with bureaus within government ministries. They also maintain close liaison with the permanent policy committee in the LDP. Major business federations in the country have allies in the Ministry of Trade and Industry (MITI). Because of these ties, it takes little overt political mobilization to convince a government official in MITI or the Ministry of Finance that further trade liberaliza-

tion is necessary for big business which produces for the international market.

Commercial Marketing - Food is a political commodity. It is also a commercial good which can provide huge profits. Events in the late 1970s in Japan suggest that extraordinary profits are sometimes made in the commerce of imported food items. A considerable amount of food imports are handled by Japan's general trading companies (Sōgō Shōsha).[16] There are about 6,000 trading companies, but 9 major firms dominate the field. Their functions go well beyond marketing and distribution to include research and development, overseas project construction, transport, joint ventures, third party trade, information gathering, resource development, financing, and market development at home. The 9 largest trading firms handle about 50 percent of Japan's exports, 60 percent of all imports, and about 20 percent of domestic wholesale and retail transactions. The total business of the top companies exceeds the amount of international trade of most countries of the world. There is considerable evidence to show that this gives Japanese commercial interests substantial market power overseas to keep prices of raw materials artificially low.[17] Since food imports are handled by these private commercial interests their activities also have an enormous impact on the availability and price of food at home.

Mitsui Bussan, for example, played a central role in developing the poultry industry in Japan. The company imported feed made from milo, maize, soybeans, wheat bran, and other basic commodities. The company also moved to guarantee the purchase of chickens raised by farmers and poultry farms. As the demand for chickens increased, Mitsui also went into wholesale and retail distribution by making agreements with producers, dealers, and retail outlets.[18]

Vast industrial complexes have also been organized by trading companies so that food such as corn, soybeans, or animal feed can be transported from silos overseas to huge storage silos built at Japanese port-cities. One plant next to the silo can produce oil, flour, sugar, and cornstarch. Another nearby plant uses these products to make noodles, bread, animal feed, millet jelly, etc. The trading company thus imports the raw materials on its own ships, and then handles both the primary manufactured product and the secondary products. Profits accumulate at each stage.[19]

What happens to food commodities after they arrive in Japan is nonetheless a bit of a mystery. Retail prices of many food items are frequently several times those in the country of origin. A reporter for a meat trade journal recently triggered a national stir when he described the incredibly complex beef-distribution system in Japan. He alleged that agricultural cooperatives and leading meat dealers were making in ordinate profits by artificially controlling prices. He also described the beef import system. The Livestock Industry Promotion Corporation is designated by the Ministry of Agriculture and Forestry as the sole importer of livestock products. Only designated dealers are allowed to distribute imported beef. A surcharge is paid to the Corporation by importers as a means of protecting domestic producers. The surcharge collected on imported beef amounted to about $104 million in 1976. What happened to this money became a hot issue. The Corporation claimed that it was used to promote the domestic livestock industry, but the public was not persuaded. Beef brought from Australia was about $1.60 per kilogram; by the time it reached the consumer it was $6 or more. The profits of trading companies dealing with imported beef have risen and consumers have become deeply suspicious and quite angry.[20]

Government Ministries - Since agricultural policy is connected with so many political and economic interests it means that government actions are not in the control of any one ministry. Coordination, compromise, and trade-offs must be forged through the same political process found in any bureaucratic setting. Thus it is possible to indicate only in general terms where the various bureaucracies stand with regard to self-sufficiency, agricultural trade, and foreign aid.

The Ministry of Foreign Affairs is unusually decentralized so that divisions and bureaus have more freedom than is found in other ministries.[21] Considerable importance is given by all officials to the American alliance, although geographic bureaus concerned with Asia and the Far East place special importance on areas within their jurisdiction. The Foreign Affairs Ministry generally takes a liberal position on trade matters but there seems to be broad support for actions to increase Japan's aid to Asia. The ministry is obviously hampered by its lack of any important domestic support groups.

The Ministry of Finance is considered the most prestigious of Japan's ministries, although such a generalization has to be qualified when it comes to agricultural policy.[22] The ministry has a reputation of being liberal on trade matters but conservative when it comes to foreign aid. The guardians of the public treasury are generally unhappy with the high level of subsidization provided farmers and annually aggrieved when rice prices continue to rise, although Japan's declining self-sufficiency ratio does not seem to be treated as a matter of grave importance.

The Ministry of Trade and Industry has been liberal on agricultural trade but for reasons of promoting Japan's international competitiveness rather than commitment to principles of free trade.[23] Generally, the ministry has been protectionist in the areas of trade and foreign capital. All the ministries have officials dealing with economic aid; but the annual government report on foreign aid is compiled by the Ministry of Trade and Industry,[24] and this probably helps to account for the distinct businesslike orientation in the country's aid policies. MITI and the Ministry of Foreign Affairs must cooperate with each other in the conduct of international economic relations. Last year, for the first time, the Ministry of Foreign Affairs issued its own official report on foreign aid. Clearly an intra-bureaucratic squabble is under way in connection with future aid priorities.

The Ministry of Agriculture and Forestry is firmly against any liberalization of food commodities trade that might adversely affect their constituents. The ministry is also eager to boost Japan's self-sufficiency in food. Its position on agricultural aid seems to be reasonably positive.

Although the ministry is influential because of political support received from the LDP and farm groups, it is not the unquestioning pawn or captive of rural zealots.

Some of the consequences of politics can be readily seen. Food prices are high in Japan. The country's protectionist policies have certainly held the growth of imports of beef, pork, citrus products, and other commodities in check and thus contributed to inflationary pressures in the economy. Some economists will argue that a good deal of the explanation for relatively low levels of nutrition in Japan can be related to high food prices. There is also growing foreign pressure to relax import barriers against foodstuffs. Protection creates unhappy allies, angry consumers, and handsome profits for some importers and food distributors.

Farmers benefit from protection but not all of them perceive themselves to be especially privileged. Like their counterparts elsewhere, many Japanese farmers are caught in a difficult price-cost squeeze. The small-scale farm system probably exacerbates the lag between rural and urban incomes. The Ministry of Agriculture and Forestry wants to increase the nation's self-sufficiency ratio but seems unable adequately to control the economic decisions of producers and the political behavior of politicians. There is widespread recognition that Japan must diversify its sources of external supply; how this will be connected with international food problems and agricultural aid programs is extremely uncertain.

Boosting Domestic Production

The economic constraints that make Japanese agriculture especially vulnerable are well known. As long as agriculture continues to require soil, the relative balance between total population and the amount of arable land in Japan will be a severe limitation. One study shows that per capita acreage available for food production is 0.05 of a hectare, the lowest of all countries surveyed including West Germany, United Kingdom, and Korea.[25] To be self-sufficient in soybeans and sorghum alone would require more land than the total acreage under rice crops. A clear challenge for the country is to develop a kind of agriculture not dependent on the soil and reliant upon newly refined agricultural techniques.

Structural problems are also a major limiting factor. The average farm size in the country is about 1.1 hectare. According to a recent white paper on agriculture, 87 percent of all farm households are engaged in agriculture on a part-time basis. Only 9 percent of all farm households were defined as "viable units" in the sense that incomes from agriculture amount to at least the average income of nonagricultural households in towns and cities. In 1976 about 54 percent of the agricultural working force was female, another 13 percent was males aged 60 or older, and 26 percent was comprised of males between 35 and 59 years of age. The number of young people who have decided to take up careers in farming has decreased from 260,000 in 1955 to 10,000 in 1975.[26] Part-time farming has permitted farm households to maintain income levels with other sectors of the economy. But such a farm structure has impeded the enlargement of farms, limited productivity gains, and inhibited adequate response to changing consumer demands.

The economic conditions of Japanese agriculture imply perhaps that the country would be well-advised to use its land, labor, and capital for nonagricultural purposes and to import almost all its food. But considerations of national security, social order, and political power require that some of the advantages of an ideal international division of labor be sacrificed. Since 1975 the government has been trying to implement a program of "integrated food policies" (*Sōgō Shokuryō Seisaku*) aimed at stabilization and development of imports, increased stockpiling, protection of fishing resources and an increase in food-sufficiency to 75 percent on a value basis by 1985.[27]

The new effort to improve domestic production followed the recommendations of the Advisory Council on Agricultural Policy (*Nōsei Shingikai*) and the 1975 National Food Conference (*Kokumn Shokuryō Kaigi*). Participants in the Conference were appointed by the Prime Minister and included representatives from producer and consumer groups, business leaders, the heads of food marketing organizations, members of the press, prefectural governors, academic specialists and chairmen of a few advisory councils used by the Ministry of Agriculture and Forestry to formulate general policies.[28] Such a gathering of eminent economic, intellectual, and political leaders frequently precedes new departures in policy. It symbolizes the existence of a broad consensus, although differences over details usually persist.

The "integrated" program to improve self-sufficiency is not a crash program in economic development. It is an example of long-term, "indicative" planning to be used as a guideline for future policy. The goals of the program include the following:

- the development of some new arable land and the restoration of double-cropping to increase the overall planted area by 836,000 hectares;

- the promotion of wheat, barley, soybean, and rapeseed production;

- the promotion of forage production through acreage payments;

-renewed efforts to encourage full-time farming;

- the use of price policies to encourage the production of food rather than as welfare policies to guarantee the incomes of part-time farmers;

- the continuation of rice-diversion programs to encourage the productin of other crops;

- assistance to the fishing industry to develop marine resources in waters near Japan;

- the development of new food resources;

- the promotion of rice consumption.

The program also calls for diversification and stabilization of food imports and a more positive attitude toward bilateral and multilateral commodity agreements.[29] Table 2 shows projected self-sufficiency ratios based on 1972 levels.

Attaining an overall growth in self-sufficiency of 2 percent in 10 years may appear modest. When growth in domestic demand (including population growth) is taken into account, however, the projections imply an increase in production of about 27 percent. A number of economists and other observers have expressed strong doubt that such levels of self-sufficiency can be achieved, especially those projected for wheat, barley, soybeans, beef, fruits, and concentrated feeds. The principal misgivings include the following:

- availability of funds: subsidies, special payments, and other funds required to boost production to such levels will not be available. Government revenues to agriculture will probably drop, especially if overall economic growth rates decline. Measures to increase domestic production are designed within the Ministry of Agriculture and Forestry; but funds for new departures involve the interests of other ministries. Rice farmers have received generous treatment because annual pricing decisions are made outside the annual budget process. Funds for increased "self-sufficiency" are allocated through the regular budgetary process which means that farm programs must compete with other national priorities.

- availablity of land: the amount of land in agriculture can be expanded by using existing farmland more extensively and by creating more farmland. An effective increase of about 836,000 hectares is needed. Few economists or other experts believe this will be possible when industry is slowly moving to rural areas and many farmers are employed part-time in nonagricultural sectors of the economy.

- expansion of farm scale: the numerical dominance of older people in the agricultural work force and the effects of land speculation, especially on the fringe of industrial and urban development areas, discourages the possibility of expanding the scale of management.

- the desire to retain their ownership of farmland keeps many farmers in their village; the high cost of land prevents full-time farmers from expanding their scale of management.

- price policies: politics will assure that price policies will continue to be used as a welfare measure to protect farm incomes. Rice politics has demonstrated that part-time farmers prefer price supports as a means to support rural incomes.

The prognosis for the next few years is thus for a continuation of a downward trend in domestic production, but at a much slower rate than the decline of the 1960s. The share of agriculture, forestry, and fisheries in the country's future GNP is expected to be somewhat larger than previously estimated. For the first time in many decades, the annual white paper on agriculture for fiscal 1975 reported that the future of farming is bright and that growth in the primary sector will be a positive element in the nation's economy for years to come.[30]

Foreign Trade

The most striking feature of Japan's position in the world economy is its almost total lack of domestic sources of crucial raw materials. Scarcity in raw materials influences in a central way its economic relations with other countries just as dependence on foreigners for basic necessities creates a pervasive sense of national insecurity at all levels of Japanese society. As we have seen, Japan imports a substantial proportion of its foodstuffs. The country's food position will thus continue to be greatly affected by the economic and political conditions in exporting countries and by general world market conditions.

The economic logic of Japan's food position dictates support of world policies of free trade, international coordination, and unhindered market access. As a major importer of agricultural commodities Japan is seeking arrangements to maintain essential supplies at relatively stable prices: long-term supply contracts, government-to-government agreements and overseas joint ventures which assure more Japanese control of production and distribution. As a good international citizen, Japan should probably also be in favor of international commodity arrangements, multinational food reserves, and improved worldwide information concerning agriculture and international stockpiling schemes. The nation's

elite will fear export embargoes, contract cancellation, new price negotiations under existing contracts and government-imposed export prices to circumvent earlier agreed-on prices.

Domestic political circumstances will provide other imperatives. Protectionist policies have been pursued in order to enhance national security, to protect farm incomes, and to help preserve the political support of the present LDP government. This has meant tariff and other restrictions inconsistent with GATT principles and high food prices inconsistent with the wishes of urban consumers and foreign-oriented businessmen. High support prices for commodities like rice and the accompanying trade protection for other commodities will probably continue in order to sustain high farm incomes.

There exist, then, widely divergent views on how international trade should be organized and what principles should pertain to it. The situation is complicated even more because other countries like to instruct Japan on how to pursue economic goals. Japan's food security, especially for grains and pulses, depends on the United States, and most experts in Japan believe the dependence will increase in coming years. Japanese officials are thus continuing to portray their country as a mature, stable, and reliable market and are anxious to establish formal trade agreements to obviate the possibility of any future soybean or other unwanted "shocks." But formal commitments from the United States are not easy to extract. Moreover, the mounting Japanese trading surplus is creating new tensions between the close allies. American officials want Japan to reduce restrictions on commodities like beef, oranges, and citrus juice. A 1978 concession by the Japanese government prompted an American congressman to warn that "token concessions" would not satisfy protectionist forces in the United States and might prompt retaliatory trade moves.[31]

There is some commercial competition among Japan's three most important trading partners in agriculture. Japan will continue to take advantage of this while also seeking bilateral import agreements on both private and official levels. Understandings of various kinds have been established with the United States, Australia, and Canada as well as with some other export countries. Competition among political enemies also intrudes on Japan's agricultural trade policies. Japan signed a $20 billion industrial trade pact with China in 1978. It was the most dramatic single link between the two countries since 1972.[32] This new link, however, might prompt some form of retaliation from the Soviet Union, perhaps through restrictions on Japan's access to Russia's fertile fishing grounds in the Pacific.

Japan has also moved to diversify its sources of external supply in order to reduce the risk of unilateral action by a single source of supply. The countries of Southeast Asia are a possible area of development. Thailand is now Japan's fourth most important source of agricultural commodities as measured in total value and only the United States sells more maize to Japan. The Thai government would like to increase sales of maize, sorghum, chilled beef, sugar, and a number of fish foods. But according to a recent study by the Japan External Trade Organization, Thai prices are relatively high and some improvement in quality is also desired.[33]

Overseas investment in agricultural development is also increasing. But Japan must move with caution. A new interest in agricultural development in Tokyo is not regarded without some suspicion and doubt in Southeast Asia. Warnings about Japan's policies of "agrarian imperialism" are sometimes expressed by government officials and intellectuals in the region. The cumulative total of Japanese private investments overseas amounted to about $16 billion at the end of the Japanese fiscal year of 1975 (April 1975 - March 1976). Almost 55 percent was in developing countries. Investment in the Republic of Korea, the Philippines, Thailand, and Indonesia was especially high.[34] Since the world food crisis more attention has been given to investment in agriculture. The Overseas Agricultural Development Association was set up in 1975 to support enterprises carried out in other countries involving the production of maize, sorghum, soybeans, and beef for export to Japan.

The Overseas Economic Cooperation Fund (OECF) has been a major instrument for the Japanese government to provide loans and investment funds for development projects in the Third World. About 85 percent of all OECF loans for foreign government and government agencies have gone to Asian countries. Loans are also given to Japanese enterprises engaged in overseas projects such as the development of a banana plantation in the Philippines and maize plantations in Indonesia. Trading companies have also been involved in agricultural development programs in such diverse countries as Indonesia, Brazil, Australia, Afghanistan, and Mexico. It is still too early to judge the overall success of this new attempt to diversify Japan's overseas sources of food.

Foreign Aid

A brief review of aid policies shows that Japanese politics is divided by multiple centers of power and interests.[35] It demonstrates also that there are few advocates of foreign aid who are indifferent to instrumental utility or unconcerned about Japan's economic and political interests. The priorities of foreign economic policy have greater importance than the "humanitarian" needs of the recipient. In this regard, Japan appears to be little different from other industrial countries including especially the United States.[36]

Actors - The political and administrative responsibility for foreign aid programs is widely shared.   The Ministry of Foreign Affairs is responsible for negotiations with foreign governments on economic cooperation. But decisions about projects and financing also include participation by the Ministries of Finance, International Trade and Industry, Agriculture and Forestry, and the Economic Planning Agency. These ministries also consult with the Overseas Economic Cooperation Fund, the Export-Import Bank and the Japanese International Cooperation Agency. These latter agencies are placed under the supervision of different ministries, thus exacerbating sectionalism in government. The External Development Cooperation Council is an advisory council to the Prime Minister and helps provide nongovernmental views on foreign aid. In addition, government officials also maintain contact with a variety of other government-affiliated organizations, the LDP, and with private businessmen. Aid disbursements must be approved by Parliament. Such pluralistic arrangements make it difficult to reconcile conflicting views, yet Japan's political style emphasizes consensual decision-making and thus discourages major departures or new innovations. Inertia might be the most important explanation of aid policies.

The record - Among the member nations of the Development Assistance Committee (DAC) of the OECD, Japan ranks fourth—after the United States, France, and West Germany—in terms of the amount of official development assistance (ODA) given (grants, technical cooperation, direct loans, and contributions to international agencies).[37] In terms of percentage share of the DAC's total, Japan accounted for 8.1 percent in 1976. However, Japan's ODA disbursements declined in 1976 by 3.7 percent in nominal terms, to $1.10 billion. As a percentage of GNP, ODA fell from 0.23 percent in 1975 to 0.20 percent in 1976, the lowest level since 1964. Japan's percentage was thirteenth among the 17 members and well below the DAC average of 0.33 percent. Private economic assistance rose by 38.5 percent in 1976 so that total official and private flows reached 0.72 percent of GNP as compared with 0.59 percent in 1975. This figure was also below average among the DAC members. Total ODA disbursements for 1977 were expected to increase substantially following the announcement by the government that it would double its ODA within five years.

The financial terms of Japan's ODA continued to soften during 1976 but still failed to meet the DAC terms recommended. The grant element of Japan's ODA was 75 percent as compared to the DAC average of 88.5 percent. This placed Japan as lowest of all member countries. The terms and conditions of direct loans are more stringent than those of other industrial countries. The share of technical cooperation in bilateral aid is also below DAC average. The large percentage of total aid that is non-ODA is generally taken to mean that Japanese aid is marked by a high degree of commercial and business interest, the pattern for some years.

According to OECD reports, Japan was involved in 42 agricultural projects as of January 1975.[38] Eighteen of these projects involved capital assistance and twenty-four involved technical assistance. Major outlays were for irrigation projects, the construction of fertilizer plants (Peru, India), and a rural development project in Korea. The Japan International Cooperation Agency (JICA) plays a central role in expanding Japanese economic and technical cooperation. Programs fall into three categories: accepting trainees from developing countries, sending experts to aid recipient countries, and grants of machinery and equipment. In 1976 JICA was involved in different ways in agricultural projects in 17 countries. Eight projects were in Indonesia and five in Thailand. About 8.2 percent of all Japanese bilateral project assistance in 1975 went to agriculture, forestry, and fisheries.[39] This percentage has been rising slowly.

Japan's economic cooperation policy places great emphasis on Asia since the region has close historical, geographical, and economic relationships with Japan. Asia accounted for 77 percent of Japan's ODA in 1976. Southeast Asia accounted for 56 percent of the 5 ASEAN nations accounted for 48 percent. Table 3 shows the amount of official development assistance given to Southeast Asian countries during the period 1974-1976. Indonesia received a little over one-fourth of all ODA. The second largest recipient was the Philippines followed by Thailand. No other nation received more than 5 percent of total ODA. The Republic of Korea (not shown here) received 3.2 percent of Japan's ODA. These countries all have a high level of private direct investment by Japanese.

Japan has also been active in the international framework created in the past two decades for the economic and social development of Asian countries, including Southeast Asia. Tokyo's leaders have emphasized multilateral channels in order to lessen the real fear of Japanese economic exploitation felt by many people in an area of vital interest to Japan. A multilateral approach broadens economic and political risks and also keeps some of the other rich, industrial countries of the world in Asia. Japan has been the largest subscriber, along with the United States, in the Asian Development Bank since its inauguration. In 1976 Japan subscribed $603 million, which was slightly over 16 percent of the total subscription of the bank. Japan is also the largest contributor to the Asian Development Fund and the Technical Assistance Special Fund. Finally, the country has been active in various other regional institutions including the Asian Productivity Center, the Colombo Plan, the Ministerial Conference for the Economic Development of Southeast Asia, the UN Economic and Social Commission for Asia and the Pacific (ESCAP), and with various regional research and training centers.

Motives - Hasegawa's study of Japan's foreign aid programs which were launched in the early 1950s asserts that aid was tailored to attain five major objectives: "(1) to spur the process of Japanese reconstruction and economic growth; (2) to establish diplomatic relations between Japan and neighboring countries; (3) to maintain a political, economic, and social system, and to stabilize policies of aid-receiving countries that are beneficial to Japan; (4) to raise per capita income in Japan; and (5) to assert Japan's influence and leadership in both regional and global communities."[40] Other studies do not deviate very much from such conclusions. One does not need to be a gloomy cynic to recognize the strong economic, if not self-serving character, of much of Japanese foreign aid. As an Indonesian Cabinet minister recently observed, Japanese trade, aid and investments are "three cards held in one hand."[41]

A number of additional observations are possible based on current patterns of Japan's aid-giving.

- Japan's concern about food and other agricultural problems has been directed primarily toward the major exporting countries, especially the United States. The LDCs in Asia have been viewed in a regional context (ASEAN) and considered as suppliers of other critical raw materials or as large markets for exports of goods and services.

- Japan concentrates its aid in countries which are important in terms of its overseas economic interests (Indonesia, Thailand, and the Philippines). In this sense, Japan's objectives are primarily economic.

- The worldwide distribution of Japanese aid indicates that a large amount of ODA is allocatd to high-income, relatively high-growth countries.

- Japanese aid agencies rely on overseas businessmen to help identify potential projects.[42] This implies that aid will tend to support Japan's economic interests.

- There is an absence of any significant native tradition of philanthropy in Japan and a widespread belief that individual nations must take primary responsibility for their own development. However, recent polls conducted in Japan show widespread support for additional national aid programs.

- National strategic interests seem to have been less directly connected to Japan's aid programs than to those of the United States, although aid to Korea is clearly connected to underlying strategic interests and the post-Vietnam situation in Asia is forcing Japanese policy-makers to think more broadly in strategic terms.

- Japan's aid is distributed for the most part to anticommunist regimes in Asia.

- International agencies in recent years have stressed the need to emphasize programs focusing on health, nutrition, shelter, education, and food; Japan's aid-givers have tended to perceive inadequacies in basic economic infrastructures as a key constraint to development. Aid programs have been shaped accordingly.

- The politics of aid makes new departures very difficult.

- Agricultural development has not been a major concern until very recently.

- A tentative review of Japan's aid programs reveals that many projects are supported without a coherent, overall set of policies.

Future - Japan's economic and political strategies in Asia are in a significant period of delicate transition. The new economic agreement with China has already been mentioned. A government advisory council on foreign aid recommended in 1976 that Japan's ODA percentage be increased to the average attained by the OECD countries by 1980. Soon thereafter, the government committed itself to double its ODA in three years. The World Bank estimated that the country's ODA would be increased in yen terms, from about ¥380 billion in 1977 to about ¥760 billion in 1980. Japan has been piling up a huge balance of payments surplus since 1976 and so there is great pressure inside and outside the country to use some of these funds for hard-pressed developing countries. However, there is as yet no official word on when the three-year period will begin or if the doubling of ODA will be achieved in dollar or yen terms.[43]

Japan has also emerged as a kind of pacemaker of economic integration for the five ASEAN countries. Prime Minister Takeo Fukuda made a widely publicized tour of Southeast Asia in 1977, in connection with the tenth anniversary of the Association. During his visit, the Prime Minister pledged a loan package of $1 billion for five industrial projects to be undertaken by each of the five ASEAN countries. The Ministry of Foreign Affairs designated the offer as part of the new "Fukuda Doctrine" and thus a "Dawn of a New Era" in Japan's relations with Southeast Asia.

Japan's new interest in the ASEAN regional grouping can be explained by a number of reasons: apprehension in Tokyo about the stability of Southeast Asia in the post-Vietnam era; an opportunity for Japan to assert its power and prestige in a regional grouping in which no other great power is directly involved; the movement of ASEAN away from political and military concerns to more economic-related matters; the location of Japan's vital economic interests and the geographical position of the ASEAN countries which lie athwart Japan's vital trade routes to Europe and the Middle East; the growing demand among ASEAN leaders for a more cooperative stance from Tokyo in trade and economic matters; the pressure from the Carter administration that Japan play a more active role in Asian affairs; and the inherent compatability of countries all more or less favoring an open economy.[44]

To what extent the "Fukuda Doctrine" will reflect a new concern for agricultural development is uncertain. All the countries in ASEAN have requested additional funds for agricultural development projects. Recent announcements by the Ministry of Foreign Affairs have also made it clear that a new emphasis would be placed on technical cooperation projects. By 1978, sufficient financial support had been provided for 17 technical cooperation projects run by the JICA in various countries to train personnel for rice farming, dry field farming, sericulture, stock farming, and afforestation. According to Japanese government reports, an agricultural development program in southern Sumatra has been well received. Under the supervision of Japanese experts, farmers from some 1,400 households work on a demonstration farm covering 100 hectares. The rice crop has increased by 40 percent and annual income rose by 60 percent in four years. About 4,600 households are growing corn, soybeans, and other crops. The project also includes an agricultural extension center where Japanese experts teach techniques to local residents and also cooperate in soil analysis and agricultural experiments.[45]

Japan's aid will not be restricted to these five Asian countries. Prime Minister Fukuda also visited Burma in 1977 and press reports indicate that Japan still hopes to improve relations with Vietnam and other Southeast Asian countries. As Japan's first economic assistance to Vietnam since it was unified, the JICA is helping to finance a project to improve corn production. The agreement was worked out with Vietnam by the National Federation of Agricultural Cooperatives.

Japan has also taken a more global approach to the food problem. The country recently contributed $55 million to the International Fund for Agriculture Development. A Centre for Integrated Rural Development in Asia and the Pacific is also being established by FAO with the cooperation of the Japanese government.

Conclusion
There are many signs that a fundamental shift is under way in Japan's food policies as a consequence of uncertainties in the international food

market. Politics as much as reasoned principles or grand strategies will largely shape future actions. More attention is certainly being given to domestic production. Nonetheless, Japan will continue to need imports and will find itself under continual pressure to let in more foreign-produced foods. A prima facie case can easily be made for extending trade between Japan and the countries of Pacific Asia (including Australia and New Zealand): (1) they are geographically proximate; (2) trade flows between Japan and the Asian Pacific countries are important and long-standing; (3) there is considerable potential for agricultural development in many Asian countries; (4) diversification of external sources of supply will probably permit Japan to be a bit more secure about food.[46] But politics and economics are not so easily separated; any important change in agricultural trade patterns will be slow in coming. In this sense, Japan is tied to the non-Asian world.

It is a simple task for the outsider to observe that Japan can do more about foreign aid, including agricultural development cooperation.[47] The country is affluent by most standards. Economic and social stability in Asia are closely connected to Japan's self-interests. Japan also has a rich and successful experience in adapting technology to the needs of small farms. The country has been a pioneer in the technology of high-yielding rice varieties and its agricultural supply firms produce a whole variety of modern machines suitable to small-scale farming. Japan has a unique opportunity to play a central role in Asian agricultural development. Given Japan's heavy dependence on foreign resources, its extremely close interdependence with developing countries through trade and investment, and in view of the international environment surrounding Japan, it seems doubtful that agricultural development can be ignored.

NOTES

1. T.J. Pempel, "Japanese foreign economic policy: the domestic bases for international behavior," *International Organization* 31 (Autumn 1977), pp. 723-774.

2. Chalmers Johnson, "The Japanese Problem," in Donald C. Hellmann, ed., *China and Japan: A New Balance of Power* (Lexington, MA: Lexington Books, 1976), pp. 51-94.

3. Saburo Okita, "Natural Resource Dependency and Japanese Foreign Policy," *Foreign Affairs* 52 (July 1974), pp. 714-724; Charles F. Gallagher, "Japan and the World Food Problem," [CFG-1-'75], *AUFS Reports*, East Asia Series, Vol. XXII, No. 1, 1975.

4. Gary Saxonhouse and Hugh Patrick, "Japan and the United States: Bilateral Tensions and Multilateral Issues in the Economic Relationship," in Hellmann, "China and Japan," p. 119.

5. Fred H. Sanderson, *Japan's Food Prospects and Policies* (Washington, D.C., The Brookings Institution, 1978), p. 12. See also Takekazu Ogura, "Implications of Japan's Declining Food Self-Sufficiency Ratio," *The Developing Economies* 14 (December 1976), pp. 419-448.

6. Statistics on Japan's food trade are taken from Japan External Trade Organization (JETRO), *White Paper on International Trade*, various issues.

7. All figures are for the period 1960-1973. See Japan, Ministry of Agriculture and Forestry, *Nihon no Shokuryo Seisaku o Kangaeru* [An Analysis of Japan's Food Policy] (Tokyo, 1976), p. 76.

8. It has been recently argued that when restrictions such as waivers, import surcharges and state trading are taken into account, liberalization of agricultural imports might be higher in Japan than in West European countries. See Hiroshi Kitamura, *Choices for the Japanese Economy* (London: The Royal Institute of International Affairs, 1976), p. 145.

9. A good review of Japanese agriculture during this period is OECD, *Agricultural Policy in Japan* (Paris, 1974).

10. See Michael W. Donnelly, "Setting the Price of Rice: A Study in Political Decisionmaking," in T.J. Pempel, ed., *Policymaking in Contemporary Japan* (Ithaca: Cornell University Press), pp. 143-200; Yujiro Hayami, "Rice Policy in Japan's Economic Development," *American Journal of Agricultural Economics* 54 (1972), pp. 19-31.

11. Statistics in the following discussion are taken from JETRO, *White Paper on International Trade, 1977*.

12. John F. Cooper and Kenneth R. Stunkel, "The Elusive Goal: Great Power Status," *The Japan Interpreter*, 13 (Winter 1975), pp. 292-314.

13. J.A.A. Stockwin, *Japan: Divided Politics in a Growth Economy* (London: Weidenfeld and Nicolsen, 1975), p. 100.

14. Kazushi Ohkawa and Henry Rosovsky, *Japanese Economic Growth* (Stanford: Stanford University Press, 1973), p. 245.

15. For details see Tanaka Toyotoshi, *Nihon no Nokyo* [Japan's Association of Agricultural Cooperatives] (Tokyo, Nokyo Kyokai, 1971).

16. On Japanese trading companies see Kikuiri Ryusuke, "Shosha: Organizers of the World Economy," *The Japan Interpreter* 8 (Autumn 1973), pp. 353-373; Lawrence B. Krause and Sueo Sekiguchi, "Japan and the World Economy," in Hugh Patrick and Henry Rosovsky, ed., *Asia's New Giant* (Washington, D.C., The Brookings Institution, 1976), especially pp. 389-397.

17. Franklin B. Weinstein, "Multinational corporations and the Third World: the case of Japan and Southeast Asia," *International Organization* 30 (Summer 1976), pp. 373-404.

18. Kikuiri, "Shosha," pp. 361-62,

19. JETRO, *The Role of Trading Companies in International Commerce* (Tokyo: JETRO Marketing Series, No. 2, 1972).

20. Yokota Tetsuji, *Gyuniku wa naze Takaika* [Why is Beef so Expensive?] (Tokyo: The Simul Press, Inc., 1977).

21. I.M. Destler, et al., *Managing An Alliance: The Politics of U.S. - Japanese Relations* (Washington, D.C., The Brookings Institution, 1976), especially chapter two.

22. John Creighton Campbell, *Contemporary Japanese Budget Politics* (Berkeley and Los Angeles: The University of California Press, 1977).

23. Chalmers Johnson, "MITI and Japanese International Economic Policy," in Robert A. Scalapino, ed., *The Foreign Policy of Modern Japan* (Berkeley and Los Angeles: The University of California Press, 1977), pp. 227-279.

24. See Japan, Ministry of Trade and Industry, *Keizai Kyoryoku no Genjo to Mondai-ten*, annual. The English language report is JETRO, *Economic Cooperation of Japan*, annual.

25. Ogura, "Implications of Japan's," p. 433.

26. Japan, Ministry of Agriculture and Forestry, *Nogyo Hakusho* (Agricultural White Paper), 1977.

27. For details of the new "integrated" food-policies see Japan, Ministry of Agriculture and Forestry, *Nihon no Shokuryo.*

28. *Ibid.*, p. 279.

29. See Sanderson, *Japan's Food Prospects*; Organization for Economic Co-operation and Development, *Review of Agricultural Policies in OECD Member Countries, 1974-76* (Paris: OECD, 1977), pp. 76-83.

30. *The Japan Economic Review*, May 15, 1977.

31. *The New York Times*, January 13, 1978.

32. *Ibid.*, February 17, 1978.

33. JETRO, *Focus Japan*, December 1977.

34. JETRO, *White Paper on International Trade* (1977), p. 43.

35. Studies of Japan's aid programs include Lawrence Olson, *Japan in Postwar Asia* (New York: Praeger Publishers, 1970); Sukihiro Hasegawa, *Japanese Foreign Aid: Policy and Practice* (New York: Praeger Publishers, 1975); Martha F. Loutfi, *The Net Cost of Japanese Foreign Aid* (New York: Praeger Publishers, 1973).

36. See R.D. McKinlay and R. Little, "A Foreign Policy Model of U.S. Bilateral Aid Allocation," *World Politics* 30 (October 1977), pp. 58-86.

37. Current information on Japan's aid programs is based on the following sources: *Keizai Kyoryoku no Genjo to Mondaiten*, 1976; JETRO, *Economic Cooperation of Japan*, 1977; and OECD, *Development Co-operation*, 1977.

38. OECD, *Development Co-operation*, 1975.

39. *Keizai Kyoryoku no Genjo to Mindaiten* (1976) p. 153.

40. Hasegawa, *Japanese Foreign Aid*, p. 11.

41. Weinstein, "Multinational corporations," p. 379.

42. For evidence concerning businessmen as roving ambassadors see William E. Bryant, *Japanese Private Economic Diplomacy* (New York: Praeger Publishers, 1975).

43. *Japan Times*, July 15, 1978.

44. See Weinstein, "Multinational corporations," and Shee Poon-Kim, "A Decade of ASEAN, 1967-1977," *Asian Survey* 17 (August 1977), pp. 753-770.

45. See Japan Information Service, *Japan Report*, Vol. 24, #2, January 16, 1978.

46. A significant study of Japan's trade with Pacific Asian countries is Thomas P. Kreshner, *Japanese Foreign Trade* (Lexington, MA, Lexington Books, 1975).

47. A recent proposal by Saburo Okita, Chairman of the Japan Economic Research Center, to double rice production in Asia has generated considerable discussion in Japan and elsewhere. See *Trialogue* (Spring 1978).

Table 1
Japan's Degree of Feed Self-Sufficiency (1960-1972)

			(unit: %)	
	1960	1965	1970	1972
Value of All Foods[a]	89	81	75	72
Concentrated Feeds	67	44	33	36
Original Calories	78	65	56	53

a. excludes marine products

Source: Japan, Ministry of Agriculture, Forestry and Fisheries.

Table 2
The Supply and Demand of Selected Food Commodities 1972 and 1985

	1972			1985		
	Domestic Consumption	Domestic Production	Self-Sufficiency Ratio	Domestic Consumption	Domestic Production	Self-Sufficiency Ratio
Rice	11,948	11,897	100	12,110	12,110	100
Wheat	5,372	284	5	5,899	553	9
Barley	1,842	324	18	2,502	890	36
Sweet and White Potatoes	5,604	5,598	100	4,927	4,927	100
Soybean	3,496	127	4	5,007	427	9
Peanuts	119	64	54	156	82	53
Other Beans	378	268	71	380	218	57
Tea	104	95	91	129	125	97
Vegetables	16,041	15,837	99	20,136	20,136	100
Fruits	7,894	6,420	81	10,416	8,789	84
Sugar	3,052	621	20	3,821	1,064	28
Fats and Oils	1,533	352	23	2,240	370	17
Milk and Milk Products	5,719	4,944	86	8,142	7,680	94
Beef	367	290	79	625	508	81
Pork	883	793	90	1,335	1,325	99
Chicken Meat	668	640	96	915	914	100
Other Meat	229	7	3	318		
Eggs	1,843	1,811	98	2,206	2,205	100
Sea Foods	10,205	10,376	101	13,521	11,953	95
Concentrated Feeds	15,516	5,628	36	20,609	5,837	28

Source: Japan, Ministry of Agriculture and Forestry *Nihon no Shokuryo* Seisaku o Kangaeru [An Analysis of Japan's Food Policy] (Tokyo: Zenkoku Nogyo Kaigisho, 1976), pp. 92-93.

Table 3

**Japan's Official Development Assistance to
Southeast Asia (1974-1976)**

(Net disbursements; Unit: US$1 million)

Country	1974	1975	1976
Burma	46.4	21.7	27.3
Khumer Republic	8.5	0.2	0.1
Indonesia	221.1	197.9	200.5
Laos	9.7	6.5	11.1
Malaysia	36.3	63.3	34.0
Philippines	73.3	70.3	75.5
Singapore	12.9	7.6	5.7
Thailand	17.4	41.2	43.1
Vietnam	54.6	17.3	28.4
Total	480.1	425.9	425.7

Source: Japan, Ministry of Foreign Affairs,
Japan's Economic Cooperation.

Mexican farmers, Plan Puebla.

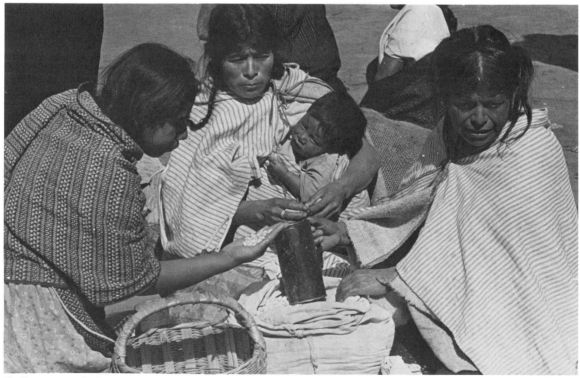

Tzoil women in the market, San Cristobal de las Casas, Chiapas, Mexico.

Changing Fashions in Bilateral Aid to Agriculture

Jon McLin

When does a country have a "food problem" of such severity as to justify the priority attention of its own leaders and of the international community? Most frequently, one or more of the following conditions must be met:

1. Undernutrition to an extent that is or is becoming unacceptable.

2. A net trade deficit in food that is or is becoming financially unsustainable.

3. A degree of dependence on imported food that is unacceptable for nonfinancial reasons, e.g., possible interruptions of supplies for political reasons or in tight market conditions.

4. A need to create agricultural employment for the rural poor because of the importance of providing jobs to increase their purchasing power, and the lack of adequate opportunity in the industrial sector.

If one or more of these conditions characterize a country, outside observers frequently conclude that the country has a food problem. Yet within the country the political weight given by governments to the various elements of the food equation may be quite different. In deciding how to deal with the food issue and the importance to attach to it, domestic political considerations will often determine the form and limit the extent of what can be done.

Thus the role of rich countries and international agencies in confronting the Third World's nutritional problems is likely to be sec-ondary, in spite of the great concern they are manifesting. Furthermore, the gap between their rhetoric and real effort is striking. Both bilateral and multilateral aid donors have been solemnly speaking of substantial increases in aid volume and of selectively focusing aid on the rural sector and the poorest countries and people. Yet increased volumes of aid to agriculture have not been sustained nor is the verbal commitment to concentrate on the poorest, least-developed countries reflected in the figures to date.

Aid Trends in General

It is on the face of it surprising, in view of the stagnation in aid levels in recent years and of the underlying difficulty of justifying higher expenditures before a skeptical public opinion, that several governments in or around 1976 committed themselves to make substantial increases in their aid programs.[1] The collective performance of the 17 countries which belong to the Development Assistance Committee (DAC) of the Organization for Economic Cooperation and Development (OECD) is farther away in 1978 than in 1965 from attaining the target figure for official development assistance (ODA) of 0.7 percent of GNP.[2] From 0.44 percent in 1965, the collective performance of the 17 countries declined to 0.34 percent by 1970 and has stayed very close to that level ever since (0.36 percent in 1975; 0.35 percent in 1976).[3]

This rate of growth has corresponded to a very slight increase in real terms (6 percent over a decade, according to DAC estimates). Yet given rapid population growth in recipient countries, aid per capita has undergone a steady reduction. Partly offsetting this decline, the grant element of official development assistance has increased from 84 percent in 1967 to 89 percent in 1976. This softening of the terms of ODA was stimulated in part by a 1972 DAC Recommendation which specified some norms (including a grant element of at least 84%, revised to 86% in a Recommendation adopted in 1978). In response to another DAC Recommendation encouraging the use of bilateral aid for purposes of procurement in other developing countries, a very few donors have untied substantial parts of their bilateral aid. But most such aid remains tied to procurement in the donor country.

While the overall level of official development assistance has not increased, a marked change has occurred in the distribution of aid by source. The dominant role played formerly by the bilateral programs of the DAC members has been whittled away both by the relatively much faster growth in the resources channeled through multilateral institutions[4] and by OPEC performance since 1973.

In the short space of a few years, OPEC members have become major providers of finance to developing countries. Their concessional disbursements (i.e., ODA) amounted in 1976 to $5.2 billion (compared to a DAC figure of $13.7 billion), down from $5.5 billion in 1975 but still equivalent to over 2 percent of their collective gross product. The overall grant element amounted to 79 percent (5 percentage points below the DAC-recommended level), and over the years there has been some abatement of the initial concentration of giving on a relatively few, principally Arab or Muslim, countries. Nevertheless, concentration remains high: in 1976 five countries (Egypt, Pakistan, Syria, India, and Jordan) received over 70 percent of OPEC's total aid disbursements.

As UNCTAD studies and others have pointed out, OPEC donors are repeating DAC experience in more than one respect. One is the concentration on a small group of favored recipients. Thirty-nine countries with special relationships to DAC countries got 28 percent of ODA-commitments during the period 1969-1972,

although they account for only 3 percent of the population of all developing countries. Similarly, the "preponderant use of bilateral channels for directing the OPEC countries concessional aid flows to other developing countries (88% in both 1974 and 1975) resembles the pattern set by the DAC countries, which channeled more than 80 percent of their ODA bilaterally as late as 1971 and...as much as 73 percent bilaterally in 1974."[5] For that part of their aid provided multilaterally, OPEC members, like the DAC group, have shown a predilection for institutions in which their influence is great. In the proposal for, and voting arrangements within, the International Fund for Agricultural Development, they have shown themselves prepared to create new institutions (as in their own various funds) with tailor-made constitutions so as to funnel their money toward a particular sector and to maintain a significant degree of control. This, too, is a page from the DAC countries' book, whose chapters could be named for the various voluntary funds of the United Nations.

During the past decade there have also been notable changes in relative performance within the DAC group. The United States share of official development assistance from all DAC countries dropped by half between 1965 and 1975 (58.1% to 29.5%),[6] the level of effort by middle-sized members was rather stable, while several smaller countries—such as Canada, the Scandinavian countries, the Netherlands—made dramatic increases in their aid budgets, in terms both absolute and relative to GNP. By 1975 Canada was providing more ODA than Britain, and the three Scandinavian countries collectively almost as much as Japan.[7]

These developments accompanied a rising level of criticism of the aid relationship by knowledgeable leaders from both North and South. Many prominent spokesmen from the Third World had come to question the importance of discretionary aid as it had been practiced for the past quarter century. Instead they began to emphasize such things as automatic transfers of resources, access to industrial country markets for their manufactures, commodity schemes aimed at improving their terms of trade and enhancing their value added through local processing, debt forgiveness, and collective self-reliance. At the same time, students of development in donor countries for a variety of reasons were questioning whether or not bilateral assistance programs were reaching those who really needed help and asking skeptically what aid's net contribution to development actually is, in view of the often short-term political purposes for which it is used.

At almost the time these criticisms were reaching their apogee, governments—especially of DAC countries—were rediscovering the merits of official development assistance programs. One political attraction of the instrument is that it at least appears to facilitate the targeting by donors of their funds for purposes, countries and groups that are most in favor, or least in disfavor, among the constituencies which must foot the bill. As support increased for targeting bilateral aid toward the poorest countries and people, and the rural and agricultural sectors, the merits of revitalizing foreign aid programs began to receive increased rhetorical emphasis.

Further, in light of the combined effects of the oil price increases and the high commodity prices of 1973 and 1974—and the changed political context in which they occurred—a number of industrial countries apparently concluded that responding to the claims of the Third World would henceforth merit a higher political priority than in the past. Compared to much of the shopping list of the Group of 77, which negotiated on behalf of the South in fora such as the United Nations Conference on Trade and Development (UNCTAD), and the Conference on International Economic Cooperation, where much of the North-South dialogue has been playing itself out, increased aid looked to the North like one of the relatively less painful concessions to make. Changing tariff and trade structures in order to accept more LDC manufactures would affect jobs in many vulnerable and politically sensitive sectors; the recession of 1973-1975 was an especially unfavorable time to talk of major concessions in that field. Artificially altering the terms of trade through managed commodity schemes implied a degree of market intervention which the larger industrial countries found repugnant and which, even if they were well disposed, they

would have found difficult or impossible to execute without causing major economic distortions. Electorates were judged unready to accept the idea of a "development tax." Debt forgiveness on a broad basis allegedly threatened the confidence on which future financial cooperation would have to be based, although subsequent decisions by several countries to cancel some of the public debt of the poorest countries indicate that views on this subject have evolved. The political attractions of the aid instrument are that it does not require structural change and is revocable; and as already mentioned, it is discretionary as regards recipients, and therefore can be targeted on those countries and for those purposes enjoying political support.

The donors have understandably not taken seriously the occasional criticisms by spokesmen of recipient countries of the principle of aid. While the rhetoric of self-reliance often conveys the image of rejecting handouts, a closer look at a representative sampling of statements reveals that at least for the near term Third World countries' desires are very much in keeping with the objectives of the DAC and of liberal sentiment in the West in general—make good on the 0.7 percent target, increase the proportion of grants and of untied aid, channel the aid toward the poorest countries and people and toward the rural sector.[8]

These were the circumstances that led governments to a renewed interest in aid and *a fortiori* to a willingness to contemplate greater relative efforts in the future. The combination of this rationale and the visible evidence that some countries take seriously the 0.7 percent target have had a noticeable effect on some of the larger DAC members whose sluggish performance relative to their economic weight has in the past dragged down the DAC average. The Carter Administration has spoken of "substantial increases" in assistance over the next five years. The Japanese government has announced a decision to double ODA disbursements (in terms of U.S. dollars) between 1977 and 1980, and simultaneously to bring its ODA disbursements as a percentage of GNP up to the DAC average. The DAC Chairman writes that other countries that "can be expected" to "make strenuous efforts to substantially increase their aid effort in the years ahead" include Belgium, Canada, Denmark, France, Australia, and Finland. Collectively, the Committee members expressed their intention in July 1977, and reaffirmed it the following October, "to increase effectively and substantially their official development assistance." The $1 billion Special Action Program in favor of the low income countries, agreed to at the conclusion of the Conference on International Economic Cooperation, and the recent (fifth) replenishment of the International Development Association are two earnests of these good intentions.

The decline in 1976 ODA in real terms is not necessarily in conflict with these affirmations, as it reflected the outcome of earlier appropriations decisions and reflected a number of special factors such as bunched expenditures.[9] But it does point up the need to judge the verbal commitments not in their own terms but against the concrete results which ensue.

Aid to Agriculture

It has become conventional since the World Food Conference to evaluate external assistance to agriculture in relation to the target figure of $5 billion which was put forward in the preparatory documentation for that meeting and for which a Conference resolution declared there was "broad support." As this has come to be taken as a benchmark, and as there is considerable confusion in the use made of it, some clarification is in order.

What that figure represented was the average annual amount of external assistance to agriculture, expressed in 1972 prices, required during the period 1975-1980 to realize an investment program estimated by the FAO Secretariat as necessary to raise the annual average rate of growth of agricultural production in the developing world from the 2.6 percent actually achieved in the period 1962-1973 to 3.5-4.0 percent in the period 1974-1985. The calculation was based on the more or less arbitrary assumption that one-third of total investment requirements would have to come from outside. The effort envisaged represented an approximate tripling of effort, as some $1.5 billion per year was by their calculation then being provided

externally for the purposes covered by their program.[10] These purposes corresponded roughly to the narrower of the two standard definitions used by the DAC in calculating aid to agriculture, namely one which excludes expenditures for items 13 through 17 on the following list.

1. Crop Development
2. Animal Husbandry
3. Fisheries
4. Forestry
5. Water Development
6. Land Development and Reclamation
7. Agricultural Services (including agricultural education and training, extension services, research, administration, planning, marketing, feasibility studies, topographical surveys, land reform and cooperation)
8. Agricultural Development Banks
9. Storage
10. Supply of means of production (includes supply of fertilizers, pesticides, seeds, agricultural tools and equipment and not included elsewhere)
11. Rural Development
12. Agriculture Unallocated (items which cannot be classified specifically under items 1 to 11)
13. Manufacturing and Maintenance of Agricultural Means of Production
14. Agro-Industries
15. Infrastructure and Transport for Agricultural Development (notably feeder roads)
16. Regional Development Projects
17. River Development Projects

The utility of comparisons of aid effort in subsequent years with the $5 billion figure is limited by several factors, the first of which is the value of the initial calculations. The problems associated with such estimates are well known and the authors themselves only claimed to be indicating "broad orders of magnitude." The figures are perhaps best used as indicators of the political priority given by donors to the food and agricultural aspects of development. Even to use them for these purposes requires attention to comparability.

Purchasing power comparability is a particular problem because of the accelerated rate of inflation and the currency instability prevailing in the mid-1970s. The DAC Secretariat has devised special deflators for aid flows (both ODA and total flows)—which for these years of the mid-1970s are considerably higher than GNP deflators. On the basis of these, the $5 billion in 1972 prices converts into around $8.2 billion in 1976 prices.[11]

A comparison of actual effort with the $5 billion goal (expressed in terms of current dollars) may best be made graphically. Assuming the actual figure of $1.5 billion estimated by the World Food Conference corresponds to all official bilateral and multilateral financial flows to agriculture, according to the narrow DAC definition, one can use DAC figures for these items for subsequent years to trace a curve which shows a sharp increase in both real and monetary terms in 1973-74, only to level off in 1974-1976 (see graph, page 216).

Thus, in real terms, the target looks as far if not farther from attainment than it did in 1973.[12] In seeking an explanation for the falloff, the FAO Secretariat hypothesizes that in 1976 "after quintupling in current terms between 1971 and 1975, the rapid increases in commitments have generally exhausted the pipeline of projects in the agricultural sector which would meet the basic criteria for external support. This explanation seems even more plausible in view of the simultaneous decline in commitments of aid to agriculture among all major donors. In the case of the OPEC countries and some multilateral agencies, notably IDA, however, total commitments to all sectors have also declined due to their overall financial position during 1975 and 1976. It is also possible that as a result of the relatively rich harvests during the past two years, the sense of crisis prevalent at the time of the World Food Conference in 1974 has diminished, and donor interest has shifted toward such issues as rural development and away from the supply of fertilizers and other production inputs; assistance for rural development is less capital intensive and includes a substantial component of nonagricultural items."[13] Whatever the validity of this explanation, the contrast is striking between, on the one hand, the confident predictions of a couple of years ago that aid to agricul-

ture would increase significantly, predictions based on what seemed the good evidence of a general trend among donors to accord preference to agriculture, and on the other, the actual aid flows.

For the agricultural sector as for aid as a whole, the bilateral programs of DAC countries have declined somewhat in relative importance as the multilateral lending institutions and OPEC members have expanded their commitments. As the tabular data show (Table 1), some 60 percent of the official assistance to agriculture in 1976 (broad definition) came from the multilateral sources. Nonetheless, the DAC share is disproportionately important because of its higher concessional content. The expansion in volume of OPEC and multilateral assistance has been accompanied by a hardening of terms. In its *Review of Field Programmes* the FAO points out that although ODA from DAC sources has maintained its highly concessional nature, ODA from OPEC and multilateral donors registered a decline in concessionality as its volume increased. Thus the developing countries' debt burden is being added to from the net flow of ODA as well.

The flow of ODA has special bearing on the general terms of aid to agriculture and the picture that emerges from recent commitments is not very encouraging. The proportion of ODA in total commitments for agriculture has averaged about two-thirds from 1974 through 1976, contributing not at all toward a softening of the overall financial terms. According to a study of the Consultative Group on Food Production and Investment in Developing Countries (CGFPI), the overall grant element of aid to agriculture declined from 61 percent in 1973 to 41 percent in 1975, especially due to the hardening of terms of OPEC country loans and a smaller share of IDA in total commitments by the World Bank (Table 2).[14]

One reason for the 1976 decline in agriculture's share of all new aid commitments, broadly defined, appears to be the increase in the shares of both multilateral and OPEC bilateral lending allocated for this purpose (Table 3).

Given the relative stagnation in the level and priority of agriculture within donors' aid budgets, it may be supposed that at least the aid is being concentrated on the poorest or "food deficit" countries. Once again, however, the figures contradict the policy-makers' rhetoric. To quote the findings of the FAO Secretariat:

In general, the poorer countries appear to have received less aid per capita as well as per hectare of cultivated area. An analysis of 56 developing countries shows that low income countries (less than $200 per capita) received half as much as the higher income countries (more than US$500 per capita) on a per capita basis, and were also significantly worse off on the basis of aid per hectare of land under cultivation. Countries with a large agricultural labour force (more than 70% of the total labour force) received less than those with a small agricultural labour force (under 40%), about half as much on a per capita basis, and one-third as much on a per hectare basis. The 18 countries identified by CGFPI as food deficit countries, together received only about 25 percent of capital aid commitments, or half as much per capita as the rest of the developing countries. . . . (Table 4).

On the basis of data from the national plans of 35 developing countries, it was noted that countries devoting a larger portion of public investment to agriculture received more aid, both per capita and per hectare of cultivated land. Although the data used must be viewed with circumspection, this finding is perhaps not altogether fortuitous. It is interesting to note, however, that if the least developed countries among the 35 countries are disaggregated, the picture is reversed (i.e., those among them who appeared to have allocated a higher proportion of total resources to agriculture had received lower allocations of aid on a per capita or per hectare of cultivated land basis). This can only be explained by the overwhelming preponderance of subsistence agriculture in these countries and difficulties encountered in identifying suitable investment projects due to lack of institutions and trained staff, among other reasons.[15]

While these conclusions apply specifically to aid to agriculture from all donors, the DAC Secretariat's analysis of aid for all purposes from its limited group of donors runs in the same direction: the lowest income group's share has declined in both 1975 and 1976, and the shares of the Least Developed (LLDCs) and Most Seriously Affected countries (MSAs) declined in 1976 (Table 5).

The beneficiaries of this discrimination have been the predominantly middle-income countries of Latin America and the Near East, whose shares of aid are not only out of proportion to their income levels but also to their shares of population or cultivable land (Table 6).

The preponderant share of aid given to agriculture has taken the form of capital assistance, although as donors have shifted to an emphasis on rural development, in which many projects feature a "package" of inputs, it becomes increasingly difficult to distinguish usefully between capital and technical assistance—and increasingly important that the two should be closely related. Useful breakdowns of the capital aid expenditures are difficult to make with available data (Table 7). But all indications confirm that projects of land and water development form the largest single category, accounting for 20-30% of the total in the period 1973-1975. Substantial sums have also been spent on both provision of fertilizer supplies and, increasingly, on the construction of fertilizer plants. This pattern of expenditures is roughly in line with the relative magnitudes called for in the FAO's 1974 document.[16] What appears not to be in line is the spending on credit, storage, and marketing, which by DAC calculations for 1974 attracted commitments of only $235 million, compared to the $1.2 billion per year called for in the FAO figures. More could usefully be done here, it appears.

Within the three-year period 1973-1975 the FAO has noticed significant changes in the pattern of new commitments:

Most notably, the proportion of commitments for manufacturing of inputs quintupled and that for rural development projects doubled while commitments for provision of production inputs and related services as well as for agro-industries, have declined sharply. The land and water development projects have maintained their predominant position in all three years.

There has been a dramatic increase in funds provided for research. Founded in 1971, the Consultative Group on International Agricultural Research supported five international research centers in its first year of operation with financial assistance amounting to $15 million. By 1976 the number of centers had grown to 11 and financial support had grown more than 4-fold, to $64 million.[17]

Selected Country Programs

Given the continued importance of the DAC donors, both through their direct aid programs and through their weight in multilateral agencies, it may be useful to note some of the features of the programs for those DAC members which on the basis of size or degree and quality of commitment are in the vanguard.

Canada. In 1975 the Canadian government adopted a new policy document on development cooperation, a statement which could serve as a text for the new fashions in aid. Food production and rural development, priorities to the poorest countries and people, basic needs, a greater share of "program" as opposed to "project" assistance, equitable distribution as well as growth, realization of the 0.7 percent target, ultimate pursuit of a "permanent system of (international) redistribution of resources"—all these are emphasized. The priorities it set began to be reflected in commitments for 1975 but by 1976 "disbursement difficulties" arose "in part from apparent absorption capacity limitation in the poorest LDCs.... The shift in emphasis in the bilateral program in favor of greater involvement in agricultural and integrated rural development initiatives...contributed to this problem as such projects are generally administratively more labor-intensive and more difficult to identify, particularly in the poorest countries."[18] Despite the heightened emphasis on program assistance, the Canadians were seeking to resolve the administrative bottlenecks themselves and hadn't adequate manpower to do so at the anticipated rate. Moreover, the larger element of local cost finance required for the kind of projects now favored created difficulties, given the fact that only 20 percent of Canada's bilateral aid program is untied. Despite these difficulties, an above-average 23 percent of Canada's ODA in 1976 (portion allocable by sector) went to agriculture.

France. A number of singular features characterize France's assistance program. It has long ranked near the top of the league for all DAC donors—at the top if only the large countries are considered—as measured by ODA as a share of GNP. Its 1976 ratio was 0.62 percent, and it has repeatedly accepted the 0.7 percent target. Yet this performance is achieved only through the dubious accounting device of including financial transfers to the overseas departments and territories; it is as if the U.S. counted Puerto Rico as a recipient of its "foreign" assistance. If these bits of French real estate are left out of the picture, the key ratio falls sharply to 0.35 percent, much closer to the DAC average of 0.33 percent. The preponderant part goes to French-speaking countries in Africa, a geographical distribution which, given the small populations of these countries, skews the pattern of per capita aid rather sharply; as several of this group are in the Least-Developed category, however, there is some equity in this concentration.

The composition of its program has been less susceptible than others to rhetorical fashion. The dominant note has been and continues to be the high proportion spent on technical assistance. Almost half its total ODA expenditures of $2.1 billion go for this purpose, and France accounts for some 36 percent of total DAC expenditure on technical assistance.

Although the level of expenditure on agriculture is not high (7.6%), it increased very rapidly from 1972-1975, and stress is now put on the importance of integrated rural development. Noteworthy among its various projects are support for large-scale development of the Senegal and Niger river basins; a substantial research effort focused mainly on specific crops (largely independent of the Consultative Group on International Agricultural Research—CGIAR); and, recently, an interest in collaborating with other donors, notably in the context of the Club des Amis du Sahel.

Federal Republic of Germany. Long criticized in the DAC as being, along with Japan and the United States, one of the heavyweight laggards, the Federal Republic made itself still more vulnerable by a 16 percent drop in ODA disbursements in 1976, which brought its ODA/GNP rate down to 0.31 percent. Moreover, it was slow to indicate what its contribution would be to the increased aid effort promised by DAC ministers in mid-1977. On the other hand, the government in 1978 decided to increase aid funds appreciably faster than the general budget over the next few years. The terms of its aid are relatively favorable, although with a grant element of 88.3 percent they are below the DAC average; it has one of the best records of any donor country in respect to the portion of its ODA that is untied.

Agriculture and rural development have been stressed in German aid policy statements for the past several years, but that commitment is imperfectly reflected in the figures. Only about 10 percent of capital aid goes to agriculture. German spokesmen state that their policy is to respond to the request of recipient countries, as they have neither the desire nor the manpower to formulate requests on behalf of the recipients. Most requests coming to them are for industrial or infrastructural projects, either because the requesting government is little interested in agriculture or because it does not think of agriculture as the German forte. An unusually large portion of their aid that is identifiably allocated to agriculture takes the form of technical assistance ($84.8 million out of $117.3 million in 1976).

The Netherlands. Dutch ODA in 1976 reached 0.82 percent of GNP—a better performance than that of any other DAC member except Sweden. It is scheduled to reach 1.0 percent by the end of the decade. The grant element is slightly below the DAC average and terms are hardening. Just over half is untied. In an effort to concentrate on the poorest countries and the poorest people, the bulk of Dutch aid is given to a group of 18 "target countries," selected because they are genuinely poor, need help, and have a social and political system that allows aid to reach the poorest people. The Dutch have consciously shifted their emphasis to agriculture and rural development, and seek especially to aid small farmers. In their rural development projects they stress the importance of cooperatives, credit, employment generation (especially for young people and women), health and education. About a quarter of Dutch aid is devoted to these purposes. For the target countries a substantial share of assistance takes the form of program aid. Under Minister Jan Pronk, the government aid program was willing to run the risk that its conditions would be interpreted as neocolonial interference in internal matters.

Sweden. The generosity of Sweden's aid program is well known. In 1976 ODA amounted to 0.82 percent of GNP, and the grant element was 99.9 percent. The determination to reach the poorest strata of the assisted countries while refraining from dictating to recipients the kind of projects that would be favored has led the government to concentrate its aid on a number of countries giving a high priority to the social aspects of development. As it works out, a high share goes to MSAs and LLDCs. The share allocated to agriculture increased in the mid-1970s to about 18 percent, but the latest trend, in response to demand from recipients, is toward aid for industrialization. A liberal policy is followed regarding the financing of local costs. Substantial use is made of church-related and other private, voluntary groups as channels for public aid. In recent years a rising, although still modest, share of the aid has been tied. The bilateral portion has also increased, as a more critical and selective view has been taken of the operations of multilateral agencies.

United Kingdom. New directions for Britain's aid program were laid down in the 1975 White Paper, entitled "More Help for the Poorest," inspired by the views of Mrs. Judith Hart, who thereafter was given the ministerial responsibilities for carrying out the policy. As the title of the document suggests, stress is put on helping the poorest countries, and people, and on agriculture and rural development. The government has calculated that the proportion of bilateral project disbursements benefiting wholly or partly the rural poor increased from 50 to 60 percent from 1974 to 1975. There has also been an increase in the share of grants relative to loans, and by 1976 the ODA grant element was a very high 95 percent. A number of difficulties were anticipated and have been encountered, at all phases of the project cycle, in applying the new strategy—limitations of personnel, sensitivities of recipient administrations regarding conditions aimed at assuring that benefits will reach the poorest, inadequate authority for local cost financing. Attempts are being made to increase the share of funds channeled through private voluntary agencies, but the first results have been meager.

United States. In spite of the marked decline in the U.S. share of DAC and of total aid over the past decade or so, its relative and absolute weight remain substantial. Although representing only 0.25 percent of GNP, its ODA disbursements in 1976 were nearly double that of the next largest donor country (Saudi Arabia). Its aid to the agricultural sector represented about a third of the DAC total.

AID's program shifted its emphasis to agriculture, nutrition, and rural poverty with the passage of the 1973 amendments to the Foreign Assistance Act. The will of key Congressional bodies to move in that direction was and has remained clear. In response to that mandate, the relative allocations for agriculture and nutrition increased. In the fiscal year 1978 requests, $586 million or 41 percent of the development assistance portion of the budget was requested for food and nutrition, and the same categories were stressed in the other segments of the aid budget, namely security supporting assistance and Public Law (PL) 480.

Other "basic needs" (health, education) accounted for much of the remainder. The reviewing Congressional committee criticized, however, the fact that "the Agency's food and nutrition proposal, although more attentive than in the past to the needs of small farmers, is still heavily laden with infrastructure projects. A case in point is the food and nutrition program proposed for Asia. There, AID had proposed to allocate $147.6 million, or 64 percent of the $229.3 million food and nutrition program for Asia, to infrastructure projects." Although the Committee's observations are themselves vulnerable to criticism (it favors small projects of rural development, yet is critical of projects involving a high proportion of local costs, as these necessarily do), it is perhaps on the mark in finding that "the high incidence of infrastructure projects in the Agency's food and nutrition proposal is an indication of the Agency's inability to effectively program funds at this time for priority projects."[19]

At the time of this writing, the Congress is about to consider two major proposals for changing the size and structure of the program: the Carter Administration's first budget which calls for large increases in several categories of development assistance; and a proposal inspired by Hubert Humphrey for taking AID out of the State Department and making other changes in the structure. The disposition of both, following the major internal and external reviews of aid policy carried out in recent months, will of course significantly affect activities in support of agriculture and rural development.

The European Community. Although the preponderant share of the Community's aid budget originates with its member states and is therefore counted in their figures (a small fraction comes from the autonomous European Investment Bank), its role is worth noting for several reasons. One is that this accounting convention may be changed as the EC puts into effect a financial system based on its "own resources." Another is that the volume of its aid programs has sharply increased over the past few years, through the entry into force of the Lomé Convention and numerous other commitments. Annual ODA disbursements now vary between $500 million and $1 billion, depending upon "bunching" factors. Thirdly, a steeply rising share of this, including the entirety of the first allocation of funds to nonassociated countries, is going to projects related to agriculture and rural development. Some 1.1 billion EUA (about $1.25 billion) will be devoted to these purposes in the period 1976-1980. Within that category, there is a shift toward projects which favor food, as opposed to cash crops for export.

OPEC. Although no qualitative assessment of OPEC aid programs is attempted here, the UNCTAD Secretariat has provided some very recent data that give an idea of trends in OPEC assistance to agricultural projects. The data list new commitments by the five large funds, which award project-oriented loans. Although project descriptions are sketchy, the share of these which appear to fall into the agricultural sector, broadly defined, is shown in Table 8. The results confirm those of CGFPI, and parallel the experience of both DAC and multilateral donors, indicating that support for agriculture has passed a peak.

* * * * *

This brief survey has shown that in a remarkably convergent, almost orchestrated fashion, the principal Western donor countries reoriented their aid programs in the mid-1970s toward a set of objectives that included priority for the poorest countries and people, especially the rural poor; an emphasis on more equitable distribution of the benefits of aid; a concern for social as well as economic development, particularly in the provision of minimal "basic needs"; a consequent preference for smaller projects with less visible boundaries; and a predilection for dealing with those developing countries which themselves shared this outlook. Many of these translate into an elevated priority for programs and projects relating to food, agriculture, and nutrition.

The uniformity of this response to the disappointing results of the first two "Development Decades" and to the food shortages that followed the anomalous crop years in 1972 and 1973 is a tribute to the policy-shaping influence of the World Food Conference and of that club of donors which is called the Development Assistance Committee. Yet such influence could not have produced this result if there had not been a domestic political logic in the policy changes. Such logic lay in the promise that these policies could constitute a response to the newly insistent demands of the developing countries, a response satisfying in its humanitarian tone and reassuring in its avoidance of basic changes in international economic structures.

Problems have arisen because the political and social environment necessary to pursue the new policies was and is not favorable. Generating, supervising, and implementing a multitude of small projects puts great demands on administrative manpower, which is most lacking precisely in the countries now given priority. Outside experts in the numbers required tend either not to be available or, if they are, to constitute such a formidable presence as to aggravate political sensitivities. The donors' requirements for detailed evidence that the benefits of the aid are reaching the target groups—necessary to satisfy parliamentary pressures and public opinion—exacerbate rather than alleviate the administrative burden. The implications of projects of this type for local cost financing and hence for further untying of aid run counter to the need for domestic political support in donor countries, which continues to depend in part on the export promotion aspect of aid. Finally, there may be involved a basic contradiction of political goals. While the general foreign policy goal of most donors toward the Third World appears to be to preserve as nearly as possible the status quo, the realization of the new philosophy of aid may in many countries require revolutionary social and political changes. All this is cause for wondering whether the future of aid is as bright as the results of recent analyses in donor countries would suggest.

Some of the elements that would help to bridge the difficulties just described are reasonably clear. Administrative and manpower bottlenecks can in part be alleviated by greater reliance on private voluntary organizations, which are able to utilize the management capabilities of their counterpart organizations in recipient countries, and on the personnel of multilateral agencies. Longer-term programming will facilitate the introduction of difficult reforms by recipients, knowing that they can rely on sustained external support for their innovations. The Club des Amis du Sahel incorporates some of these and other (by implication, more populous) regions. What is at issue is the extent to which either side will be able to deliver on its end of a bargain in which more, and more predictable, external assistance is distributed in support of reform measures within recipient countries that will allow that assistance to have its intended effects.

NOTES

1. When not otherwise specified, "aid" is used in this paper to refer to official financial flows, irrespective of the degree of concessionality, to developing countries. Most frequently, I will be discussing "official development assistance" (ODA), using the Development Assistance Committee's definition of that term (grants and loans with a grant element of at least 25%, based on a discount of 10%), and will so specify.

2. Except for Austria, Italy, Switzerland, and the United States, all other DAC members have, with various qualifications, accepted the 0.7 percent target.

3. *Development Co-operation, 1977 Review* (Paris: OECD, 1977). Hereinafter referred to as DAC Chairman's Report. Where not otherwise indicated, statistics used here are taken from these volumes.

4. "While DAC countries' ODA doubled in current prices over the last 10 years, net disbursements by multilateral institutions in favor of developing countries (concessional and nonconcessional) were increasing almost 6-fold, from about $1 billion in 1965 to nearly $6 billion in 1975." DAC Chairman's Report, 1976, p. 163.

5. UNCTAD, *Financial Solidarity for Development: Efforts and Institutions of the Members of OPEC*, TD/B/627, New York, 1977.

6. DAC Chairman's Report, 1976, p. 155.

7. *Ibid.*

8. See, e.g., Mahbub ul Haq, *The Third World and the International Economic Order*, Overseas Development Council, 1976; *What Now: The 1975 Dag Hammarskhold Report*; the 1976 Manila Declaration and Program of Action of the Group of 77.

9. Preliminary DAC data for 1977 show that ODA remained at about the same level in real terms as in 1976, and declined in terms of GNP. OECD Press Release A(78) 24 of June 19, 1978.

10. The figure was advanced and explained in U.N. World Food Conference paper E/Conf. 54/4, *The World Food Problem: Proposals for National and International Action*.

11. The Secretariat of the World Food Council, using unspecified deflators, came up with a slightly different figure of $8.3 billion at 1975 prices.

12. The FAO has compiled data using the broad definition, which also show a decline in 1976 relative to the same measure in previous years (Table 1).

13. FAO, *Review of Field Programmes, 1976-1977*, p. 55.

14. *Ibid.*, p. 56.

15. *Ibid.*, p. 59.

16. E/Conf. 54/4, *op. cit.* In addition to the allocations by type of expenditure, figures are presented in Table 7 for the percentage of allocable to the food sector, as distinct from nonfood agricultural expenditure. These results of a CGFPI study reassuringly indicate the pre-eminence of basic food production in aid programs for agriculture.

17. The eleven are: The International Rice Research Institute (IRRI), Los Banos, Philippines; The International Maize and Wheat Improvement Center (CIMMYT), El Batán, Mexico; The International Center for Tropical Agriculture (CIAT), Palmira, Colombia; The International Institute of Tropical Agriculture (IITA), Ibadan, Nigeria; The International Potato Center (CIP), Lima, Peru; The International Crops Research Institute for the Semi-Arid Tropics (ICRISAT), Hyderabad, India; The International Laboratory for Research on Animal Diseases (ILRAD), Nairobi, Kenya; The International Livestock Center for Africa (ILCA), Addis Ababa, Ethiopia; The West Africa Rice Development Association (WARDA), Monrovia, Liberia; The International Board for Plant Genetic Resources (IBPGR), Rome, Italy; and The International Centre for Agricultural Research in Dry Areas (CARDA), Cairo, Egypt. *Consultative Group on International Agricultural Research*, CGIAR, New York, 1976, pp. 4-5. (Available from United Nations Development Program.)

18. Development Assistance Committee, *Annual Aid Review*, Memorandum of Canada, 1977.

19. U.S. Congress, Senate, Appropriations Committee. *Report on Foreign Assistance Bill, 1978.*

Table 1

Official Bilateral and Multilateral Assistance to Agriculture, Narrow and Broad Definition
ODA and OOF Commitments, 1974, 1975, & 1976[1]

($ million)

Donor	1974 Narrow Definition			1974 Broad Definition			1975 Narrow Definition			1975 Broad Definition			1976 Narrow Definition			1976 Broad Definition		
	ODA	OOF	Total	ODA	OOF	Total	ODA	OOF	Total	ODA	OOF	Total	ODA	OOF	Total	ODA	OOF	Total
DAC Bilateral	1,214.31	157.31	1,371.62	1,557.06	167.52	1,724.58	1,150.6	18.8	1,169.4	1,574.5	31.3	1,605.8	1,067.9	146.5	1,214.4	1,341.6	175.4	1,517.0
of which:																		
Capital Assistance	474.14	157.31	611.45	816.89	167.52	996.29	460.1	18.8	478.9	886.8	31.3	918.1	560.8	146.5	707.3	834.5	175.4	1,009.9
Fertilizer Supply	373.07		373.07	373.07		373.07	291.8		291.8	289.0		289.0	172.3		172.3	172.3		172.3
Technical Co-operation	367.10		367.10	367.10		367.10	398.7		398.7	398.7		398.7	334.8		334.8	334.8		334.8
DAC Bilateral & EEC	1,348.06	157.31	1,505.37	1,700.26	167.52	1,867.78	1,216.7	18.8	1,235.5	1,641.3	31.3	1,672.6	1,141.0	146.5	1,287.5	1,422.1	175.4	1,597.5
EEC	133.75		133.75	143.20		143.20	66.1		66.1	66.8		66.8	73.1		73.1	80.5		80.5
OPEC Bilateral	103.09		103.09	165.55	170.36	335.91	232.4		232.4	534.8	200.0	734.8	89.2		89.2	199.7	162.1	361.8
Multilateral Agencies	674.94	830.35	1,505.29	993.54	981.55	1,975.09	617.0	1,095.8	1,712.8	1,056.4	1,846.0	2,902.4	799.3	926.8	1,726.1	1,101.9	1,457.5	2,559.4
of which:																		
UNDP	111.00		111.00	111.00		111.00	60.0		60.0	60.0		60.0	102.0		102.0	102.0		102.0
IDA	331.55		331.55	617.25		617.25	404.3		404.3	657.2		657.2	376.0		376.0	452.0		452.0
IBRD		758.05	758.05		871.95	871.95		837.5	837.5		1,494.3	1,494.3	81.0	759.5	840.5	167.3	1,229.8	1,397.1
IDB	179.87	43.70	223.57	179.87	43.70	223.57	106.1	188.0	294.1	215.6	201.8	417.4	160.4	107.8	268.2	258.9	127.8	386.7
AsDB	36.85	27.20	64.05	69.75	64.20	133.95	10.0	65.5	75.4	82.0	141.1	223.1	70.7	58.4	129.1	106.9	90.4	197.3
AfDB	15.67	1.40	17.07	15.67	1.70	17.37	36.6	4.8	41.5	41.6	8.8	50.4	9.2	1.1	10.3	14.8	9.5	24.3
OPEC-funded Multi-lateral Agencies		18.40	18.40	27.65		27.65	23.9		23.9	64.5		64.5	38.8		38.8	72.5		72.5
of which:																		
AFESD		18.40	18.40	27.65		27.65	10.9		10.9	51.5		51.5	23.9		23.9	33.1		33.1
ADEBA							13.0		13.0	13.0		13.0	14.9		14.9	39.4		39.4
Total Bilateral and Multilateral	2,126.09	1,006.06	3,132.15	2,887.00	1,319.43	4,206.43	2,090.0	1,114.6	3,204.6	3,297.0	2,077.3	5,374.3	2,068.3	1,073.3	3,141.6	2,796.2	1,795.0	4,591.2

1. ODA - Official development assistance; OOF - Other official flows.

Source: Development Co-operation Directorate, Paris, OECD, 1978.

Table 2

Average Grant Elements of Capital Commitments for Agriculture by Donor Groups

	1973		1974		1975		1976[b]	
	Amount US$ Million	Grant Element (%)	Amount US$ Million	Grant Element (%)	Amount US$Million	Grant Element (%)	Amount US$ Million	Grant Element (%)
DAC Bilateral & EEC[a]	541.4	82.7	920.8	69.8	1,002.4	71.6		N.A.
OPEC Bilateral	34.9	54.0	313.5	25.7	826.3	36.2	396.9	46.0
Multilateral	1,334.9	53.2	2,056.6	42.9	2,864.7	31.3	2,534.1	36.0
TOTAL	1,911.2	61.6	3,290.9	48.6	4,693.4	40.8		

a. Excludes amounts for which the required information is not available.
b. Provisional.

Source: Consultative Group on Food Production and Investment in Developing Countries (CGFPI), *Analysis of Resource Flows in Agriculture, Document A,* from the fourth meeting, September 7-9, 1977, Washington, D.C., Table 6.1, p. 14. Hereafter cited as CGFPI.

Table 3

Share of Agriculture in Total Commitments

	1973	1974	1975	1976
		Percent		
DAC Bilateral	10.0	14.1	12.9	(12.9)
OPEC Bilateral	17.0	17.7	22.4	18.3
Multilateral	26.0	30.9	34.5	29.5
TOTAL	16.2	20.9	22.1	(18.5)

Note: Data for 1976 added, based on indications in 1977 DAC Chairman's Report that share allocated to agriculture was essentially unchanged in 1976.

Source: CGFPI, Table 1.3, page 5.

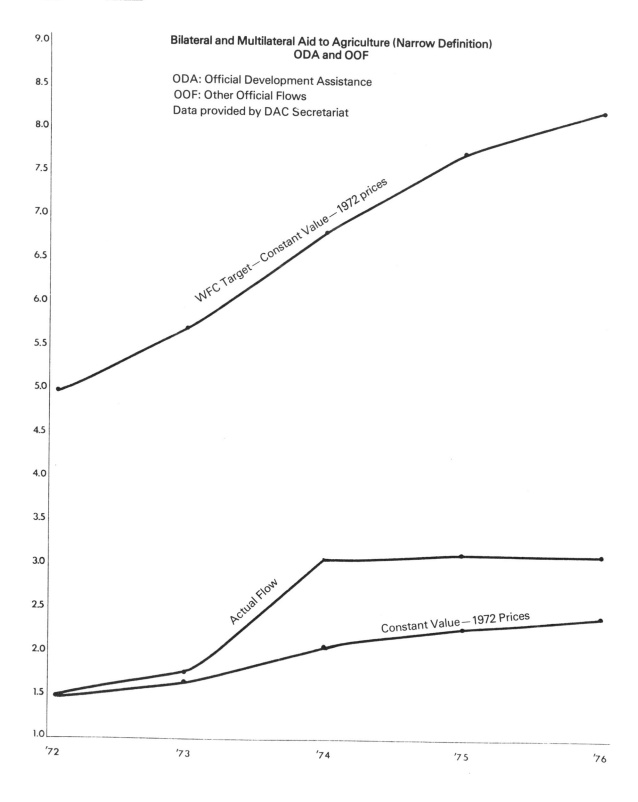

Bilateral and Multilateral Aid to Agriculture (Narrow Definition)
ODA and OOF

ODA: Official Development Assistance
OOF: Other Official Flows
Data provided by DAC Secretariat

WFC Target—Constant Value—1972 prices

Actual Flow

Constant Value—1972 Prices

Table 4

Capital Commitments for Agriculture to Priority Food-Deficit Countries[a]

(Annual Average 1973-1975)

	DAC Bilateral & EEC	OPEC Bilateral	Multilateral	Total	Per Capita (US$)
		US$ Million			
Afghanistan*	8.8	0.5	12.0	21.3	1.25
Bangladesh*	80.2	14.2	47.7	142.1	1.86
Burundi	5.4	0.3	1.7	7.4	2.02
Chad	0.6		8.0	8.6	2.15
Ethiopia*	12.3		26.7	39.0	1.43
Guinea	0.6		2.3	2.9	0.54
Haiti	3.6			3.6	0.80
India*	91.2		319.7	410.9	0.69
Mali	8.2	0.6	12.5	21.3	3.89
Nepal	3.3	0.1	5.2	8.6	0.70
Niger	3.5		0.7	4.2	0.94
Rwanda	1.6	1.1	2.8	5.5	1.35
Somalia	2.2	5.2	3.5	10.9	3.52
Sri Lanka*	21.5	8.6	22.3	52.4	3.91
Tanzania	34.5		31.7	66.2	4.61
Upper Volta	3.2	0.3	8.0	11.5	1.97
Yemen, A.R.		5.6	7.0	12.6	1.97
Yemen, P.D.R.		10.0	1.7	11.7	7.18
18 Priority Countries	280.7	46.5	513.5	840.7	1.04
Other Developing Countries	697.0	346.9	1,565.1	2,609.0	2.22
TOTAL[b]	977.7	393.4	2,078.6	3,449.7	1.74
% to Priority Countries	28.7	11.8	24.7	24.4	

a. Priority Food-Deficit Countries fall into two categories. The first consists of those five countries (marked *) for which the 1974 per capita GNP did not exceed $150; which have a population of more than 10 million; and face by 1985 a deficit of more than one million tons of cereals just to maintain the present inadequate level of nutrition. The second category is composed of 13 smaller low-income countries whose individual food deficits, though small in absolute terms, pose a major problem at the national level because their per capita dietary energy supplies are not enough now to meet even an average of 95 percent of their nutritional requirements.

b. Excludes amounts for which detailed breakdown by destination is not available.

Source: CGFPI, Table 4.1, page 9.

Table 5

Geographic Allocation of DAC Bilateral ODA
by Categories of Developing Countries

	% of total gross disbursements						
	1970	1971	1972	1973	1974	1975	1976
29 LLDCs[a]	6.8	7.4	10.8	12.1	12.9	16.7	13.4
45 MSAs[b]	33.5	32.3	31.2	32.2	35.5	40.4	38.5
GNP per capita:							
<$265	45.2	47.1	43.3	42.9	47.9	44.0	38.5
$ 265-$520	13.7	13.5	16.4	15.8	15.7	18.3	19.7
$ 520-$1,075	21.4	19.3	18.3	16.3	13.7	13.2	13.0
>$1,075	10.9	10.8	12.6	15.2	12.9	15.8	19.3
Unallocated	8.7	9.5	9.3	9.7	9.9	8.7	9.5

a. LLDC means per capita GNP of $100 or less, share of manufacturing in GDP of 10% or less and literacy ratio of 20% or less.
b. MSAs are those among LLDCs most seriously affected by recent economic crisis (1973-74).

Source: DAC Chairman's Report 1977, *Development Cooperation Review, 1977*, OECD, Table IV-12, page 72.

Table 6

Regional Distribution of Capital Aid Commitments
to Agriculture (1973-1975)
(percent of total)

Region	Aid Commitments	Population	Land under Cultivation
Africa	18	16	28
Asia & Far East	44	57	39
Latin America	24	17	21
Near East	14	10	12
Total	100	100	100

Source: FAO, *Review of Field Programmes*, 1977-78, p. 58.

Table 7

Objectives of Capital Commitments for Agriculture

(Annual Average 1974 and 1975)

	Commitments				
	DAC Bilateral	OPEC Bilateral	Multilateral	Total	Percentage to Food Sector
	US$ Million				
Land & Water Development					
Irrigation, Drainage, Flood Control	90.7	63.1	732.4	886.2	87.1
Land Clearance, Settlement	26.8	13.1	117.8	157.7	39.0
Crop Development					
Food Crops	40.0		49.6	89.6	93.6
Non-Food Crops, Beverages	35.1	23.0	78.1	136.2	4.3
Crop Storage & Processing	26.0		64.0	90.0	76.9
Livestock, Dairy & Animal Health	34.4	32.5	180.1	247.0	95.5
Fisheries	19.7	12.3	65.0	97.0	100.0
Forestry & Forest Industries	45.0	26.1	66.5	137.6	0.0
Agricultural Development					
Rural Development	148.6	5.0	186.2	339.8	63.3
Credit & Banking	9.6		242.8	252.4	78.5
Research, Extension, Training	17.2	0.3	64.7	82.2	87.4
General Agricultural Development	166.9	37.1	129.5	333.5	72.7
Fertilizer Production & Distribution	195.6	356.9	468.0	1,020.5	83.3
Agricultural Inputs					
Fertilizer Supplies	308.1			308.1	83.3
Machinery & Other Inputs	68.2			68.2	83.3
Other	101.5		56.3	157.8	40.3
Total	1,333.4	569.4	2,501.0	4,403.8	
Percentage Going to the Food Sector	71.7	75.9	75.6	74.5	

Source: CGFPI, Table 5.2, p. 11.

Table 8

Commitments for Agricultural Projects (US $ million)

(% of all commitments)

	1973	1974	1975	1976	1977
Kuwait Fund for Arab Economic Development	32.9 (56%)	44.5 (31%)	144.0 (47%)	40.2 (13%)	50.7 (16%)
United Arab Emirates Fund		10.1 (21%)	10.2 (22%)	27.6 (22%)	
Saudi Fund for Development			95.7 (34%)	114.9 (27%)	73.7 (11%)
Arab Bank for Economic Development in Africa				24.4 (31%)	11.2 (52%)
Arab Fund for Economic & Social Development		51.6 (40%)	15.0 (8%)	101.6 (32%)	
Total	32.9	106.2	264.9	308.7	135.7

Source: Calculated by the author from data supplied by the
UNCTAD Secretariat.

The World Bank and Agricultural Development

Richard E. Stryker

During the decade since Robert McNamara's accession to the presidency of the World Bank Group,[1] the Bank has emerged as the leading international institution for development financing. Annual lending and investment commitments have increased ninefold since 1968, from just under $1 billion to $8.7 billion in FY1978. Cumulative lending operations, which stood at about $13 billion at the outset of the McNamara era, surpassed $60 billion in 1978. The Bank now accounts for nearly 20 percent of total net aid to Third World countries (almost one-quarter of the net aid from DAC countries), roughly double its relative contribution ten years ago. During FY1978 alone the Bank financed over 275 separate projects in 75 countries. To administer this financial complex, the size of the Bank's staff has more than tripled since 1968, to some 2,500 professionals and about an equal number of supporting personnel. If the Bank President has his way, the pace of growth will not slacken during his third five-year term. He projects commitments of $9.8 billion for FY1979, and bank disbursements during 1979-1983 should match the total cumulative operations of 1948-1978 (in current dollars).

The influence of the Bank extends well beyond any quantitative accounting of its operations. Its country reports, evaluating borrower's economic and policy performances; its expertise in designing and evaluating development projects; its coordinating role in aid consortia and interagency activities affecting Third World economies; and the efforts of its President to stake out a broad ranging leadership role for the institution, not just as a financial body but as the central and most innovative source for elaborating and operationalizing development strategies—all these, above and beyond its financing weight, make the Bank an increasingly formidable international actor.

Indeed, the perceived role of the Bank is such, particularly in tandem with its august sister institution, the International Monetary Fund (IMF), that talk of a "World Bank World" circulates in some quarters. Such a "World" would, arguably, be more developmentally oriented than the present system, dominated as it is by bilateral rivalries and neocolonial spheres of influence.[2] On the other hand, despite its claims of "political impartiality," and of a decision-making process "based only on economic considerations," the Bank is a profoundly political institution. Its actions have far-reaching, and certainly not always progressive, consequences for Third World countries and for the international order.

This is in no sense a democratic or broadly representative organization. Its sources of funding and weighted voting mechanisms concentrate decision-making authority in the hands of the wealthy capitalist countries, in particular the United States. The authorized capitalization of the IBRD comprises 340,000 authorized shares, of which 266,597 had been subscribed as of June 30, 1978. Ten percent of the capital subscriptions have been called and paid in; the remaining ninety percent is subject to call by the Bank only when required to meet lending obligations. The voting power of member countries is determined by the size of the capital subscription and the extent to which it is pledged in freely usable currencies (see Table 1).[3] The voting structure of the IDA differs somewhat from that of the IBRD, with the weight of the United States slightly less dominant. To whatever extent the World Bank has become the focus of international development efforts, and its President the "conscience of the world" in his antipoverty mission, their roles have never been authorized by nor are they accountable to their Third World clients.[4]

The sense of mission in McNamara's Bank is undeniable. While the intellectual ferment over the need to reorient development strategies in the late 1960s and early 1970s did not originate in the World Bank, the new approaches—emphasizing impoverished target groups, basic needs, and combining redistributive with growth policies— were quickly embraced by McNamara. These ideas have been refined by Bank staff and associates, circulated in publications under Bank auspices, and incorporated in the public image projected by the Bank. The new development strategies have an important urban policy dimension, but the heaviest stress is on agriculture and rural development.

The largest and poorest segment of Third World populations resides in the countryside. The challenge set by McNamara is to reach these impoverished rural masses and increase their productivity. This will enable poor countries to feed themselves to an ever greater extent, while simultaneously reducing absolute poverty, narrowing domestic income distribution gaps, and improving nutritional levels. Poverty, inequality, and hunger are assumed, for strategic purposes anyway, to result from low productivity (and high population growth) among these disadvantaged target groups. Upgrading their productive capacity (and reducing their fertility) can reverse the vicious circles of underdevelopment according to current Bank doctrine.

Priority to Agriculture

In light of the new thinking about development priorities, the Bank is eager to point out its recent shifts in lending by sector. Long renowned, and frequently criticized, for an almost exclusive devotion to financing physical infrastructure, the Bank has diversified its lending significantly in the 1970s. As explained by John Adler, a top Bank official since 1950, the earlier priority

was a "natural" for the Bank. The absence, or severe inadequacy, of infrastructure facilities was one of the clearly identifiable differences between developing and developed countries, and infrastructure investment lent itself ideally to the "specific project" financing called for in the Articles [of Agreement setting up the Bank].[5]

An equally important factor was the Bank's "dogmatic preference" for private ownership and enterprise in the industrial and agricultural sectors and its "essentially *laissez-faire* notion of the development process."[6] The role of government was to be carefully limited, concerned primarily with providing infrastructure so that private capital could proceed with directly productive investments. Not until 1963, under the presidency of George Woods, did the Bank become involved to any extent in lending for agriculture and industry, along with social sectors like education. Whereas infrastructure projects received nearly three-fourths of all Bank lending to less developed countries during the 15 year period of 1948-1963, that proportion had fallen to just over one-half by McNamara's first 5-year term, and has been just over one-third in recent years. Agriculture has clearly been the leading beneficiary of this shift, with its proportion of total lending rising from less than one-tenth in the early period to about one-third currently. Data on sectoral operations are summarized in Table 2.

There are several, generally competing, explanations for the increasing priority to agricultural lending by the World Bank. One, preferred by Robert McNamara and some other Bank representatives, concentrates on the moral and intellectual enlightenment of development experts in recent years. While not an autonomous process, the elaboration of new strategies focused on agriculture and on basic needs is sometimes explained as a progressive response to the ever more clearly perceived complexity of development problems and to the human dimension of those problems. A second explanation is more modest, namely that the world food crisis of

1972-1974 finally goaded Bank officials and others into belated recognition of the centrality of agriculture in Third World development and international stability. A third, more radical, perspective emphasizes the link between renewed agribusiness interest in Third World agriculture and World Bank financing of capital-intensive, export-oriented agricultural projects and the infrastructure necessary to support them. There is an element of truth in each of these views, but they do not merit equal weighting.

New Development Strategies

A growing disenchantment with conventional liberal theories of development, on both analytical and prescriptive grounds, was evident by the mid-1960s. The relevance of Western experience, the narrow economic growth orientation, the faith in "trickle down" effects of growth, the highly restricted conception of government's proper role in development, and other aspects of liberal theory were increasingly disputed, even rejected. The leaders of this revisionist movement to develop a more reformist, socially integrated, and rural focused perspective included Marxists, structuralists, and various humanistic, utopian, and Christian branches of liberalism.

Little indication of this intellectual and moral ferment appeared in the Bank until several years after McNamara's tenure commenced. Indeed, despite the gradual shifts in lending priorities which appeared during the Woods and early McNamara presidencies, the Bank remained stolidly conventional in its overall approach to the development process. The major strategic reorientation was not in agriculture at all, where lending was concentrated on expansion of commodity exports and livestock, most often under the control of large-scale, even foreign owners (discussed further below). Rather, McNamara chose to dramatize the issue of the population boom. In a series of public addresses in 1969-70, he singled out rapid population growth as the major obstacle to Third World progress, apparently ignoring the broader social context of development problems for a time.[7]

The rhetoric emanating from the Bank began to catch up with the new development thinking proceeding outside, following the recruitment of Mahbub ul Haq in 1970. While Haq's influence within the Bank is probably exaggerated for Third World consumption, he is reputed to have had an important role in swaying McNamara toward his current reformist stance. As the most visible "house radical," Haq has certainly had an important public role in popularizing the new approaches to development and seeking to identify the Bank with them. Whether his former orthodoxy as a Pakistani planner renders his conversion to revisionist views more or less credible, the impact of his 1971-72 speeches on the need for new development strategies was considerable. He talked about development as the eradication of poverty rather than the pursuit of economic growth, as the generation of employment more than of GNP, and as requiring the injection of distributional issues "into the very pattern and organization of production." He even praised the Chinese experience (before the Nixon visit) as exemplary of the strategy outlined. From a World Bank official, this was quite a break with tradition![8]

In succeeding years, a veritable flood of speeches, articles, working papers, and books on these lines has issued from the Bank: *Redistribution With Growth, Assault on World Poverty, Malnutrition and Poverty*, compilations on *The Size Distribution of Income* among nations, and others.[9] Particularly in the area of rural development, an extensive collection of sector policy papers has been produced. These cover topics such as land reform, agricultural credit, village water supply, rural electrification, land settlement, nonfarm employment, education, and health. Special attention has been drawn to small farmer problems by Uma Lele, one of the Bank's leading agricultural economists, who has synthesized the recent experience with "new style," multisectoral projects aimed at such farmers in Africa; and by Daniel Benor and others, who have systematized innovative agricultural extension programs to reach the mass of small farmers in South Asia.[10] No review of this vast literature can be attempted here, but the Bank has forged to the forefront of development thought today. The distribution and direction of lending operations *is* being subjected to moral and intellectual trends to an ever greater extent.

A study of Bank publications is not necessarily a reliable guide to Bank policies, however. As one observer has noted, most of the studies mentioned above "have not been discussed or approved by the Board [of Governors] nor by Management. Moreover, most of these publications do not lead to operationally useful guidelines for the Bank's main line of business: to (co-)finance specific development projects."[11] The sector policy papers are an exception to the first caveat, in that they were submitted to the Bank's Executive Directors prior to publication. Indeed, since 1976, the official *Annual Reports* open with the following claim:

While the Bank has traditionally financed all kinds of infrastructure facilities..., its present development strategy places a greatly increased emphasis on investments which can directly affect the well-being of the masses of poor people of developing countries by making them more productive and by including them as active participants in the development process. This strategy is increasingly evident in the rural development, agriculture, and education projects....

Nevertheless, these papers and the whole poverty-focused thrust are still surprisingly controversial among the Bank's professional staff. Some express genuine concern that because of the emphasis on poverty and the small farm sector, the Bank has reduced lending for lumpy, capital-intensive investments in infrastructure which may still be required to complement loans of more direct benefit to small farmers. Others point simply to the questions being raised by representatives of major shareholders. In late 1976, for example, the retiring executive directors from both Japan and the United States voiced strong reservations about the "new style" projects and expanded Bank lending. And the *Wall Street Journal* attacked several costly multisector Bank projects in Indonesia in a widely quoted article in late 1977.[12] The question of the extent to which the "new style" has been reflected in concrete rural development projects will be explored further on.

The Food Crisis

The world food crisis of 1972-1974 coincided with the major surge in World Bank lending for agriculture. To some extent, the lending shift was influenced by the trends in development thinking sketched above. But the food crisis was worth a thousand books and speeches as an impetus to new rural priorities. The current view within the Bank is that "the shortages of 1972-1974 were to a large degree transitory. They were the outcome of coincidental factors which do not presage a fundamental deterioration in the world's ability to feed itself." Recent foodgrain harvests have been more encouraging, especially in 1976 and 1977. Nonetheless, "world per capita production of cereals... is lower than in the 1972-1974 period. Most of the recent production gains appear to have been attributable to favorable weather. There is no evidence to suggest that a new, higher global production trend has been established."[13]

Aggregate world production is much less significant than its global distribution, of course. The surplus, concentrated in North America, cannot be easily transferred to the deficit areas of the Third World. By 1985, the foodgrain deficit of the underdeveloped countries is projected to reach about 75 million tons, double the current deficit. Concessionary transfers of food aid are unlikely to expand notably in coming years; the trend is in the opposite direction. The cost of commercial food imports on the scale indicated would be simply prohibitive for the poorer countries, to say nothing of the logistical and ideological barriers. Moreover, the estimated nutritional deficit would not be reduced even if the market deficit could be.

The case for depending primarily on domestic production is strengthened by the income linkage to nutrition. Market availability of foodgrains will not ensure that the poorest groups will be able to increase their consumption. The majority reside in rural areas and are directly or indirectly dependent on agriculture for their livelihood. The direct means to improve their situation is to increase their productivity and income, thereby ensuring their access to the increased food output.[14]

Despite the rhetoric about rural development and the statistical shifts in lending from infrastructure to agriculture, the World Bank was little involved with projects to enhance staple crop production in the Third World until very recently. Through the mid- and later-1960s, Bank lending for agriculture was concentrated on livestock and export crops. During FY1964-1968, the proportion of total agricultural lending oriented to the promotion of domestic food crops was less than 22 percent. More strikingly,

The sharp increase in lending for agriculture during FY69-73 was not accompanied by any significant shift in intra-sectoral priorities. During that time the share of foodgrain lending increased marginally to just one-fourth of the total for agriculture. The emphasis remained on non-foodgrain crops, even in food deficit countries.[15]

By the 1974-75 fiscal years, however, total agricultural lending had tripled in amount, and about one-half of this total is estimated to have been devoted to domestic food projects. Subsequent data have not yet been published. Recent Bank writings have expressed growing concern over the marketing, energy, transport, and other constraints on any very rapid increases in Third World food production, and these aspects may well receive increased attention in the future. However, if the Bank shifts away from direct lending to assist small farmers toward a more indirect approach to lending for agriculture, the distribution of benefits would strongly favor larger, more well-established farmers.[16]

Perhaps of even greater import, the ratio of concessionary resources from the International Development Association (IDA) within total Bank Group lending and within total agricultural lending has not kept pace with the rapid increase in IBRD activity during the past few years. Since the countries with the most severe food deficits correspond closely to the countries which cannot afford IBRD loans on near-commercial terms, and therefore must rely on IDA funding, the relative decline in IDA's share of bank lending for agriculture means that the most urgent domestic food projects are not receiving priority, even though the absolute amount of financing available to them has increased substantially (see Table 3).

Agribusiness

A third explanation for the World Bank's increased emphasis on agricultural lending is that it serves the interests of the great capitalist agribusinesses and a relatively small number of commercial farmers within the developing countries themselves. In this view, the moral and intellectual claims of Bank officials are a sham, and the food deficit more an opportunity than a crisis.[17]

Since the mid-1960s multinational corporations (MNCs) have increased their investment in local production and international marketing of traditional tropical crops (industrial raw materials, fruits, sugar) and livestock. New prospects have been opened up, too, for example in palm oil and in vegetables for the northern "off-season." This new frontier perspective was captured perfectly by the South African journal *To The Point International* in an article on "The Sahel: Today's Disaster Area...Tomorrow's Glorious Garden?" (October 5, 1974):

Space-age farms, modern cattle ranches and lush market gardens in the middle of the Sahara.... This is no mirage. It is what experts from six of the world's most backward nations have conjured up for the future.... The plan calls for giant dams to harness the Senegal and Niger Rivers and provide power; advanced irrigation systems to water the dust bowls; and forest walls to check the southward march of the Sahara. It could eventually turn the rural subsistence economies of the west African nations...into a vegetable garden for Europe and a vast beef belt.[18]

A multitude of processing industries has been stimulated by the new attention to agricultural development. Although private investment data are hard to come by, a list of agricultural projects insured or financed by the U.S. Overseas Private Investment Corporation since 1973 indicates a rising level of activity (see Table 4).[19] Reports from private bankers suggest that the wishes and desires of government leaders are having an effect on commercial investment and financing undertakings. One banker, whose organization has a long record of financing agricultural projects in Third World countries, indicated that, because of changing policy priorities in host countries, he anticipated a reduction in large plantation-type investments and an increase in the number of grain storage and marketing projects his bank would finance. Others have indicated, however, that if a host country wishes to undertake a capital intensive agricultural production project and seeks outside financing, there is still scope for the outside lender to influence the country's decision regarding the character of the project, provided that it is commercially viable.[20]

Development of "Green Revolution" technology has also created a new clientele for multinational products and services. Overseas sales of farm equipment, seeds, fertilizers, pesticides and insecticides have boomed, along with the supporting services of international consultants, technical assistants, advertisers, sales personnel, and engineers.

The World Bank is the leading multinational provider of the requisite rural infrastructure (irrigation facilities, dams, feeder roads) and agricultural credit. The Bank is also the coordinator of the Consultative Group on International Agricultural Research (CGIAR), an umbrella agency grouping a dozen research and training institutes engaged in improving and propagating the new high-yielding varieties at the core of the Green Revolution. In these activities, the Bank can be viewed as promoting the penetration of capitalist-style agriculture into Third World economies. In the words of Ernest Feder, the current emphasis on reaching small farmers can be explained as an effort "to make capitalist-style 'entrepreneurs' of the peasant-producers."[21] Neither the Bank, nor most agricultural development experts outside the Bank, would be likely to disagree that capitalist economic principles guide its lending in Third World countries. Despite giving homage to labor-intensive and self-reliant development strategies, Bank economists believe that improvement in the agricultural performance of small farmers will only come about if they are given market incentives to invest in new technologies and the resources to make these initial investments.

Bank lending also opens up export opportunities for suppliers of agricultural inputs and is

explicitly acknowledged to do so. Indeed, the major purpose of "deepening" extension work, in the eyes of Bank officials, is to "demonstrate to farmers the economic benefit of improved technology," which "quickly generates demand for a greater variety of increasingly sophisticated production inputs and services."[22]

Pressure from donor countries clearly affects Bank procurement policy. It is also the case, however, that in earlier years when the Bank's agricultural lending was mostly to very large projects, there was very little scope for local procurement. Since shifting to smaller projects and less capital-intensive technology, more opportunities for local suppliers could open up. Nevertheless, the Bank still insists on competitive international bidding on most contracts financed by Bank loans (rather than preferential inducements for local producers) and imposes severe restrictions on local cost financing, thus encouraging capital-intensive imports.

The somewhat distinctive function of the International Finance Corporation (IFC) should be mentioned here. While nearly all Bank activities in the primary sector may be said to promote agribusiness at least indirectly, direct financing of agribusiness (among other private enterprises) is the special province of the IFC. As one staff member puts it, "The IFC is the arm of the World Bank which provides debt and equity finance to projects sponsored by the private sector in developing countries.... Agribusiness ventures financed by the IFC are considered to be large and generally corporate enterprises which manage the production and/or processing of agricultural goods for domestic consumption or for export."[23]

Investments in the milling and storing of grains have recently begun to rank high in the roster of IFC commitments. However, the majority of agribusiness ventures involving IFC participation are concerned with preparing food commodities for export, particularly sugar (see Table 5). Exemplary of recent IFC commitments is a series of three equity investments in 1972-1974, and 1976 in "Bud Senegal," an African affiliate of the multinational Bud Antle Company. The company's West African operations, in Senegal, Mali, and Ivory Coast, are concerned with "growing and *exporting* vegetables...as favorable market conditions exist in Europe for off-season vegetables.... The hope was that these [tomatoes, eggplants, green beans, strawberries, and melons] could supply the European winter markets."[24]

Agribusiness commitments have not figured prominently in past IFC investment activity, but the proportion is now beginning to increase. Only about 6 percent of total IFC commitments, both equity investments and loans, during 1957-1978, were directed to food and food processing firms; but the proportion was over 10 percent in FY1977 and 15 percent in FY1978.[25] At the end of 1977, McNamara hired a special African adviser to oversee a new phase of expansion in IFC, with agribusiness investments in Africa uppermost in mind. The adviser is Henri Konan Bédié, the former Economy and Finance Minister of the Ivory Coast, the most export- and agribusiness-oriented regime in Black Africa.[26]

The Rural Poor and Food Production

A central issue in agricultural development is the relationship between the goals of increasing food production and reducing rural poverty. The dilemma of the Green Revolution is that its successes in attaining the first goal, uneven and precarious though they are, seem to have been at the expense of progress toward the second goal. The reasons for this lie partly in the characteristics of the new seeds, which require a "package" of supporting inputs—irrigation, fertilizers, insecticides, etc.—and, thus, bias innovation in favor of those farmers with access to the capital needed to purchase the costly items and in favor of those areas with an abundant and controlled water supply. This bias is reinforced, though it could be significantly tempered, by the thrust of government policy in most Third World countries. Larger farmers have been favored over small farmers and agricultural laborers quite systematically, if not always intentionally. Agricultural credit policies, inappropriate factor prices, and foreign exchange rates render capital goods imports cheap relative to labor; further, research, extension, investment, and credit designed to promote Green Revolution technology

leave smaller unorganized farmers less competitive and induce larger farmers to substitute machines and chemicals for labor. The Green Revolution was conceived as a progressive technological revolution, "but from a socioeconomic point of view it has largely become transformed into a commercial revolution...often at the expense of peasant farming."[27]

The World Bank has taken the lead in attempting to counter the preceding interpretation of the Green Revolution, both in its publication on the economic and technological benefits to date of the new seeds and in its development of "new style" rural projects to redirect the social benefits of agricultural modernization. In other words, the development theory propounded by the Bank today is that there is no necessary tradeoff between growth and equality, that policies can be and are being designed to reconcile these two paramount goals. The linkage between the goals, outlined at the outset of this paper, is that neither increased aggregate output nor improved income and nutritional levels among the mass of the rural population is possible unless their productivity is raised. In McNamara's oft-quoted Nairobi speech, in September 1973, he stressed that:

Disparities in income will simply widen unless action is taken which will directly benefit the poorest...[There] is no viable alternative to increasing the productivity of small-scale agriculture if any significant advance is to be made in solving the problems of absolute poverty in rural areas...[It] is obvious that no attempt to increase the productivity of subsistence agriculture can succeed in an environment of overall economic stagnation.... The point is that the reverse is also true—and it is time we recognized it. Without rapid progress in smallholder agriculture throughout the developing world, there is little hope either of achieving long-term stable economic growth or of significantly reducing the levels of absolute poverty.[28]

The Bank President then proposed a comprehensive strategy for rural development to be initiated by Third World governments with the support of international agencies, led by the

World Bank. The basic elements of this strategy for increasing the productivity of smallholder agriculture are the development of improved rural organizational capacity (by government agencies and among farmers); land and tenancy reforms; better access to agricultural credit; assured water supplies; expansion of extension services and applied research; greater access to public services of all kinds; pricing policies to provide agricultural production incentives; and regional policies to coordinate the spatial dimension of development processes. Together, these policies, targeted at the over 100 million small farm families of the Third World, are at the core of the "integrated" or "new style" rural development projects with which the Bank has launched its assault on world poverty.

McNamara's optimism in his Nairobi speech, that "small farms can be as productive as large farms," and that growth and equality can therefore be pursued simultaneously, must be qualified in the light of more detailed Bank statements and actual policies. The first sector policy paper on agriculture, in 1972, stressed the "practical limitations to expansion of small-farm production." Provision of the necessary services to enable small farmers to improve their productivity "requires massive resources," both financial and human, neither of which has been forthcoming. Moreover, the adoption of many modern agricultural inputs requires "a certain minimum scale of operations if they are to be used efficiently," less perhaps for reasons of technological than financial and administrative economies of scale. The strategy of integrated smallholder development is optimal in theory due to the interdependence among policy elements, the "minimum package" of inputs and services needed to cross the threshold of effectiveness, and the spatial dimension of social development, but it has severe deficiencies in practice. Above all, given the extreme scarcity of resources, integrated regional projects are far too costly and concentrated, and difficult to replicate on a wider scale. Finally, land reforms, comprising redistribution, improved tenant security, and consolidation of smallholdings, are almost certainly prerequisite (in many societies) to meaningful rural development, but "the Bank's overall influence on these matters is bound to be slight."[29]

Subsequent efforts to explicate the Bank's rural development strategy have also qualified the public optimism of McNamara's pronouncements. The 1975 sector policy paper on rural development, while stressing that the "twin goals" of increasing food production and reducing rural poverty do not *necessarily* conflict, cautions that production imperatives and financial constraints will continue to require considerable Bank lending directed at larger-scale farmers.[30]

The Bank claimed, in both 1975 and 1976, that about one-half of total agricultural lending is "now specifically aimed at increasing the productivity and hence, standards of living, of large numbers of the rural poor."[31] The 1977 *Annual Report* is more specific, defining rural development projects within agriculture as those "in which more than half the direct benefits are expected to accrue to the rural poor. In FY1977, the share rose to 61 percent, but the ratio declined again, to 53 percent, in FY1978.[32] This still means, however, that 40-50 percent of recent projects within the agricultural sector have little or no poverty-focused impact, and leakage to nonpoor farmers within the remainder may approach 50 percent. That is, clearly, a worst-case reading of the situation, though it is probably not an unreasonable one given the past history of appropriation of benefits by larger farmers, especially in Latin America and South Asia.

Calculations by Bank officials that the "new style" projects initiated during 1975-1977 will double the incomes of 40, 50, or 60 million individuals below the poverty line in the Third World provoke unavoidable skepticism. Similarly, the claims of increments to annual foodgrain production attributable to Bank operations are impressive, but, as the Bank warns, "estimates only." By FY1977, 5 million tons of additional foodgrains were claimed across the Third World from the previous 3 years' projects, and an eventual increase of 8.5 million tons in Africa and Asia was projected from FY1974-75 projects alone. More realistic is the ensuing caveat that the new-style projects assigned by the Bank "are in their infancy—two to three years old, at best.... It is, therefore, still too early to assess, with finality, the impact on farm production and farmer incomes flowing from the Bank's rural development strategy.[33] In fact, the increased complexity in the new poverty-focused projects— in their design, implementation, administration, and evaluation—is of such a different order from the mere "engineering" complexities of traditional infrastructure projects that the learning process is likely to be tortuous and lengthy. Expertise in the generation of electricity involves a large but reasonably well demarcated set of variables, highly transferable across political, cultural, and other borders. "Expertise" in the eradication of poverty, on the other hand, comes up against virtually unlimited ramifications and unanticipated consequences, and transferability is always in doubt. Given that governments must guarantee repayment even if projects fail, the Bank's new experiments, at least those financed on hard terms, may soon become less attractive.[34]

In assessing the longer-run credibility of the Bank's assault on poverty, it is critical, of course, to determine the extent to which lending is reoriented not simply to the amorphous rubric, "agriculture," and to the ambiguous "new style" projects, but to the most needy countries and the most effectively reformist regimes. Here, the distinction between the IBRD and the IDA must be re-emphasized. The latter is a development fund in which eligibility for loans is based upon "need," as measured by per capita income levels. The threshold above which countries are unlikely to qualify for IDA credits (though not absolutely excluded) has been raised over time to reflect inflationary levels. It is currently $520 per capita in 1975 dollars. Virtually all IDA credits (c. $14 billion through FY1978) have been allocated to countries below the thresholds established over time, though some 5 percent has gone to middle-income countries, mostly in the 1960s and concentrated on Turkey and South Korea. Another 20 percent has gone to countries with per capita incomes in the $200-$550 range (Indonesia, Egypt...), leaving 75 percent for the poorest countries, somewhat more in the past few years (see Table 6).

IBRD loans, at near-commercial rates, do not incorporate need except in the broad sense that

the Bank has defined its clientele for the past 30 years as "the developing countries." They range from the impoverished African and Asian nations with per capita incomes below $200 to several European and other nations with very high per capita incomes (e.g., Finland, over $5,000, Israel, $3,800, Greece, $2,300, and Yugoslavia, $1,500). Within this range, eligibility for loans is based on general determinations of creditworthiness and specific evaluations of project proposals. These criteria militate against the poorest countries, which cannot really afford IBRD loans in any case. Only 10 percent of all IBRD loans to current borrowers (less recently) have gone to countries with per capita incomes below $200, almost entirely to India and Pakistan. In principle, the Bank does not lend to countries able to obtain financing on reasonable terms elsewhere in the international capital markets. In fact, rather than being a "lender of last resort," the IBRD competes with commercial banks for business in the most dynamic middle-income countries, such as Brazil, Mexico, South Korea, and Yugoslavia. The leading beneficiaries in the allocation of IBRD funds include a few countries in the poorest and lower-middle income categories (India, Indonesia, Philippines, Thailand). But most of the "big winners" are in higher income brackets—Brazil, Mexico, Iran, Argentina, and Yugoslavia, all over $1,000; and South Korea, Colombia, and Turkey, all over $550. Excluding Iran, which is no longer a borrower, the 10 other countries just cited account for over 50 percent of all IBRD loans to current borrowers, and their proportion has been rising in the 1970s (see Table 7).

The ratio of IDA credits to IBRD loans has averaged 13 during the 1970s, though the rapid increases in Bank lending to commercial borrowers and the recurrent uncertainties over IDA replenishments provide a continuing concern about maintaining that ratio. Projections for FY1978/1980 by McNamara include some $2.5 billion annually in IDA credits (thanks to the fifth replenishment of $7.6 billion), equivalent to 25 percent of total Bank Group commitments over the period. *The poorest countries* (one-fourth of the current borrowers, *with nearly one-half of the population of all borrowing countries*) receive only *one-fourth* of all Bank Group commitments, excluding IFC investments. This proportion has changed little over the years, despite the new poverty-focused image.

As for reorienting lending to reformist regimes, where governments display both administrative capacity to manage socioeconomic policy effectively and political commitment to reducing poverty and inequality, the record is not very encouraging. In part, of course, this is because authoritarian political structures still characterize most underdeveloped countries, both large and small. But the Bank remains little influenced by the degree of political repression in borrowing countries which are politically allied with the West.

The Bank should not be accused of rewarding repression, but political stability and economic orthodoxy facilitate external financing; and these conditions, in turn, may require repressive measures. Among the dozen or so leading recipients of total IBRD/IDA funds, only Yugoslavia, India, and Colombia can reasonably claim to have reformist regimes. On the other hand, lending to the reformist regimes of Chile under Allende, Peru under Valasco, and Sri Lanka under Madame Bandaranaike was suspended entirely. The Bank has supported projects in two socialist countries (Yugoslavia and Romania), extended a small IDA credit to Laos in late 1977, and lent on a reasonable scale to a few radical African regimes (Tanzania, Algeria, Ethiopia). But in continuing to concentrate much of its resources on relatively nonreformist regimes that, moreover, have ample access to commercial capital markets, the Bank reduces its leverage to pursue broader kinds of development strategy. The allocation of IDA credits is more in keeping with both need and relative governmental commitment to poverty alleviation, but as one observer has pointed out:

The politically-determined rigidity of the present geographical distribution [spread across 55 poor and near-poor countries], together with the extreme scarcity of concessionary aid, permits very limited variation in lending between countries to award "outstanding initiatives" on the poverty front.[35]

*   *   *   *   *

The financial and policy influence of the World Bank on the less developed countries has grown significantly under the McNamara presidency of the past decade, and it is likely to grow further for the foreseeable future. This influence can be easily exaggerated, however, due to the visibility of the dollars and the rhetoric. There may well be increasing incompatibility between the goal of maximum financial expansion and the goal of seriously assaulting poverty. The former stimulates quantitative fetishism and, thus, unavoidably, the continuing attractiveness of lending for traditional types of projects with high foreign-exchange costs in countries with good credit ratings. In this domain, the Bank is finding itself outflanked by the more free-wheeling and aggressively expansionist Euro-currency market. A serious war on world poverty, on the other hand, requires the kind of rethinking evidenced by the Bank in recent years, the elaboration of more socially complex "new style" projects, experimentation with more labor-intensive rural and urban development strategies, and a redirection of resources to regimes supportive of these objectives in the poorest countries. In *this* domain, the Bank still operates on a small and uncertain scale, and finds itself in a contradiction between the implications of reform and the constraints of its own institutional position. In its starkest form, the contradiction is that

Although the Bank advocates major policy changes necessary for an effective rural strategy, it will suspend lending if political turmoil accompanies a movement leading to change in a country's internal distribution of power.[36]

A major problem is that of U.S. power and interference with policy decisions which rightfully belong to the entire Bank membership. Although its voting rights amount to just under one-quarter of the total, the U.S. exercises disproportionate influence on Bank policy. The current emphasis on basic human needs, participatory programs, and rural development stems in large part from the recent surge of interest in these aspects of development within the United States. On the other hand, the power alliances of the United States have a significant impact on the distribution of Bank lending among and within countries. This situation can be corrected only if the world moves toward a more egalitarian international distribution of power and a broadening of the base of control within

the World Bank and other development institutions.

NOTES

1. The World Bank Group is comprised of the International Bank for Reconstruction and Development (IBRD), the International Development Association (IDA), and the International Finance Corporation (IFC). While they are under common management, they have distinctive roles and should not be confused. IDA is the "soft loan" component of the Bank, and there is now a "Third Window" with loans on terms intermediate between those of IDA and the commercial rates of the IBRD. IFC is a relatively minor component of the Bank Group, concerned with mobilizing investment capital for promoting private sector activities in Third World countries. References to "the Bank" in the text will usually be inclusive of the entire Bank Group, though the separate agency names will be used for clarity at times.

The sources consulted in preparing this paper are numerous and will be cited specifically where appropriate. In order to avoid excessive noting, however, the following general sources should be cited at the outset: World Bank, *Annual Reports* (1972-1978), with updated *Fact Sheet* (December 31, 1977); World Bank, *Summary Proceedings*, Annual Meetings of the Boards of Governors (1975-1978); IFC, *Annual Reports* (1975-1978); IDA, *International Development Association* (April 1977); World Bank, *Questions and Answers* (March 1976); and the massive semiofficial history by Edward Mason and Robert Asher, *The World Bank Since Bretton Woods* (Washington, D.C.: Brookings, 1973). In addition, thanks to the American Universities Field Staff, I was able to spend two days conducting interviews at the Bank in February 1978, where a number of officials and considerable documentation were made available to me. I would like to acknowledge my appreciation to these individuals, particularly to Paul Danquah, Uma Lele, Theodore Goering, Walter Schaefer Kehnert, Konan Bédié, and Mary Stephano.

2. See the Tanzanian statement "Cooperation Against Poverty," in Charles Wilber, ed., *The Political Economy of Development and Underdevelopment* (New York: Random House, 1973), pp. 386-87.

3. World Bank *Annual Report* 1978, p. 149.

4. See Joseph Lelyveld, "McNamara's Style at the World Bank," *New York Times* (November 30, 1975); and John White, "International Agencies: The Case for Proliferation," in G.K. Helleiner, ed., *A World Divided* (Cambridge: Cambridge University Press, 1976), pp. 275-293.

5. John Adler, "Development Theory and the Bank's Development Strategy," *Finance and Development*, 14, 4 (December 1977), p. 32.

6. Adler, "The World Bank's Concept of Development," in Jagdish Bhagwati and Richard Eckaus, eds., *Development and Planning* (London: Allen and Unwin, 1972), pp. 34-36.

7. See, especially, McNamara's Address at the University of Notre Dame (May 1969). Later pronouncements on population from the Bank have incorporated the more balanced scholarly analyses of recent years, in which population is only one (and a largely dependent) social variable. See McNamara's M.I.T. Address on *Accelerating Population Stabilization Through Social and Economic Progress* (Washington, D.C.: Overseas Development Council, 1977).

8. See Mahbub ul Haq, *The Poverty Curtain* (New York: Columbia University Press, 1976), in which the two speeches are reprinted (quote at page 34), along with his later elaboration of the new development strategies and the content of "a new international economic order."

9. Hollis Chenery, et al., eds., *Redistribution With Growth* (London: Oxford University Press, 1974); World Bank, *Assault on World Poverty* (Baltimore: Johns Hopkins, 1975); Shlomo Reutlinger and Marcelo Selowsky, *Malnutrition and Poverty* (Baltimore: Johns Hopkins, 1976); Shail Jain, *Size Distribution of Income* (Baltimore: Johns Hopkins, 1975).

10. See recent sector policy papers on *Rural Enterprise and NonFarm Employment* (January 1978), *Agricultural Land Settlement* (January 1978), *Village Water Supply* (March 1976), *Rural Electrification* (October 1975), *Land Reform* (May 1975), *Agricultural Credit* (May 1975), *Rural Development* (February 1975, and others; Uma Lele, *The Design of Rural Development* (Baltimore: Johns Hopkins, 1975); Daniel Benor and James Harrison, *Agricultural Extension* (World Bank, May 1977); and Michael Cerna and Benjamin Tepping, *A System for Monitoring and Evaluating Agricultural Extension Projects* (World Bank Staff Working Paper No. 272, December 1977).

11. Aart J.M. Van de Laar, "The World Bank and the World's Poor," *World Development*, 4, 10/11, 1976, p. 838.

12. See reports in the *Far Eastern Economic Review* (December 10, 1976 and January 7, 1977), and in the *New York Times* (December 27, 1976), on the speeches by the retiring Japanese and American executive directors. *The Wall Street Journal* article, written by Barry Newman, is entitled, "In Indonesia, Attempts by World Bank to Aid Poor Often Go Astray" (November 10, 1977).

13. S.J. Burki and T.J. Goering, *A Perspective on the Foodgrain Situation in the Poorest Countries* (World Bank Staff Working Paper No. 251, April 1977), pp. 1, 10.

14. *Ibid.*, p. 18.

15. *Ibid.*, p. 41. My emphasis.

16. *Ibid.*, pp. 37, 42; Lele, *op. cit.*, pp. 32, 112; and interviews with Bank officials.

17. See, e.g., Ernest Feder, "Capitalism's Last-Ditch Effort to Save Underdeveloped Agricultures," *Journal of Contemporary Asia*, 7, 1 (1977), pp. 57-78; Susan George, *How the Other Half Dies* (Montclair, N.J.: Allenheld, Osmun, & Co., 1977), chapter 10; and Frances Moore Lappé and Joseph Collins, *Food First: Beyond the Myth of Scarcity* (Boston: Houghton, Mifflin, 1977), chapter 41.

18. Quoted in Immanuel Wallerstein, "The Three Stages of African Involvement in the World Economy," in Wallerstein and Peter Gutkind, eds., *The Political Economy of Contemporary Africa* (Beverly Hills: Sage, 1976), p. 49.

19. See OPIC Annual Reports, cited in *U.S. Food and Beverage Industry Report*, prepared by Richard Gilmore for the U.N. Center on Transnational Corporations, Overseas Development Council (January 1978).

20. Aspen Institute for Humanistic Studies, *Report of the Workshop on Public/Private Collaboration and Third World Food Systems*, Aspen, Colorado, August 20-26, 1978. I am grateful to Barbara Huddleston for this and the preceding citation.

21. Feder, *op. cit.*, p. 58.

22. Burki and Goering, *op. cit.*, p. 34.

23. John Lowe, "The IFC and the Agri-business Sector," *Finance and Development*, 14, 1 (March 1977), pp. 25-26.

24. Susan George, *op. cit.*, p. 210. Emphasis in original. Also see Lappé and Collins, *op. cit.*, pp. 259-60.

25. IFC, *Annual Reports* (1977-78).

26. See my forthcoming book, *Neocolonialism and Development: A Study of the Ivory Coast Political Economy* (Indiana University Press).

27. Among the numerous studies of the Green Revolution, see especially Keith Griffin, *The Political Economy of Agrarian Change* (Cambridge, Mass.: Harvard University Press, 1974), p. 208

28. Robert McNamara, *Address to the Board of Governors* (Nairobi, Kenya, September 24, 1973).

29. World Bank, "Agriculture," in *World Bank Operations* (Baltimore: Johns Hopkins, 1972), pp. 24, 27-29, 36, 45.

30. *Rural Development*, pp. 21, 62-63.

31. *Ibid.*, p. 66; *Questions and Answers*, p. 24.

32. *Annual Report* (1977), p. 11.

33. *Ibid.*, pp. 11-12; Burki and Goering, *op. cit.*, p. 43; McNamara *Accelerating Population Stabilization*, p. 30.

34. See Van de Laar, *op. cit.*, p. 848; and Van de Laar, "The World Bank: Which Way?" *Development and Change*, 7 (1976), p. 91.

35. Van de Laar, "World Bank and World's Poor," p. 848.

36. *Ibid.*, p. 849.

Table 1

Voting Power of IBRD Members, June 30, 1978

Executive Director	Alternate	Casting Votes of	Total Votes	Percent
Appointed				
Edward R. Fried	William P. Dixon	United States	68,130	23.7
William S. Ryrie	Ronald F.R. Deare	United Kingdom	26,250	9.2
Hans Janssen[1]	Hans-Dieter Hanfland	Germany (Federal Rep. of)	13,903	4.9
Jacques Henry Wahl	Pierre-Henri Cassou	France	13,042	4.5
Susumu Murayama	Fumiya Iwasaka	Japan	10,480	3.7
Elected				
Earl G. Drake (Canada)	Edward M. Agostini (Guyana)	Bahamas,[2] Barbados,[2] Canada, Guyana, Ireland, Jamaica[2]	14,820	5.2
Giorgio Rota (Italy)	Miguel Martín-Fernández (Spain)	Italy, Portugal,[2] Spain	13,446	4.7
Anthony Lj.A. Looijen (Netherlands)	Gavra D. Popovic[3] (Yugoslavia)	Cyprus, Israel, Netherlands, Romania,[2] Yugoslavia	13,114	4.6
M. Narasimhan (India)	M. Syeduz-Zaman (Bangladesh)	Bangladesh, India, Sri Lanka	11,644	4.1
Elinar Magnussen (Norway)	Valgeir Arsaelsson (Iceland)	Denmark, Finland, Iceland, Norway, Sweden	10,990	3.8
Jacques de Groote (Belgium)	Tunc Bilget (Turkey)	Austria, Belgium, Luxembourg Turkey	10,727	3.7
Thavil Khutrakul (Thailand)	Bharat B. Pradhan (Nepal)	Burma, Fiji, Indonesia, Korea (Republic of), Lao People's Democratic Republic, Malaysia, Nepal, Singapore,[2] Thailand, Viet Nam	10,463	3.6
Said E. El-Naggar (Arab Republic of Egypt)	Saleh A. Al-Hegelan (Saudi Arabia)	Bahrain,[2] Egypt (Arab Republic of), Iraq, Jordan, Kuwait, Lebanon, Pakistan, Qatar,[2] Saudi Arabia, Syrian Arab Republic, United Arab Emirates,[2] Yemen Arab Republic	10,123	3.5
Timothy T. Thahane (Lesotho)	A.H. Madinga (Malawi)	Botswana, Burundi, Equatorial Guinea, Ethiopia, The Gambia, Guinea, Kenya, Lesotho, Liberia, Malawi, Nigeria, Sierra Leone, Sudan, Swaziland, Tanzania, Trinidad and Tobago, Uganda, Zambia	9,766	3.4

Yahia Khelif (Algeria)	Kwaku Gyasi-Twum (Ghana)	Afghanistan, Algeria, Ghana, Greece, Iran, Libya, Morocco, Oman, Tunisia, Yemen (People's Democratic Republic of	8,800	3.1
R.A. Johnston (Australia)	Gerald S. Aburn (New Zealand)	Australia, New Zealand, Papua New Guinea, Western Samoa	8,620	3.0
Ernesto Franco-Holguín (Colombia)	Ramón Martínez-Aponte (Dominican Republic)	Brazil, Colombia, Dominican Republic, Ecuador, Philippines	8,416	2.9
Eduardo Pesqueira	Oscar G. Espinosa	Costa Rica, El Salvador, Guatemala, Haiti, Honduras, Mexico, Nicaragua, Panama, Peru, Venezuela[2]	8,343	2.9
Armand Razafindrabe (Madagascar)	(vacant)	Benin, Cameroon, Central African Empire, Chad, Congo (People's Republic of the), Gabon, Ivory Coast, Madagascar, Mali, Mauritania, Mauritius, Niger, Rwanda, Senegal, Somalia, Togo, Upper Volta, Zaire	8,276	2.9
Julio C. Gutierrez (Paraguay)	Eduardo R. Conesa (Argentina)	Argentina, Bolivia, Chile, Paraguay, Uruguay [2]	7,575	2.6
			286,928	100.0

Note: Cambodia (464 votes), Republic of China (7,750 votes), and South Africa (2,980 votes) did not participate in the 1976 regular election of Executive Directors. Comoros (266 votes), Guinea-Bissau (277 votes), Maldives (256 votes), Sao Tome and Principe (264 votes), and Suriname (412 votes) became members after that Election.

1. Has resigned effective August 13, 1978; to be succeeded by Eberhard Kurth.

2. Member of the Bank only.

3. Has resigned effective July 31, 1978; to be succeeded by Mindrag Stojiljković.

Source: *World Bank Annual Report 1978*, p. 183.

Table 2

Sectoral Distribution of IBRD/IDA Lending[a]

| | (Percent) | | | | | |
	1948-63	1964-68	1969-73	1974-78	1978	Cumul. 1948-78
Agriculture	8.4	12.6	19.7	31.0	38.9	24.6
Infrastructure[b]	73.7	62.8	53.0	36.6	233.7	46.2
Other[c]	17.9	24.6	27.3	32.4	27.4	29.2

| | ($U.S. million) | | | | | |
	1948-63	1964-68	1969-73	1974-78	1978	Cumul. 1948-78
Agriculture	436	621	2,507	10,012	3,270	13,576
Infrastructure[b]	3,847	3,100	6,737	11,831	2,835	25,515
Other[c]	935	1,212	3,456	10,490	2,306	16,093
Total	5,218	4,933	12,700	32,333	8,411	55,184

a. *Current borrowers only*, i.e., less developed country borrowers, excluding postwar reconstruction and other loans to developed countries ($3,265 millions) and excluding loans to the IFC ($550 millions).

b. Transportation, electric power, telecommunications, water supply and sewage.

c. Industry, development finance companies, education, urbanization, tourism, population, and nonproject sectors.

Source: Calculated by the author from World Bank *Fact Sheet* (December 31, 1977), and *Annual Report*, 1978.

Table 3

Average Annual Share of IDA in Agricultural Lending

| | Agricultural Lending | | | Percent of IDA in |
Period	From IDA	From IBRD	Total	Total
	($ Million)			
FY61-68	38	41	79	48.1
FY69-73	261	257	518	50.4
FY74-78	675	1,329	2,004	33.7

Source: World Bank Policy Planning and Program Review Department, cited in S.J. Burki and T.J. Goering, *A Perspective on the Foodgrain Situation in the Poorest Countries* (World Bank Staff Working Paper No. 251, April 1977), p. 41; and World Bank, *Annual Reports*, 1977-78.

Table 4

Agricultural Projects of U.S. Corporations Financed or Insured by the Overseas Private Investment Corporation, 1973-1977
(Table includes only those projects having an investment value exceeding $1,000,000)

Company	Country	Project	Size of Investment	Largest Single Current Coverage
1973 Insurance Program				
Chase International Investment Corporation	Iran	Production and marketing of agricultural products and livestock	1,200,000	600,000
Coca-Cola Export Corp.	Indonesia	Soft drink base	2,500,000	250,000
Del Monte International Inc.	Kenya	Growing and processing of pineapples and other agricultural products	23,250,000	14,790,000
Hawaiian Agronomics Co. Inc. and The Diamond A Cattle Co.	Iran	Production and marketing of agricultural products	3,400,000	700,000
Hormel International Corp.	Philippines	Expansion of food processing plant	2,018,000	631,966
International Dairy Engineering Company	Iran	Processing of fresh and frozen dairy products and other foods	1,500,000	1,500,000
Kellogg Company	Guatemala	Manufacture of cereal and related products	1,050,000	805,000
Pacific International Food Company	Korea	Grain elevator	1,000,000	500,000
Seaboard Overseas Ltd.	Liberia	Flour mill	1,750,000	1,099,000
Standard Fruit Company	Nicaragua	Banana plantation	3,000,000	3,000,000
1973 Finance Program				Amount of Financing
Cargill Agricola S.A.	Brazil	Soybean processing	5,400,000	2,500,000
Development Company Ltd.	Ghana	Tuna fishing	1,000,000	615,000
Seaboard Overseas Ltd.	Nigeria	Flour mill	4,000,000	2,000,000
P.O. United Coconut (TINA)	Indonesia	Coconut processing plant	1,300,000	500,000
1974 Insurance Program				Largest Coverage
Del Monte Corp.	Kenya	Facility for growing canning and processing of pineapple	7,750,000	12,777,200

1974 Insurance Program cont.

Foremost-McKesson, Inc.	Indonesia	Manufacture of dairy products	8,100,000	9,600,000
King Ranch Inc.	Venezuela	Cattle ranch	1,985,000	1,940,000
Oceanography Mariculture Industries Inc.	Dominican Republic	Fish farm	1,600,000	1,600,000

1975 Insurance Program

Central Soya	Brazil	Manufacture of livestock and poultry feeds	2,250,000	2,250,000
Ralston Purina Co.	Brazil	Manufacture of animal feeds	1,178,077	1,178,077
Ralston Purina Co.	Panama	Shrimp farm operation	1,800,000	2,952,000

1975 Finance Program

Amount of Financing

Accra Plains Agricultural Development Co., Ltd.	Ghana	Rice, sorghum, and soybean growing and processing	25,000,000	7,400,000
Confederation of Latin American Cooperatives (COLAC)	Latin America-Regional	Credit union inter-lending to people outside the credit structure	11,016,000	1,250,000
Fabrica de Laticinios Eunice, Ltda.	Brazil	Milk, cheese, and butter processing plant	1,220,000	200,000
Pioneer Cannery, Ltd.	Ghana	Tuna cannery	1,375,000	200,000
Premier Tobacco Industries, Ltd.	Pakistan	Expansion-tobacco processing	2,180,000	1,200,000
Rafhan Maize Products	Pakistan	Corn processing	3,303,000	2,000,000
Sam Yang Baker Tank Terminal Co., Ltd.	Korea	Edible oil storage terminal facility	1,550,000	550,000
Societe d'Investissement Rwandais du The	Rwanda	Tea processing	1,580,000	515,000
Taylor & Associates of Costa Costa Rica, Inc.	Costa Rica	Frozen vegetable processing	2,502,000	1,502,000

1976 Insurance Program

Largest Coverage

Continental Enterprises (Bermuda) Ltd.	Brazil	Feed mill	1,050,849	1,182,600
Continental Seafoods, Inc.	Nigeria	Shrimp fishing and process	2,268,000	1,836,000
Foremost-McKesson, Inc.	Saudi Arabia	Manufacture of dairy products	1,230,435	2,145,870

1976 Insurance Program cont.

				Largest Coverage
Union Carbide International Capital Corp.	Indonesia	Harvest and process shrimp	1,800,000	1,980,000

1977 Insurance Program

Beker Overseas Limited	Brazil	Manufacture of fertilizer (expansion)	1,565,924	4,554,854
Continental Enterprises	Brazil	Soybean milling	32,670,000	43,470,000
Del Monte Corporation	Greece	Processing and canning fruits and vegetables (expanded	2,900,700	3,673,400
Marine Shipping Company	Egypt	Grain unloading operation	2,000,000	2,000,000
Pfizer Corporation	Kenya	Manufacture of animal feed supplements (expansion	1,044,000	1,882,800

1977 Finance Program

				Amount of Financing
Alexander and Baldwin Agribusiness, Inc.	Cameroon	Experimental corn farm	1,000,000	150,000

Source: OPIC Annual Reports, 1973-75, cited in *U.S. Food and Beverage Industry Report,* prepared by Richard Gilmore for the UN Center on Transitional Corporation, Overseas Development Council, January 1978.

Overseas Private Investment Corporation 1977 Annual Report, pp. 20-24.

Table 5

IFC Commitments in Agribusiness, by Subsector[a]

Subsector (number of	Amount ($ millions)	Percent
Sugar (10)	68.1	55
Meat & Animal Products (5)	18.9	15
Grains (9)	12.2	10
Retail Food (2)	7.2	6
Oils (2)	3.6	3
Tomatoes (3)	2.6	2
Commercial Farming (5)	2.2	2
Other (2) (Soybeans and Tea)	9.5	7
TOTAL (38)	$124.3	100%

a. Commitments through FY1978.

Sources: John W. Lowe, "The IFC and the Agribusiness Sector," *Finance and Development*, 14, 1 March 1977), p. 26; and IFC, *Annual Reports* (1977-78).

Table 6

Allocation of IDA Credits by Income Level
($U.S. millions)

Poorest (below $200)	1961-78	Percent	1976-78	Percent
India	$5,558	41	$2,117	40
Bangladesh	916	7	448	9
Pakistan	916	7	324	6
Ethiopia	368	3	108	2
Tanzania	353	3	185	4
Zaire	202	1	78	1
(twenty others)	1,811	13	1,016	20
Total	10,124	74	4,276	82
Lower-Middle ($200-$550)				
Indonesia	632	5	70	1
Egypt	434	3	218	4
Sudan	296	2	123	2
Kenya	246	2	98	2
(twenty-seven others)	1,351	10	468	9
Total	2,969	22	977	18
Middle ($550-$900)				
Turkey	179	1		
South Korea	111			
(eleven others)	329	3	23	
Total	619	4	23	—
TOTALS (Sixty-nine countries)	$13,710	100	$5,276	100

a. Current borrowers only.

Source: Calculated by the author from data on the World Bank *Fact Sheet* (December 31, 1977); the *Annual Reports* (1974-1978); and the World Bank *Atlas* (1977).

Table 7

Allocation of IBRD Loans by Income Level[a]
($U.S. millions)

Upper-Middle (above $900)	1948-78	Percent	1976-78	Percent
Brazil	$3,945	9	$1,628	10
Mexico	3,262	8	1,042	6
Yugoslavia	1,952	5	810	5
Iran	1,211	3		
Argentina	1,017	2	485	3
Romania	883	2	593	3
(twenty-four others)	4,935	12	1,117	7
Total	17,205	41	5,675	34
Middle ($550-$900)				
South Korea	2,008	5	1,208	7
Colombia	1,932	5	716	4
Turkey	1,495	4	586	3
Malaysia	951	2	238	2
Algeria	803	2	493	3
Peru	573	1	234	1
(nine others)	1,918	5	945	6
Total	9,680	24	4,420	26
Lower-Middle ($200-$550)				
Indonesia	1,772	4	1,392	8
Philippines	1,644	4	995	6
Thailand	1,193	3	534	3
Nigeria	912	2	152	1
Morocco	884	2	401	2
Egypt	731	2	513	3
Zambia	542	1	86	1
Kenya	508	1	288	2
(twenty-three others)	2,524	6	1,147	7
Total	10,710	25	5,508	33
Poorest (below $200)				
India	2,346	6	809	5
Pakistan	884	2	175	1
(twenty-four others)	919	2	156	1
Total	4,149	10	1,140	7
TOTALS (102 countries)	$41,578	100	$16,743	100

a. Current borrowers only.

Source: Calculated by the author from data on the World Bank *Fact Sheet* (December 31, 1977); the *Annual Reports* (1974-1978); and the World Bank *Atlas* (1977).

Conference Participants, "Politics of Food"

Center for Mediterranean Studies
American Universities Field Staff, Rome, Italy
Director: E.A.Bayne

Participants

Chairman: John M.Thompson (United States), Associate Director, American Universities Field Staff.

Project Coordinator: Jon B. McLin (United States), American Universities Field Staff Associate for European Community and International Organization Affairs, Geneva.

* * * * *

Meliza Agabin (Philippines), Deputy Director, Technical Board for Agricultural Credit, Republic of the Philippines.

Pran Chopra (India), journalist; formerly chief editor, *The Statesman* and one-time editorial director, The Press Foundation of Asia.

Grant Cottam (United States), Professor of Botany and Chairman of Instructional Programs, Institute of Environmental Studies, University of Wisconsin-Madison.

Michael W. Donnelly (United States), Assistant Professor of Political Science, University of Toronto, formerly with the Social Science Research Council.

René Dumont (France), Professor of Agronomy, *Institut du Développement Economique et Social* and *Institut d'Études, Politiques*, Paris. Author of *La Chine surpeuplée, Revolution dans les Campagnes Chinoises, Chine: La Révolution Culturelle*, etc.

LaVern W. Faidley (United States), Agricultural Engineer, Agricultural Services Division, Agriculture Department, Food and Agriculture Organization, Rome.

Ronald Francisco (United States), Assistant Professor of Political Science, University of Kansas; Fellow, Institute for the Study of World Politics, Co-author of *The Future of Agriculture in the U.S.S.R. and Eastern Europe*, etc.

Marcus Franda (United States), American Universities Field Staff Associate for India and Bangladesh, New Delhi. Author of *Radical Politics in West Bengal* and *India's Rural Development*, etc.

Brewster Grace (United States), American Universities Field Staff Associate for Southeast Asia.

Keith Griffin (United Kingdom), Acting Warden, Queen Elizabeth House, University of Oxford; formerly World Employment Program, International Labor Organization. Author of *Political Economy of Agrarian Change, Underdevelopment in Spanish America*, etc.

Ahmed A. Goueli (Egypt), Statistics Department, Egyptian Ministry of Agriculture and Department of Agricultural Economics, Zagazig University; consultant, The Ford Foundation.

Howard Handelman (United States), American Universities Field Staff Faculty Associate for Latin America. Author of *Struggle in the Andes: Peasant Political Mobilization in Peru*, etc.

Barbara Huddleston (United States), International Food Policy Research Institute, Washington, D.C.; formerly United States Department of Agriculture.

Thomas Poleman (United States), Professor of Agricultural Economics, Cornell University. Author of *Food, Population and Employment: The Impact of the Green Revolution, The Papaloapan Project*, etc.

Albert Ravenholt (United States), American Universities Field Staff Associate for East and Southeast Asia, Manila. Author of *The Philippines; a Young Republic on the Move*, etc.

O. Sabry, Assistant Coordinator (Technical), World Conference on Agrarian Reform and Rural Development, Food and Agriculture Organization, Rome.

Thomas G. Sanders (United States), American Universities Field Staff Associate for Latin America, Merida, Yucatan, Mexico. Author of *Secular Consciousness and National Conscience, Mexico's Development Decade,* etc.

Richard E. Stryker (United States), Associate Professor of Political Science, Indiana University. Author of *Neo-Colonialism as a Development Strategy: The Political Economy of the Ivory Coast,* etc.

Harry E. Walters (United States), Acting Deputy Executive Director, United Nations World Food Council, Rome.

John Waterbury (United States), American Universities Field Staff Associate for the Arab World, Cairo. Author of *Egypt: Burdens of the Past, Options for the Future* and *Hydropolitics of the Nile Valley,* etc.

Mary L. Wolff (United States), Associate Program Director, Aspen Institute for Humanistic Studies, Program in Science, Technology and Humanism, Boulder.

Fernando L. Zeggara (Bolivia), Economist, Policy Analysis Division, Economic and Social Policy Department, Food and Agriculture Organization, Rome.

Observers

Anne Grace (United States), Agricultural Economist, Agency for International Development, Manila.

Garlan E. Hoskin (United States), Executive Associate, American Universities Field Staff.

William Moody (United States), Director, International Programs, The Rockefeller Brothers Fund.

Louis Solomon (United States), Associate Producer, "Global Papers" Television Project.

Manon Spitzer (United States), Editor and Director of Publications, American Universities Field Staf

John Stremlau (United States), Assistant Director, International Relations Division, The Rockefeller Foundation.

Staff

Lori J. Ross, Secretary.
Ruth Bachli-Pearson, Conference Assistant.
Carl McLean Stern, Audio Technician.